Table Of Contents

P9-DEG-917

COLLECTOR'S
VALUE GUIDE™

HALLMARK
Keepsake Ornaments

Collector Handbook and
Secondary Market Price Guide

FOURTH EDITION

HALLMARK
Keepsake Ornaments

This publication is not affiliated with Hallmark Cards, Inc. or any of its affiliates, subsidiaries, distributors or representatives. Any opinions expressed are solely those of the authors, and do not necessarily reflect those of Hallmark Cards, Inc. Product names and product designs are the property of Hallmark Cards, Inc., Kansas City, Missouri.

Front cover (left to right): "Winter Fun with BARBIE™ and KELLY™ Ornament" (2000), "Hooray for the U.S.A." (2000) and "Snow Buddies" (3rd edition in *Snow Buddies* Keepsake series, 2000).

Back cover (top to bottom): "1941 Murray® Airplane" (Kiddie Car Classic, 1992) and "Full of Love" (Spring Ornament, 1991).

First page: "The Detective" (3rd edition in *Spotlight on Snoopy* Keepsake series, 2000).

EDITORIAL

Managing Editor: Jeff Mahony
Associate Editors: Melissa A. Bennett
Jan Cronan
Gia C. Manalio
Paula Stuckart
Contributing Editor: Mike Micciulla
Assistant Editors: Heather N. Carreiro
Jennifer Filipek
Joan C. Wheal
Editorial Assistants: Timothy R. Affleck
Beth Hackett
Nicole LeGard Lenderking
Steven Shinkaruk

WEB (collectorbee.com)

Web Reporter: Samantha Bouffard
Web Graphic Designer: Ryan Falis

R&D

R&D Specialist: Priscilla Berthiaume
R&D Graphic Designer: Angi Shearstone

ART

Creative Director: Joe T. Nguyen
Assistant Art Director: Lance Doyle
Senior Graphic Designers: Susannah C. Judd
David S. Maloney
Carole Mattia-Slater
David Ten Eyck
Graphic Designers: Jennifer J. Bennett
Sean-Ryan Dudley
Kimberly Eastman
Marla B. Gladstone
Caryn Johnson
Robert Kyerematen
Jeremy Maendel
Chery-Ann Poudrier

PRODUCTION

Production Manager: Scott Sierakowski
Product Development
Manager: Paul Rasid

ISBN 1-888-914-81-5

CheckerBee PUBLISHING

306 Industrial Park Road
Middletown, CT 06457

www.collectorbee.com

Foreword By
Clara Johnson Scroggins

Clara Johnson Scroggins is known throughout the country for her extensive collection of Hallmark Keepsake Ornaments. Active in ornament collecting for more than 30 years, she has written nine books about Hallmark Keepsake Ornaments and spends much of her time on the lecture circuit, speaking to ornament collectors and clubs around the country.

Dear Friends,

We have begun a new year, a new decade and a new century. With those changes, we have paid goodbyes to Lynn Wylie, Tex Ann Kraft and Anne Rothers in the Keepsake Ornament Collector's Club, and have welcomed Claire Brand, General Manager, Keepsakes; Mark Amren, Keepsake Ornament Collector's Club Manager; and Michelle Brown, Communications/Events Coordinator, Keepsake Ornaments Collector's Club.

With the expansion of the Keepsakes Artists department, we have many beautiful and meaningful collectibles to look forward to that will help us capture all of the wonderful memories of our lives and the moments that are yet to come. So hold on and hang tight because we are in for an exciting adventure in Keepsakes collecting!

Clara

Introducing The Collector's Value Guide™

T his year marks the 27th anniversary of Hallmark Keepsake Ornaments and the fourth edition of the Hallmark Keepsake Ornaments Collector's Value Guide™. This all-inclusive handbook provides everything you need to become an expert in the field of one of the largest and most recognized collectibles in the country.

The Collector's Value Guide™ not only supplies comprehensive information about every Keepsake Ornament, but also about Spring Ornaments, Merry Miniatures and Kiddie Car Classics. Each piece in this handbook is highlighted by a full-color picture, as well as material type, artist, stock number and issue price. Finally, updated 2000 secondary market prices are given to help you determine the value of your collection.

What's Inside

- A look at the newest additions to the Hallmark Keepsake series as well as the final editions for retiring series

- Exclusive interviews with Keepsake Artists Tammy Haddix, John "Collin" Francis and Robert Chad

- Biographies of all the artists who sculpt the Keepsake Ornaments, including information about the four newest sculptors to join the Studio: Julie Forsyth, Rich LaPierre, Sharon Visker and Chris Webb

- A tour of the Hallmark Visitor's Center and the Crown Center complex in which it is located

- And much more!

History Of Hallmark

W ith a shoebox full of postcards, a pocket full of dreams and not much else, 18-year-old Joyce Hall headed to Kansas City in 1910 to pursue his dream of becoming a successful businessman. Although the road to success was long and hard, his dream eventually came true. He now has offices around the globe, and some say Hall's is the ultimate success story.

Humble Beginnings

Joyce Hall started out far removed from the greeting cards, collectibles and ornaments that have made Hallmark a household name. As a teenager, this Nebraska native ran a small mail-order business out of a tiny room in the YMCA. He sent packets of 100 homemade postcards with printed invoices to retailers around the country. And although many retailers kept the cards without paying for them, and others simply returned the merchandise completely, about one third of the dealers sent in checks and within a few months, Hall had earned more than $200.

The Making Of A Legend

Always the entrepreneur, Hall was not content to sit back and bask in his success. By 1915, he had established Hall Brothers and was manufacturing better quality cards for such holidays as Christmas and Valentine's Day. Packaged with envelopes, these illus-

trated greeting cards saw enormous success. Hall's brothers, Rollie and Bill Hall, came on board to help run the company, which had grown to include 120 employees. Within six years, Hall Brothers moved from four tiny offices to a six-story plant.

Two years later, the Hallmark name made its debut and, thanks to a national advertising campaign spearheaded by Joyce Hall,

The Keepsake Ornament Collector's Club began in 1987 as a way to bring collectors together to share the excitement of collecting. Members receive special club ornaments, the opportunity to purchase additional exclusive ornaments, a quarterly newsletter, an early release of the "Dream Book" and invitations to special Hallmark events and signings.

Hallmark became associated with a high-quality product. In 1944, the company slogan made its first appearance, cementing Hallmark's reputation of producing products for those times "when you care to send the very best."

During the next 20 years, the line expanded from greeting cards and gift wrap to paper party goods. On Christmas Eve in 1951, the first "Hallmark Hall Of Fame" special made its debut to bring social values into television programming. The productions, still air today and have received several awards, including more Emmy awards than any other program on television.

A Great Place To Work

Since 1921, Hallmark has been considered a great place to work. It has held company picnics and other events to boost company morale. In 1956, it strengthened its reputation for excellent employee relations when it began its Hallmark Career Rewards Program. Today, Hallmark employees own one-third of the corporation and enjoy benefits that go beyond basic insurance and profit sharing. The company has consistently been listed as one of America's "Top Ten Places to Work" by several publications.

A Success Story

In 1966, Joyce Hall handed over his duties as Chief Executive Officer to his son, Donald J. Hall, who has continued to lead the company in exploring new markets, including the highly successful

Hallmark Keepsake Ornaments. The younger Hall made several acquisitions, including jigsaw puzzle manufacturer Springbok Editions in 1967 and Crayola Crayon® manufacturer Binney & Smith in 1984.

🕊 A Midwestern Disneyland 🦌

To help improve the surroundings of the three-million-square-foot corporate offices of Hallmark, the company tore down empty businesses and abandoned parking lots in the local area and built the Crown Center, an 85-acre business and entertainment metropolis located on the edge of downtown Kansas City. The Center consists of hotels, shops, theaters and restaurants as well as the popular Visitors Center, a museum of Hallmark history.

Hallmark continued its dedication in 1994, to family entertainment by creating Hallmark Entertainment Inc., a company created to produce the family-oriented television programming that it supports through its "Hallmark Hall Of Fame" series. The company is also one of the largest supporters of the new Science City museum in Kansas City, which helps promote education for both young and old in the field of science.

From Joyce Hall's tiny office in the YMCA to the corporate powerhouse it is today, Hallmark has been dedicated to providing the highest quality entertainment and products. It is this commitment that is sure to help keep the family-owned business a success for years to come.

COMMUNITY WORK

Each year, Hallmark uses the wood from the Crown Center Christmas tree to make a set of ornaments, the proceeds of which go to charity. The company also holds an annual food drive, which averages 5,000 pounds of food per year. And Hallmark employees participate in a special program to build and refurbish homes of the less fortunate in the local area.

A Closer Look
At The Hallmark Line

Upon their debut in 1973, Hallmark Ornaments changed the face of contemporary collectibles forever. The company implemented innovations in the field of holiday ornaments by deviating from traditional glass ball designs produced by other companies. Hallmark printed illustrations on their ornaments, traditional holiday images that evoked a feeling of warmth and comfort in most people. Included among these early designs were works by Norman Rockwell, Betsey Clark and Currier & Ives.

Throughout the years, Hallmark has kept up with the latest trends, ensuring continued success among new generations of collectors. While traditional holiday scenes handcrafted onto gold, silver and glass ornaments still serve as the backbone of the ornament collection, popular cartoon characters, contemporary sports and pop culture activities all have taken center stage over the years as well.

Keepsake Ornaments

Hallmark Keepsake Ornaments make up the majority of Hallmark's ornament line. Introduced in 1973, the collection features several ornaments designed in the traditional glass ball pattern, as well as several hand crafted with materials such as wood and cloth.

Each year, collectors look forward to the release of the Hallmark "Dream Book," a full-color catalog that previews the ornaments to be issued in the upcoming year. The "Dream Book" is usually available by March, although the ornaments featured inside are often only available from late summer until Christmas.

The booklet introduces the year's ornaments, which may range from a pewter tree that commemorates "Baby's First Christmas" to a miniature version of "Chewbacca™" of Star Wars™ fame. There are many collectible series within the Keepsake line that consist of pieces with related themes, such as *At the Ballpark* or *Rocking Horse*. In each series, one piece (known as an "edition") is added each year until the series ends with the final edition. In addition to series, Hallmark also releases several unannounced collections. These are pieces that follow a certain theme but are not designated as an official series by Hallmark. Some examples of unannounced series include Mickey & Co., the Child's Age Collection and Mr. Potato Head®.

Magic Ornaments

The term "Magic Ornaments" refers to pieces that have special effects, such as light or music, as part of their appeal. These pieces made their debut as "The Lighted Collection" in 1984. Shortly thereafter, motion was added to selected pieces, followed in 1989 by the incorporation of sound. Nine series featuring these special pieces have been introduced into the ornament collection to date. Keepsake Magic Ornaments are easily recognizable in the "Dream Book," as they are marked with a starburst.

Crown Reflections

In 1998, a collection of blown glass ornaments known as Crown Reflections made its debut. Based on traditional European designs from more than a century ago, these pieces are carefully sculpted and hand painted by the Keepsake Studio artists. The line grew in 1999 with the release of several new designs, including many based on the popular Kiddie Car Classics collection of die-cast model cars. A Crown Reflections series of blown glass balls known as "Holiday Traditions" completes the collection.

Li'l Blown Glass

Inspired by the Crown Reflections blown glass ornaments that saw success in 1998 and 1999, the Li'l Blown Glass collection made its debut in 2000 with miniature versions of the intricate decorations. These 25 pieces rang from traditional holiday images of "Li'l Mr. Claus" and "Li'l Roly-Poly Santa" to colorful fruits and sets of different colored stars. As with their larger Crown Reflections counterparts, the Li'l Blown Glass pieces are sculpted with the finest detail and hand painted.

Laser Gallery

Originally introduced as Laser Creations in 1999, the Laser Gallery consists of delicate holiday ornaments crafted from archival paper. The ornaments in this collection are created by a tiny laser beam, which cuts through the paper and forms the design. The pattern is then assembled by hand in a manner that allows it to reflect light and shadows in a truly unique way. The majority of pieces in this collection contain light clips, which can be turned on to bring a warm glow to any holiday tree.

Showcase Ornaments

Beginning in 1993, Hallmark introduced a line of metal and porcelain ornaments that depict specific religious and folk art themes. These pieces were only available through Hallmark Gold Crown® Stores. Although the line is no longer in production, several current ornamental designs have adopted the style of the Showcase Ornaments.

Miniature Ornaments

The second largest collection in the Keepsake Ornament family, Miniature Ornaments, have the same intricate detail and variety of modern and traditional themes as the full-size Keepsake Ornaments. Miniature ornaments generally range from 1/2" to 1-3/4" in size and are often harder to find than their larger counterparts as they are released in limited numbers. Several series featuring miniature ornaments have also been released over the years.

🌿 Other Hallmark Ornaments 🌿

In addition to the hundreds of ornaments that can be purchased through Gold Crown stores each year, Hallmark releases a number of special pieces that only can be obtained by certain methods or at special outlets. Here's a look at these types of ornaments:

Collector's Club Ornaments – Members of the Keepsake Ornaments Collector's Club are entitled to special exclusive pieces as a benefit of membership. Some ornaments are a benefit of membership, some may be purchased at different times throughout the year and some require collectors to attend selected events. Often, pieces obtained through the Keepsake Ornaments Collector's Club complement series within the general line.

Premiere Exclusives – More than 200 ornaments were selected to be revealed on July 15, 2000 at Gold Crown stores around the country. Collectors attending the 8th National Keepsake Ornament

HAPPY ANNIVERSARY CHARLIE BROWN
REACH Program pieces, also known as Open House pieces, have come in the form of Merry Miniatures figurines since 1996. With the 50th anniversary celebration of Peanuts® in 2000, the pieces return to ornament form to honor Charlie Brown, Snoopy, Linus, Lucy and Woodstock from the Peanuts® gang.

Premiere Event on this day were slated to receive two special premiere ornaments: "Frosty Friends," which features a set of two ornaments and a display piece; and "Little Red Riding Hood – 1991," a Merry Miniature from the Madame Alexander® Collection.

REACH Program pieces – The REACH Program begins in conjunction with the annual Holiday Open House weekend at Hallmark Gold Crown Stores around the country. In 2000, this event is scheduled for November 11 and 12. This year's five REACH Program pieces are based on the characters from the Peanuts® comic strip, available at different times during the three-week promotion.

Special Event Pieces – The Hallmark Keepsake Artists also sculpt some limited edition pieces for special events where collectors can meet the artists, win prizes and purchase exclusive event pieces. Sometimes, these pieces are ornaments from the general line that are painted in different colors, while other times they are completely unique pieces.

Some of the most popular special events are the Artists On Tour appearances, which have been held since 1994. In the past, Hallmark hosted several annual events around the country on different dates. The format changed for 2000 with 20 events simultaneously occurring throughout the country during the weekend of October 6 and 7. The Artists On Tour events always draw a crowd, as collectors have the opportunity to meet with, and receive signatures from, their favorite Keepsake Artists.

🌱 Spring Ornaments 🌿

Soft pastel colors and Easter themes are hallmarks of the Spring Ornament Collection. The line was introduced in 1991 as "Easter Ornaments," as the pieces in the collection focused solely on eggs, bunnies and other traditional Easter images. But as the line grew, spring-themed pieces were added and now collectors can find everything from budding flowers to favorite storybook characters, such as Winnie the Pooh and Peter Rabbit™, emerging from hibernation to celebrate the new season. The Spring Ornament line contains 18 series, from *Eggs In Sports* to *Fairy Berry Bears*.

🍂 Merry Miniatures 🍂

Unlike the ornament collection, a line of small figurines takes center stage in this popular collection, which has been in existence since 1974. While earlier pieces featured simple names and concepts – such as "Child," "Duck," and "Witch" – the line in recent years has become progressively more original, featuring recognizable characters such as Mickey Mouse and Alice in Wonderland. Merry Miniatures have also been selected as Hallmark Ornament Premiere pieces and Gold Crown Open House exclusives (also known as REACH Program pieces).

Merry Miniatures welcomed 2000 with several changes to the line. This year, the pieces, which were sold in packaging from 1995 through 1999, no longer come in colorful cardboard boxes, arriving instead in clear plastic containers. Also, for the first time in the Merry Miniatures history, two new annual collections have been added. Happy Hatters features 12 capped youngsters who will be available at different times throughout this year, while the Madame Alexander® Collection spotlights eight figurines based on designs from the popular Madame Alexander® doll collection.

🍂 Kiddie Car Classics 🍂

These die-cast metal models of classic cars are sure to drive any serious car fanatic wild! The collection has been a hit since the line's inception in 1992 as cars race off shelves within hours of their appearance. Each car is about 8" in length and boasts realistic features, such as rubber tires, movable pedals, bright paint and working headlights.

Kiddie Car Classics has several sub-categories, such as Kiddie Car Classics, Miniature Kiddie Car Classics, Sidewalk Cruisers and the Don Palmiter Custom Collection, named after the artist. Luxury, Limited and Numbered Editions are further highlights of the line. Gear up for the latest 2000 introductions, which include "1935 American Tandem," "1958 Custom Corvette" and "1934 Christmas Classic."

Other Hallmark Collections

Hallmark also offers a quickly-growing group of themed collectible lines in recent years. Legends In Flight™ spotlights the development of aircraft through the years with model airplanes, while Great American Railways™ does the same for the locomotive through a line of model trains. School Days Lunch Boxes™ focuses on popular tin lunch box designs (each with a matching beverage holder) from the 1950s, '60s, '70s and '80s.

For 2000, Hallmark introduces three new collections. Through a series of ornaments, coin and figurine sets as well as a collector's kit, the American Spirit Collection™ celebrates the popular 50 State Quarters Program™ issued by the U.S. Mint in 1999.

The Peanuts® Collection commemorates the 50th anniversary and retirement of the beloved Peanuts® comic strip, which ended production in early 2000. Miniature pewter figurines, framed comic strips and 6" jointed porcelain figurines are just some of the many items available in this collection that features the lovable Charlie Brown, Snoopy, Linus and Lucy.

After many years of gracing storybook covers, Dr. Seuss' famous characters come to life through figurines, coin banks and bookends in Hallmark's The Dr. Seuss™ Collection. All of the crew is here, from "The Grinch Who Stole Christmas™" to "The Cat In The Hat™."

Welcome To The
New Keepsake Series

Hallmark began its first series, *Betsey Clark*, in 1973 and since 1978, has released a new series every year. These series have found their way into almost all of Hallmark's different lines, including Keepsake Ornaments, Crown Reflections, Magic Ornaments, Miniature Ornaments and Spring Ornaments.

Most series last for a minimum of three years, although there are exceptions, such as *African-American Holiday BARBIE*™ whose first, and final, release occurred in 1998. However, most ornament series exceed the minimum. The longest-running series, *Here Comes Santa*, is still current and has had 22 pieces released since its introduction in 1979. Other popular long-running series include *Frosty Friends*, which was introduced in 1980 and is still current; and *Nostalgic Houses and Shops*, introduced in 1984 and also still current.

Some of the most popular Hallmark ornaments belong to a series. Often, these pieces achieve some of the highest values on the secondary market. The first edition of each series is usually the most highly sought after and, therefore, the most valuable. It is almost impossible to predict which series will rise to the top, especially among this year's candidates. Here's a look at the first editions of the new 2000 series:

🌿 New Keepsake Series 🍃

BARBIE™ Ornament — This is the newest series to honor one of America's favorite dolls. Patricia Andrews, the artist behind many other classic BARBIE™ ornaments, is the sculptor of this series' first edition, due to be released in November of 2000.

Cool Decade — Count down to the next decade with these ten "chilly" ornaments. This first piece, sculpted by Tammy Haddix, is the perfect way to commemorate the new decade as well as the new millennium. The 2000 release features a jolly walrus complete with a santa hat.

Fashion Afoot — This series of miniature shoes, which are also hinged boxes, are the height of fashion. This year's edition is a Victorian-style button-up boot, sculpted by Joanne Eschrich. A proper lady mouse with gloves, kerchief and plumed hat appears ready to "step out" on the town.

Robot Parade — These highly detailed robots are sure to bring back memories of favorite childhood toys. Sculpted by Nello Williams, the first in this series is a bright red, pressed tin robot with a movable head and arms. It even has workable wheels on the bottom of its feet!

Toymaker Santa — Santa has a lot of toys to make before Christmas, and collectors can look forward to seeing him with a new toy each year. The first piece in this series, sculpted by Ken Crow, shows Santa taking a test drive on a newly-made toy train.

New Miniature Series

Ice Block Buddies — This series of miniature arctic animals is a wonderful way to mark each passing year. You can start your collection with this adorable wreath-wearing seal sculpted by Linda Sickman.

MONOPOLY® Game: Advance to Go! — Everyone's favorite board game now comes in a new miniature series. What better way to represent this high stakes real estate game than with money? This year's piece is a handcrafted pewter "Sack of Money" sculpted by Sharon Pike.

Last Call For The Final Editions

When Hallmark retires a series, it lets collectors know in advance by designating the last piece as the "final" edition. Listed here are the 12 series that will end in 2000, together with the names of the final ornaments.

🍃 Keepsake Series 🍃

Holiday BARBIE™ Collectors Club — "Based on the 1992 Happy Holidays BARBIE™ Doll"

Madame Alexander® Holiday Angels — "Twilight Angel"

Majestic Wilderness — "Foxes in the Forest"

The Old West — "Mountain Man"

Romantic Vacations — "Donald and Daisy at Lovers' Lodge"

Scarlett O'Hara™ — "Scarlett O'Hara™"

Unforgettable Villains — "*Sleeping Beauty's* Maleficent"

🍃 Miniature Series 🍃

Miniature Clothespin Soldier — "Sailor"

Nutcracker Ballet — "Sugarplum Fairy"

Nutcracker Guild — "Nutcracker Guild"

Teddy-Bear Style — "Teddy-Bear Style"

🍃 Crown Reflections Series 🍃

Holiday Traditions — "Christmas Rose"

Q&A With Hallmark Artists

CheckerBee Publishing recently spoke with three Hallmark Keepsake Artists – Tammy Haddix, John "Collin" Francis and Robert Chad. Here's what they had to say:

🌿 Tammy Haddix 🌿

CheckerBee Publishing: Many of your pieces incorporate a family theme. How has your family influenced your work?

Tammy Haddix: My family has always influenced my work. They've always encouraged and inspired me. When I try to come up with concepts for ornaments, I think "OK, what would I want to give my family or my friends?" They've always been really supportive and really excited about what I do.

CP: How has your son Zachary influencd your work?

TH: It seems like any time I sculpt a little elf or something, I'm always looking at his picture and trying to make it look like him.

CP: As the sculptor of the lovable *Snow Buddies* series, do you find it easier to create ornaments in a series than general ornaments?

TH: Sometimes it can be hard to create series pieces, but the *Snow Buddies* were easy because there were so many woodland animals that I could pair with the snowmen. Series ornaments have to go for three years and sometimes there are not enough ideas to repeat the idea. It's a challenge to make each one as good or better than the last one, and to see how they look as a group, how they evolve and change.

CP: From the Keepsake Ornaments that you've sculpted so far, it appears that you're an animal lover. Do you have any pets?

TH: Yes, we have two dogs. We have a sheltie named Sherman that we got when he was a puppy, right before I met my husband. And then we adopted another dog, a springer spaniel named Shelby. She was abandoned and found at a lake. Those are my son's buddies now.

CP: Pieces such as "Warm Kindness" and "Angelic Trio" present a sense of warmth, love and goodwill. How do you incorporate that sense of personality into the characters you sculpt?

TH: Every time I start an ornament, I really want to bring it to life with some emotion, so when somebody looks at it they will think, "Oh, isn't that just really sweet." That's always my goal, to give it some kind of personality or warmth.

CP: Do you have a favorite piece that you've sculpted?

TH: My "Snow Buddies" pieces are my favorite. I was really glad when the series went past three years. It was really good to know that people liked it, that they're getting the same feeling that I have for it.

CP: Do you ever get sculptor's block? How do you overcome it?

TH: Sometimes, I'll sit down to sculpt something and I'll know what I want it to look like but it just won't come together. I just can't seem to get it to happen. Well, then I usually put it away for a little while, go research or look at a magazine and just get away from it and rest my brain. Then I come back to it with a fresh eye, which really helps.

CP: What are some of your memories of your time spent at the Keepsake Studio?

TH: Mostly the Artists On Tour, getting to travel with the other artists and getting to know them better. And then getting to develop some relationships with collectors. They're a lot of fun; they're some really neat people. And they're so excited about what we do, it just makes it really fun. It's like, "Wow, they really like this stuff."

ꙮ John "Collin" Francis ꙮ

CheckerBee Publishing: When did you know that you wanted to be an artist and what led you to Hallmark?

John "Collin" Francis: I actually started out to be a civil engineer. My freshman year in college, I was rooming with a guy who was taking an art minor and I really liked what he was doing a lot better than what I was doing. So my sophomore year in college, I switched my major to art. I finished my art at Hastings College in Nebraska and had started working on my masters degree at Kansas University. I finished one day of classes and there was the letter from the Armed Forces telling me to go report to the Armed Forces building in Kansas City to go to Vietnam, but I flunked my physical. While I was waiting for them to classify me, I came to Hallmark. They put me to work as an engraver and I've stayed there ever since.

CP: So it was supposed to be temporary?

JCF: It was going to be, but I like Hallmark a lot. They were hiring lots of people back in the '60s so I went to night school here at the Art Institute and improved my color and painting and drawing skills. Finally, I got a break and got to start out in an art department after about five years as an engraver.

CP: You've sculpted three of the four pieces in the *Hockey Greats* series, including "Eric Lindros" for this year. Are you a hockey fan?

JCF: I got interested when I started sculpting the pieces. I hadn't been a hockey fan before because I'm from Wyoming and there isn't much hockey going on out there. But I've seen a couple of games and I love it. I was in sports all through grade school, junior high, high school – Little League, football, baseball, track – oh, everything.

CP: How do you choose the designs for your *Lighthouse Greetings* series each year?

JCF: What we've been doing, and it didn't start out that way, is working our way clockwise around the country, around the coastline. The very first lighthouse isn't part of the series. It came out early on, in 1994. They wanted to see how this cute little lighthouse with a little penguin with a spyglass and Mr. and Mrs. Claus standing out there in front would do, and people really enjoyed it so we started the series two years later. We don't just completely copy what a lighthouse looks like. We use some features from different lighthouses and then make a composite. So now we've been down the East Coast and up around the West Coast to the Great Lakes. Now I've headed down to Florida and I'm in the Gulf.

CP: You've said in the past that you're an avid birdwatcher.

JCF: Yes, a neighborhood kind of birdwatcher. I don't know a lot about birds around the world or that sort of thing, but I do know a lot about our birds right here in Missouri.

CP: Did this hobby inspire your 2000 piece "Birds in Harmony"?

JCF: That sketch was done by another artist and they just decided that I would be a good candidate because they know how much I like birds. I feed the birds right here on my windowsill. In fact, I'm looking at a little house finch right now. He's taking a drink out of a little tub of water that I've got wired to the side of the window.

CP: Do you have a favorite piece that you've sculpted?

JCF: My favorite piece would probably be the little bunnies on the poinsettia, "Gentle Dreamers." I think a lot of the collectors enjoy it the most, too. I have people walk up to me and say, "Of all the pieces you've done, that was kind of special to me" – and it just kind of became special to me, too.

✍ Robert Chad ❦

CheckerBee Publishing: How did you make the move from being an animator and a printmaker to becoming a Hallmark Keepsake Artist?

Robert Chad: Desperation! I was printmaking, but realized I couldn't make a living with that. Then I went to animation and after three years, realized it was way too hard and very hard to make a living unless I went to Disney or worked for somebody big. But I got bored with drawing, generally speaking. All my drawings back in those days were really three-dimensional. I used to try to make the images pop off the piece of paper. So it was kind of a natural thing for me to go into sculpture. I wasn't looking for the job, and in fact, I had never sculpted until this job showed up. I had dabbled in it, so I basically did a couple of little sculpts and that's how I got the job. I had freelanced with Hallmark for six to eight years all over the company, all different areas, but just about all of it was two-dimensional.

CP: Do you have any input on how Mary Hamilton comes up with the ideas and the names for her *Mary's Angels* pieces?

RC: Well, Mary does sketches and that's pretty much her entire input. Sometimes, I might go back to her if I can't figure out what she's drawn. That's pretty much how I got my job here. The first one in that series was my trial by fire. It took me one full month to sculpt it when it should have taken more like two weeks. But it took me a month of seven days a week, ten hours a day because I really wanted the job. That first one, it's called "Buttercup." No one wanted to do it, no one wanted to do that cute look, so I was the new guy and I didn't have a choice, it was assigned to me. And it's lasted 15 years now. I'm sculpting number 15 right now.

CP: You're well known for your talent in sculpting cartoon characters. Who is your favorite cartoon character to sculpt and why?

RC: The one that's in the line this year – Gossamer. I have, for 10 years or so, been asking to do Gossamer but he's one of those "outside" characters. He's the last on my list for obscure characters. I did Marvin the Martian and I did Michigan J. Frog and Gossamer – those are three very obscure characters. At first, they wouldn't touch them with a 10-foot pole and then Marvin the Martian gained popularity. He's always been my favorite ever since I was a little kid watching the old cartoons. And now I'm done because I don't really want to do any more. I've done all the ones I care about.

CP: Are there any other designs or characters that you look forward to creating in the future?

RC: Once again, the thing that's in the line this year is "Santa's Chair." I really liked doing that. There's more of that kind of work coming.

CP: Where did you get the inspiration for "Santa's Chair" and how long did it take you to create it since it's so highly detailed?

RC: Probably the inspiration initially comes from the interior background paintings from Disney's "Pinocchio," which have hand-carved little characters in the wooden objects. There's a calliope in the movie and if you look you can see little characters carved into the calliope. I think it took me three weeks to a month to do that piece because there is so much detail on it.

CP: You've said that your hobbies include traveling. What is your favorite travel destination?

RC: My favorite travel destination is my next one and it's unknown. Two years ago, I went to France on a sculpture workshop, went out in the Loire Valley to a little chateau and sculpted for two weeks. That was fun. That was a nice vacation. Probably I'll do that again, but in Italy to carve stone for a couple of weeks. But first, I've got to put a roof on my house. That's this year.

Meet The Hallmark Artists

I f you're a dedicated Hallmark ornament collector, you probably know every piece in this year's "Dream Book" by heart. But how well do you know the artists who create them? Here's a look at the Hallmark sculptors, including four artists who joined the Keepsake Studio full-time in 1999.

🎨 Patricia Andrews 🎨

A lifelong fan of Barbie dolls, Patricia Andrews was the perfect candidate to sculpt the doll's likeness for Hallmark. Because she's sculpted more than her share of the 40-year-old doll, she's earned a reputation as "The Barbie Lady." Andrews has also sculpted other glamorous ladies during her 13 years in the Keepsake Studio, including those in the *Scarlett O'Hara*™ and *Marilyn Monroe* series. She finds inspiration in old movies (black and white films are her favorite) and from her husband, fellow Keepsake Artist Dill Rhodus, who she says is her greatest influence and supporter.

This year, Andrews adds to her repertoire of famous females with "Jeannie I Dream Of Jeannie" and "Angel of Promise," the third in a series of angels sculpted by Andrews to benefit the Cards For The Cure™ program to fund breast cancer research.

🎨 Nina Aubé 🎨

As a child, Nina Aubé was a practical joker, playing tricks and teasing her sisters. Today, she puts her mischievous side to use through her artwork. She is the creator of the popular *Mischievous Kittens* series and several ornaments that explore the antics of both humans and animals. Aubé has sculpted more than 100 Merry Miniatures figurines, and remembers the first time her name was associated with the products, as well as the overwhelming response she received from collectors.

Aubé finds inspiration in her pets, including her cockatiel, Opie, who insists on riding around on her shoulder every day when she comes home from work. Aubé also likes to travel, read, watch movies and garden. Among her sculptures for 2000 are "A Reader to the Core" and "Stroll Around the Pole."

Katrina Bricker

Katrina Bricker considers family to be an important part of her life. Some of her favorite childhood memories include taking trips to the zoo, going on nature walks and fishing with her two sets of grandparents. She considers her dog, Molly, to be her prized possession. And now Bricker and her husband Paul Albright (also a Hallmark employee) have a new reason to celebrate: the birth of their son, Adam, in August of 1999.

Bricker is also an avid equestrian who has a collection of horse figurines. This year, she brings "Mom and Dad," "Kristi Yamaguchi" and "Surprise Package" to the 2000 collection.

Robert Chad

Originally a printmaker and an animator, Robert Chad has applied his talent for creating cartoon figures by sculpting ornaments for the Keepsake Studio since 1987. He was struck with the "cartoon bug" as a child and would watch cartoons and then try to copy the designs on paper. While Looney Tunes™ and Spiderman™ are some of his favorite images to create, Chad is involved in a variety of designs and mediums, from the long-running *Mary's Angels* series to the 1993 porcelain "Bringing Home the Tree."

An art lover as well as an artist, Chad has a small art collection at home, including two Cecil Forbes sketches that he treasures. He also counts traveling, watching movies and listening to music among his hobbies. This year, look for his work in pieces such as "Bugs Bunny and Gossamer," "Mary's Angels" and "Hooray for the U.S.A."

🍃 Ken Crow 🍃

Ken Crow is a child at heart. The vibrant artist loves to play with toys – most notably his collection of puppets. Usually spotted with his stuffed crow companion on his shoulder, Crow values his collection of characters, which includes a Jerry Mahoney ventriloquist dummy that his parents gave to him when he was a child, and a Santa marionette that he used to entertain guests at the Hallmark 25th Anniversary Convention in 1998. He says he would become a puppeteer if he could make a living at it.

At his job in the Keepsake Studio, Crow makes a living by bringing inanimate objects to life through his sculptures. He feels fortunate to have the talent and ability to immortalize life, as seen in "Our Little Blessings," a special ornament dedicated to his children. Crow's portfolio for 2000 includes such pieces as "G.I. Joe® Action Pilot," "Toymaker Santa" and "Time For Joy."

🍃 Joanne Eschrich 🍃

Joanne Eschrich grew up near Boston and fondly remembers snowy winters and ice skating with her three sisters and two brothers. She brings those childhood memories to life every Christmas through her creation of Keepsake Ornaments.

Eschrich's two daughters, Jamie and Anna, also influence the types of pieces that she designs. Whether it is the excitement of the first snowfall of the winter or the challenge of a ballet rehearsal, Eschrich captures the emotions of special moments that others can relate to and want to immortalize. Eschrich adds "Caroler's Best Friend," "Snow Girl" and "All Things Beautiful," which features a miniature readable storybook, to the collection this year.

⇗ John "Collin" Francis ⇜

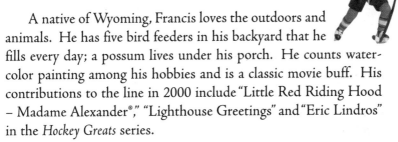

While he has sculpted a variety of ornaments and figurines in his 14 years with the Keepsake Studio, John "Collin" Francis is probably best known for his Merry Miniatures and his Madame Alexander® designs. He especially enjoys sculpting the Madame Alexander® dolls, he says, because they represent angels who carry on the true meaning and spirit of Christmas.

A native of Wyoming, Francis loves the outdoors and animals. He has five bird feeders in his backyard that he fills every day; a possum lives under his porch. He counts water-color painting among his hobbies and is a classic movie buff. His contributions to the line in 2000 include "Little Red Riding Hood – Madame Alexander®," "Lighthouse Greetings" and "Eric Lindros" in the *Hockey Greats* series.

⇗ Tammy Haddix ⇜

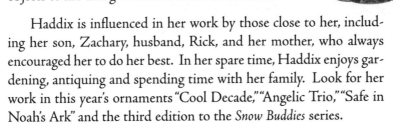

Tammy Haddix wanted to be an artist for Hallmark since she was 5 years old. She got the opportunity when a Hallmark representative recruited her from the Kansas City Art Institute during a visit to the school. Since then, Haddix has turned her dreams into reality as she enters her fourth year in the Keepsake Studio. She says her favorite part of the job is her ability to bring inanimate objects to life and give them a sense of emotion.

Haddix is influenced in her work by those close to her, includ-ing her son, Zachary, husband, Rick, and her mother, who always encouraged her to do her best. In her spare time, Haddix enjoys gar-dening, antiquing and spending time with her family. Look for her work in this year's ornaments "Cool Decade," "Angelic Trio," "Safe in Noah's Ark" and the third edition to the *Snow Buddies* series.

⮞ Kristina Kline ❦

Kristina Kline came to the Keepsake Ornament Studio in 1995, and since then has made a name for herself. This comes as no surprise to Keepsake studio manager Jack Benson and fellow artist Robert Chad who spotted her talent while teaching a sculpting class at the Kansas City Art Institute where Kline was a student. Her class project, a sculpture of a teddy bear and cat, won her an internship with Hallmark; she became a full-time artist soon after.

Kline surrounds herself with tokens of family and comfort when thinking of new ideas for ornaments. Her most valued possessions include a quilt made by her mother and a Hallmark pin given to her by her father. For 2000, she has sculpted "Our First Christmas," "Gifts for the Grinch," and "Imperial Stormtrooper™" from the Star Wars™ films.

⮞ Tracy Larsen ❦

Tracy Larsen says he would like to incorporate more of his original designs into his sculpting. Since he came to the Keepsake Studio in 1995, he has been doing just that. He broke new ground when he created three of the first Keepsake Ornaments to be sculpted out of blown glass ("Frankincense," "Gold" and "Myrrh"), and won hearts all over America with his "Howdy Doody™" and "Larry, Moe and Curly The Three Stooges™" designs. He is also the artist behind the "Collector's Plate" unannounced series. Larsen's designs for 2000 include "Larry, Moe and Curly. The Three Stooges™," "Grandma's House" and "A Visit from St. Nicholas."

In his spare time, Larsen enjoys painting, playing sports and spending time with his wife and children (the fifth of whom, a daughter named Sophia, was born in October of 1999).

Joyce Lyle

Joyce Lyle names "The Sound of Music" and "The Music Man" among her favorite movies, but she has found fame in the Keepsake Studio for her traditional holiday pieces and her depiction of characters from another classic musical – "The Wizard of Oz." Lyle's sculptures of "Glinda, The Good Witch™," "Wicked Witch of the West™" and "The Lollipop Guild™" are so realistic that you almost expect them to come to life, perhaps because she watched the film over and over until she got the look exactly right. She also relates to the movie's theme: "there's no place like home." With six siblings, five children and three grandchildren, her home is filled with a lot of love.

Lyle is active in choral and hand-bell choirs within her church and community, and she serves as director for the local children's choir. Among her 2000 releases are "The Lullabye League" and "Snowy Garden."

Lynn Norton

Lynn Norton has been building models since he was 8 years old, when he was introduced to the hobby by his great-grandfather. Since then, the artist has built a variety of planes, trains, automobiles and other modes of transportation, many of which he has sculpted as Hallmark ornaments.

Originally an engraver for Hallmark, Norton joined the Keepsake Studio in 1987 as a technical artist. He sculpted his first ornament, a replica of the Star Trek™ "Starship Enterprise," in 1991. A longtime Star Trek™ fan, Norton built the model himself, using his engraving skills to create windows and detail lines in the ornament. Since then, Norton has sculpted several other models and ornaments for Hallmark, including this year's "Borg™ Cube STAR TREK: Voyager" and "Spirit of St. Louis."

✈ Don Palmiter ✦

During his first years as an artist with the Keepsake Studio in the late 1980s, Don Palmiter sculpted figurines before finding his true calling: Kiddie Car Classics. Palmiter is the primary artist and researcher for the successful collection of die-cast metal model automobiles and has created more than 50 pieces to date, including those in the Sidewalk Cruisers collection.

A classic car fanatic since childhood, Palmiter is also the sculptor behind the *Classic American Cars* ornament series. He bases many of his designs on his own collection of classic automobiles, which has included a 1962 Corvair, a 1963 Rolls Royce Silver Cloud and a 1968 Corvette. Palmiter also enjoys spending time with his family, interior decorating and antiquing, which – like his collection of classic cars – inspires a sense of nostalgia and warm memories from the past.

✈ Sharon Pike ✦

Sharon Pike feels lucky that she can combine her love for animals and her humorous outlook on life with her work every day. A member of the Keepsake Studio since 1983, she has sculpted all sorts of animals, including this year's "Gold-Star Teacher" and "Loggin' On to Santa."

Pike also applies her creativity to making jewelry, painting and attending art shows, and is a fan of the theater and science fiction. She says she is inspired by other artists and her pet cats, including a calico named C.C. who is her most prized possession, and her recently deceased cat named Skunk who lives on through many of the ornaments he inspired.

Dill Rhodus

Known as the Studio's "resident sport nut," Dill Rhodus has always had a passion for sports. His father was a minor league baseball player so sports played an important role in the family's life. Rhodus still enjoys sports of all kinds (especially golf) and carries that passion into his work. He has sculpted a variety of athletes, including those in the *Football Legends* and *At the Ballpark* series. Also known for his creation of several Star Wars™ pieces, it is no surprise that Rhodus' 2000 ornaments include "Obi-Wan Kenobi™" and "Gungan™ Submarine," among others.

Rhodus' other passion is his family, which includes his wife, fellow Keepsake Artist Patricia Andrews, and his two daughters, Elizabeth and Andrea. In his spare time, he enjoys coaching his daughters' soccer teams and gardening.

Anita Marra Rogers

Anita Marra Rogers knew that she had made the right career move the minute she walked into the Keepsake Studio in 1987. She enjoys the fact that she can express her personality through her work, and has made a name for herself as a talented sculptor of both people and animals.

Her ability to sculpt accurate portrayals of humans has allowed her to design pieces based on many well-known characters, including "The Beatles Gift Set," "Captain James T. Kirk" and "Mr. Spock." This year, she adds "Catwoman™," "Lieutenant Commander Worf™ STAR TREK: Deep Space Nine™" and "Harley-Davidson® BARBIE™ Ornament" to her credits. She also enjoys creating ornaments based on animals, such as her *Puppy Love* series. Rogers enjoys baking, traveling, collecting and solving puzzles.

⇗ Ed Seale ⇖

Ed Seale began working in the Keepsake Artist Studio in 1980, when the department was called the Trim-A-Home department. Since then, he has created many successful designs, including ornaments in the immensely popular *Frosty Friends* series. He is also well-known for his habit of sculpting animals in situations where one would expect to find humans. His inspiration has come from time aboard his catamaran, his experiences growing up in Toronto and his memories, which he considers to be his most prized possessions. Among Seale's 2000 additions to the collection are "Close-Knit Friends," "Adobe Church," "Seaside Scenes" and "Dale Earnhardt."

Now semi-retired, Seale says the best part about working at the Keepsake Studio has been his interactions with fellow Keepsake Artists and the collectors he's met and inspired. He has served as a mentor for many of the new Keepsake Artists and has touched the lives of numerous collectors with his ornaments.

⇗ Linda Sickman ⇖

In her 24 years with the Keepsake Studio, Linda Sickman has sculpted more than 300 designs, but her most famous may be those in her *Rocking Horse* series. Sickman was glad to return to this concept in 1998, when she designed a new series of horse-themed ornaments called *A Pony For Christmas*.

Sickman has also worked with pieces based on transportation, including several in the Kiddie Car Corner collection. Wheeled designs come naturally to Sickman, who spent much of her childhood travelling on trains and riding tractors at her grandparents' farm. A collector of tin toys, she has used this medium to create several ornaments, such as those in the *Tin Locomotive* and *Yuletide Central* series. Her contributions to the 2000 line include "Cool Character" and "Memories of Christmas," both sculpted from pressed tin.

Bob Siedler

A sculptor with the Keepsake Studio since 1982, Bob Siedler enjoys the challenge of variety that comes with each year's introductions. Since new designs are added annually, he finds sculpting always fresh and exciting. Siedler says he gets his ideas for new pieces by observing people's behavior.

Some of his best-known pieces are those of licensed products such as Snoopy, who, Siedler says, "has his own unique attitude." In addition to the third edition of the *Spotlight On Snoopy* series, Siedler has sculpted this year's "A Snoopy® Christmas" Reach ornaments and "Mr. Monopoly™." An active golfer and snow skier, Siedler also created the NFL collection for 2000.

Sue Tague

Although she has worked on all kinds of artistic projects for Hallmark – including painting, drawing and designing – Sue Tague is most passionate about her current career: sculpting. A full-time member of the Keepsake Studio since 1994, Tague had experienced most elements of the job before she reached this position. She had actively designed ornaments for the Studio as far back as 1978 and sculpted several Merry Miniatures along the way.

Outside of work, Tague designs dolls and puppets. Look for her work in the 2000 ornaments "Backpack Bear," "King of the Ring" and "Dancin' In Christmas."

Duane Unruh

Duane Unruh has a lengthy history in athletics, which he puts to use in the Keepsake Studio every day. His father was a college and high school coach for 40 years, laying the groundwork for Unruh, who was a high school coach and enjoyed a 24-year career

in the school system before joining Hallmark. After his retirement, Unruh began a second career as a sculptor. Growing up during the Depression, he made many of his own toys, and as an adult, he enjoyed woodworking and sculpting. It was only natural that he follow his heart to the Keepsake Studio, where he is a senior designer.

Unruh enjoys all aspects of his work, from research to detailing the final design. His contributions for 2000 include "Arnold Palmer" and "Karl Malone," the sixth edition of the *Hoop Stars* series.

LaDene Votruba

Holidays have always been special to LaDene Votruba. Her entire family would get together at the family farm in rural Wilson, Kansas, and enjoy a festive meal together. These memories come to life through her ornaments. Whether she's designing pieces for spring or winter, her celebratory feelings for the season express themselves loud and clear.

Votruba finds inspiration in everything she does, from reading, shopping and walking in the country to antiquing and making jewelry. Votruba also owns a home library full of books and magazines, which she scans for ideas in times of "artist's block." Her 2000 ornaments include "Graceful Glory," "Sister to Sister" and the miniature ornament "Precious Penguin."

Nello Williams

As a child, Nello Williams dreamed of becoming a Disney animator. He is now fulfilling his dream by bringing his favorite Disney characters to life in another way – through sculpting Hallmark Keepsake Ornaments. In addition to his work on the Disney team, William also sculpts ornaments that reflect the more humorous side of his personality. He prides himself on his ability to make others smile and laugh, which is evident in many of his 2000 ornaments, including "Sleigh X-2000," "The Yellow Submarine" and "Green Eggs and Ham™" from the miniature collection.

COLLECTOR'S
VALUE GUIDE™

A life long music buff, Williams plays the guitar and keyboard, writes songs and composes music. In 1999, he brought his musical talents to the workplace when he wrote and directed the sound effects for the 1999 musical ornament "Jazzy Jalopy."

The New Keepsake Studio Artists

Four new artists recently joined the Keepsake Studio as full-time sculptors. Here's a brief introduction to each artist:

Julie Forsyth – This New Jersey native came to Hallmark in 1978 as a sculptor for the Little Gallery line of fine collectibles. After leaving the Studio to have children, she returned to Hallmark and the Keepsake Studio two years ago.

Rich LaPierre – Originally from Massachusetts, LaPierre was hired by Hallmark right out of cartoon school. He has now been with the company for 15 years. While he serves primarily as the artist behind the School Days Lunch Boxes, LaPierre has sculpted a number of ornaments for the 2000 line.

Sharon Visker – Visker began her career with Hallmark 16 years ago, working for the specialty and design departments. She eventually did woodcarving and made the transition to three-dimensional work. A native of Colorado, Visker graduated from Utah's Brigham Young University with an illustration degree.

Chris Webb – A graduate of the Kansas City Art Institute, Webb always wanted to be an artist. This St. Louis native now spends his time designing "anything with wheels." A classic car enthusiast, he enjoys restoring and building automobiles in his spare time.

Hallmark Top Ten

This section showcases the ten most valuable Hallmark Ornaments based on their secondary market values. It should come as no surprise that the majority of these are first editions of a collectible series. How many are in your collection?

KANSAS CITY SANTA (1991)
Convention Ornament
No stock number
Original Price: N/C
MARKET VALUE: $975

SANTA'S MOTORCAR (1979)
1st in the *Here Comes Santa* series
#900QX1559
Original Price: $9
MARKET VALUE: $690

TIN LOCOMOTIVE (1982)
1st in the *Tin Locomotive* series
#1300QX4603
Original Price: $13
MARKET VALUE: $670

A COOL YULE (1980)
1st in the *Frosty Friends* series
#650QX1374
Original Price: $6.50
MARKET VALUE: $665

ROCKING HORSE (1981)
1st in the *Rocking Horse* series
#900QX4222
Original Price: $9
MARKET VALUE: $635

FROSTY FRIENDS (1981)
2nd in the *Frosty Friends* series
#800QX4335
Original Price: $8
MARKET VALUE: $495

TRUEST JOYS OF CHRISTMAS (1977)
5th in the *Betsey Clark* series
#350QX2642
Original Price: $3.50
MARKET VALUE: $450

ROCKING HORSE (1982)
2nd in the *Rocking Horse* series
#1000QX5023
Original Price: $10
MARKET VALUE: $440

THE BELLSWINGER (1979)
1st in *The Bellringers* series
#1000QX1479
Original Price: $10
MARKET VALUE: $410

ANTIQUE TOYS (1978)
1st in the *Carrousel Series*
#600QX1463
Original Price: $6
MARKET VALUE: $405

How To Use Your Collector's Value Guide™

1. Locate your piece in the Value Guide. Keepsake Ornaments are listed first in two sections: series (listed in alphabetical order by series name) and general ornaments (listed in reverse chronological order). For each year, the general ornaments are grouped as follows (if applicable): Keepsake, Magic, Crown Reflections, Li'l Blown Glass, Showcase, Laser Creations, Miniature and miscellaneous. Spring Ornaments, Merry Miniatures and Kiddie Car Classics follow in separate sections. An alphabetical index begins on page 345.

2. Fill in the price you paid for the piece in the "Price Paid" column. The original retail price is the first 3 or 4 digits of the Hallmark stock number. For example, a piece with stock number 450QXM5937 would have a retail price of $4.50. An N/A means that the information is not available.

3. Record the current market value of your piece in the "Value" column. "N/E" means the market value is not yet established for that piece.

4. Calculate the total value of each page by adding the boxes. Use a pencil so you can change the totals as your collection grows.

5. Transfer the totals to the "Total Value Of My Collection" worksheets, found on pages 324-328. Add these together to find the total value of your collection.

Hallmark Artist Key

ANDR	Patricia Andrews
AUBE	Nina Aubé
BAUR	Tim Bauer
BISH	Ron Bishop
BLAC	Thomas Blackshear
BRIC	Katrina Bricker
BRWN	Andrew Brownsword
CHAD	Robert Chad
CROW	Ken Crow
DLEE	Donna Lee
DUTK	Peter Dutkin
ESCH	Joanne Eschrich
FORS	Julie Forsyth
FRAL	Tobin Fraley
FRAN	John "Collin" Francis
HADD	Tammy Haddix
HAMI	Mary Hamilton
JLEE	Julia Lee
JOHN	Cathy Johnson
KLIN	Kristina Kline
LAPR	Rich LaPierre
LARS	Tracy Larsen
LYLE	Joyce Lyle
MAHO	Jim Mahon
MCGE	Diana McGehee
N/A	not available
NORT	Lynn Norton
PALM	Don Palmiter
PATT	Joyce Pattee
PIKE	Sharon Pike
PYDA	Michele Pyda-Sevcik
RGRS	Anita Marra Rogers
RHOD	Dill Rhodus
SCHU	Lee Schuler
SEAL	Ed Seale
SICK	Linda Sickman
SIED	Bob Siedler
TAGU	Sue Tague
UNRU	Duane Unruh
VARI	various artists
VISK	Sharon Visker
VOTR	LaDene Votruba
WEBB	Chris Webb
WILL	Nello Williams

Madonna and Child and St. John (1st, 1984)
Beaded Satin • MCGE
650QX3494 • Value $20

African-American Holiday BARBIE™	
Price Paid	Value

All-American Trucks

1.	
2.	
3.	
4.	
5.	
6.	
7.	

All God's Children®

8.	
9.	
10.	

Art Masterpiece

11.	$6.50	$20
12.		
13.		

At The Ballpark

14.	
15.	
16.	
17.	
	$20

Totals

Keepsake Series

Ornaments which are part of a Hallmark Keepsake Series have proven over time to be among the most popular Hallmark Ornaments ever produced. The year 2000 introduces six new series to delight collectors and bids farewell to seven series that honor their final editions in 2000.

1

African-American Holiday BARBIE™ (1st & final, 1998)
Handcrafted • ANDR
1595QX6936 • **Value $26**

2

1956 Ford Truck (1st, 1995)
Handcrafted • PALM
1395QX5527 • **Value $38**

3

1955 Chevrolet Cameo (2nd, 1996)
Handcrafted • PALM
1395QX5241 • **Value $31**

4

1953 GMC (3rd, 1997)
Handcrafted • PALM
1395QX6105 • **Value $27**

5

1937 Ford V-8 (4th, 1998)
Handcrafted • PALM
1395QX6263 • **Value $26**

6

1957 Dodge® Sweptside D100 (5th, 1999)
Handcrafted • PALM
1395QX6269 • **Value $22**

7
New!

1978 Dodge® L'il Red Express Truck (6th, 2000)
Handcrafted • PALM
1395QX6581 • **Value $13.95**

8

Christy (1st, 1996)
Handcrafted • N/A
1295QX5564 • **Value $26**

9

Nikki (2nd, set/2, 1997)
Handcrafted • N/A
1295QX6142 • **Value $24**

10

Ricky (3rd & final, 1998)
Handcrafted • N/A
1295QX6363 • **Value $23**

11

Madonna and Child and St. John (1st, 1984)
Bezeled Satin • MCGE
650QX3494 • **Value $20**

12

Madonna of the Pomegranate (2nd, 1985)
Bezeled Satin • MCGE
675QX3772 • **Value $17**

13

Madonna and Child with the Infant St. John (3rd & final, 1986)
Bezeled Satin • MCGE
675QX3506 • **Value $30**

14

Nolan Ryan (1st, 1996)
Handcrafted • RHOD
1495QXI5711 • **Value $37**

15

Hank Aaron (2nd, 1997)
Handcrafted • RHOD
1495QX6152 • **Value $29**

16

Cal Ripken Jr. (3rd, 1998)
Handcrafted • RHOD
1495QXI4033 • **Value $26**

17

Ken Griffey Jr. (4th, 1999)
Handcrafted • RHOD
1495QXI4037 • **Value $20**

	Price Paid	Value
African-American Holiday BARBIE™		
1.		
All-American Trucks		
2.		
3.		
4.		
5.		
6.		
7.		
All God's Children®		
8.		
9.		
10.		
Art Masterpiece		
11.		
12.		
13.		
At the Ballpark		
14.		
15.		
16.		
17.		
Totals		

VALUE GUIDE — HALLMARK KEEPSAKE ORNAMENTS

1

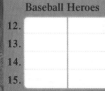

New!

**Mark McGwire
(5th, 2000)**
Handcrafted • RHOD
1495QXI5361 • **Value $14.95**

2

BARBIE™ (1st, 1994)
Handcrafted • ANDR
1495QX5006 • **Value $46**

3

**Solo in the Spotlight
(2nd, 1995)**
Handcrafted • ANDR
1495QXI5049 • **Value $28**

4

**Brunette Debut – 1959
(club edition, 1995)**
Handcrafted • ANDR
1495QXC5397 • **Value $65**

5

**Featuring the
Enchanted Evening
BARBIE® Doll (3rd, 1996)**
Handcrafted • ANDR
1495QXI6541 • **Value $30**

6

**Wedding Day 1959-1962
(4th, 1997)**
Handcrafted • ANDR
1595QXI6812 • **Value $30**

7

**BARBIE™ and KEN™
Wedding Day (set/2, com-
plements the series, 1997)**
Handcrafted • ANDR/PALM
3500QXI6815 • **Value $52**

8

Silken Flame™ (5th, 1998)
Handcrafted • ANDR
1595QXI4043 • **Value $28**

9

**Gay Parisienne™
BARBIE™ Ornament
(6th, 1999)**
Handcrafted • ANDR
1595QXI5301 • **Value $23**

10

New!

**Commuter Set™
(7th, 2000, set/2)**
Handcrafted • ANDR
1595QX6814 • **Value $15.95**

11

New!

PHOTO UNAVAILABLE

**BARBIE™ Ornament
(1st, 2000)**
Handcrafted • ANDR
1595QXI6821 • **Value $15.95**

12

Babe Ruth (1st, 1994)
Handcrafted • RHOD
1295QX5323 • **Value $58**

13

Lou Gehrig (2nd, 1995)
Handcrafted • RHOD
1295QX5029 • **Value $23**

14

Satchel Paige (3rd, 1996)
Handcrafted • RHOD
1295QX5304 • **Value $22**

15

**Jackie Robinson
(4th & final, 1997)**
Handcrafted • RHOD
1295QX6202 • **Value $24**

16

**The Bellswinger
(1st, 1979)**
Handcrafted/Porcelain • N/A
1000QX1479 • **Value $410**

17

**The Bellringers
(2nd, 1980)**
Handcrafted/Porcelain • N/A
1500QX1574 • **Value $86**

18

**Swingin' Bellringer
(3rd, 1981)**
Handcrafted/Ceramic • N/A
1500QX4415 • **Value $100**

	Price Paid	Value
At the Ballpark		
1.		
BARBIE™		
2.		
3.		
4.		
5.		
6.		
7.		
8.		
9.		
10.		
BARBIE™ Ornament		
11.		
Baseball Heroes		
12.		
13.		
14.		
15.		
The Bellringers		
16.		
17.		
18.		
Totals		

VALUE GUIDE — HALLMARK KEEPSAKE ORNAMENTS

#		
1 **Angel Bellringer** **(4th, 1982)** *Handcrafted/Ceramic* • DLEE 1500QX4556 • **Value $100**	**2**  **Teddy Bellringer** **(5th, 1983)** *Handcrafted/Porcelain* • N/A 1500QX4039 • **Value $135**	**3** **Elfin Artist** **(6th & final, 1984)** *Porcelain* • N/A 1500QX4384 • **Value $52**

4 **Christmas 1973**
(1st, 1973)
Glass • N/A
250XHD1102 • **Value $130**

5  **Musicians (2nd, 1974)**
Glass • N/A
250QX1081 • **Value $80**

6 **Caroling Trio (3rd, 1975)**
Glass • N/A
300QX1331 • **Value $72**

7 **Christmas 1976**
(4th, 1976)
Glass • N/A
300QX1951 • **Value $112**

8 **Truest Joys of**
Christmas (5th, 1977)
Glass • N/A
350QX2642 • **Value $450**

9 **Christmas Spirit**
(6th, 1978)
Satin • N/A
350QX2016 • **Value $62**

10 **Holiday Fun (7th, 1979)**
Satin • N/A
350QX2019 • **Value $42**

11 **Joy-in-the-Air**
(8th, 1980)
Glass • N/A
400QX2154 • **Value $32**

12 **Christmas 1981**
(9th, 1981)
Glass • N/A
450QX8022 • **Value $32**

13 **Joys of Christmas**
(10th, 1982)
Satin • N/A
450QX2156 • **Value $34**

14 **Christmas Happiness**
(11th, 1983)
Glass • N/A
450QX2119 • **Value $32**

15 **Days are Merry**
(12th, 1984)
Glass • N/A
500QX2494 • **Value $33**

16 **Special Kind of Feeling**
(13th & final, 1985)
Glass • PIKE
500QX2632 • **Value $35**

17 **Betsey Clark: Home For**
Christmas (1st, 1986)
Glass • PIKE
500QX2776 • **Value $34**

18 **Betsey Clark: Home For**
Christmas (2nd, 1987)
Glass • PIKE
500QX2727 • **Value $24**

19 **Betsey Clark: Home For**
Christmas (3rd, 1988)
Glass • PIKE
500QX2714 • **Value $23**

20 **Betsey Clark: Home For**
Christmas (4th, 1989)
Glass • N/A
500QX2302 • **Value $36**

The Bellringers

	Price Paid	Value
1.		
2.		
3.		

Betsey Clark

4.		
5.		
6.		
7.		
8.		
9.		
10.		
11.		
12.		
13.		
14.		
15.		
16.		

Betsey Clark: Home For Christmas

17.		
18.		
19.		
20.		

Totals

1

Betsey Clark: Home For Christmas (5th, 1990)
Glass • N/A
500QX2033 • **Value $24**

2

Betsey Clark: Home For Christmas (6th & final, 1991)
Glass • N/A
500QX2109 • **Value $28**

3

Betsey's Country Christmas (1st, 1992)
Glass • N/A
500QX2104 • **Value $26**

4

Betsey's Country Christmas (2nd, 1993)
Glass • N/A
500QX2062 • **Value $19**

5

Betsey's Country Christmas (3rd & final, 1994)
Glass • N/A
500QX2403 • **Value $16**

6

Antique Toys (1st, 1978)
Handcrafted • N/A
600QX1463 • **Value $405**

7

Christmas Carrousel (2nd, 1979)
Handcrafted • N/A
650QX1467 • **Value $190**

8

Merry Carrousel (3rd, 1980)
Handcrafted • N/A
750QX1414 • **Value $172**

9

Skaters' Carrousel (4th, 1981)
Handcrafted • N/A
900QX4275 • **Value $92**

10

Snowman Carrousel (5th, 1982)
Handcrafted • SEAL
1000QX4783 • **Value $102**

11

Santa and Friends (6th & final, 1983)
Handcrafted • SICK
1100QX4019 • **Value $52**

12

Cat Naps (1st, 1994)
Handcrafted • RHOD
795QX5313 • **Value $40**

13

Cat Naps (2nd, 1995)
Handcrafted • RHOD
795QX5097 • **Value $25**

14

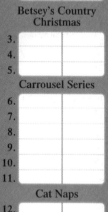

Cat Naps (3rd, 1996)
Handcrafted • RHOD
795QX5641 • **Value $20**

15

Cat Naps (4th, 1997)
Handcrafted • BRIC
895QX6205 • **Value $19**

16

Cat Naps (5th & final, 1998)
Handcrafted • BRIC
895QX6383 • **Value $20**

17

A Celebration of Angels (1st, 1995)
Handcrafted • ANDR
1295QX5077 • **Value $26**

18

A Celebration of Angels (2nd, 1996)
Handcrafted • ANDR
1295QX5634 • **Value $26**

19

A Celebration of Angels (3rd, 1997)
Handcrafted • ANDR
1395QX6175 • **Value $22**

20

A Celebration of Angels (4th & final, 1998)
Handcrafted • ANDR
1395QX6366 • **Value $23**

Betsey Clark: Home For Christmas

	Price Paid	Value
1.		
2.		

Betsey's Country Christmas

3.		
4.		
5.		

Carrousel Series

6.		
7.		
8.		
9.		
10.		
11.		

Cat Naps

12.		
13.		
14.		
15.		
16.		

A Celebration Of Angels

17.		
18.		
19.		
20.		

Totals

1

Christmas Kitty
(1st, 1989)
Porcelain • RGRS
1475QX5445 • **Value $31**

2

Christmas Kitty
(2nd, 1990)
Porcelain • RGRS
1475QX4506 • **Value $34**

3

Christmas Kitty
(3rd & final, 1991)
Porcelain • RGRS
1475QX4377 • **Value $28**

4

St. Nicholas (1st, 1995)
Handcrafted • RGRS
1495QX5087 • **Value $30**

5

Christkindl (2nd, 1996)
Handcrafted • VOTR
1495QX5631 • **Value $28**

6

Kolyada
(3rd & final, 1997)
Handcrafted • VOTR
1495QX6172 • **Value $26**

7

1957 Corvette (1st, 1991)
Handcrafted • PALM
1275QX4319 • **Value $215**

8

1966 Mustang (2nd, 1992)
Handcrafted • PALM
1275QX4284 • **Value $54**

9

1956 Ford Thunderbird
(3rd, 1993)
Handcrafted • PALM
1275QX5275 • **Value $38**

10

1957 Chevrolet Bel Air
(4th, 1994)
Handcrafted • PALM
1295QX5422 • **Value $33**

11

1969 Chevrolet Camaro
(5th, 1995)
Handcrafted • PALM
1295QX5239 • **Value $24**

12

1958 Ford Edsel
Citation Convertible
(club edition, 1995)
Handcrafted • PALM
1295QXC4167 • **Value $78**

13

1959 Cadillac De Ville
(6th, 1996)
Handcrafted • PALM
1295QX5384 • **Value $29**

14

1969 Hurst Oldsmobile
442 (7th, 1997)
Handcrafted • PALM
1395QX6102 • **Value $27**

15

1970 Plymouth®
Hemi 'Cuda (8th, 1998)
Handcrafted • PALM
1395QX6256 • **Value $27**

16

1955 Chevrolet®
Nomad® Wagon
(9th, 1999)
Handcrafted • PALM
1395QX6367 • **Value $22**

17

New!

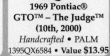

1969 Pontiac®
GTO™ – The Judge™
(10th, 2000)
Handcrafted • PALM
1395QX6584 • **Value $13.95**

18

The Clauses on Vacation
(1st, 1997)
Handcrafted • SIED
1495QX6112 • **Value $28**

19

The Clauses on Vacation
(2nd, 1998)
Handcrafted • SIED
1495QX6276 • **Value $23**

20

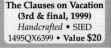

The Clauses on Vacation
(3rd & final, 1999)
Handcrafted • SIED
1495QX6399 • **Value $20**

Keepsake Series

1
British (1st, 1982)
Handcrafted • SICK
500QX4583 • **Value $135**

2
Early American (2nd, 1983)
Handcrafted • SICK
500QX4029 • **Value $51**

3
Canadian Mountie (3rd, 1984)
Handcrafted • SICK
500QX4471 • **Value $32**

4
Scottish Highlander (4th, 1985)
Handcrafted • SICK
550QX4715 • **Value $30**

5
French Officer (5th, 1986)
Handcrafted • SICK
550QX4063 • **Value $30**

6
Sailor (6th & final, 1987)
Handcrafted • SICK
550QX4807 • **Value $30**

7
Light Shines at Christmas (1st, 1987)
Porcelain • VOTR
800QX4817 • **Value $72**

8
Waiting for Santa (2nd, 1988)
Porcelain • VOTR
800QX4061 • **Value $47**

Clothespin Soldier

	Price Paid	Value
1.		
2.		
3.		
4.		
5.		
6.		

Collector's Plate

7.		
8.		
9.		
10.		
11.		
12.		

Cool Decade

13.		
14.		

CRAYOLA® Crayon

15.		
16.		
17.		
18.		
19.		

9
Morning of Wonder (3rd, 1989)
Porcelain • VOTR
825QX4612 • **Value $29**

10
Cookies for Santa (4th, 1990)
Porcelain • VOTR
875QX4436 • **Value $31**

11
Let It Snow! (5th, 1991)
Porcelain • VOTR
875QX4369 • **Value $27**

12
Sweet Holiday Harmony (6th & final, 1992)
Porcelain • VOTR
875QX4461 • **Value $25**

13
New!
Cool Decade (1st, 2000)
Handcrafted • HADD
795QX6764 • **Value $7.95**

14
New!
Cool Decade (club edition, 2000)
Handcrafted • HADD
795QX6764 • **Value $7.95**

15
Bright Journey (1st, 1989)
Handcrafted • SICK
875QX4352 • **Value $65**

16
Bright Moving Colors (2nd, 1990)
Handcrafted • CROW
875QX4586 • **Value $51**

17
Bright Vibrant Carols (3rd, 1991)
Handcrafted • CROW
975QX4219 • **Value $43**

18
Bright Blazing Colors (4th, 1992)
Handcrafted • CROW
975QX4264 • **Value $40**

19
Bright Shining Castle (5th, 1993)
Handcrafted • CROW
1075QX4422 • **Value $30**

Totals

sake Series

1

Bright Playful Colors
(6th, 1994)
Handcrafted • CROW
1095QX5273 • **Value $30**

2

Bright 'n' Sunny Tepee
(7th, 1995)
Handcrafted • ANDR
1095QX5247 • **Value $26**

3

Bright Flying Colors
(8th, 1996)
Handcrafted • CROW
1095QX5391 • **Value $28**

4

Bright Rocking Colors
(9th, 1997)
Handcrafted • TAGU
1295QX6235 • **Value $28**

5

Bright Sledding Colors
(10th & final, 1998)
Handcrafted • TAGU
1295QX6166 • **Value $25**

6

Native American
BARBIE™ (1st, 1996)
Handcrafted • ANDR
1495QX5561 • **Value $30**

7

Chinese BARBIE™
(2nd, 1997)
Handcrafted • RGRS
1495QX6162 • **Value $27**

8

Mexican BARBIE™
(3rd, 1998)
Handcrafted • RGRS
1495QX6356 • **Value $26**

9
Russian BARBIE™
Ornament
(4th & final, 1999)
Handcrafted • RGRS
1495QX6369 • **Value $21**

10

The Cat in the Hat
(1st, 1999, set/2)
Handcrafted • WILL
1495QXI6457 • **Value $22**

11
New!

One Fish Two Fish
Red Fish Blue Fish™
(2nd, 2000)
Handcrafted • WILL
1495QX6781 • **Value $14.95**

12
Cinderella (1st, 1997)
Handcrafted • CROW
1495QXD4045 • **Value $32**

13

Walt Disney's
Sleeping Beauty
(3rd & final, 1999)
Handcrafted • N/A
1495QXD4097 • **Value $23**

14
Walt Disney's
Snow White **(2nd, 1998)**
Handcrafted • N/A
1495QXD4056 • **Value $27**

15

Fabulous Decade
(1st, 1990)
Handcrafted/Brass • SEAL
775QX4466 • **Value $40**

16
Fabulous Decade
(2nd, 1991)
Handcrafted/Brass • SEAL
775QX4119 • **Value $42**

17
Fabulous Decade
(3rd, 1992)
Handcrafted/Brass • SEAL
775QX4244 • **Value $50**

18
Fabulous Decade
(4th, 1993)
Handcrafted/Brass • PIKE
775QX4475 • **Value $25**

19

Fabulous Decade
(5th, 1994)
Handcrafted/Brass • SEAL
795QX5263 • **Value $27**

20

Fabulous Decade
(6th, 1995)
Handcrafted/Brass • SEAL
795QX5147 • **Value $22**

CRAYOLA® Crayon	Price Paid	Value
1.		
2.		
3.		
4.		
5.		

Dolls Of The World		
6.		
7.		
8.		
9.		

Dr. Seuss® Books		
10.		
11.		

The Enchanted Memories Collection		
12.		
13.		
14.		

Fabulous Decade		
15.		
16.		
17.		
18.		
19.		
20.		

Totals

Fabulous Decade (7th, 1996)
Handcrafted/Brass • SEAL
795QX5661 • **Value $23**

Fabulous Decade (8th, 1997)
Handcrafted/Brass • PIKE
795QX6232 • **Value $19**

Fabulous Decade (9th, 1998)
Handcrafted/Brass • PIKE
795QX6393 • **Value $25**

Fabulous Decade (10th & final, 1999)
Handcrafted/Brass • PIKE
795QX6357 • **Value $20**

New!

Fashion Afoot (1st, 2000)
Handcrafted • ESCH
1495QX8341 • **Value $14.95**

David and Goliath (1st, 1999)
Handcrafted • LARS
1395QX6447 • **Value $22**

New!

Jonah and the Great Fish (2nd, 2000)
Handcrafted • LARS
1395QX6701 • **Value $13.95**

Joe Montana (1st, 1995)
Handcrafted • RHOD
1495QXI5759 • **Value $50**

Fabulous Decade

	Price Paid	Value
1.		
2.		
3.		
4.		

Fashion Afoot

5.		

Favorite Bible Stories

6.		
7.		

Football Legends

8.		
9.		
10.		
11.		
12.		
13.		
14.		

Frosty Friends

15.		
16.		
17.		
18.		
19.		
20.		

Joe Montana (Kansas City, 1995)
Handcrafted • RHOD
1495QXI6207 • **Value $102**

Troy Aikman (2nd, 1996)
Handcrafted • RHOD
1495QXI5021 • **Value $29**

Joe Namath (3rd, 1997)
Handcrafted • RHOD
1495QXI6182 • **Value $28**

Emmitt Smith (4th, 1998)
Handcrafted • RHOD
1495QXI4036 • **Value $27**

Dan Marino (5th, 1999)
Handcrafted • RHOD
1495QXI4029 • **Value $20**

New!

John Elway (6th, 2000)
Handcrafted • RHOD
1495QXI6811 • **Value $14.95**

A Cool Yule (1st, 1980)
Handcrafted • BLAC
650QX1374 • **Value $665**

Frosty Friends (2nd, 1981)
Handcrafted • N/A
800QX4335 • **Value $495**

Frosty Friends (3rd, 1982)
Handcrafted • SEAL
800QX4523 • **Value $295**

Frosty Friends (4th, 1983)
Handcrafted • SEAL
800QX4007 • **Value $320**

Frosty Friends (5th, 1984)
Handcrafted • SEAL
800QX4371 • **Value $95**

Frosty Friends (6th, 1985)
Handcrafted • SEAL
850QX4822 • **Value $84**

Totals

1

Frosty Friends (7th, 1986)
Handcrafted • SIED
850QX4053 • **Value $76**

2

Frosty Friends (8th, 1987)
Handcrafted • SEAL
850QX4409 • **Value $63**

3

Frosty Friends (9th, 1988)
Handcrafted • SEAL
875QX4031 • **Value $69**

4

Frosty Friends (10th, 1989)
Handcrafted • SEAL
925QX4572 • **Value $65**

5

Frosty Friends (11th, 1990)
Handcrafted • SEAL
975QX4396 • **Value $39**

6

Frosty Friends (12th, 1991)
Handcrafted • PIKE
975QX4327 • **Value $45**

7

Frosty Friends (13th, 1992)
Handcrafted • JLEE
975QX4291 • **Value $35**

8

Frosty Friends (14th, 1993)
Handcrafted • JLEE
975QX4142 • **Value $33**

9

Frosty Friends (complements the series, 1993)
Handcrafted • SEAL
2000QX5682 • **Value $48**

10

Frosty Friends (15th, 1994)
Handcrafted • SEAL
995QX5293 • **Value $33**

11

Frosty Friends (16th, 1995)
Handcrafted • SEAL
1095QX5169 • **Value $29**

12

Frosty Friends (17th, 1996)
Handcrafted • SEAL
1095QX5681 • **Value $26**

13

Frosty Friends (18th, 1997)
Handcrafted • SEAL
1095QX6255 • **Value $25**

14

Frosty Friends (19th, 1998)
Handcrafted • SEAL
1095QX6226 • **Value $25**

15

Frosty Friends (20th, 1999)
Handcrafted • SEAL
1295QX6297 • **Value $23**

16

New!

Frosty Friends (21st, 2000)
Handcrafted • SEAL
1095QX6601 • **Value $10.95**

17

New!

Frosty Friends (Premiere, set/3, 2000)
Porcelain/Pewter • SEAL
1895QX8524 • **Value $18.95**

18

New!

Husky (club edition, miniature, 2000)
Pewter • N/A
(N/C) No stock # • **Value N/E**

19

Gift Bearers (1st, 1999)
Porcelain • TAGU
1295QX6437 • **Value $23**

20

New!

Gift Bearers (2nd, 2000)
Porcelain • TAGU
1295QX6651 • **Value $12.95**

Frosty Friends

	Price Paid	Value
1.		
2.		
3.		
4.		
5.		
6.		
7.		
8.		
9.		
10.		
11.		
12.		
13.		
14.		
15.		
16.		
17.		
18.		

Gift Bearers

	Price Paid	Value
19.		
20.		

Totals

49

Keepsake Series

1

St. Nicholas (1st, 1989)
Glass • VOTR
500QX2795 • Value $26

2

St. Lucia (2nd, 1990)
Glass • VOTR
500QX2803 • Value $24

3

Christkindl (3rd, 1991)
Glass • VOTR
500QX2117 • Value $24

4

Kolyada (4th, 1992)
Glass • VOTR
500QX2124 • Value $23

5

The Magi (5th & final, 1993)
Glass • VOTR
500QX2065 • Value $23

6

Greatest Story (1st, 1990)
Porcelain/Brass • VOTR
1275QX4656 • Value $28

7

Greatest Story (2nd, 1991)
Porcelain/Brass • VOTR
1275QX4129 • Value $27

8

Greatest Story (3rd & final, 1992)
Porcelain/Brass • VOTR
1275QX4251 • Value $25

9

Donald's Surprising Gift (1st, 1997)
Handcrafted • BRIC
1295QXD4025 • Value $27

10

Ready for Christmas (2nd, 1998)
Handcrafted • N/A
1295QXD4006 • Value $23

11

Minnie Trims the Tree (3rd & final, 1999)
Handcrafted • N/A
1295QXD4059 • Value $20

12

Hark! It's Herald (1st, 1989)
Handcrafted • CROW
675QX4555 • Value $27

13

Hark! It's Herald (2nd, 1990)
Handcrafted • CROW
675QX4463 • Value $22

14

Hark! It's Herald (3rd, 1991)
Handcrafted • RGRS
675QX4379 • Value $25

15

Hark! It's Herald (4th & final, 1992)
Handcrafted • JLEE
775QX4464 • Value $21

16

Heritage Springer® (1st, 1999)
Die-Cast Metal • PALM
1495QXI8007 • Value $30

17
New!

Fat Boy® (2nd, 2000)
Die-Cast Metal • PALM
1495QXI6774 • Value $14.95

18

Heart of Christmas (1st, 1990)
Handcrafted • SEAL
1375QX4726 • Value $78

19

Heart of Christmas (2nd, 1991)
Handcrafted • SEAL
1375QX4357 • Value $30

20

Heart of Christmas (3rd, 1992)
Handcrafted • SEAL
1375QX4411 • Value $28

	Price Paid	Value
The Gift Bringers		
1.		
2.		
3.		
4.		
5.		
Greatest Story		
6.		
7.		
8.		
Hallmark Archives		
9.		
10.		
11.		
Hark! It's Herald		
12.		
13.		
14.		
15.		
Harley Davidson® Motorcycle Milestones		
16.		
17.		
Heart Of Christmas		
18.		
19.		
20.		
Totals		

1

Heart of Christmas
(4th, 1993)
Handcrafted • SEAL
1475QX4482 • **Value $27**

2

Heart of Christmas
(5th & final, 1994)
Handcrafted • SEAL
1495QX5266 • **Value $29**

3

Heavenly Angels
(1st, 1991)
Handcrafted • LYLE
775QX4367 • **Value $27**

4

Heavenly Angels
(2nd, 1992)
Handcrafted • LYLE
775QX4454 • **Value $30**

5

Heavenly Angels
(3rd & final, 1993)
Handcrafted • LYLE
775QX4945 • **Value $21**

6

Santa's Motorcar
(1st, 1979)
Handcrafted • MAHO
900QX1559 • **Value $690**

7

Santa's Express
(2nd, 1980)
Handcrafted • MAHO
1200QX1434 • **Value $225**

8

Rooftop Deliveries
(3rd, 1981)
Handcrafted • MAHO
1300QX4382 • **Value $345**

9

Jolly Trolley (4th, 1982)
Handcrafted • SICK
1500QX4643 • **Value $150**

10

Santa Express (5th, 1983)
Handcrafted • DLEE
1300QX4037 • **Value $295**

11

Santa's Deliveries
(6th, 1984)
Handcrafted • SICK
1300QX4324 • **Value $94**

12

Santa's Fire Engine
(7th, 1985)
Handcrafted • SICK
1400QX4965 • **Value $70**

13

Kringle's Kool Treats
(8th, 1986)
Handcrafted • SIED
1400QX4043 • **Value $75**

14

Santa's Woody (9th, 1987)
Handcrafted • CROW
1400QX4847 • **Value $88**

15

Kringle Koach
(10th, 1988)
Handcrafted • CROW
1400QX4001 • **Value $50**

16

Christmas Caboose
(11th, 1989)
Handcrafted • CROW
1475QX4585 • **Value $52**

17

Festive Surrey
(12th, 1990)
Handcrafted • SICK
1475QX4923 • **Value $45**

18

Santa's Antique Car
(13th, 1991)
Handcrafted • SICK
1475QX4349 • **Value $56**

19

Kringle Tours
(14th, 1992)
Handcrafted • SICK
1475QX4341 • **Value $37**

20

Happy Haul-idays
(15th, 1993)
Handcrafted • SICK
1475QX4102 • **Value $35**

Heart Of Christmas

	Price Paid	Value
1.		
2.		

Heavenly Angels

3.		
4.		
5.		

Here Comes Santa

6.		
7.		
8.		
9.		
10.		
11.		
12.		
13.		
14.		
15.		
16.		
17.		
18.		
19.		
20.		

Totals

1

**Shopping With Santa
(complements the
series, 1993)**
Handcrafted • SICK
2400QX5675 • **Value $47**

2

**Makin' Tractor Tracks
(16th, 1994)**
Handcrafted • SICK
1495QX5296 • **Value $55**

3

**Santa's Roadster
(17th, 1995)**
Handcrafted • SICK
1495QX5179 • **Value $31**

4

Santa's 4 x 4 (18th, 1996)
Handcrafted • SEAL
1495QX5684 • **Value $32**

5

**The Claus-Mobile
(19th, 1997)**
Handcrafted • TAGU
1495QX6262 • **Value $28**

6

**Santa's Bumper Car
(20th, 1998)**
Handcrafted • TAGU
1495QX6283 • **Value $24**

7

**Santa's Golf Cart
(21st, 1999)**
Handcrafted • RHOD
1495QX6337 • **Value $21**

8

New!

**Sleigh X-2000
(22nd, 2000)**
Handcrafted • WILL
1495QX6824 • **Value $14.95**

9

**Wayne Gretzky
(1st, 1997)**
Handcrafted • UNRU
1595QXI6275 • **Value $33**

10

**Mario Lemieux
(2nd, 1998)**
Handcrafted • FRAN
1595QXI6476 • **Value $25**

11

**Gordie Howe®
(3rd, 1999)**
Handcrafted • FRAN
1595QXI4047 • **Value $20**

12

New!

**Eric Lindros
(4th, 2000)**
Handcrafted • FRAN
1595QXI6801 • **Value $15.95**

13

**Holiday BARBIE™
(1st, 1993)**
Handcrafted • ANDR
1475QX5725 • **Value $178**

14

**Holiday BARBIE™
(2nd, 1994)**
Handcrafted • ANDR
1495QX5216 • **Value $56**

15

**Holiday BARBIE™
(3rd, 1995)**
Handcrafted • ANDR
1495QXI5057 • **Value $36**

16

**Holiday BARBIE™
(4th, 1996)**
Handcrafted • ANDR
1495QXI5371 • **Value $33**

17

**Holiday BARBIE™
(5th, 1997)**
Handcrafted • ANDR
1595QXI6212 • **Value $30**

18

**Holiday BARBIE™
(6th & final, 1998)**
Handcrafted • ANDR
1595QXI4023 • **Value $32**

Here Comes Santa

	Price Paid	Value
1.		
2.		
3.		
4.		
5.		
6.		
7.		
8.		

Hockey Greats

9.		
10.		
11.		
12.		

Holiday BARBIE™

13.		
14.		
15.		
16.		
17.		
18.		

Totals

VALUE GUIDE — HALLMARK KEEPSAKE ORNAMENTS

1

Based on the 1988 Happy Holidays® BARBIE® Doll (1st, club edition, 1996)
Handcrafted • ANDR
1495QXC4181 • **Value $80**

2

Based on the 1989 Happy Holidays® BARBIE® Doll (2nd, club edition, 1997)
Handcrafted • ANDR
1595QXC5162 • **Value $53**

3

Based on the 1990 Happy Holidays® BARBIE® Doll (3rd, club edition, 1998)
Handcrafted • ANDR
1595QXC4493 • **Value $45**

4

Based on the 1991 Happy Holidays® Barbie™ Doll (4th, club edition, 1999)
Handcrafted • ANDR
1595QXC4507 • **Value $30**

5

New!
Based on the 1992 Happy Holidays® BARBIE® Doll (5th & final, club edition, 2000)
Handcrafted • ANDR
1595QXC4494 • **Value $15.95**

6

Holiday Heirloom (1st, LE-34,600, 1987)
Crystal/Silver-Plated • UNRU
2500QX4857 • **Value $30**

7

Holiday Heirloom (2nd, club edition, LE-34,600, 1988)
Crystal/Silver-Plated • N/A
2500QX4064 • **Value $34**

8

Holiday Heirloom (3rd & final, club edition, LE-34,600, 1989)
Crystal/Silver-Plated • N/A
2500QXC4605 • **Value $36**

9

Cardinalis (1st, 1982)
Wood • N/A
700QX3133 • **Value $395**

10

Black-Capped Chickadees (2nd, 1983)
Wood • N/A
700QX3099 • **Value $75**

11

Ring-Necked Pheasant (3rd, 1984)
Wood • N/A
725QX3474 • **Value $33**

12

California Partridge (4th, 1985)
Wood • N/A
750QX3765 • **Value $32**

13

Cedar Waxwing (5th, 1986)
Wood • N/A
750QX3216 • **Value $30**

14

Snow Goose (6th, 1987)
Wood • VOTR
750QX3717 • **Value $27**

15

Purple Finch (7th & final, 1988)
Wood • N/A
775QX3711 • **Value $29**

16

Shaquille O'Neal (1st, 1995)
Handcrafted • N/A
1495QXI5517 • **Value $48**

17

Larry Bird (2nd, 1996)
Handcrafted • N/A
1495QXI5014 • **Value $32**

18

Magic Johnson (3rd, 1997)
Handcrafted • N/A
1495QXI6832 • **Value $30**

19

Grant Hill (4th, 1998)
Handcrafted • UNRU
1495QXI6846 • **Value $25**

20

Scottie Pippen (5th, 1999)
Handcrafted • UNRU
1495QXI4177 • **Value $22**

Holiday BARBIE™ – Collector's Club

	Price Paid	Value
1.		
2.		
3.		
4.		
5.		

Holiday Heirloom

6.		
7.		
8.		

Holiday Wildlife

9.		
10.		
11.		
12.		
13.		
14.		
15.		

Hoop Stars

16.		
17.		
18.		
19.		
20.		

Totals

Keepsake Series

1

New!
Karl Malone (6th, 2000)
Handcrafted • UNRU
1495QXI6901 • **Value $14.95**

2

Joyful Santa (1st, 1999)
Handcrafted • CHAD
1495QX6949 • **Value $22**

3

New!
Joyful Santa (2nd, 2000)
Handcrafted • ANDR
1495QX6784 • **Value $14.95**

4

Murray® "Champion" (1st, 1994)
Die-Cast Metal • PALM
1395QX5426 • **Value $70**

5

Murray® Fire Truck (2nd, 1995)
Die-Cast Metal • PALM
1395QX5027 • **Value $32**

6

Murray® Airplane (3rd, 1996)
Die-Cast Metal • PALM
1395QX5364 • **Value $28**

7

1937 Steelcraft Auburn by Murray® (club edition, 1996)
Die-Cast Metal • PALM
1595QXC4174 • **Value $60**

8

Murray® Dump Truck (4th, 1997)
Die-Cast Metal • PALM
1395QX6195 • **Value $27**

Hoop Stars

	Price Paid	Value
1.		

Joyful Santa

2.		
3.		

Kiddie Car Classics

4.		
5.		
6.		
7.		
8.		
9.		
10.		
11.		
12.		
13.		
14.		
15.		

The Language Of Flowers

16.		
17.		
18.		
19.		

9

1937 Steelcraft Airflow by Murray® (club edition, 1997)
Die-Cast Metal • PALM
1595QXC5185 • **Value $51**

10

1955 Murray® Tractor and Trailer (5th, 1998)
Die-Cast Metal • PALM
1695QX6376 • **Value $30**

11

1935 Steelcraft by Murray® (club edition, 1998)
Die-Cast Metal • PALM
1595QXC4496 • **Value $42**

12

1968 Murray® Jolly Roger Flagship (6th, 1999)
Die-Cast Metal • PALM
1395QX6279 • **Value $22**

13

1939 Garton® Ford Station Wagon (club edition, 1999)
Die-Cast Metal • PALM
1595QXC4509 • **Value $28**

14

New!
1924 Toledo Fire Engine #6 (7th, 2000)
Die-Cast Metal • PALM
1395QX6691 • **Value $13.95**

15

1938 Garton® Lincoln Zephyr (club edition, 2000)
Handcrafted • PALM
1595QXC4501 • **Value $15.95**

16

Pansy (1st, 1996)
Handcrafted • TAGU
1595QK1171 • **Value $55**

17

Snowdrop Angel (2nd, 1997)
Handcrafted • TAGU
1595QX1095 • **Value $30**

18

Iris Angel (3rd, 1998)
Handcrafted • TAGU
1595QX6156 • **Value $26**

19

Rose Angel (4th & final, 1999)
Handcrafted • TAGU
1595QX6289 • **Value $22**

Totals		

VALUE GUIDE — HALLMARK KEEPSAKE ORNAMENTS

1

700E Hudson Steam Locomotive (1st, 1996)
Die-Cast Metal • N/A
1895QX5531 • **Value $70**

2

1950 Santa Fe F3 Diesel Locomotive (2nd, 1997)
Die-Cast Metal • N/A
1895QX6145 • **Value $42**

3

Pennsylvania GG-1 Locomotive (3rd, 1998)
Die-Cast Metal • N/A
1895QX6346 • **Value $33**

4

746 Norfolk and Western Steam Locomotive (4th, 1999)
Die-Cast Metal • N/A
1895QX6377 • **Value $27**

5
New!

Lionel® General Steam Locomotive (5th, 2000)
Die-Cast Metal • N/A
1895QX6684 • **Value $18.95**

6

Cinderella – 1995 (1st, 1996)
Handcrafted • FRAN
1495QX6311 • **Value $43**

7

Little Red Riding Hood – 1991 (2nd, 1997)
Handcrafted • FRAN
1495QX6155 • **Value $32**

8

Mop Top Wendy (3rd, 1998)
Handcrafted • FRAN
1495QX6353 • **Value $28**

9

Red Queen – Alice in Wonderland (4th, 1999)
Handcrafted • FRAN
1495QX6379 • **Value $23**

10
New!

Christmas Holly (5th, 2000)
Handcrafted • FRAN
1495QX6611 • **Value $14.95**

11

Glorious Angel (1st, 1998)
Handcrafted • FRAN
1495QX6493 • **Value $29**

12

Angel of The Nativity (2nd, 1999)
Handcrafted • FRAN
1495QX6419 • **Value $28**

13
New!

Twilight Angel (3rd & final, 2000)
Handcrafted • FRAN
1495QX6614 • **Value $14.95**

14

Snowshoe Rabbits in Winter (1st, 1997)
Handcrafted • N/A
1295QX5694 • **Value $33**

15
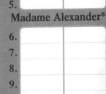
Timber Wolves at Play (2nd, 1998)
Handcrafted • N/A
1295QX6273 • **Value $25**

16

Curious Raccoons (3rd, 1999)
Handcrafted • N/A
1295QX6287 • **Value $23**

17
New!

Foxes in the Forest (4th & final, 2000)
Handcrafted • N/A
1295QX6794 • **Value $12.95**

18

Marilyn Monroe (1st, 1997)
Handcrafted • ANDR
1495QX5704 • **Value $31**

19

Marilyn Monroe (2nd, 1998)
Handcrafted • ANDR
1495QX6333 • **Value $27**

20

Marilyn Monroe (3rd & final, 1999)
Handcrafted • ANDR
1495QX6389 • **Value $24**

LIONEL® Train	Price Paid	Value
1.		
2.		
3.		
4.		
5.		
Madame Alexander®		
6.		
7.		
8.		
9.		
10.		
Madame Alexander® Holiday Angels		
11.		
12.		
13.		
Majestic Wilderness		
14.		
15.		
16.		
17.		
Marilyn Monroe		
18.		
19.		
20.		
Totals		

1
Buttercup (1st, 1988)
Handcrafted • CHAD
500QX4074 • **Value $53**

2
Bluebell (2nd, 1989)
Handcrafted • CHAD
575QX4545 • **Value $95**

3
Rosebud (3rd, 1990)
Handcrafted • CHAD
575QX4423 • **Value $48**

4
Iris (4th, 1991)
Handcrafted • CHAD
675QX4279 • **Value $47**

5
Lily (5th, 1992)
Handcrafted • CHAD
675QX4274 • **Value $57**

6
Ivy (6th, 1993)
Handcrafted • CHAD
675QX4282 • **Value $29**

7
Jasmine (7th, 1994)
Handcrafted • CHAD
695QX5276 • **Value $25**

8
Camellia (8th, 1995)
Handcrafted • CHAD
695QX5149 • **Value $22**

Mary's Angels

	Price Paid	Value
1.		
2.		
3.		
4.		
5.		
6.		
7.		
8.		
9.		
10.		
11.		
12.		
13.		

9
Violet (9th, 1996)
Handcrafted • CHAD
695QX5664 • **Value $21**

10
Daisy (10th, 1997)
Handcrafted • CHAD
795QX6242 • **Value $20**

11
Daphne (11th, 1998)
Handcrafted • CHAD
795QX6153 • **Value $20**

12
Heather (12th, 1999)
Handcrafted • CHAD
795QX6329 • **Value $18**

13
New!
Marguerite (13th, 2000)
Handcrafted • CHAD
795QX6571 • **Value $7.95**

14
**Merry Olde Santa
(1st, 1990)**
Handcrafted • SEAL
1475QX4736 • **Value $86**

Merry Olde Santa

14.		
15.		
16.		
17.		
18.		
19.		
20.		

15
**Merry Olde Santa
(2nd, 1991)**
Handcrafted • JLEE
1475QX4359 • **Value $90**

16
**Merry Olde Santa
(3rd, 1992)**
Handcrafted • UNRU
1475QX4414 • **Value $39**

17
**Merry Olde Santa
(4th, 1993)**
Handcrafted • RGRS
1475QX4842 • **Value $38**

18
**Merry Olde Santa
(5th, 1994)**
Handcrafted • CHAD
1495QX5256 • **Value $35**

19
**Merry Olde Santa
(6th, 1995)**
Handcrafted • ANDR
1495QX5139 • **Value $30**

20
**Merry Olde Santa
(7th, 1996)**
Handcrafted • CROW
1495QX5654 • **Value $29**

Totals

VALUE GUIDE — HALLMARK KEEPSAKE ORNAMENTS

1
Merry Olde Santa
(8th, 1997)
Handcrafted • LYLE
1495QX6225 • **Value $30**

2
Merry Olde Santa
(9th, 1998)
Handcrafted • UNRU
1595QX6386 • **Value $30**

3
Merry Olde Santa
(10th & final, 1999)
Handcrafted • RHOD
1595QX6359 • **Value $25**

4
Bandleader Mickey
(1st, 1997)
Handcrafted • SIED
1395QXD4022 • **Value $26**

5
Minnie Plays the Flute
(2nd, 1998)
Handcrafted • N/A
1395QXD4106 • **Value $23**

6
Donald Plays the
Cymbals (3rd, 1999)
Handcrafted • N/A
1395QXD4057 • **Value $21**

7 *New!*
Baton Twirler Daisy
(4th, 2000)
Handcrafted • N/A
1395QXD4034 • **Value $13.95**

8
Miniature Crèche
(1st, 1985)
Wood/Straw • SEAL
875QX4825 • **Value $36**

9
Miniature Crèche
(2nd, 1986)
Porcelain • SEAL
900QX4076 • **Value $62**

10
Miniature Crèche
(3rd, 1987)
Brass • SEAL
900QX4819 • **Value $39**

11
Miniature Crèche
(4th, 1988)
Acrylic • UNRU
850QX4034 • **Value $35**

12
Miniature Crèche
(5th & final, 1989)
Handcrafted • RGRS
925QX4592 • **Value $23**

13
Mischievous Kittens
(1st, 1999)
Handcrafted • AUBE
995QX6427 • **Value $26**

14 *New!*
Mischievous Kittens
(2nd, 2000)
Handcrafted • AUBE
995QX6641 • **Value $9.95**

15 *New!*
Mischievous Kittens
(Premiere, gray, comple-
ments the series, 2000)
Handcrafted • AUBE
(N/C) QX6427 • **Value N/E**

16
Humpty Dumpty
(1st, 1993)
Handcrafted • SEAL/VOTR
1375QX5282 • **Value $43**

17
Hey Diddle, Diddle
(2nd, 1994)
Handcrafted • SEAL
1395QX5213 • **Value $45**

18
Jack and Jill (3rd, 1995)
Handcrafted • SEAL/VOTR
1395QX5099 • **Value $29**

19
Mary Had a Little Lamb
(4th, 1996)
Handcrafted • SEAL/VOTR
1395QX5644 • **Value $29**

20
Little Boy Blue
(5th & final, 1997)
Handcrafted • SEAL/VOTR
1395QX6215 • **Value $28**

	Price Paid	Value
Merry Olde Santa		
1.		
2.		
3.		
Mickey's Holiday Parade		
4.		
5.		
6.		
7.		
Miniature Creche		
8.		
9.		
10.		
11.		
12.		
Mischievous Kittens		
13.		
14.		
15.		
Mother Goose		
16.		
17.		
18.		
19.		
20.		
Totals		

1

**Merry Mistletoe Time
(1st, 1986)**
Handcrafted • UNRU
1300QX4026 • **Value $107**

2

**Home Cooking
(2nd, 1987)**
Handcrafted • UNRU
1325QX4837 • **Value $68**

3

**Shall We Dance
(3rd, 1988)**
Handcrafted • UNRU
1300QX4011 • **Value $55**

4

Holiday Duet (4th, 1989)
Handcrafted • UNRU
1325QX4575 • **Value $55**

5

Popcorn Party (5th, 1990)
Handcrafted • UNRU
1375QX4393 • **Value $75**

6

**Checking His List
(6th, 1991)**
Handcrafted • UNRU
1375QX4339 • **Value $48**

7

**Gift Exchange
(7th, 1992)**
Handcrafted • UNRU
1475QX4294 • **Value $43**

8

**A Fitting Moment
(8th, 1993)**
Handcrafted • FRAN
1475QX4202 • **Value $43**

Mr. And Mrs. Claus

	Price Paid	Value
1.		
2.		
3.		
4.		
5.		
6.		
7.		
8.		
9.		
10.		

Norman Rockwell

11.		
12.		
13.		
14.		
15.		
16.		
17.		
18.		
19.		

Totals

9

**A Handwarming
Present (9th, 1994)**
Handcrafted • UNRU
1495QX5283 • **Value $38**

10

**Christmas Eve Kiss
(10th & final, 1995)**
Handcrafted • UNRU
1495QX5157 • **Value $31**

11

**Santa's Visitors
(1st, 1980)**
Cameo • N/A
650QX3061 • **Value $240**

12

The Carolers (2nd, 1981)
Cameo • N/A
850QX5115 • **Value $50**

13

**Filling the Stockings
(3rd, 1982)**
Cameo • N/A
850QX3053 • **Value $33**

14

**Dress Rehearsal
(4th, 1983)**
Cameo • N/A
750QX3007 • **Value $38**

15

**Caught Napping
(5th, 1984)**
Cameo • MCGE
750QX3411 • **Value $36**

16

Jolly Postman (6th, 1985)
Cameo • MCGE
750QX3745 • **Value $35**

17

Checking Up (7th, 1986)
Cameo • PIKE
775QX3213 • **Value $30**

18

**The Christmas Dance
(8th, 1987)**
Cameo • PALM
775QX3707 • **Value $25**

19

**And to All a Good
Night (9th & final, 1988)**
Cameo • N/A
775QX3704 • **Value $26**

VALUE GUIDE — HALLMARK KEEPSAKE ORNAMENTS

1

Victorian Dollhouse (1st, 1984)
Handcrafted • DLEE
1300QX4481 • **Value $218**

2

Old-Fashioned Toy Shop (2nd, 1985)
Handcrafted • DLEE
1375QX4975 • **Value $150**

3

Christmas Candy Shoppe (3rd, 1986)
Handcrafted • DLEE
1375QX4033 • **Value $300**

4

House on Main St. (4th, 1987)
Handcrafted • DLEE
1400QX4839 • **Value $83**

5

Hall Bro's Card Shop (5th, 1988)
Handcrafted • DLEE
1450QX4014 • **Value $66**

6

U.S. Post Office (6th, 1989)
Handcrafted • DLEE
1425QX4582 • **Value $70**

7

Holiday Home (7th, 1990)
Handcrafted • DLEE
1475QX4696 • **Value $78**

8

Fire Station (8th, 1991)
Handcrafted • DLEE
1475QX4139 • **Value $70**

9

Five and Ten Cent Store (9th, 1992)
Handcrafted • DLEE
1475QX4254 • **Value $44**

10

Cozy Home (10th, 1993)
Handcrafted • DLEE
1475QX4175 • **Value $47**

11

Tannenbaum's Dept. Store (complements the series, 1993)
Handcrafted • DLEE
2600QX5612 • **Value $55**

12

Neighborhood Drugstore (11th, 1994)
Handcrafted • DLEE
1495QX5286 • **Value $37**

13

Town Church (12th, 1995)
Handcrafted • PALM
1495QX5159 • **Value $32**

14

Accessories for Nostalgic Houses and Shops (set/3, 1995)
Handcrafted • JLEE
895QX5089 • **Value $18**

15

Victorian Painted Lady (13th, 1996)
Handcrafted • PALM
1495QX5671 • **Value $29**

16

Cafe (14th, 1997)
Handcrafted • PALM
1695QX6245 • **Value $30**

17

Grocery Store (15th, 1998)
Handcrafted • PALM
1695QX6266 • **Value $28**

18

Halls Station (complements the series, 1998)
Handcrafted • PALM
2500QX6833 • **Value $44**

19

House on Holly Lane (16th, 1999)
Handcrafted • PALM
1695QX6349 • **Value $24**

20

New!

Schoolhouse (17th, 2000)
Handcrafted • PALM
1495QX6591 • **Value $14.95**

Nostalgic Houses And Shops

	Price Paid	Value
1.		
2.		
3.		
4.		
5.		
6.		
7.		
8.		
9.		
10.		
11.		
12.		
13.		
14.		
15.		
16.		
17.		
18.		
19.		
20.		

Totals

Keepsake Series

1

**Pony Express Rider
(1st, 1998)**
Handcrafted • UNRU
1395QX6323 • **Value $28**

2

Prospector (2nd, 1999)
Handcrafted • UNRU
1395QX6317 • **Value $21**

3

New!

**Mountain Man
(3rd & final, 2000)**
Handcrafted • UNRU
1595QX6594 • **Value $15.95**

4

Owliver (1st, 1992)
Handcrafted • SIED
775QX4544 • **Value $21**

5

Owliver (2nd, 1993)
Handcrafted • SIED
775QX5425 • **Value $20**

6

**Owliver
(3rd & final, 1994)**
Handcrafted • SIED
795QX5226 • **Value $20**

7

Italy (1st, 1991)
Handcrafted • SICK
1175QX5129 • **Value $26**

8

Spain (2nd, 1992)
Handcrafted • SICK
1175QX5174 • **Value $23**

The Old West

	Price Paid	Value
1.		
2.		
3.		

Owliver

4.		
5.		
6.		

Peace On Earth

7.		
8.		
9.		

The PEANUTS® Gang

10.		
11.		
12.		
13.		

A Pony For Christmas

14.		
15.		
16.		

Porcelain Bear

17.		
18.		
19.		
20.		

9

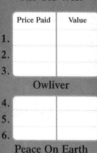

Poland (3rd & final, 1993)
Handcrafted • SICK
1175QX5242 • **Value $25**

10

**The PEANUTS® Gang
(1st, 1993)**
Handcrafted • RHOD
975QX5315 • **Value $58**

11

**The PEANUTS® Gang
(2nd, 1994)**
Handcrafted • BISH
995QX5203 • **Value $27**

12

**The PEANUTS® Gang
(3rd, 1995)**
Handcrafted • SIED
995QX5059 • **Value $25**

13

**The PEANUTS® Gang
(4th & final, 1996)**
Handcrafted • FRAN
995QX5381 • **Value $20**

14

**A Pony for Christmas
(1st, 1998)**
Handcrafted • SICK
1095QX6316 • **Value $26**

15

**A Pony for Christmas
(2nd, 1999)**
Handcrafted • SICK
1095QX6299 • **Value $21**

16

New!

**A Pony for Christmas
(3rd, 2000)**
Handcrafted • SICK
1295QX6624 • **Value $12.95**

17

**Cinnamon Teddy
(1st, 1983)**
Porcelain • DUTK
700QX4289 • **Value $82**

18

**Cinnamon Bear
(2nd, 1984)**
Porcelain • N/A
700QX4541 • **Value $55**

19

**Porcelain Bear
(3rd, 1985)**
Porcelain • DUTK
750QX4792 • **Value $60**

20

**Porcelain Bear
(4th, 1986)**
Porcelain • N/A
775QX4056 • **Value $44**

Totals

1

Porcelain Bear
(5th, 1987)
Porcelain • N/A
775QX4427 • **Value $40**

2

Porcelain Bear
(6th, 1988)
Porcelain • PIKE
800QX4044 • **Value $40**

3

Porcelain Bear
(7th, 1989)
Porcelain • PIKE
875QX4615 • **Value $38**

4

Porcelain Bear
(8th & final, 1990)
Porcelain • N/A
875QX4426 • **Value $35**

5

Puppy Love (1st, 1991)
Handcrafted/Brass • RGRS
775QX5379 • **Value $65**

6

Puppy Love (2nd, 1992)
Handcrafted/Brass • RGRS
775QX4484 • **Value $42**

7

Puppy Love (3rd, 1993)
Handcrafted/Brass • RGRS
775QX5045 • **Value $30**

8

Puppy Love (4th, 1994)
Handcrafted/Brass • RGRS
795QX5253 • **Value $25**

9

Puppy Love (5th, 1995)
Handcrafted/Brass • RGRS
795QX5137 • **Value $25**

10

Puppy Love (6th, 1996)
Handcrafted/Brass • RGRS
795QX5651 • **Value $21**

11

Puppy Love (7th, 1997)
Handcrafted/Brass • RGRS
795QX6222 • **Value $21**

12

Puppy Love (8th, 1998)
Handcrafted/Brass • RGRS
795QX6163 • **Value $18**

13

Puppy Love (9th, 1999)
Handcrafted • RGRS
795QX6327 • **Value $18**

14

New!

Puppy Love (10th, 2000)
Handcrafted • RGRS
795QX6554 • **Value $7.95**

15

Dasher (1st, 1986)
Handcrafted • SIED
750QX4223 • **Value $152**

16

Dancer (2nd, 1987)
Handcrafted • SIED
750QX4809 • **Value $55**

17

Prancer (3rd, 1988)
Handcrafted • SIED
750QX4051 • **Value $39**

18

Vixen (4th, 1989)
Handcrafted • SIED
775QX4562 • **Value $23**

19

Comet (5th, 1990)
Handcrafted • SIED
775QX4433 • **Value $30**

20

Cupid (6th, 1991)
Handcrafted • SIED
775QX4347 • **Value $29**

Porcelain Bear	Price Paid	Value
1.		
2.		
3.		
4.		
Puppy Love		
5.		
6.		
7.		
8.		
9.		
10.		
11.		
12.		
13.		
14.		
Reindeer Champs		
15.		
16.		
17.		
18.		
19.		
20.		
Totals		

Keepsake Series

1

Donder (7th, 1992)
Handcrafted • SIED
875QX5284 • **Value $34**

2

Blitzen
(8th & final, 1993)
Handcrafted • SIED
875QX4331 • **Value $27**

3

New!

Robot Parade (1st, 2000)
Handcrafted/Pressed Tin • WILL
1495QX6771 • **Value $14.95**

4

Rocking Horse (1st, 1981)
Handcrafted • SICK
900QX4222 • **Value $635**

5

Rocking Horse (2nd, 1982)
Handcrafted • SICK
1000QX5023 • **Value $440**

6

Rocking Horse (3rd, 1983)
Handcrafted • SICK
1000QX4177 • **Value $310**

7

Rocking Horse (4th, 1984)
Handcrafted • SICK
1000QX4354 • **Value $95**

8

Rocking Horse (5th, 1985)
Handcrafted • SICK
1075QX4932 • **Value $85**

Reindeer Champs

	Price Paid	Value
1.		
2.		

Robot Parade

3.		

Rocking Horse

4.		
5.		
6.		
7.		
8.		
9.		
10.		
11.		
12.		
13.		
14.		
15.		
16.		
17.		
18.		
19.		
20.		

9

Rocking Horse (6th, 1986)
Handcrafted • SICK
1075QX4016 • **Value $82**

10

Rocking Horse (7th, 1987)
Handcrafted • SICK
1075QX4829 • **Value $80**

11

Rocking Horse (8th, 1988)
Handcrafted • SICK
1075QX4024 • **Value $68**

12

Rocking Horse (9th, 1989)
Handcrafted • SICK
1075QX4622 • **Value $58**

13

Rocking Horse
(10th, 1990)
Handcrafted • SICK
1075QX4646 • **Value $100**

14

Rocking Horse
(11th, 1991)
Handcrafted • SICK
1075QX4147 • **Value $48**

15

Rocking Horse
(12th, 1992)
Handcrafted • SICK
1075QX4261 • **Value $46**

16

Rocking Horse
(13th, 1993)
Handcrafted • SICK
1075QX4162 • **Value $38**

17

Rocking Horse
(14th, 1994)
Handcrafted • SICK
1095QX5016 • **Value $28**

18

Rocking Horse
(15th, 1995)
Handcrafted • SICK
1095QX5167 • **Value $28**

19

Pewter Rocking Horse
(15th Anniversary
Edition, 1995)
Pewter • SICK
2000QX6167 • **Value $41**

20

Rocking Horse
(16th & final, 1996)
Handcrafted • SICK
1095QX5674 • **Value $27**

Totals

1

Donald and Daisy in Venice (1st, 1998)
Handcrafted • LARS
1495QXD4103 • **Value $26**

2

Mickey and Minnie in Paradise (2nd, 1999)
Handcrafted • N/A
1495QXD4049 • **Value $20**

3

New!

Donald and Daisy at Lovers' Lodge (3rd & final, 2000)
Handcrafted • N/A
1495QXD4031 • **Value $14.95**

4

Scarlett O'Hara™ (1st, 1997)
Handcrafted • ANDR
1495QX6125 • **Value $30**

5

Scarlett O'Hara™ (2nd, 1998)
Handcrafted • ANDR
1495QX6336 • **Value $27**

6

Scarlett O'Hara™ (3rd, 1999)
Handcrafted • ANDR
1495QX6397 • **Value $23**

7

New!

Scarlett O'Hara™ (4th & final, 2000)
Handcrafted • ANDR
1495QX6671 • **Value $14.95**

8

The Flight at Kitty Hawk (1st, 1997)
Handcrafted • NORT
1495QX5574 • **Value $33**

9

1917 Curtiss JN-4D "Jenny" (2nd, 1998)
Handcrafted • NORT
1495QX6286 • **Value $28**

10

Curtiss R3C-2 Seaplane (3rd, 1999)
Handcrafted • NORT
1495QX6387 • **Value $23**

11

New!

Spirit of St. Louis (4th, 2000)
Handcrafted • NORT
1495QX6634 • **Value $14.95**

12

Ice Hockey Holiday (1st, 1979)
Handcrafted • N/A
800QX1419 • **Value $162**

13

Ski Holiday (2nd, 1980)
Handcrafted • FRAN
900QX1541 • **Value $170**

14

SNOOPY® and Friends (3rd, 1981)
Handcrafted • FRAN
1200QX4362 • **Value $130**

15

SNOOPY® and Friends (4th, 1982)
Handcrafted • SEAL
1300QX4803 • **Value $120**

16

Santa SNOOPY® (5th & final, 1983)
Handcrafted • SICK
1300QX4169 • **Value $97**

17

Snow Buddies (1st, 1998)
Handcrafted • HADD
795QX6853 • **Value $27**

18

Snow Buddies (2nd, 1999)
Handcrafted • HADD
795QX6319 • **Value $22**

19

New!

Snow Buddies (3rd, 2000)
Handcrafted • HADD
795QX6654 • **Value $7.95**

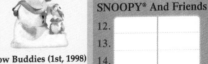

Romantic Vacations	Price Paid	Value
1.		
2.		
3.		
Scarlett O'Hara™		
4.		
5.		
6.		
7.		
Sky's The Limit		
8.		
9.		
10.		
11.		
SNOOPY® And Friends		
12.		
13.		
14.		
15.		
16.		
Snow Buddies		
17.		
18.		
19.		
Totals		

Keepsake Series

1

Joe Cool (1st, 1998)
Handcrafted • SIED
995QX6453 • **Value $24**

2

Famous Flying Ace (2nd, 1999)
Handcrafted • SIED
995QX6409 • **Value $22**

3
New!

The Detective (3rd, 2000)
Handcrafted • SIED
995QX6564 • **Value $9.95**

4

Luke Skywalker™ (1st, 1997)
Handcrafted • RHOD
1395QXI5484 • **Value $33**

5

Princess Leia™ (2nd, 1998)
Handcrafted • RHOD
1395QXI4026 • **Value $28**

6

Han Solo™ (3rd, 1999)
Handcrafted • ANDR
1395QXI4007 • **Value $22**

7
New!

Obi-Wan Kenobi™ (4th, 2000)
Handcrafted • RHOD
1495QXI6704 • **Value $14.95**

8

Jeff Gordon (1st, 1997)
Handcrafted • SEAL
1595QXI6165 • **Value $42**

Spotlight On SNOOPY

	Price Paid	Value
1.		
2.		
3.		

STAR WARS™

4.		
5.		
6.		
7.		

Stock Car Champions

8.		
9.		
10.		

Thimble Series

11.		
12.		
13.		
14.		
15.		
16.		
17.		
18.		
19.		
20.		

9
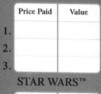
Richard Petty (2nd, 1998)
Handcrafted • SEAL
1595QXI4143 • **Value $30**

10

Bill Elliott (3rd & final, 1999)
Handcrafted • SEAL
1595QXI4039 • **Value $25**

11

Mouse in a Thimble (1st, 1978, re-issued in 1979)
Handcrafted • N/A
250QX1336 • **Value $300**

12

A Christmas Salute (2nd, 1979, re-issued in 1980)
Handcrafted • N/A
300QX1319 • **Value $180**

13

Mouse in a Thimble (1979, re-issued from 1978)
Handcrafted • N/A
300QX1336 • **Value $295**

14

Thimble Elf (3rd, 1980)
Handcrafted • N/A
400QX1321 • **Value $185**

15

A Christmas Salute (1980, re-issued from 1979)
Handcrafted • N/A
400QX1319 • **Value $180**

16

Thimble Angel (4th, 1981)
Handcrafted • N/A
450QX4135 • **Value $158**

17

Thimble Mouse (5th, 1982)
Handcrafted • N/A
500QX4513 • **Value $78**

18

Thimble Elf (6th, 1983)
Handcrafted • N/A
500QX4017 • **Value $40**

19

Thimble Angel (7th, 1984)
Handcrafted • N/A
500QX4304 • **Value $62**

20

Thimble Santa (8th, 1985)
Handcrafted • SIED
550QX4725 • **Value $38**

1

Thimble Partridge
(9th, 1986)
Handcrafted • N/A
575QX4066 • **Value $27**

2

Thimble Drummer
(10th, 1987)
Handcrafted • SIED
575QX4419 • **Value $30**

3

Thimble Snowman
(11th, 1988)
Handcrafted • SIED
575QX4054 • **Value $26**

4

Thimble Puppy
(12th & final, 1989)
Handcrafted • RGRS
575QX4552 • **Value $29**

5

Victorian Christmas
Thomas Kinkade, Painter
of Light™ (1st, 1997)
Porcelain • SEAL
1095QXI6135 • **Value $26**

6

Victorian Christmas II,
Thomas Kinkade, Painter
of Light™ (2nd, 1998)
Ceramic • N/A
1095QX61343 • **Value $26**

7

Victorian Christmas III
Thomas Kinkade,
Painter of Light™
(3rd & final, 1999)
Ceramic • N/A
1095QX6407 • **Value $19**

8

Tin Locomotive (1st, 1982)
Pressed Tin • SICK
1300QX4603 • **Value $670**

9

Tin Locomotive (2nd, 1983)
Pressed Tin • SICK
1300QX4049 • **Value $295**

10

Tin Locomotive (3rd, 1984)
Pressed Tin • SICK
1400QX4404 • **Value $89**

11

Tin Locomotive (4th, 1985)
Pressed Tin • SICK
1475QX4972 • **Value $84**

12

Tin Locomotive (5th, 1986)
Pressed Tin • SICK
1475QX4036 • **Value $82**

13

Tin Locomotive (6th, 1987)
Pressed Tin • SICK
1475QX4849 • **Value $66**

14

Tin Locomotive (7th, 1988)
Pressed Tin • SICK
1475QX4004 • **Value $55**

15

Tin Locomotive
(8th & final, 1989)
Pressed Tin • SICK
1475QX4602 • **Value $60**

16

Tobin Fraley Carousel
(1st, 1992)
Porcelain/Brass • FRAL
2800QX4891 • **Value $58**

17

Tobin Fraley Carousel
(2nd, 1993)
Porcelain/Brass • FRAL
2800QX5502 • **Value $47**

18

Tobin Fraley Carousel
(3rd, 1994)
Porcelain/Brass • FRAL
2800QX5223 • **Value $58**

19

Tobin Fraley Carousel
(4th & final, 1995)
Porcelain • FRAL
2800QX5069 • **Value $50**

	Price Paid	Value
Thimble Series		
1.		
2.		
3.		
4.		
Thomas Kinkade		
5.		
6.		
7.		
Tin Locomotive		
8.		
9.		
10.		
11.		
12.		
13.		
14.		
15.		
Tobin Fraley Carousel		
16.		
17.		
18.		
19.		
Totals		

Keepsake Series

1

Farm House (1st, 1999)
Pressed Tin • SICK
1595QX6439 • **Value $24**

2

Red Barn (complements the series, 1999)
Pressed Tin • SICK
1595QX6947 • **Value $24**

3

New!

Bait Shop With Boat (2nd, 2000)
Pressed Tin • SICK
1595QX6631 • **Value $15.95**

4

New!

Toymaker Santa (1st, 2000)
Handcrafted • CROW
1495QX6751 • **Value $14.95**

5

The Fireman (1st, 1995)
Die-Cast Metal • CROW
1695QK1027 • **Value $42**

6

Uncle Sam (2nd, 1996)
Die-Cast Metal • CROW
1695QK1084 • **Value $34**

7

Santa Claus (3rd & final, 1997)
Die-Cast Metal • CROW
1695QX1215 • **Value $26**

8

Partridge in a Pear Tree (1st, 1984)
Acrylic • N/A
600QX3484 • **Value $290**

9

Two Turtle Doves (2nd, 1985)
Acrylic • PIKE
650QX3712 • **Value $75**

10

Three French Hens (3rd, 1986)
Acrylic • VOTR
650QX3786 • **Value $50**

11

Four Colly Birds (4th, 1987)
Acrylic • PIKE
650QX3709 • **Value $39**

12

Five Golden Rings (5th, 1988)
Acrylic • PIKE
650QX3714 • **Value $29**

13

Six Geese A-Laying (6th, 1989)
Acrylic • N/A
675QX3812 • **Value $24**

14

Seven Swans A-Swimming (7th, 1990)
Acrylic • N/A
675QX3033 • **Value $30**

15

Eight Maids A-Milking (8th, 1991)
Acrylic • N/A
675QX3089 • **Value $30**

16

Nine Ladies Dancing (9th, 1992)
Acrylic • PYDA
675QX3031 • **Value $25**

17

Ten Lords A-Leaping (10th, 1993)
Acrylic • CHAD
675QX3012 • **Value $25**

18

Eleven Pipers Piping (11th, 1994)
Acrylic • N/A
695QX3183 • **Value $19**

19

Twelve Drummers Drumming (12th & final, 1995)
Acrylic • N/A
695QX3009 • **Value $19**

Town and Country

	Price Paid	Value
1.		
2.		
3.		

Toymaker Santa

4.		

Turn-of-the-Century Parade

5.		
6.		
7.		

The Twelve Days Of Christmas

8.		
9.		
10.		
11.		
12.		
13.		
14.		
15.		
16.		
17.		
18.		
19.		

Totals

1

U.S. Christmas Stamps (1st, 1993)
Enamel/Copper • SICK
1075QX5292 • **Value $29**

2

U.S. Christmas Stamps (2nd, 1994)
Enamel/Copper • N/A
1095QX5206 • **Value $26**

3

U.S. Christmas Stamps (3rd & final, 1995)
Enamel/Copper • N/A
1095QX5067 • **Value $23**

4

Cruella de Vil Walt Disney's *101 Dalmatians* (1st, 1998)
Handcrafted • ESCH
1495QXD4063 • **Value $26**

5

Snow White's Jealous Queen (2nd, 1999)
Handcrafted • N/A
1495QXD4089 • **Value $20**

6

New!

Sleeping Beauty's Maleficent (3rd & final, 2000)
Handcrafted • N/A
1495QXD4001 • **Value $14.95**

7

Feliz Navidad (1st, 1985)
Handcrafted • DLEE
975QX4902 • **Value $100**

8

Vrolyk Kerstfeest (2nd, 1986)
Handcrafted • SIED
1000QX4083 • **Value $67**

9

Mele Kalikimaka (3rd, 1987)
Handcrafted • DLEE
1000QX4827 • **Value $33**

10

Joyeux Noël (4th, 1988)
Handcrafted • DLEE
1000QX4021 • **Value $34**

11

Fröhliche Weihnachten (5th, 1989)
Handcrafted • DLEE
1075QX4625 • **Value $32**

12

Nollaig Shona (6th & final, 1990)
Handcrafted • DLEE
1075QX4636 • **Value $29**

13

A Visit From Piglet (1st, 1998)
Handcrafted • N/A
1395QXD4086 • **Value $25**

14

Honey Time (2nd, 1999)
Handcrafted • N/A
1395QXD4129 • **Value $20**

15

New!

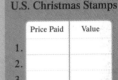

A Blustery Day (3rd, 2000)
Handcrafted • N/A
1395QXD4021 • **Value $13.95**

16

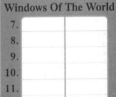

Playing With Pooh (1st, 1999)
Handcrafted • N/A
1395QXD4197 • **Value $23**

17

New!

Story Time With Pooh (2nd, 2000)
Handcrafted • N/A
1395QXD4024 • **Value $13.95**

18

Winter Surprise (1st, 1989)
Handcrafted • FRAN
1075QX4272 • **Value $25**

19

Winter Surprise (2nd, 1990)
Handcrafted • FRAN
1075QX4443 • **Value $24**

U.S. Christmas Stamps	Price Paid	Value
1.		
2.		
3.		
Unforgettable Villains		
4.		
5.		
6.		
Windows Of The World		
7.		
8.		
9.		
10.		
11.		
12.		
Winnie the Pooh		
13.		
14.		
15.		
Winnie the Pooh and Christopher Robin, Too		
16.		
17.		
Winter Surprise		
18.		
19.		
Totals		

Keepsake Series

1

Winter Surprise (3rd, 1991)
Handcrafted • LYLE
1075QX4277 • **Value $29**

2

Winter Surprise (4th & final, 1992)
Handcrafted • FRAN
1175QX4271 • **Value $27**

3

Wooden Lamb (1st, 1984)
Wood • N/A
650QX4394 • **Value $45**

4

Wooden Train (2nd, 1985)
Wood • DUTK
700QX4722 • **Value $48**

5

Wooden Reindeer (3rd, 1986)
Wood • CROW
750QX4073 • **Value $30**

6

Wooden Horse (4th, 1987)
Wood • SIED
750QX4417 • **Value $27**

7

Wooden Airplane (5th, 1988)
Wood • DUTK
750QX4041 • **Value $24**

8

Wooden Truck (6th & final, 1989)
Wood • N/A
775QX4595 • **Value $20**

9

Yuletide Central (1st, 1994)
Pressed Tin • SICK
1895QX5316 • **Value $55**

10

Yuletide Central (2nd, 1995)
Pressed Tin • SICK
1895QX5079 • **Value $34**

11

Yuletide Central (3rd, 1996)
Pressed Tin • SICK
1895QX5011 • **Value $40**

12

Yuletide Central (4th, 1997)
Pressed Tin • SICK
1895QX5812 • **Value $34**

13

Yuletide Central (5th & final, 1998)
Pressed Tin • SICK
1895QX6373 • **Value $42**

Winter Surprise

	Price Paid	Value
1.		
2.		

Wood Childhood Ornaments

3.		
4.		
5.		
6.		
7.		
8.		

Yuletide Central

9.		
10.		
11.		
12.		
13.		

Totals		

Magic Series

The first Magic collectible series, featuring ornaments with light, sound and motion, was introduced in 1985. Since then, a total of nine series have made their debut, although only two series ("Candlelight Services" and "Lighthouse Greetings") remain current. No new series were introduced for 2000.

1

The Stone Church
(1st, 1998)
Handcrafted • SEAL
1895QLX7636 • **Value $50**

2

Colonial Church
(2nd, 1999)
Handcrafted • SEAL
1895QLX7387 • **Value $28**

3

New!

Adobe Church
(3rd, 2000)
Handcrafted • SEAL
1895QLX7334 • **Value $18.95**

4

Chris Mouse (1st, 1985)
Handcrafted • SIED
1250QLX7032 • **Value $93**

5

Chris Mouse Dreams
(2nd, 1986)
Handcrafted • DUTK
1300QLX7056 • **Value $82**

6

Chris Mouse Glow
(3rd, 1987)
Handcrafted • SIED
1100QLX7057 • **Value $64**

7

Chris Mouse Star
(4th, 1988)
Handcrafted • SIED
875QLX7154 • **Value $63**

8

Chris Mouse Cookout
(5th, 1989)
Handcrafted • RGRS
950QLX7225 • **Value $62**

9

Chris Mouse Wreath
(6th, 1990)
Handcrafted • RGRS
1000QLX7296 • **Value $43**

10

Chris Mouse Mail
(7th, 1991)
Handcrafted • SIED
1000QLX7207 • **Value $41**

11

Chris Mouse Tales
(8th, 1992)
Handcrafted • RGRS
1200QLX7074 • **Value $30**

12

Chris Mouse Flight
(9th, 1993)
Handcrafted • RGRS
1200QLX7152 • **Value $33**

13

Chris Mouse Jelly
(10th, 1994)
Handcrafted • RGRS
1200QLX7393 • **Value $30**

14

Chris Mouse Tree
(11th, 1995)
Handcrafted • RGRS
1250QLX7307 • **Value $28**

15

Chris Mouse Inn
(12th, 1996)
Handcrafted • SIED
1450QLX7371 • **Value $29**

16

Chris Mouse Luminaria
(13th & final, 1997)
Handcrafted • SIED
1495QLX7525 • **Value $29**

Candlelight Services

	Price Paid	Value
1.		
2.		
3.		

Chris Mouse

4.		
5.		
6.		
7.		
8.		
9.		
10.		
11.		
12.		
13.		
14.		
15.		
16.		

Totals

Magic Series

1

The Nutcracker Ballet – Sugarplum Fairy (1st, 1986)
Handcrafted • N/A
1750QLX7043 • **Value $85**

2

A Christmas Carol (2nd, 1987)
Handcrafted • N/A
1600QLX7029 • **Value $75**

3

Night Before Christmas (3rd, 1988)
Handcrafted • DLEE
1500QLX7161 • **Value $45**

4

Little Drummer Boy (4th, 1989)
Handcrafted • DLEE
1350QLX7242 • **Value $44**

5

The Littlest Angel (5th & final, 1990)
Handcrafted • FRAN
1400QLX7303 • **Value $51**

6

Forest Frolics (1st, 1989)
Handcrafted • PIKE
2450QLX7282 • **Value $90**

7

Forest Frolics (2nd, 1990)
Handcrafted • PIKE
2500QLX7236 • **Value $72**

8

Forest Frolics (3rd, 1991)
Handcrafted • PIKE
2500QLX7219 • **Value $70**

9

Forest Frolics (4th, 1992)
Handcrafted • PIKE
2800QLX7254 • **Value $65**

10

Forest Frolics (5th, 1993)
Handcrafted • PIKE
2500QLX7165 • **Value $55**

11

Forest Frolics (6th, 1994)
Handcrafted • PIKE
2800QLX7436 • **Value $60**

12

Forest Frolics (7th & final, 1995)
Handcrafted • PIKE
2800QLX7299 • **Value $50**

13

Freedom 7 (1st, 1996)
Handcrafted • SEAL
2400QLX7524 • **Value $70**

14

Friendship 7 (2nd, 1997)
Handcrafted • SEAL
2400QLX7532 • **Value $52**

15

Apollo Lunar Module (3rd, 1998)
Handcrafted • N/A
2400QLX7543 • **Value $46**

16

Lunar Rover Vehicle (4th & final, 1999)
Handcrafted • SEAL
2400QLX7377 • **Value $38**

17

Lighthouse Greetings (1st, 1997)
Handcrafted • FRAN
2400QLX7442 • **Value $73**

18

Lighthouse Greetings (2nd, 1998)
Handcrafted • FRAN
2400QLX7536 • **Value $45**

19

Lighthouse Greetings (3rd, 1999)
Handcrafted • FRAN
2400QLX7379 • **Value $35**

20

New!

Lighthouse Greetings (4th, 2000)
Handcrafted • FRAN
2400QLX7344 • **Value $24**

Christmas Classics

	Price Paid	Value
1.		
2.		
3.		
4.		
5.		

Forest Frolics

6.		
7.		
8.		
9.		
10.		
11.		
12.		

Journeys Into Space

13.		
14.		
15.		
16.		

Lighthouse Greetings

17.		
18.		
19.		
20.		

Totals

1

PEANUTS® (1st, 1991)
Handcrafted • RHOD
1800QLX7229 • **Value $82**

2

PEANUTS® (2nd, 1992)
Handcrafted • RHOD
1800QLX7214 • **Value $58**

3

PEANUTS® (3rd, 1993)
Handcrafted • RHOD
1800QLX7155 • **Value $50**

4

PEANUTS® (4th, 1994)
Handcrafted • RHOD
2000QLX7406 • **Value $46**

5

**PEANUTS®
(5th & final, 1995)**
Handcrafted • RHOD
2450QLX7277 • **Value $50**

6

**Lighting the Tree
(1st, 1986)**
Handcrafted • N/A
2200QLX7033 • **Value $100**

7

**Perfect Portrait
(2nd, 1987)**
Handcrafted • N/A
1950QLX7019 • **Value $70**

8

**On With the Show
(3rd & final, 1988)**
Handcrafted • DLEE
1950QLX7191 • **Value $44**

9

**Tobin Fraley Holiday
Carousel (1st, 1994)**
Handcrafted • UNRU
3200QLX7496 • **Value $70**

10

**Tobin Fraley Holiday
Carousel (2nd, 1995)**
Handcrafted • FRAL
3200QLX7269 • **Value $60**

11

**Tobin Fraley Holiday
Carousel
(3rd & final, 1996)**
Handcrafted • FRAN
3200QLX7461 • **Value $52**

Crown Reflections

Introduced by Hallmark in 1998, the Crown Reflections series was formed to recreate the beauty of traditional, blown glass ornaments of yesteryear. The "Holiday Traditions" series continues this year with the addition of "Christmas Rose," which is the final edition in the series.

12

**Red Poinsettias
(1st, 1998)**
Blown Glass • N/A
3500QBG6906 • **Value $47**

13

**Pink Poinsettias
(complements the
series, 1998)**
Blown Glass • N/A
2500QBG6926 • **Value $36**

14

**White Poinsettias
(complements the
series, 1998)**
Blown Glass • N/A
2500QBG6923 • **Value $36**

15

**Festival of Fruit
(2nd, 1999)**
Handcrafted • N/A
3500QBG6069 • **Value $36**

16

New!

**Christmas Rose
(3rd & final, 2000)**
Blown Glass • N/A
3500QBG4054 • **Value $35**

PEANUTS®

	Price Paid	Value
1.		
2.		
3.		
4.		
5.		

Santa And Sparky

6.		
7.		
8.		

Tobin Fraley Holiday Carousel

9.		
10.		
11.		

Holiday Traditions

12.		
13.		
14.		
15.		
16.		

Totals

Miniature Series

There are two new Miniature Series making their debut in 2000 ("Ice Block Buddies" and "MONOPOLY® Game: Advance to Go!"), which brings the collection to a total of 38 series since it began in 1988. Four series are retiring from the collection this year, which leaves 13 current series to continue into 2001.

1

**Alice in Wonderland
(1st, 1995)**
Handcrafted • ANDR
675QXM4777 • **Value $18**

2

Mad Hatter (2nd, 1996)
Handcrafted • ANDR
675QXM4074 • **Value $16**

3

White Rabbit (3rd, 1997)
Handcrafted • ANDR
695QXM4142 • **Value $15**

4

**Cheshire Cat
(4th & final, 1998)**
Handcrafted • ANDR
695QXM4186 • **Value $14**

5

**Antique Tractors
(1st, 1997)**
Die-Cast Metal • SICK
695QXM4185 • **Value $18**

Alice In Wonderland

	Price Paid	Value
1.		
2.		
3.		
4.		

Antique Tractors

5.		
6.		
7.		
8.		

The Bearymores

9.		
10.		
11.		

Centuries Of Santa

12.		
13.		
14.		
15.		
16.		
17.		

6

**Antique Tractors
(2nd, 1998)**
Die-Cast Metal • SICK
695QXM4166 • **Value $15**

7

**Antique Tractors
(3rd, 1999)**
Die-Cast Metal • SICK
695QXM4567 • **Value $13**

8

New!

**Antique Tractors
(4th, 2000)**
Die-Cast Metal • SICK
695QXM5994 • **Value $6.95**

9

**The Bearymores
(1st, 1992)**
Handcrafted • RGRS
575QXM5544 • **Value $21**

10

**The Bearymores
(2nd, 1993)**
Handcrafted • RGRS
575QXM5125 • **Value $18**

11

**The Bearymores
(3rd & final, 1994)**
Handcrafted • RGRS
575QXM5133 • **Value $16**

12

**Centuries of Santa
(1st, 1994)**
Handcrafted • SICK
600QXM5153 • **Value $27**

13

**Centuries of Santa
(2nd, 1995)**
Handcrafted • SICK
575QXM4789 • **Value $20**

14

**Centuries of Santa
(3rd, 1996)**
Handcrafted • SICK
575QXM4091 • **Value $16**

15

**Centuries of Santa
(4th, 1997)**
Handcrafted • SICK
595QXM4295 • **Value $13**

16

**Centuries of Santa
(5th, 1998)**
Handcrafted • SICK
595QXM4206 • **Value $12**

17

**Centuries of Santa
(6th & final, 1999)**
Handcrafted • SICK
595QXM4589 • **Value $12**

VALUE GUIDE — HALLMARK KEEPSAKE ORNAMENTS

1

Christmas Bells
(1st, 1995)
Handcrafted/Metal • SEAL
475QXM4007 • **Value $24**

2

Christmas Bells
(2nd, 1996)
Handcrafted/Metal • SEAL
475QXM4071 • **Value $18**

3

Christmas Bells
(3rd, 1997)
Handcrafted/Metal • SEAL
495QXM4162 • **Value $14**

4

Christmas Bells
(4th, 1998)
Handcrafted/Metal • SEAL
495QXM4196 • **Value $12**

5

Christmas Bells
(5th, 1999)
Handcrafted/Metal • SEAL
495QXM4489 • **Value $11**

6
New!

Christmas Bells
(6th, 2000)
Handcrafted/Metal • SEAL
495QXM5964 • **Value $4.95**

7

Holiday Flurries
(1st, 1999)
Handcrafted • SICK
695QXM4547 • **Value $15**

8
New!

Holiday Flurries
(2nd, 2000)
Handcrafted • SICK
695QXM5311 • **Value $6.95**

9
New!

Ice Block Buddies
(1st, 2000)
Handcrafted • SICK
595QXM6011 • **Value $5.95**

10

Kittens in Toyland
(1st, 1988)
Handcrafted • CROW
500QXM5621 • **Value $25**

11

Kittens in Toyland
(2nd, 1989)
Handcrafted • CROW
450QXM5612 • **Value $21**

12

Kittens in Toyland
(3rd, 1990)
Handcrafted • CROW
450QXM5736 • **Value $20**

13

Kittens in Toyland
(4th, 1991)
Handcrafted • CROW
450QXM5639 • **Value $16**

14

Kittens in Toyland
(5th & final, 1992)
Handcrafted • CROW
450QXM5391 • **Value $17**

15

The Kringles (1st, 1989)
Handcrafted • RGRS
600QXM5625 • **Value $28**

16

The Kringles (2nd, 1990)
Handcrafted • RGRS
600QXM5753 • **Value $24**

17

The Kringles (3rd, 1991)
Handcrafted • RGRS
600QXM5647 • **Value $26**

18

The Kringles (4th, 1992)
Handcrafted • RGRS
600QXM5381 • **Value $20**

19

The Kringles
(5th & final, 1993)
Handcrafted • RGRS
575QXM5135 • **Value $17**

Christmas Bells

	Price Paid	Value
1.		
2.		
3.		
4.		
5.		
6.		

Holiday Flurries

7.		
8.		

Ice Block Buddies

9.		

Kittens In Toyland

10.		
11.		
12.		
13.		
14.		

The Kringles

15.		
16.		
17.		
18.		
19.		

Totals

Miniature Series

1

**Locomotive and Tender
(1st, 1999, set/2)**
Die-Cast Metal • SEAL
1095QXM4549 • **Value $20**

2

New!
**Horse Car and Milk Car
(set/2, 2nd, 2000)**
Die-Cast Metal • SEAL
1295QXM5971 • **Value $12.95**

3

**March of the Teddy
Bears (1st, 1993)**
Handcrafted • UNRU
450QXM4005 • **Value $20**

4

**March of the Teddy
Bears (2nd, 1994)**
Handcrafted • UNRU
450QXM5106 • **Value $18**

5

**March of the Teddy
Bears (3rd, 1995)**
Handcrafted • UNRU
475QXM4799 • **Value $15**

6

**March of the Teddy
Bears (4th & final, 1996)**
Handcrafted • UNRU
475QXM4094 • **Value $13**

7

**Miniature Clothespin
Soldier (1st, 1995)**
Handcrafted • SICK
375QXM4097 • **Value $18**

8

**Miniature Clothespin
Soldier (2nd, 1996)**
Handcrafted • SICK
475QXM4144 • **Value $14**

9

**Miniature Clothespin
Soldier (3rd, 1997)**
Handcrafted • SICK
495QXM4155 • **Value $12**

10

**Miniature Clothespin
Soldier (4th, 1998)**
Handcrafted • SICK
495QXM4193 • **Value $10**

11

**Miniature Clothespin
Soldier (5th, 1999)**
Handcrafted • SICK
495QXM4579 • **Value $10**

12

New!
**Sailor
(6th & final, 2000)**
Handcrafted • SICK
495QXM5334 • **Value $4.95**

13

**Electra-Glide®
(1st, 1999)**
Die-Cast Metal • PALM
795QXI6137 • **Value $17**

14

New!
**1962 Duo-Glide™
(2nd, 2000)**
Die-Cast Metal • PALM
795QXI6001 • **Value $7.95**

15

**Murray® "Champion"
(1st, 1995)**
Die-Cast Metal • PALM
575QXM4079 • **Value $20**

16

**Murray® "Fire Truck"
(2nd, 1996)**
Die-Cast Metal • PALM
675QXM4031 • **Value $17**

17

**Murray Inc.® "Pursuit"
Airplane (3rd, 1997)**
Die-Cast Metal • PALM
695QXM4132 • **Value $15**

18

**Murray Inc.® Dump
Truck (4th, 1998)**
Die-Cast Metal • PALM
695QXM4183 • **Value $14**

19

**1955 Murray® Tractor
and Trailer (5th, 1999)**
Die-Cast Metal • PALM
695QXM4479 • **Value $12**

20

New!
**1968 Murray® Jolly
Roger Flagship
(6th, 2000)**
Die-Cast Metal • WEBB
695QXM5944 • **Value $6.95**

**LIONEL® 746 Norfolk
And Western**

	Price Paid	Value
1.		
2.		

**March Of The
Teddy Bears**

3.		
4.		
5.		
6.		

**Miniature Clothespin
Soldier**

7.		
8.		
9.		
10.		
11.		
12.		

**Harley-Davidson®
Motorcycle**

13.		
14.		

**Miniature Kiddie Car
Classics**

15.		
16.		
17.		
18.		
19.		
20.		

Totals

Miniature Series

1

1937 Steelcraft Auburn (1st, 1998)
Die-Cast Metal • PALM
695QXM4143 • **Value $15**

2

1937 Steelcraft Airflow by Murray® (2nd, 1999)
Die-Cast Metal • PALM
695QXM4477 • **Value $13**

3
New!

1935 Steelcraft by Murray® (3rd, 2000)
Die-Cast Metal • WEBB
695QXM5951 • **Value $6.95**

4
New!

Sack of Money (1st, 2000)
Pewter • PIKE
895QXM5341 • **Value $8.95**

5

The Nativity (1st, 1998)
Pewter • UNRU
995QXM4156 • **Value $19**

6

The Nativity (2nd, 1999)
Pewter • UNRU
995QXM4497 • **Value $17**

7
New!

The Nativity (3rd, 2000)
Pewter • UNRU
995QXM5961 • **Value $9.95**

8

Nature's Angels (1st, 1990)
Handcrafted/Brass • SEAL
450QXM5733 • **Value $26**

9

Nature's Angels (2nd, 1991)
Handcrafted/Brass • PIKE
450QXM5657 • **Value $23**

10

Nature's Angels (3rd, 1992)
Handcrafted/Brass • PIKE
450QXM5451 • **Value $21**

11

Nature's Angels (4th, 1993)
Handcrafted/Brass • ANDR
450QXM5122 • **Value $18**

12

Nature's Angels (5th, 1994)
Handcrafted/Brass • VOTR
450QXM5126 • **Value $14**

13

Nature's Angels (6th, 1995)
Handcrafted/Brass • ANDR
475QXM4809 • **Value $17**

14

Nature's Angels (7th & final, 1996)
Handcrafted/Brass • PIKE
475QXM4111 • **Value $13**

15

The Night Before Christmas (1st, 1992, w/display house)
Handcrafted • UNRU
1375QXM5541 • **Value $32**

16

The Night Before Christmas (2nd, 1993)
Handcrafted • UNRU
450QXM5115 • **Value $20**

17

The Night Before Christmas (3rd, 1994)
Handcrafted • UNRU
450QXM5123 • **Value $16**

18

The Night Before Christmas (4th, 1995)
Handcrafted • UNRU
475QXM4807 • **Value $20**

19

The Night Before Christmas (5th & final, 1996)
Handcrafted • UNRU
575QXM4104 • **Value $14**

Miniature Kiddie Car Luxury Edition

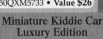

	Price Paid	Value
1.		
2.		
3.		

MONOPOLY® Game: Advance to Go!

4.		

The Nativity

5.		
6.		
7.		

Nature's Angels

8.		
9.		
10.		
11.		
12.		
13.		
14.		

The Night Before Christmas

15.		
16.		
17.		
18.		
19.		

Totals

Miniature Series

1

Locomotive (1st, 1989)
Handcrafted • SICK
850QXM5762 • **Value $47**

2

Coal Car (2nd, 1990)
Handcrafted • SICK
850QXM5756 • **Value $35**

3

**Passenger Car
(3rd, 1991)**
Handcrafted • SICK
850QXM5649 • **Value $52**

4

Box Car (4th, 1992)
Handcrafted • SICK
700QXM5441 • **Value $30**

5

Flatbed Car (5th, 1993)
Handcrafted • SICK
700QXM5105 • **Value $26**

6

Stock Car (6th, 1994)
Handcrafted • SICK
700QXM5113 • **Value $23**

7

**Milk Tank Car
(7th, 1995)**
Handcrafted • SICK
675QXM4817 • **Value $19**

8

Cookie Car (8th, 1996)
Handcrafted • SICK
675QXM4114 • **Value $18**

9

Candy Car (9th, 1997)
Handcrafted • SICK
695QXM4175 • **Value $15**

10

**Caboose
(10th & final, 1998)**
Handcrafted • SICK
695QXM4216 • **Value $15**

11

**Noel R.R. Locomotive
1989-1998 (Anniversary
Edition, 1998)**
Pewter • SICK
1095QXM4286 • **Value $21**

12

**The Nutcracker Ballet
(1st, 1996, w/display stage)**
Handcrafted • VOTR
1475QXM4064 • **Value $29**

13

**Herr Drosselmeyer
(2nd, 1997)**
Handcrafted • VOTR
595QXM4135 • **Value $13**

14

Nutcracker (3rd, 1998)
Handcrafted • VOTR
595QXM4146 • **Value $14**

15

Mouse King (4th, 1999)
Handcrafted • VOTR
595QXM4487 • **Value $13**

16

New!

**Sugarplum Fairy
(5th & final, 2000)**
Handcrafted • VOTR
595QXM5984 • **Value $5.95**

17

**Nutcracker Guild
(1st, 1994)**
Handcrafted • SICK
575QXM5146 • **Value $23**

18

**Nutcracker Guild
(2nd, 1995)**
Handcrafted • SICK
575QXM4787 • **Value $18**

19

**Nutcracker Guild
(3rd, 1996)**
Handcrafted • SICK
575QXM4084 • **Value $15**

20

**Nutcracker Guild
(4th, 1997)**
Handcrafted • SICK
695QXM4165 • **Value $14**

Noel R.R.

	Price Paid	Value
1.		
2.		
3.		
4.		
5.		
6.		
7.		
8.		
9.		
10.		
11.		

The Nutcracker Ballet

12.		
13.		
14.		
15.		
16.		

Nutcracker Guild

17.		
18.		
19.		
20.		

Totals

1
Nutcracker Guild (5th, 1998)
Handcrafted • SICK
695QXM4203 • **Value $14**

2
Nutcracker Guild (6th, 1999)
Handcrafted • SICK
695QXM4587 • **Value $13**

3 New!
Nutcracker Guild (7th & final, 2000)
Handcrafted • SICK
695QXM5991 • **Value $6.95**

4
Family Home (1st, 1988)
Handcrafted • DLEE
850QXM5634 • **Value $45**

5
Sweet Shop (2nd, 1989)
Handcrafted • JLEE
850QXM5615 • **Value $29**

6
School (3rd, 1990)
Handcrafted • JLEE
850QXM5763 • **Value $25**

7
Inn (4th, 1991)
Handcrafted • JLEE
850QXM5627 • **Value $29**

8
Church (5th, 1992)
Handcrafted • JLEE
700QXM5384 • **Value $35**

9
Toy Shop (6th, 1993)
Handcrafted • JLEE
700QXM5132 • **Value $20**

10
Hat Shop (7th, 1994)
Handcrafted • ANDR
700QXM5143 • **Value $20**

11
Tudor House (8th, 1995)
Handcrafted • JLEE
675QXM4819 • **Value $18**

12
Village Mill (9th, 1996)
Handcrafted • RHOD
675QXM4124 • **Value $16**

13
Village Depot (10th & final, 1997)
Handcrafted • LARS
695QXM4182 • **Value $15**

14
On the Road (1st, 1993)
Pressed Tin • SICK
575QXM4002 • **Value $22**

15
On the Road (2nd, 1994)
Pressed Tin • SICK
575QXM5103 • **Value $18**

16
On the Road (3rd, 1995)
Pressed Tin • SICK
575QXM4797 • **Value $16**

17
On the Road (4th, 1996)
Pressed Tin • SICK
575QXM4101 • **Value $14**

18
On the Road (5th, 1997)
Pressed Tin • SICK
595QXM4172 • **Value $13**

19
On the Road (6th & final, 1998)
Pressed Tin • SICK
595QXM4213 • **Value $12**

20
Penguin Pal (1st, 1988)
Handcrafted • SIED
375QXM5631 • **Value $27**

Nutcracker Guild		
	Price Paid	Value
1.		
2.		
3.		

Old English Village		
4.		
5.		
6.		
7.		
8.		
9.		
10.		
11.		
12.		
13.		

On The Road		
14.		
15.		
16.		
17.		
18.		
19.		

Penguin Pal		
20.		
Totals		

Miniature Series

1

Penguin Pal (2nd, 1989)
Handcrafted • N/A
450QXM5602 • **Value $21**

2

Penguin Pal (3rd, 1990)
Handcrafted • N/A
450QXM5746 • **Value $19**

3

Penguin Pal (4th & final, 1991)
Handcrafted • SIED
450QXM5629 • **Value $17**

4

Rocking Horse (1st, 1988)
Handcrafted • SICK
450QXM5624 • **Value $47**

5

Rocking Horse (2nd, 1989)
Handcrafted • SICK
450QXM5605 • **Value $33**

6

Rocking Horse (3rd, 1990)
Handcrafted • SICK
450QXM5743 • **Value $29**

7

Rocking Horse (4th, 1991)
Handcrafted • SICK
450QXM5637 • **Value $29**

8

Rocking Horse (5th, 1992)
Handcrafted • SICK
450QXM5454 • **Value $24**

9

Rocking Horse (6th, 1993)
Handcrafted • SICK
450QXM5112 • **Value $20**

10

Rocking Horse (7th, 1994)
Handcrafted • SICK
450QXM5116 • **Value $20**

11

Rocking Horse (8th, 1995)
Handcrafted • SICK
450QXM4827 • **Value $17**

12

Rocking Horse (9th, 1996)
Handcrafted • SICK
475QXM4121 • **Value $15**

13

Rocking Horse (10th & final, 1997)
Handcrafted • SICK
495QXM4302 • **Value $13**

14

Santa's Little Big Top (1st, 1995)
Handcrafted • CROW
675QXM4779 • **Value $20**

15

Santa's Little Big Top (2nd, 1996)
Handcrafted • CROW
675QXM4081 • **Value $15**

16

Santa's Little Big Top (3rd & final, 1997)
Handcrafted • CROW
695QXM4152 • **Value $15**

17

Seaside Scenes (1st, 1999)
Handcrafted • SEAL
795QXM4649 • **Value $15**

18
New!

Seaside Scenes (2nd, 2000)
Handcrafted • SEAL
795QXM5974 • **Value $7.95**

19

Snowflake Ballet (1st, 1997)
Handcrafted • ANDR
595QXM4192 • **Value $18**

20

Snowflake Ballet (2nd, 1998)
Handcrafted • ANDR
595QXM4173 • **Value $14**

	Price Paid	Value
Penguin Pal		
1.		
2.		
3.		
Rocking Horse		
4.		
5.		
6.		
7.		
8.		
9.		
10.		
11.		
12.		
13.		
Santa's Little Big Top		
14.		
15.		
16.		
Seaside Scenes		
17.		
18.		
Snowflake Ballet		
19.		
20.		
Totals		

Value Guide — Hallmark Keepsake Ornaments

1
Snowflake Ballet
(3rd & final, 1999)
Handcrafted • ANDR
595QXM4569 • **Value $12**

2
Teddy-Bear Style
(1st, 1997)
Handcrafted • UNRU
595QXM4215 • **Value $15**

3
Teddy-Bear Style
(2nd, 1998)
Handcrafted • UNRU
595QXM4176 • **Value $12**

4
Teddy-Bear Style
(3rd, 1999)
Handcrafted • UNRU
595QXM4499 • **Value $11**

5 New!
Teddy-Bear Style
(4th & final, 2000)
Handcrafted • UNRU
595QXM5954 • **Value $5.95**

6
Thimble Bells
(1st, 1990)
Porcelain • PYDA
600QXM5543 • **Value $24**

7
Thimble Bells
(2nd, 1991)
Porcelain • PYDA
600QXM5659 • **Value $22**

8
Thimble Bells
(3rd, 1992)
Porcelain • LYLE
600QXM5461 • **Value $20**

9
Thimble Bells
(4th & final, 1993)
Porcelain • VOTR
575QXM5142 • **Value $15**

10
Welcome Friends
(1st, 1997)
Handcrafted • PIKE
695QXM4205 • **Value $17**

11
Welcome Friends
(2nd, 1998)
Handcrafted • PIKE
695QXM4153 • **Value $15**

12
Welcome Friends
(3rd & final, 1999)
Handcrafted • PIKE
695QXM4577 • **Value $13**

13
**Winter Fun With
SNOOPY® (1st, 1998)**
Handcrafted • LARS
695QXM4243 • **Value $17**

14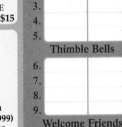
**Winter Fun With
SNOOPY® (2nd, 1999)**
Handcrafted • LARS
695QXM4559 • **Value $15**

15 New!
**Winter Fun With
SNOOPY® (3rd, 2000)**
Handcrafted • LARS
695QXM5324 • **Value $6.95**

16
Dorothy's Ruby Slippers
(1st, 1999)
Handcrafted • KLIN
595QXM4599 • **Value $26**

17 New!
The Tin Man's Heart
(2nd, 2000)
Handcrafted • RGRS
595QXM5981 • **Value $5.95**

18
Woodland Babies
(1st, 1991)
Handcrafted • CROW
600QXM5667 • **Value $24**

19
Woodland Babies
(2nd, 1992)
Handcrafted • PALM
600QXM5444 • **Value $17**

20
Woodland Babies
(3rd & final, 1993)
Handcrafted • FRAN
575QXM5102 • **Value $16**

Snowflake Ballet

	Price Paid	Value
1.		

Teddy-Bear Style

2.		
3.		
4.		
5.		

Thimble Bells

6.		
7.		
8.		
9.		

Welcome Friends

10.		
11.		
12.		

Winter Fun With SNOOPY®

13.		
14.		
15.		

Wonders of Oz™

16.		
17.		

Woodland Babies

18.		
19.		
20.		

Totals

2000

This year, 350 new ornaments join the ranks, including 25 in the new Li'l Blown Glass series of miniature blown glass ornaments. In addition, three new collections make their debut this year: the American Spirit™ Collection, Peanuts® Gallery and The Dr. Seuss™ Collection. See the collectibles series section for more 2000 ornaments.

1

102 Dalmatians
Handcrafted • N/A
1295QXI5231 • **Value $12.95**

2

1955 Murray® Dump Truck
Blown Glass • N/A
3500QBG4081 • **Value $35**

3

1962 BARBIE™ Hatbox Doll Case
Handcrafted • N/A
995QX6791 • **Value $9.95**

4

Alice Meets the Cheshire Cat
Handcrafted • N/A
1495QXD4011 • **Value $14.95**

5

All Things Beautiful
Handcrafted/Paper • ESCH
1395QX8351 • **Value $13.95**

6

Angel-Blessed Tree
Handcrafted • RGRS
895QX8241 • **Value $8.95**

7

Angel of Promise
Porcelain • ANDR
1495QXI4144 • **Value $14.95**

8

Angelic Trio
Handcrafted • HADD
1095QX8234 • **Value $10.95**

9

Arnold Palmer
Handcrafted • UNRU
1495QXI4324 • **Value $14.95**

10

Baby's First Christmas
Handcrafted • FRAN
795QX6914 • **Value $7.95**

11

Baby's First Christmas
Handcrafted • HADD
895QX8031 • **Value $8.95**

12

Baby's First Christmas
Handcrafted • SEAL
1095QX8034 • **Value $10.95**

13

Baby's First Christmas
Handcrafted • AUBE
1895QX8041 • **Value $18.95**

14

Baby's Second Christmas
Handcrafted • FRAN
795QX6921 • **Value $7.95**

15

Backpack Bear
Blown Glass • TAGU
3000QBG4071 • **Value $30**

16

Balthasar – The Magi
(re-issued from 1999)
Porcelain • N/A
1295QX8037 • **Value $12.95**

17

BARBIE™ Angel of Joy™ Ornament
Handcrafted • RGRS
1495QXI6861 • **Value $14.95**

General Keepsake

	Price Paid	Value
1.		
2.		
3.		
4.		
5.		
6.		
7.		
8.		
9.		
10.		
11.		
12.		
13.		
14.		
15.		
16.		
17.		
Totals		

1

Blue Glass Angel
Glass • TAGU
795QX8381 • **Value $7.95**

2

Bob the Tomato™ and Larry the Cucumber™
Handcrafted • LYLE
995QXI4334 • **Value $9.95**

3

Bringing Her Gift
Handcrafted • KLIN
1095QX8334 • **Value $10.95**

4

Bugs Bunny and Gossamer
Handcrafted • CHAD
1295QX6574 • **Value $12.95**

5

Busy Bee Shopper
Handcrafted • CHAD
795QX6964 • **Value $7.95**

6

Buzz Lightyear
Handcrafted • N/A
1495QXI5234 • **Value $14.95**

7

Caroler's Best Friend
Handcrafted • ESCH
1295QX8354 • **Value $12.95**

8

Caspar – The Magi (re-issued from 1999)
Porcelain • N/A
1295QX8039 • **Value $12.95**

9

Celebrate His Birth!
Glass • HADD
695QX2464 • **Value $6.95**

10

Child's Fifth Christmas
Handcrafted • CROW
795QX6934 • **Value $7.95**

11

Child's Fourth Christmas
Handcrafted • CROW
795QX6931 • **Value $7.95**

12

Child's Third Christmas
Handcrafted • FRAN
795QX6924 • **Value $7.95**

13

The Christmas Belle
Porcelain • AUBE
1095QX8311 • **Value $10.95**

14

Christmas Tree Surprise
Porcelain • TAGU
1695QX8321 • **Value $16.95**

15

A Class Act
Handcrafted • HADD
795QX8074 • **Value $7.95**

16

Close-Knit Friends (set/2)
Handcrafted • SEAL
1495QX8204 • **Value $14.95**

17

Cool Character
Pressed Tin • SICK
1295QX8271 • **Value $12.95**

18

Dad
Handcrafted • CHAD
895QX8071 • **Value $8.95**

19

Dale Earnhardt
Handcrafted • SEAL
1495QXI6754 • **Value $14.95**

20

Dancin' In Christmas
Handcrafted • TAGU
795QX6971 • **Value $7.95**

General Keepsake

	Price Paid	Value
1.		
2.		
3.		
4.		
5.		
6.		
7.		
8.		
9.		
10.		
11.		
12.		
13.		
14.		
15.		
16.		
17.		
18.		
19.		
20.		

Totals

1

Darth Maul™
Handcrafted • ANDR
1495QXI6885 • **Value $14.95**

2

Daughter
Porcelain • ESCH
895QX8081 • **Value $8.95**

3

Dog Dish Dilemma
Handcrafted • N/A
1295QXD4044 • **Value $12.95**

4

Dousin' Dalmatian
Handcrafted • SEAL
995QX8024 • **Value $9.95**

5

Dressing Cinderella
Handcrafted • N/A
1295QXD4109 • **Value $12.95**

6

Feliz Navidad
Handcrafted • RGRS
895QX8214 • **Value $8.95**

7

The Fishing Hole
Handcrafted • VISK
1295QX6984 • **Value $12.95**

8

Friendly Greeting
Handcrafted /Pressed Tin • ESCH
995QX8174 • **Value $9.95**

9

Friends in Harmony
Handcrafted • FRAN
995QX8001 • **Value $9.95**

10

Frosty Friends (set/2)
Blown Glass • SEAL
4000QBG4094 • **Value $40**

11

G.I. Joe® Action Pilot
Handcrafted • CROW
1395QX6734 • **Value $13.95**

12

Gifts for the Grinch
Handcrafted • KLIN
1295QXI5344 • **Value $12.95**

13

Gingerbread Church
Handcrafted • LAPR
995QX8244 • **Value $9.95**

14

Godchild
Handcrafted • TAGU
795QX8161 • **Value $7.95**

15

Gold-Star Teacher
Handcrafted • PIKE
795QX6951 • **Value $7.95**

16

Golfer Supreme
Handcrafted • SEAL
1095QX6991 • **Value $10.95**

17

The Good Book
Handcrafted • UNRU
1395QX8254 • **Value $13.95**

18

Graceful Glory
Handcrafted • VOTR
1895QX8304 • **Value $18.95**

19

Granddaughter
Porcelain • FORS
895QX8091 • **Value $8.95**

20

Grandma's House
Porcelain • LARS
1095QX8141 • **Value $10.95**

General Keepsake

	Price Paid	Value
1.		
2.		
3.		
4.		
5.		
6.		
7.		
8.		
9.		
10.		
11.		
12.		
13.		
14.		
15.		
16.		
17.		
18.		
19.		
20.		

Totals

1

Grandson
Porcelain • FORS
895QX8094 • **Value $8.95**

2

**Harley-Davidson®
BARBIE™ Ornament**
Handcrafted • RGRS
1495QXI8554 • **Value $14.95**

3

A Holiday Gathering
Porcelain • N/A
1095QX8561 • **Value $10.95**

4

Holly Berry Bell
Porcelain • FORS
1495QX8291 • **Value $14.95**

5

**The Holy Family (set/3,
re-issued from 1999)**
Porcelain • N/A
2500QX6523 • **Value $25**

6

Hooray for the U.S.A.
Handcrafted • CHAD
995QX8281 • **Value $9.95**

7

**Hopalong Cassidy
(set/2)**
Pressed Tin/Handcrafted • N/A
1495QX6714 • **Value $14.95**

8

**Hot Wheels™
1968 Deora™ (green)**
Handcrafted • UNRU
1495QXI6891 • **Value $14.95**

9

**Hot Wheels™
1968 Deora™ (red)**
Handcrafted • UNRU
1495QXI6891 • **Value $14.95**

10

Imperial Stormtrooper™
Handcrafted • KLIN
1495QXI6711 • **Value $14.95**

11

**Jeannie I Dream of
Jeannie (set/2)**
Handcrafted • ANDR
1495QXI8564 • **Value $14.95**

12

King of the Ring
Handcrafted • TAGU
1095QX6864 • **Value $10.95**

13

**Kris "Cross-Country"
Kringle**
Handcrafted • VISK
1295QX6954 • **Value $12.95**

14

Kristi Yamaguchi
Handcrafted • BRIC
1395QXI6854 • **Value $13.95**

15

**Larry, Moe, and Curly
(set/3)**
Handcrafted • LARS
3000QX6851 • **Value $30**

16

**Lieutenant Commander
Worf™ STAR TREK:
Deep Space Nine™**
Blown Glass • RGRS
3000QBG4064 • **Value $30**

17

**LIONEL® 4501
Southern Mikado
Steam Locomotive**
Blown Glass • N/A
3500QBG4074 • **Value $35**

18

Loggin' On to Santa
Handcrafted • PIKE
895QX8224• **Value $8.95**

19

The Lone Ranger™
Handcrafted • UNRU
1595QX6941 • **Value $15.95**

20

"Lucy Is Enciente"
Handcrafted • VOTR
1595QX6884 • **Value $15.95**

General Keepsake

	Price Paid	Value
1.		
2.		
3.		
4.		
5.		
6.		
7.		
8.		
9.		
10.		
11.		
12.		
13.		
14.		
15.		
16.		
17.		
18.		
19.		
20.		

Totals

VALUE GUIDE — HALLMARK KEEPSAKE ORNAMENTS

1

The Lullabye League
(set/3)
Handcrafted • LYLE
1995QX6604 • **Value $19.95**

2

Max (complements the
"The Snowmen of
Mitford" from 1999)
Handcrafted • N/A
795QX8584 • **Value $7.95**

3

Melchior – The Magi
(re-issued from 1999)
Porcelain • N/A
1295QX6819 • **Value $12.95**

4

Memories of Christmas
Pressed Tin • SICK
1295QX8264 • **Value $12.95**

5

Merry Ballooning
Pressed Tin • BRIC
1695QX8384 • **Value $16.95**

6

Mickey's Bedtime
Reading
Handcrafted • N/A
1095QXD4077 • **Value $10.95**

7

Mickey's Sky Rider
Handcrafted • N/A
1895QXD4159 • **Value $18.95**

8

Millennium Time
Capsule
Handcrafted • UNRU
1095QX8044 • **Value $10.95**

9

Mom
Handcrafted • CHAD
895QX8064 • **Value $8.95**

10

Mom and Dad
Porcelain • BRIC
995QX8061 • **Value $9.95**

11

Mother and Daughter
Porcelain • RGRS
995QX8154 • **Value $9.95**

12

Mr. Monopoly™
Handcrafted • SIED
1095QX8101 • **Value $10.95**

13
Mrs. Claus's Holiday
Handcrafted • KLIN
995QX8011 • **Value $9.95**

14

New Home
Handcrafted • SEAL
895QX8171 • **Value $8.95**

15

New Millennium Baby
Handcrafted • VOTR
1095QX8581 • **Value $10.95**

16

The Newborn Prince
Handcrafted • N/A
1395QXD4194 • **Value $13.95**

17

North Pole Network
Handcrafted • SEAL
1095QX6994 • **Value $10.95**

18

Northern Art Bear
Handcrafted • LAPR
895QX8294 • **Value $8.95**

19
Off to Neverland!
Handcrafted • N/A
1295QXD4004 • **Value $12.95**

20

Our Christmas Together
Porcelain • KLIN
995QX8054 • **Value $9.95**

General Keepsake

	Price Paid	Value
1.		
2.		
3.		
4.		
5.		
6.		
7.		
8.		
9.		
10.		
11.		
12.		
13.		
14.		
15.		
16.		
17.		
18.		
19.		
20.		

Totals

1

Our Family
Handcrafted • AUBE
795QX8211 • **Value $7.95**

2

Our First Christmas Together
Acrylic • VOTR
795QX3104 • **Value $7.95**

3

Our First Christmas Together
Handcrafted • SIED
895QX8051 • **Value $8.95**

4

Our First Christmas Together
Handcrafted • UNRU
1095QX8701 • **Value $10.95**

5

Our Lady of Guadalupe
Handcrafted • VISK
1295QX8231 • **Value $12.95**

6

Piglet's Jack-in-the-Box
Handcrafted • N/A
1495QXD4187 • **Value $14.95**

7

Pooh Chooses the Tree
Handcrafted • N/A
1295QXD4157 • **Value $12.95**

8

Qui-Gon Jinn™
Handcrafted • ANDR
1495QXI6741 • **Value $14.95**

9

A Reader to the Core
Handcrafted • AUBE
995QX6974 • **Value $9.95**

10

Rhett Butler™
Handcrafted • ANDR
1295QX6674 • **Value $12.95**

11

Safe In Noah's Ark
Handcrafted • HADD
1095QX8514 • **Value $10.95**

12

Santa's Chair
Handcrafted • CHAD
1295QX8314 • **Value $12.95**

13

Scooby-Doo™
Handcrafted • RGRS
1295QXI8394 • **Value $12.95**

14

Scuffy the Tugboat™ (w/book)
Handcrafted • VOTR
1195QX6871 • **Value $11.95**

15

Self-Portrait
Handcrafted • PIKE
1095QX6644 • **Value $10.95**

16

Seven of Nine™ STAR TREK: Voyager
Handcrafted • RGRS
1495QX6844 • **Value $14.95**

17

The Shepherds (set/2)
Porcelain • N/A
2500QX8361 • **Value $25**

18

Sister to Sister
Porcelain • VOTR
1295QX8144 • **Value $12.95**

19

Snow Girl
Handcrafted • ESCH
995QX8274 • **Value $9.95**

20

Snowy Garden
Handcrafted • LYLE
1395QX8284 • **Value $13.95**

General Keepsake

	Price Paid	Value
1.		
2.		
3.		
4.		
5.		
6.		
7.		
8.		
9.		
10.		
11.		
12.		
13.		
14.		
15.		
16.		
17.		
18.		
19.		
20.		

Totals

1

Son
Porcelain • ESCH
895QX8084 • Value **$8.95**

2

Stroll Round the Pole
Handcrafted • AUBE
1095QX8164 • Value **$10.95**

3

Super Friends™ (set/2)
Handcrafted/Pressed Tin • N/A
1495QX6724 • Value **$14.95**

4

Surprise Package
Handcrafted • BRIC
1095QXI8391 • Value **$10.95**

5

The Tender
Die-Cast Metal • N/A
1395QX6834 • Value **$13.95**

6

Tending Her Topiary
Handcrafted • KLIN
995QX8004 • Value **$9.95**

7

Thimble Soldier
Blown Glass • N/A
2200QBG4061 • Value **$22**

8

Time for Joy
Handcrafted • CROW
2400QX6904 • Value **$24**

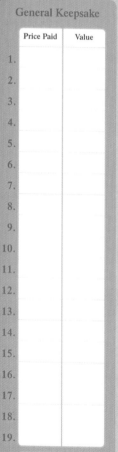

9

Together We Serve
Handcrafted • WILL
995QX8021 • Value **$9.95**

10

Tonka® Dump Truck
Die-Cast Metal • N/A
1395QX6681 • Value **$13.95**

11

Toy Shop Serenade
Handcrafted • HADD
1695QX8301 • Value **$16.95**

12

Tree Guy
Handcrafted • CHAD
895QX6961 • Value **$8.95**

13

**A Visit from
St. Nicholas**
Porcelain • LARS
1095QX8344 • Value **$10.95**

14

Warm Kindness
Porcelain • HADD
895QX8014 • Value **$8.95**

15

Warmed by Candleglow
Glass • LARS
695QX2471 • Value **$6.95**

16

**Winter Fun with
BARBIE™ and
KELLY™ Ornament**
Handcrafted • ESCH
1595QXI6561 • Value **$15.95**

17

Winterberry Santa
Handcrafted • CHAD
1495QXI4331 • Value **$14.95**

18

The Yellow Submarine
Handcrafted • WILL
1395QXI6841 • Value **$13.95**

19

Yule Tide Runner
Handcrafted • KLIN
995QX6981 • Value **$9.95**

VALUE GUIDE — HALLMARK KEEPSAKE ORNAMENTS

2000 Collection

1

Angels Over Bethlehem
Handcrafted • RHOD
1895QLX7563 • **Value $18.95**

2

**Big Twin Evolution®
Engine**
Handcrafted • PALM
2400QXI7571 • **Value $24**

3

The Blessed Family
Porcelain • LARS
1895QLX7564 • **Value $18.95**

4

**Borg™ Cube
STAR TREK: Voyager**
Handcrafted • NORT
2400QLX7354 • **Value $24**

5

The Great Oz
Handcrafted • CROW
3200QLX7361 • **Value $32**

6

Gungan™ Submarine
Handcrafted • RHOD
2400QXI7351 • **Value $24**

7

Mary's Angels
Handcrafted • CHAD
1895QLX7561 • **Value $18.95**

8

Millennium Express
Handcrafted • CROW
4200QLX7364 • **Value $42**

9

Angel Light
Archival Paper • N/A
795QLZ4311 • **Value $7.95**

10

Fun-Stuffed Stocking
Archival Paper • N/A
595QLZ4291 • **Value $5.95**

11

Heavenly Peace
Archival Paper • N/A
695QLZ4314 • **Value $6.95**

12

Jack-in-the-Box
Archival Paper • N/A
895QLZ4321 • **Value $8.95**

13

Lovely Dove
Archival Paper • N/A
795QLZ4294 • **Value $7.95**

14

The Nativity
Archival Paper • N/A
895QLZ4301 • **Value $8.95**

15

The Nutcracker
Archival Paper • N/A
595QLZ4284 • **Value $5.95**

16

A Visit From Santa
Archival Paper • N/A
895QLZ4281 • **Value $8.95**

17

Li'l Apple
Blown Glass • N/A
795QBG4261 • **Value $7.95**

18

Li'l Cascade – Red
Blown Glass • N/A
795QBG4241 • **Value $7.95**

19

Li'l Cascade – White
Blown Glass • N/A
795QBG4244 • **Value $7.95**

20

Li'l Christmas Tree
Blown Glass • N/A
795QBG4361 • **Value $7.95**

General Magic	Price Paid	Value
1.		
2.		
3.		
4.		
5.		
6.		
7.		
8.		
Laser Gallery		
9.		
10.		
11.		
12.		
13.		
14.		
15.		
16.		
Li'l Blown Glass		
17.		
18.		
19.		
20.		
Totals		

1

Li'l Gift – Green Bow
Blown Glass • N/A
795QBG4344 • **Value $7.95**

2

Li'l Gift – Red Bow
Blown Glass • N/A
795QBG4341 • **Value $7.95**

3

Li'l Grapes
Blown Glass • N/A
795QBG4141 • **Value $7.95**

4

Li'l Jack-in-the-Box
Blown Glass • N/A
795QBG4274 • **Value $7.95**

5

Li'l Mr. Claus
Blown Glass • N/A
795QBG4364 • **Value $7.95**

6

Li'l Mrs. Claus
Blown Glass • N/A
795QBG4371 • **Value $7.95**

7

Li'l Partridge
Blown Glass • N/A
795QBG4374 • **Value $7.95**

8

Li'l Pear
Blown Glass • N/A
795QBG4254 • **Value $7.95**

Li'l Blown Glass

	Price Paid	Value
1.		
2.		
3.		
4.		
5.		
6.		
7.		
8.		
9.		
10.		
11.		
12.		
13.		
14.		
15.		
16.		
17.		
18.		
19.		
20.		

9

Li'l Pineapple
Blown Glass • N/A
795QBG4251 • **Value $7.95**

10

Li'l Robot
Blown Glass • N/A
795QBG4271 • **Value $7.95**

11

Li'l Roly-Poly Penguin
Blown Glass • N/A
795QBG4281 • **Value $7.95**

12

Li'l Roly-Poly Santa
Blown Glass • N/A
795QBG4161 • **Value $7.95**

13

Li'l Roly-Poly Snowman
Blown Glass • N/A
795QBG4284 • **Value $7.95**

14

Li'l Santa – Traditional
Blown Glass • N/A
795QBG4354 • **Value $7.95**

15

Li'l Snowman – Traditional
Blown Glass • N/A
795QBG4351 • **Value $7.95**

16

Li'l Stars – Metallic Look (set/3)
Blown Glass • N/A
995QBG4221 • **Value $9.95**

17

Li'l Stars – Patriotic (set/3)
Blown Glass • N/A
995QBG4214 • **Value $9.95**

18

Li'l Stars – Traditional (set/3)
Blown Glass • N/A
995QBG4224 • **Value $9.95**

19

Li'l Swirl – Green
Blown Glass • N/A
795QBG4234 • **Value $7.95**

20

Li'l Swirl – Red
Blown Glass • N/A
795QBG4231 • **Value $7.95**

Totals

VALUE GUIDE — HALLMARK KEEPSAKE ORNAMENTS

1
Li'l Teddy Bear
Blown Glass • N/A
795QBG4264 • **Value $7.95**

2
Bugs Bunny and Elmer Fudd
Handcrafted • CHAD
995QXM5934 • **Value $9.95**

3
Catwoman™
Handcrafted • RGRS
995QXM6021 • **Value $9.95**

4
Celestial Bunny
Porcelain • AUBE
695QXM6641 • **Value $6.95**

5
Devoted Donkey
Handcrafted • SICK
695QXM6044 • **Value $6.95**

6
Green Eggs and Ham™ (set/3)
Handcrafted • WILL
1995QXM6034 • **Value $19.95**

7
Jedi Council Members: Saesee Tiin™, Yoda™ and Ki-Adi-Mundi™ (set/3)
Handcrafted • BRIC
1995QXI6744 • **Value $19.95**

8
Kindly Lions
Handcrafted • SICK
595QXM5314 • **Value $5.95**

9
Loyal Elephant
Handcrafted • SICK
695QXM6041 • **Value $6.95**

10
Mickey and Minnie Mouse (set/2)
Handcrafted • N/A
1295QXD4041 • **Value $12.95**

11
Mr. Potato Head™
Handcrafted • SIED
595QXM6014 • **Value $5.95**

12
Precious Penguin
Crystal/Pewter • VOTR
995QXM6104 • **Value $9.95**

13
Santa's Journey Begins
Handcrafted • CROW
995QXM6004 • **Value $9.95**

14
Silken Flame™ BARBIE™ Ornament and Travel Case (set/2)
Handcrafted • ANDR
1295QXM6031 • **Value $12.95**

15
Star Fairy
Handcrafted • ESCH
495QXM6101 • **Value $4.95**

16
Tigger-ific Tidings to Pooh
Handcrafted • N/A
895QXD4014 • **Value $8.95**

17
Welcoming Angel
Handcrafted • ESCH
595QXM5321 • **Value $5.95**

18
Angelic Bell
Handcrafted • BRIC
1695QXC4504 • **Value $16.95**

19
Bell-Bearing Elf (early renewal gift)
Handcrafted • CROW
QXC4514 • **Value N/E**

	Price Paid	Value
Li'l Blown Glass		
1.		
General Miniature		
2.		
3.		
4.		
5.		
6.		
7.		
8.		
9.		
10.		
11.		
12.		
13.		
14.		
15.		
16.		
17.		
Collector's Club		
18.		
19.		
Totals		

2000 Collection

1

A Friend Chimes In
(keepsake of membership)
Handcrafted • TAGU
QXC4491 • **Value N/E**

2

Jingle Bell Kringle
(keepsake of membership)
Handcrafted • CROW
QXC4481 • **Value N/E**

3

The Proud Collector
(exclusive to local clubs)
N/A • SEAL
QXC4511 • **Value N/E**

4

Ringing Reindeer
(keepsake of membership)
Handcrafted • ESCH
QXC4484 • **Value N/E**

5

**Treasure Tree (LE-25,000,
mail order exclusive)**
Handcrafted • VARI
N/A • **Value $65**

6

**Charlie Brown
Ornament**
Handcrafted • SIED
495QRP4191 • **Value $4.95**

7

Linus Ornament
Handcrafted • SIED
495QRP4204 • **Value $4.95**

8

Lucy Ornament
Handcrafted • SIED
495QRP4174 • **Value $4.95**

9

Snoopy Ornament
Handcrafted • SIED
495QRP4184 • **Value $4.95**

10

**Woodstock On
Doghouse – Display
Piece**
Handcrafted • SIED
495QRP4211 • **Value $4.95**

11

Connecticut
Double-Stamped Metal • N/A
1295QMP9404 • **Value $12.95**

12

Delaware
Double-Stamped Metal • N/A
1295QMP9400 • **Value $12.95**

13

Georgia
Double-Stamped Metal • N/A
1295QMP9403 • **Value $12.95**

14

Maryland
Double-Stamped Metal • N/A
1295QMP9426 • **Value $12.95**

15

Massachusetts
Double-Stamped Metal • N/A
1295QMP9423 • **Value $12.95**

16

New Hampshire
Double-Stamped Metal • N/A
1495QMP9432 • **Value $14.95**

17

New Jersey
Double-Stamped Metal • N/A
1295QMP9402 • **Value $12.95**

18

Pennsylvania
Double-Stamped Metal • N/A
1295QMP9401 • **Value $12.95**

19

South Carolina
Double-Stamped Metal • N/A
1295QMP9429 • **Value $12.95**

20

Virginia
Double-Stamped Metal • N/A
N/A • **Value N/E**

Collector's Club

	Price Paid	Value
1.		
2.		
3.		
4.		
5.		

Open House Ornaments

6.		
7.		
8.		
9.		
10.		

**American Spirit
Collection™**

11.		
12.		
13.		
14.		
15.		
16.		
17.		
18.		
19.		
20.		

Totals

1

American Spirit Collection Coin and Figurine Sets (10 assorted)
Gift Set/Pewter • N/A

1. Connecticut
1695QMP9410 • **Value $16.95**
2. Delaware
1695QMP9406 • **Value $16.95**
3. Georgia
1695QMP9409 • **Value $16.95**
4. Maryland
1695QMP9427 • **Value $16.95**
5. Massachusetts
1695QMP9424 • **Value $16.95**
6. New Hampshire
1895QMP9433 • **Value $18.95**
7. New Jersey
1695QMP9408 • **Value $16.95**
8. Pennsylvania
1695QMP9407 • **Value $16.95**
9. South Carolina
1695QMP9430 • **Value $16.95**
10. Virginia
N/A • **Value N/E**

2

5-piece Citizen Set
Double-Stamped Metal • N/A
595QMP9448 • **Value $5.95**

3

American Spirit Collection Citizen Sets (10 assorted)
Gift Set • N/A

1. Connecticut
195QMP9421 • **Value $1.95**
2. Delaware
195QMP9417 • **Value $1.95**
3. Georgia
195QMP9420 • **Value $1.95**
4. Maryland
195QMP9428 • **Value $1.95**
5. Massachusetts
195QMP9425 • **Value $1.95**
6. New Hampshire
195QMP9434 • **Value $1.95**
7. New Jersey
195QMP9419 • **Value $1.95**
8. Pennsylvania
195QMP9418 • **Value $1.95**
9. South Carolina
195QMP9431 • **Value $1.95**
10. Virginia
N/A • **Value N/E**

4

American Spirit Collection D/P Citizen Sets (10 assorted)
Gift Set • N/A

1. Connecticut
295QMP9447 • **Value $2.95**
2. Delaware
295QMP9443 • **Value $2.95**
3. Georgia
295QMP9446 • **Value $2.95**
4. Maryland
295QMP9450 • **Value $2.95**
5. Massachusetts
295QMP9449 • **Value $2.95**
6. New Hampshire
395QMP9452 • **Value $3.95**
7. New Jersey
295QMP9445 • **Value $2.95**
8. Pennsylvania
295QMP9444 • **Value $2.95**
9. South Carolina
295QMP9451 • **Value $2.95**
10. Virginia
N/A • **Value N/E**

American Spirit Collection™

	Price Paid	Value
1.		
2.		
3.		
4.		
5.		

5

50 State Quarters™ Collector's Kit
Embossed Metal • N/A
1495QMP9416 • **Value $14.95**

6

Artists On Tour Friday Evening Ornament
N/A • N/A
N/A • **Value N/E**

7

Signature Snowman
N/A • HADD
N/A • **Value $9.95**

Artists On Tour Pieces

6.		
7.		

8

Collegiate Collection (10 assorted)
Acrylic/Brass • N/A

1. Alabama® Crimson Tide®
995QSR2344 • **Value $9.95**
2. Florida Gators®
995QSR2324 • **Value $9.95**
3. Florida State® Seminoles®
995QSR2341 • **Value $9.95**
4. Michigan Wolverines™
995QSR2271 • **Value $9.95**
5. Nebraska Cornhuskers™
995QSR2321 • **Value $9.95**
6. North Carolina® Tar Heels®
995QSR2304 • **Value $9.95**
7. Notre Dame® Fighting Irish™
995QSR2284 • **Value $9.95**
8. Penn State® Nittany Lions®
995QSR2311 • **Value $9.95**
9. Tennessee Volunteers®
995QSR2334 • **Value $9.95**
10. The University of Kentucky® Wildcats™
995QSR2291 • **Value $9.95**

Collegiate Collection

8.		

Totals

2000 Collection

1

The Cat in the Hat™
Porcelain • CROW
1200QSU2026 • **Value $12**

2

The Ends
N/A • CHAD
4500QSU2038 • **Value $45**

3

A Faithful Friend
Porcelain • ESCH
1200QSU2029 • **Value $12**

4

Funny Fish
Porcelain • WILL
2000QSU2033 • **Value $20**

5

The Great Birthday Bird
Porcelain • BRIC
1200QSU2028 • **Value $12**

6

The Grinch™
Porcelain • PIKE
1200QSU2055 • **Value $12**

7

Hat Tricks!
Porcelain • CHAD
1500QSU2027 • **Value $15**

8

Hop on Pop™
Porcelain • KLIN
2000QSU2031 • **Value $20**

The Dr. Seuss™ Collection	Price Paid	Value
1.		
2.		
3.		
4.		
5.		
6.		
7.		
8.		
9.		
10.		
11.		
12.		
13.		
14.		
15.		
Harry Potter		
16.		
17.		
18.		
19.		
Totals		

9

Max the Reindeer
N/A • HADD
1800QSU2056 • **Value $18**

10

Merry Grinchmas!
N/A • PIKE
2000QSU2030 • **Value $20**

11

On a Train?
Porcelain • RHOD
1800QSU2036 • **Value $18**

12

On Top of the World
Porcelain • WILL
2000QSU2034 • **Value $20**

13

Sam and Ham
Porcelain • WILL
2000QSU2032 • **Value $20**

14

A Seuss Safe
Porcelain • CROW
1500QSU2037 • **Value $15**

15

Socks and Blocks
Porcelain • WILL
2000QSU2035 • **Value $20**

16

Harry Potter
N/A • N/A
N/A • **Value N/E**

17

Hermione
N/A • N/A
N/A • **Value N/E**

18

Owl
N/A • N/A
N/A • **Value N/E**

19

Professor Dumbledore
N/A • N/A
N/A • **Value N/E**

1

Blériot XI
Handcrafted • N/A
2500QHA1009 • **Value $25**

2

Curtiss R3C-2 Seaplane
Handcrafted • N/A
3200QHA1002 • **Value $32**

3

F-86F Sabre
Handcrafted • N/A
2700QHA1010 • **Value $27**

4

F4U-ID Corsair
Handcrafted • N/A
3200QHA1008 • **Value $32**

5

**Ryan NYP
"Spirit of St. Louis"**
Handcrafted • N/A
3000QHA1004 • **Value $30**

6

SPAD XIII "Smith IV"
Handcrafted • N/A
3200QHA1003 • **Value $32**

7

Vega 5B
Handcrafted • N/A
3000QHA1007 • **Value $30**

8

**NFL Collection
(10 assorted)**
Handcrafted/Brass • SIED

1. Cleveland Browns
   995QSR5161 • **Value $9.95**
2. Dallas Cowboys
   995QSR5121 • **Value $9.95**
3. Denver Broncos
   995QSR5111 • **Value $9.95**
4. Green Bay Packers
   995QSR5114 • **Value $9.95**
5. Kansas City Chiefs
   995QSR5131 • **Value $9.95**
6. Miami Dolphins
   995QSR5144 • **Value $9.95**
7. Minnesota Vikings
   995QSR5164 • **Value $9.95**
8. Pittsburgh Steelers
   995QSR5124 • **Value $9.95**
9. San Francisco 49ers
   995QSR5134 • **Value $9.95**
10. Washington Redskins
    995QSR5151 • **Value $9.95**

9

**Ornament Charms
(24 assorted)**
N/A • N/A

1. Believe
   QX2831 • **Value $.95**
2. Brass Cross
   QX2734 • **Value $.95**
3. Brass Heart
   QX2821 • **Value $.95**
4. Brother
   QX2641 • **Value $.95**
5. Congrats!
   QX2824 • **Value $.95**
6. Dad
   QX2621 • **Value $.95**
7. Daughter
   QX2644 • **Value $.95**
8. Friends Forever
   QX2701 • **Value $.95**
9. Granddaughter
   QX2654 • **Value $.95**
10. Grandma
    QX2624 • **Value $.95**
11. Grandpa
    QX2631 • **Value $.95**
12. Grandson
    QX2661 • **Value $.95**
13. Great Teacher!
    QX2674 • **Value $.95**
14. Happy Birthday
    QX2704 • **Value $.95**
15. Happy Holidays
    QX2684 • **Value $.95**
16. I Love You
    QX2694 • **Value $.95**
17. Mom
    QX2601 • **Value $.95**
18. Nephew
    QX2671 • **Value $.95**
19. Niece
    QX2664 • **Value $.95**
20. Peace on Earth
    QX2711 • **Value $.95**
21. Sister
    QX2634 • **Value $.95**
22. Son
    QX2651 • **Value $.95**
23. Thank You
    QX2681 • **Value $.95**
24. Thinking of You
    QX2691 • **Value $.95**

Legends in Flight™

	Price Paid	Value
1.		
2.		
3.		
4.		
5.		
6.		
7.		

NFL Collection

8.		

Ornament Charms

9.		

Totals

2000 Collection

1

Being There
Pewter • BRIC
1500QPC4005 • **Value $15**

2

Celebrate!
N/A • N/A
1295QPC4015 • **Value $12.95**

3

Charlie Brown
(LE-24,500)
Porcelain • N/A
2500QPC4025 • **Value $25**

4

Don't Give Up!
N/A • N/A
1295QPC4016 • **Value $12.95**

5

Fall Ball
Porcelain • WILL
2000QPC4010 • **Value $20**

6

**Five Decades of
Charlie Brown**
Pewter • SIED
1300QPC4002 • **Value $13**

7

Five Decades of Lucy
Pewter • SIED
1300QPC4003 • **Value $13**

8

Five Decades of Snoopy
Pewter • SIED
1300QPC4001 • **Value $13**

9

Flying High
Pewter • CHAD
1500QPC4004 • **Value $15**

10

Golf is Life!
N/A • N/A
1295QPC4012 • **Value $12.95**

11

The Great Pumpkin
Porcelain • RGRS
2000QPC4022 • **Value $20**

12

Hanging On!
N/A • N/A
1295QPC4014 • **Value $12.95**

13

Hugs
Porcelain • PIKE
1500QPC4007 • **Value $15**

14

It Takes All Kinds!
N/A • N/A
1295QPC4013 • **Value $12.95**

15

Joe Cool and Friend
Porcelain • FRAN
1500QPC4011 • **Value $15**

16

Jolly Holidays
Porcelain/Metal • LAPR
2000QPC4023 • **Value $20**

17

A Joyful Song
(LE-24,500)
Porcelain • SIED
2500QPC4024 • **Value $25**

18

Linus (LE-24,500)
Porcelain • N/A
2500QPC4019 • **Value $25**

19

Lucy (LE-24,500)
Porcelain • N/A
2500QPC4018 • **Value $25**

20

**On the Course
(1st in *Snoopy
and Friends Series*)**
Porcelain • AUBE
2000QPC4008 • **Value $20**

Peanuts® Gallery

	Price Paid	Value
1.		
2.		
3.		
4.		
5.		
6.		
7.		
8.		
9.		
10.		
11.		
12.		
13.		
14.		
15.		
16.		
17.		
18.		
19.		
20.		
Totals		

1

Sally
Porcelain • N/A
2500QPC4020 • **Value $25**

2

Seventh Inning Stretch
Porcelain • SIED
1500QPC4009 • **Value $15**

3

Snoopy (LE-24,500)
Porcelain • N/A
2500QPC4021 • **Value $25**

4

The Winning Team
(LE-24,500)
Porcelain/Acrylic • RGRS
3000QPC4006 • **Value $30**

5

1950s Hopalong Cassidy
Pressed Tin • N/A
1095QHM8809 • **Value $10.95**

6

1950s Mickey Mouse Circus
Pressed Tin • N/A
1095QHM8816 • **Value $10.95**

7

1960s Yellow Submarine™ (LE-24,500)
Pressed Tin • N/A
1195QHM8901 • **Value $11.95**

8

1963 The Jetsons™ (LE-24,500)
Pressed Tin • N/A
1195QHM8900 • **Value $11.95**

9

1969 Disney Fire Fighters (LE-24,500)
Pressed Tin • N/A
1195QHM8904 • **Value $11.95**

10

1980 The Empire Strikes Back
Pressed Tin • N/A
1095QHM8820 • **Value $10.95**

11

Batman™ and Robin™ Lunch Box with Drink Container (LE-19,500)
Pressed Tin • N/A
1395QHM8808 • **Value $13.95**

12

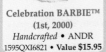

Snoopy Doghouse (LE-24,500)
Pressed Tin • N/A
1195QHM8905 • **Value $11.95**

13

Winnie the Pooh
Pressed Tin • N/A
1095QHM8821 • **Value $10.95**

14

The Wizard of Oz™ (LE-19,500)
Pressed Tin • N/A
1395QHM8822 • **Value $13.95**

15

Celebration BARBIE™ (1st, 2000)
Handcrafted • ANDR
1595QXI6821 • **Value $15.95**

16

700 E J Hudson Steam Locomotive (100th Anniversary Piece)
Die-Cast Metal • N/A
2200QXI5261 • **Value $22**

17

Ken Griffey Jr.
Handcrafted • N/A
1495QXI5251 • **Value $14.95**

18

Millennium Snowma'am
Handcrafted • N/A
895QXI5241 • **Value $8.95**

19

Mitford Snowmen (set/4)
Handcrafted • N/A
1995QXI5244 • **Value $19.95**

	Price Paid	Value
Peanuts® Gallery		
1.		
2.		
3.		
4.		
School Days Lunch Boxes™		
5.		
6.		
7.		
8.		
9.		
10.		
11.		
12.		
13.		
14.		
Special Edition Pieces		
15.		
16.		
17.		
18.		
19.		
Totals		

1999

With 212 pieces added to the Keepsake collection in 1999, there was an ornament for everyone! Two new lines joined the Hallmark Keepsake family this year: Laser Creations, a series of ornaments cut by laser light; and Legends of Flight, a group of die-cast model airplanes. See the collectible series section for more 1999 ornaments.

1

**1949 Cadillac®
Coupe deVille**
Die-Cast Metal • WILL
1495QX6429 • **Value $29**

2

**40th Anniversary
BARBIE® Ornament**
Handcrafted • ANDR
1595QXI8049 • **Value $28**

3

Adding the Best Part
Handcrafted • CROW
795QX6569 • **Value $15**

4

**African-American
Millennium Princess
BARBIE® Ornament**
Handcrafted • RGRS
1595QXI6449 • **Value $30**

5

All Sooted Up
Handcrafted • KLIN
995QX6837 • **Value $16**

General Keepsake

	Price Paid	Value
1.		
2.		
3.		
4.		
5.		
6.		
7.		
8.		
9.		
10.		
11.		
12.		
13.		
14.		
15.		
16.		
17.		

6

Angel in Disguise
Handcrafted • AUBE
895QX6629 • **Value $15**

7

Angel of Hope
Porcelain • ANDR
1495QXI6339 • **Value $25**

8

Angel Song
Handcrafted • VOTR
1895QX6939 • **Value $30**

9

**Baby Mickey's Sweet
Dreams**
Handcrafted • N/A
1095QXD4087 • **Value $18**

10

Baby's First Christmas
Handcrafted • HADD
795QX6649 • **Value $15**

11

Baby's First Christmas
Handcrafted • FRAN
795QX6667 • **Value $15**

12

Baby's First Christmas
Handcrafted • VOTR
895QX6657 • **Value $15**

13

Baby's First Christmas
Porcelain • TAGU
995QX6659 • **Value $16**

14

Baby's First Christmas
Handcrafted • ANDR
1895QX6647 • **Value $33**

15

**Baby's Second
Christmas**
Handcrafted • FRAN
795QX6669 • **Value $14**

16

**Balthasar – The Magi
(re-issued in 2000)**
Porcelain • LYLE
1295QX6819 • **Value $12.95**

17

**BARBIE® Doll
Dreamhouse™
Playhouse Ornament**
Handcrafted • ANDR
1495QXI8047 • **Value $28**

Totals

1

Best Pals
Handcrafted • AUBE
1895QX6879 • **Value $44**

2

Bowling's a Ball
Handcrafted • KLIN
795QX6577 • **Value $14**

3

Caspar – The Magi
(re-issued in 2000)
Porcelain • LYLE
1295QX8039 • **Value $12.95**

4

Chewbacca™
Handcrafted • RHOD
1495QXI4009 • **Value $27**

5

Child of Wonder
Handcrafted • UNRU
1495QX6817 • **Value $28**

6

Child's Fifth Christmas
Handcrafted • CROW
795QX6679 • **Value $14**

7

Child's Fourth Christmas
Handcrafted • CROW
795QX6687 • **Value $14**

8

Child's Third Christmas
Handcrafted • CROW
795QX6677 • **Value $14**

9

The Christmas Story
Handcrafted • UNRU
2200QX6897 • **Value $36**

10

Clownin' Around
CRAYOLA® Crayon
Handcrafted • TAGU
1095QX6487 • **Value $21**

11

Cocoa Break
HERSHEY's™
Handcrafted • KLIN
1095QX8009 • **Value $21**

12

Counting On Success
Handcrafted • PIKE
795QX6707 • **Value $13**

13

Cross of Hope
Pewter/Lead Crystal • UNRU
995QX6557 • **Value $19**

14

Dad
Pressed Tin • BRIC
895QX6719 • **Value $15**

15

Dance for the Season
Handcrafted • ESCH
995QX6587 • **Value $16**

16

Daughter
Handcrafted • ESCH
895QX6729 • **Value $15**

17

Dorothy and Glinda,
the Good Witch™
Handcrafted • LYLE
2400QX6509 • **Value $40**

18

Dumbo's First Flight
Handcrafted • N/A
1395QXD4117 • **Value $22**

19

The Family Portrait
Handcrafted • N/A
1495QXD4149 • **Value $25**

20
Feliz Navidad Santa
Handcrafted • TAGU
895QX6999 • **Value $17**

General Keepsake		
	Price Paid	Value
1.		
2.		
3.		
4.		
5.		
6.		
7.		
8.		
9.		
10.		
11.		
12.		
13.		
14.		
15.		
16.		
17.		
18.		
19.		
20.		
Totals		

1
Flame-Fighting Friends
Handcrafted • TAGU
1495QX6619 • **Value $22**

2
The Flash™
Handcrafted • RGRS
1295QX6469 • **Value $21**

3
For My Grandma
Handcrafted • LYLE
795QX6747 • **Value $14**

4
Forecast for Fun
Handcrafted/Glass • TAGU
1495QX6869 • **Value $23**

5
**G.I. Joe®,
Action Soldier™**
Handcrafted • CROW
1395QX6537 • **Value $22**

6
Godchild
Handcrafted • TAGU
795QX6759 • **Value $14**

7
Goofy As Santa's Helper
Handcrafted • N/A
1295QXD4079 • **Value $20**

8
Granddaughter
Handcrafted • SEAL
895QX6739 • **Value $15**

9
Grandson
Handcrafted • SEAL
895QX6737 • **Value $15**

10
Handled With Care
Handcrafted • RHOD
895QX6769 • **Value $14**

11
Hello, Hello (set/2)
Handcrafted • SEAL
1495QX6777 • **Value $19**

12
**The Holy Family (set/3,
re-issued from 1998)**
Porcelain • LYLE
2500QX6523 • **Value $25**

13
Howdy Doody™ (set/2)
Pressed Tin/Handcrafted • N/A
1495QX6519 • **Value $21**

14
In The Workshop
Handcrafted • AUBE
995QX6979 • **Value $14**

15
Jazzy Jalopy
Handcrafted • CROW
2400QX6549 • **Value $45**

16
**Jet Threat™ Car With
Case (set/2)**
Handcrafted • UNRU
1295QX6527 • **Value $21**

17
Jolly Locomotive
Die-Cast Metal • CROW
1495QX6859 • **Value $28**

18
Joyous Angel
Handcrafted • VOTR
895QX6787 • **Value $17**

19
A Joyous Christmas
Glass • N/A
595QX6827 • **Value $14**

20
King Malh – Third King
Handcrafted • ANDR
1395QX6797 • **Value $26**

General Keepsake

	Price Paid	Value
1.		
2.		
3.		
4.		
5.		
6.		
7.		
8.		
9.		
10.		
11.		
12.		
13.		
14.		
15.		
16.		
17.		
18.		
19.		
20.		
Totals		

VALUE GUIDE — HALLMARK KEEPSAKE ORNAMENTS

1

Kringle's Whirligig
Handcrafted • CROW
1295QX6847 • **Value $20**

2

Larry, Moe, and Curly (set/3)
Handcrafted • LARS
3000QX6499 • **Value $44**

3

Lieutenant Commander Worf™
Handcrafted • RGRS
1495QXI4139 • **Value $22**

4

Little Cloud Keeper
Porcelain • HADD
1695QX6877 • **Value $28**

5

The Lollipop Guild™ (set/3)
Handcrafted • LYLE
1995QX8029 • **Value $35**

6

"Lucy Gets In Pictures"
Handcrafted • VOTR
1395QX6547 • **Value $26**

7

Mary's Bears
Handcrafted • TAGU
1295QX5569 • **Value $19**

8

Melchoir – The Magi (re-issued in 2000)
Porcelain • LYLE
1295QX6819 • **Value $12.95**

9

Merry Motorcycle
Pressed Tin • SICK
895QX6637 • **Value $16**

10

Military on Parade
Handcrafted • CROW
1095QX6639 • **Value $21**

11

Milk 'n' Cookies Express
Handcrafted • CHAD
895QX6839 • **Value $15**

12

Millennium Princess BARBIE® Ornament
Handcrafted • RGRS
1595QXI4019 • **Value $42**

13

Millennium Snowman
Handcrafted • SEAL
895QX8059 • **Value $50**

14

Mom
Pressed Tin • BRIC
895QX6717 • **Value $15**

15

Mom and Dad
Handcrafted • SEAL
995QX6709 • **Value $18**

16

Mother and Daughter
Precious Metal • VOTR
895QX6757 • **Value $20**

17

Muhammad Ali
Handcrafted • UNRU
1495QXI4147 • **Value $24**

18

A Musician of Note
Handcrafted • HADD
795QX6567 • **Value $14**

19

My Sister, My Friend
Handcrafted • TAGU
995QX6749 • **Value $15**

20

Naboo Starfighter™
Handcrafted • WEBB
1895QXI7613 • **Value $38**

| General Keepsake | |
Price Paid	Value
1.	
2.	
3.	
4.	
5.	
6.	
7.	
8.	
9.	
10.	
11.	
12.	
13.	
14.	
15.	
16.	
17.	
18.	
19.	
20.	
Totals	

1

New Home
Handcrafted • SEAL
995QX6347 • **Value $17**

2

Noah's Ark
Handcrafted • ESCH
1295QX6809 • **Value $22**

3

North Pole Mr. Potato Head™
Handcrafted • N/A
1095QX8027 • **Value $20**

4

North Pole Star
Handcrafted • CHAD
895QX6589 • **Value $16**

5

On Thin Ice
Handcrafted • PIKE
1095QX6489 • **Value $20**

6

Our Christmas Together
Handcrafted • KLIN
995QX6689 • **Value $17**

7

Our First Christmas Together
Acrylic • VOTR
795QX3207 • **Value $14**

8

Our First Christmas Together
Handcrafted • TAGU
895QX6697 • **Value $15**

General Keepsake

	Price Paid	Value
1.		
2.		
3.		
4.		
5.		
6.		
7.		
8.		
9.		
10.		
11.		
12.		
13.		
14.		
15.		
16.		
17.		
18.		
19.		
20.		

9

Our First Christmas Together
Handcrafted • UNRU
2200QX6699 • **Value $36**

10

Outstanding Teacher
Handcrafted • KLIN
895QX6627 • **Value $15**

11

Pepé LePew and Penelope
Handcrafted • CHAD
1295QX6507 • **Value $23**

12

Piano Player Mickey
Handcrafted • N/A
2400QXD7389 • **Value $48**

13

Pinocchio and Geppetto
Handcrafted • N/A
1695QXD4107 • **Value $24**

14

Playful Snowman
Handcrafted • SICK
1295QX6867 • **Value $24**

15

The Poky Little Puppy™ (w/book)
Handcrafted • VOTR
1195QX6479 • **Value $21**

16

Praise the Day
Handcrafted • TAGU
1495QX6799 • **Value $22**

17

Presents From Pooh
Handcrafted • N/A
1495QXD4093 • **Value $25**

18

Queen Amidala™
Handcrafted • RHOD
1495QXI4187 • **Value $27**

19

Reel Fun
Handcrafted • TAGU
1095QX6609 • **Value $19**

20

Rhett Butler™
Handcrafted • ANDR
1295QX6467 • **Value $24**

Totals

1

Scooby-Doo™ (set/2)
Handcrafted/Pressed Tin • N/A
1495QX6997 • **Value $25**

2

Sew Handy
Handcrafted • TAGU
895QX6597 • **Value $25**

3

Sleddin' Buddies
Handcrafted • CROW
995QX6849 • **Value $18**

4

The Snowmen of
Mitford (set/3)
Handcrafted • N/A
1595QXI8587 • **Value $48**

5

Son
Handcrafted • ESCH
895QX6727 • **Value $15**

6

Special Dog
Handcrafted • KLIN
795QX6767 • **Value $14**

7

Spellin' Santa
Handcrafted • WILL
995QX6857 • **Value $16**

8

Sprinkling Stars
Handcrafted • AUBE
995QX6599 • **Value $17**

9

Sundae Golfer
Handcrafted • TAGU
1295QX6617 • **Value $18**

10

Surfin' the Net
Handcrafted • SEAL
995QX6607 • **Value $18**

11

Sweet Friendship
Handcrafted • HADD
995QX6779 • **Value $18**

12

Sweet Skater
Handcrafted • TAGU
795QX6579 • **Value $14**

13

The Tender LIONEL®
746 Norfolk and
Western
Die-Cast Metal • N/A
1495QX6497 • **Value $28**

14

Tigger Plays Soccer
Handcrafted • N/A
1095QXD4119 • **Value $20**

15

A Time of Peace
Handcrafted • LARS
895QX6807 • **Value $20**

16

Tonka® 1956 Suburban
Pumper No. 5
Die-Cast Metal • N/A
1395QX6459 • **Value $26**

17

Welcome to 2000
Handcrafted • LARS
1095QX6829 • **Value $50**

18

Wintertime Treat
Handcrafted • UNRU
1295QX6989 • **Value $21**

19

Woody's Roundup
Handcrafted • N/A
1395QXI4207 • **Value $23**

20

Darth Vader's
TIE Fighter
Handcrafted • RHOD
2400QXI7399 • **Value $45**

General Keepsake	Price Paid	Value
1.		
2.		
3.		
4.		
5.		
6.		
7.		
8.		
9.		
10.		
11.		
12.		
13.		
14.		
15.		
16.		
17.		
18.		
19.		
General Magic		
20.		
Totals		

1

Let It Snow!
Porcelain • LARS
1895QLX7427 • **Value $36**

2

Runabout – U.S.S. Rio Grande
Handcrafted • NORT
2400QXI7593 • **Value $48**

3

Warm Welcome
Handcrafted • HADD
1695QLX7417 • **Value $30**

4

1950 LIONEL® Santa Fe F3 Diesel Locomotive
Blown Glass • N/A
3500QBG6119 • **Value $50**

5

1955 Murray® Ranch Wagon
Blown Glass • N/A
3500QBG6077 • **Value $50**

6

Childhood Treasures (set/3)
Blown Glass • N/A
3000QBG4237 • **Value $42**

7

Frankincense (re-issued from 1998)
Blown Glass • N/A
2200QBG6896 • **Value $30**

8

Frosty Friends
Blown Glass • N/A
3500QBG6067 • **Value $52**

9

Gold (re-issued from 1998)
Blown Glass • N/A
2200QBG6836 • **Value $30**

10

Harvest of Grapes
Blown Glass • N/A
2500QBG6047 • **Value $35**

11

The Holy Family
Blown Glass • N/A
3000QBG6127 • **Value $40**

12

Jolly Snowman
Blown Glass • N/A
2000QBG6059 • **Value $35**

13

Myrrh (re-issued from 1998)
Blown Glass • N/A
2200QBG6893 • **Value $30**

14

U.S.S. Enterprise™ NCC-1701
Blown Glass • N/A
2500QBG6117 • **Value $70**

15

Village Church
Blown Glass • N/A
3000QBG6057 • **Value $45**

16

Yummy Memories (set/8)
Blown Glass • N/A
4500QBG6049 • **Value $60**

17

Angelic Messenger
Archival Paper • N/A
795QLZ4287 • **Value $13**

18

Christmas In Bloom
Archival Paper • N/A
895QLZ4257 • **Value $15**

19

Don't Open Till 2000
Archival Paper • N/A
895QLZ4289 • **Value $22**

20

Inside Santa's Workshop
Archival Paper • N/A
895QLZ4239 • **Value $15**

General Magic

	Price Paid	Value
1.		
2.		
3.		

General Crown Reflections

4.		
5.		
6.		
7.		
8.		
9.		
10.		
11.		
12.		
13.		
14.		
15.		
16.		

General Laser Creations

17.		
18.		
19.		
20.		

Totals

1

Ringing In Christmas
Archival Paper • N/A
695QLZ4277 • **Value $13**

2

**A Visit From
St. Nicholas**
Archival Paper • N/A
595QLZ4229 • **Value $13**

3

A Wish For Peace
Archival Paper • N/A
695QLZ4249 • **Value $13**

4

Yuletide Charm
Archival Paper • N/A
595QLZ4269 • **Value $13**

5

Betsey's Perfect 10
Handcrafted • KLIN
495QXM4609 • **Value $10**

6

Celestial Kitty
Porcelain • AUBE
695QXM4639 • **Value $11**

7

**Classic Batman™ and
Robin™ (set/2)**
Handcrafted • CHAD
1295QXM4659 • **Value $20**

8

Crystal Claus
Silver Plated/Crystal • VOTR
995QXM4637 • **Value $19**

9

Girl Talk (set/2)
Handcrafted • N/A
1295QXD4069 • **Value $19**

10

Love to Share
Handcrafted • SICK
695QXM4557 • **Value $11**

11

Marvin The Martian
Handcrafted • CHAD
895QXM4657 • **Value $14**

12

**Max Rebo Band™
(set/3)**
Handcrafted • BRIC
1995QXI4597 • **Value $30**

13

**Merry Grinch-mas!
(set/3)**
Handcrafted • WILL
1995QXI4627 • **Value $27**

14

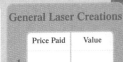

Roll-a-Bear
Handcrafted • SICK
695QXM4629 • **Value $11**

15

Santa Time
Handcrafted • UNRU
795QXM4647 • **Value $13**

16

Skating with Pooh
Handcrafted • N/A
695QXD4127 • **Value $11**

17

Taz and the She-Devil
Handcrafted • CHAD
895QXM4619 • **Value $13**

18

**Travel Case and
BARBIE™ Ornament
(set/2)**
Handcrafted • ANDR
1295QXI6129 • **Value $19**

19

Trusty Reindeer
Handcrafted • SICK
595QXM4617 • **Value $13**

General Laser Creations

	Price Paid	Value
1.		
2.		
3.		
4.		

General Miniature

5.		
6.		
7.		
8.		
9.		
10.		
11.		
12.		
13.		
14.		
15.		
16.		
17.		
18.		
19.		

Totals

103

1999 Collection

1

Arctic Artist
(keepsake of membership)
Handcrafted • HADD
QXC4527 • **Value $16**

2

Snow Day–PEANUTS®
(set/2, club edition)
Handcrafted • RHOD
1895QXC4517 • **Value $42**

3

Snowy Surprise
(keepsake of membership)
Handcrafted • HADD
QXC4529 • **Value $16**

4

The Toymaker's Gift
(keepsake of membership)
Handcrafted • CHAD
QXC4519 • **Value $16**

5

Waiting for a Hug
(early renewal gift)
Handcrafted • CHAD
QXC4537 • **Value $14**

6

Jolly Locomotive
(green)
Handcrafted • CROW
(N/C) No stock # • **Value N/E**

7

Zebra Fantasy
Handcrafted • SICK
1495QX6559 • **Value $29**

8

1968 Murray® Jolly Roger Flagship
Die-Cast Metal • PALM
(N/C) No stock # • **Value N/E**

9

Gold Locomotive
(miniature)
N/A • N/A
(N/C) No stock # • **Value N/E**

10

Hollow Log Café
Handcrafted • N/A
(N/C) No stock # • **Value N/E**

11

North Pole Pond
Handcrated • N/A
(N/C) No stock # • **Value N/E**

12

A Pony for Christmas
Handcrafted • SICK
(N/C) No stock # • **Value N/E**

13

Snowy Plaza
Handcrafted • N/A
(N/C) No stock # • **Value N/E**

14

Yummy Memories
Blown Glass • KLIN
(N/C) No stock # • **Value N/E**

15

Holiday Sensation™ BARBIE® Doll
(3rd & final,
Holiday Homecoming
Collector Series)
Handcrafted • N/A
5000QHB3403 • **Value N/E**

16

The Cat in the Hat
Dr. Seuss™ Books
Ceramic/Brass • N/A
995QXI8579 • **Value $18**

17

I Love Lucy®
Ceramic/Brass • N/A
995QXI8567 • **Value $18**

Collector's Club

	Price Paid	Value
1.		
2.		
3.		
4.		
5.		

Premiere Ornaments

6.		
7.		

Artists On Tour Pieces

8.		
9.		
10.		
11.		
12.		
13.		
14.		

BARBIE™ Collectibles

15.		

Century Stamp Ornaments

16.		
17.		

VALUE GUIDE — HALLMARK KEEPSAKE ORNAMENTS

1

Silken Flame™ BARBIE Ornament
Ceramic/Brass • N/A
995QXI8559 • **Value $18**

2

Superman™
Ceramic/Brass • N/A
995QXI8569 • **Value $18**

3
U.S.S. Enterprise™ NCC-1701 STAR TREK™
Ceramic/Brass • N/A
995QXI8557 • **Value $18**

4

Yellow Submarine THE BEATLES
Ceramic/Brass • N/A
995QXI8577 • **Value $18**

5

Collegiate Collection
Handcrafted • AUBE

1. Arizona® Wildcats™
995QSR2429 • **Value N/E**
2. Duke™ Blue Devils®
995QSR2437 • **Value N/E**
3. Florida State® Seminoles®
995QSR2439 • **Value N/E**
4. Georgetown Hoyas
995QSR2447 • **Value N/E**
5. Kentucky Wildcats®
995QSR2449 • **Value N/E**
6. Michigan Wolverines™
995QSR2457 • **Value N/E**
7. Nebraska Cornhuskers™
995QSR2459 • **Value N/E**
8. North Carolina Tar Heels™
995QSR2467 • **Value N/E**
9. Notre Dame Fighting Irish™
995QSR2427 • **Value N/E**
10. Penn State Nittany Lions™
995QSR2469 • **Value N/E**

6

Kenny Rogers Christmas From The Heart (concert piece)
Pewter • N/A
(N/C) No stock # • **Value N/E**

7

1954 Lionel® Catalog Cover Tin Sign
Pressed Tin • N/A
1800QHT3707 • **Value N/E**

8

Lionel® 671 Turbine Steam Locomotive (LE-29,500, 4th in *20th Century Series*)
Handcrafted • N/A
11500QHT7806 • **Value N/E**

9

Lionel® 726 Berkshire Steam Locomotive (Artists On Tour)
Die-Cast Metal • N/A
(N/C) No stock # • **Value N/E**

10

Lionel® 773 Hudson Steam Locomotive (LE-29,500, 5th & final in *20th Century Series*)
Handcrafted • N/A
12500QHT7807 • **Value N/E**

11

Lionel® 2333 New York Central F3A-A Diesel Locomotives (LE-29,500, 3rd in *20th Century Series*)
Die-Cast Metal • N/A
10000QHT7802 • **Value N/E**

12

Oceanside Depot (LE-29,500)
Handcrafted • N/A
6500QHT3501 • **Value N/E**

13
Curtiss P-40 Warhawk
Handcrafted • N/A
3000QHA1000 • **Value N/E**

14
F-14A Tomcat (LE-24,500)
Handcrafted • N/A
4800QHA1006 • **Value N/E**

15

Fokker Dr.I "Red Baron"
Handcrafted • N/A
3800QHA1005 • **Value N/E**

16

Wright Flyer
Handcrafted • N/A
3500QHA1001 • **Value N/E**

Century Stamp Ornaments	Price Paid	Value
1.		
2.		
3.		
4.		
Collegiate Collection		
5.		
Event Pieces		
6.		
Great American Railways™		
7.		
8.		
9.		
10.		
11.		
12.		
Legends In Flight		
13.		
14.		
15.		
16.		
Totals		

1999 Collection

1

**NBA Collection
(10 assorted)**
Handcrafted • KLIN

1. Charlotte Hornets™
1095QSR1057 • **Value N/E**
2. Chicago Bulls™
1095QSR1019 • **Value N/E**
3. Detroit Pistons™
1095QSR1027 • **Value N/E**
4. Houston Rockets™
1095QSR1029 • **Value N/E**

5. Indiana Pacers™
1095QSR1037 • **Value N/E**
6. Los Angeles Lakers™
1095QSR1039 • **Value N/E**
7. New York Knicks™
1095QSR1047 • **Value N/E**
8. Orlando Magic™
1095QSR1059 • **Value N/E**

9. Seattle SuperSonics™
1095QSR1067 • **Value N/E**
10. Utah Jazz™
1095QSR1069 • **Value N/E**

2

**NFL Collection
(15 assorted)**
Handcrafted • HADD

1. Carolina Panthers™
1095QSR5217 • **Value N/E**
2. Chicago Bears™
1095QSR5219 • **Value N/E**
3. Dallas Cowboys™
1095QSR5227 • **Value N/E**
4. Denver Broncos™
1095QSR5229 • **Value N/E**
5. Green Bay Packers™
1095QSR5237 • **Value N/E**

6. Kansas City Chiefs™
1095QSR5197 • **Value N/E**
7. Miami Dolphins™
1095QSR5239 • **Value N/E**
8. Minnesota Vikings™
1095QSR5247 • **Value N/E**
9. New England Patriots™
1095QSR5279 • **Value N/E**
10. New York Giants™
1095QSR5249 • **Value N/E**

11. Oakland Raiders™
1095QSR5257 • **Value N/E**
12. Philadelphia Eagles™
1095QSR5259 • **Value N/E**
13. Pittsburgh Steelers™
1095QSR5267 • **Value N/E**
14. San Francisco 49ers™
1095QSR5269 • **Value N/E**
15. Washington Redskins™
1095QSR5277 • **Value N/E**

NBA Collection	
Price Paid	**Value**
1.	

NFL Collection	
2.	

School Days Lunch Boxes	
3.	
4.	
5.	
6.	
7.	
8.	
9.	
10.	
11.	

3

1950s Donald Duck
Pressed Tin • N/A
1095QHM8806 • **Value N/E**

4

**1960s Mickey's
School Days**
Pressed Tin • N/A
1095QHM8804 • **Value N/E**

5

1960s Star Trek™
Pressed Tin • N/A
1095QHM8810 • **Value N/E**

6

1962 Barbie™
Pressed Tin • N/A
1095QHM8807 • **Value N/E**

7

1970s Snow White
Pressed Tin • N/A
1095QHM8814 • **Value N/E**

8

1973 Super Friends™
Pressed Tin • N/A
1095QHM8815 • **Value N/E**

9

1977 Star Wars™
Pressed Tin • N/A
1095QHM8817 • **Value N/E**

10

1980 Peanuts®
Pressed Tin • N/A
1095QHM8812 • **Value N/E**

11

**A Charlie Brown
Christmas**
Pressed Tin • N/A
N/A • **Value N/E**

Totals

1

Looney Tunes Rodeo
Pressed Tin • N/A
1095QHM8805 • **Value N/E**

2

Scooby-Doo™
Pressed Tin • N/A
1095QHM8818 • **Value N/E**

3

Between Friends
Resin • N/A
1800QHC8219 • **Value N/E**

4

Congratulations!
Resin • N/A
2200QHC8233 • **Value N/E**

5

Love Like No Other
Resin • RGRS
2200QHC8224 • **Value N/E**

6

Sweet Memories
Resin • HADD
2200QHC8231 • **Value N/E**

1998

Among the highlights for 1998 were a number of special Anniversary Edition pieces commemorating the 25th year of Hallmark Keepsake Ornaments. In addition to the 165 new ornaments in the Keepsake line, there were 12 new Magic and 25 new Miniature ornaments. See the collectible series section for more 1998 ornaments.

7

#1 Student
Handcrafted • N/A
795QX6646 • **Value $15**

8

1998 Corvette® Convertible
Handcrafted • PALM
1395QX6416 • **Value $28**

9

Angelic Flight (LE-25,000)
Crystal/Silver-Plated • ANDR
8500QXI4146 • **Value $130**

10

Baby's First Christmas
Handcrafted • FRAN
795QX6603 • **Value $16**

11

Baby's First Christmas
Handcrafted • KLIN
895QX6596 • **Value $18**

12

Baby's First Christmas
Handcrafted • TAGU
995QX6233 • **Value $16**

School Days Lunch Boxes

	Price Paid	Value
1.		
2.		

Spoonful of Stars

3.		
4.		
5.		
6.		

General Keepsake

7.		
8.		
9.		
10.		
11.		
12.		

Totals		

1

Baby's First Christmas
Handcrafted • ESCH
995QX6586 • **Value $17**

2

Baby's Second Christmas
Handcrafted • CROW
795QX6606 • **Value $16**

3

Boba Fett™
Handcrafted • RHOD
1495QXI4053 • **Value $28**

4

Bouncy Baby-sitter
Handcrafted • SIED
1295QXD4096 • **Value $22**

5

Bugs Bunny
Handcrafted • CHAD
1395QX6443 • **Value $23**

6

Building a Snowman
Handcrafted • SIED
1495QXD4133 • **Value $27**

7

Buzz Lightyear
Handcrafted • CROW
1495QXD4066 • **Value $32**

8

Captain Kathryn Janeway™
Handcrafted • RGRS
1495QXI4046 • **Value $28**

9

Catch of the Season
Handcrafted • SEAL
1495QX6786 • **Value $24**

10

Chatty Chipmunk
Handcrafted • CROW
995QX6716 • **Value $17**

11

Checking Santa's Files
Handcrafted • TAGU
895QX6806 • **Value $16**

12

A Child Is Born
Handcrafted • VOTR
1295QX6176 • **Value $19**

13

Child's Fifth Christmas
Handcrafted • CROW
795QX6623 • **Value $15**

14

Child's Fourth Christmas
Handcrafted • CROW
795QX6616 • **Value $15**

15

Child's Third Christmas
Handcrafted • CROW
795QX6613 • **Value $15**

16

A Christmas Eve Story Becky Kelly
Handcrafted • TAGU
1395QXD6873 • **Value $23**

17

Christmas Request
Handcrafted • FRAN
1495QX6193 • **Value $23**

18

Christmas Sleigh Ride
Die-Cast Metal • CROW
1295QX6556 • **Value $24**

19

Cinderella's Coach
Handcrafted • WILL
1495QXD4083 • **Value $24**

20

Compact Skater
Handcrafted • TAGU
995QX6766 • **Value $17**

General Keepsake

	Price Paid	Value
1.		
2.		
3.		
4.		
5.		
6.		
7.		
8.		
9.		
10.		
11.		
12.		
13.		
14.		
15.		
16.		
17.		
18.		
19.		
20.		
Totals		

VALUE GUIDE — HALLMARK KEEPSAKE ORNAMENTS

1

Country Home Marjolein Bastin
Handcrafted • FRAN
1095QX5172 • **Value $20**

2

Cross of Peace
Metal • KLIN
995QX6856 • **Value $17**

3

Cruising into Christmas
Handcrafted/Tin • CROW
1695QX6196 • **Value $28**

4

Dad
Handcrafted • KLIN
895QX6663 • **Value $16**

5

Daughter
Handcrafted • AUBE
895QX6673 • **Value $16**

6

Daydreams
Handcrafted • BRIC
1395QXD4136 • **Value $25**

7

Decorating Maxine-Style
Handcrafted • N/A
1095QXE6883 • **Value $20**

8

Downhill Dash
Handcrafted • CROW
1395QX6776 • **Value $23**

9

Fancy Footwork
Handcrafted • VOTR
895QX6536 • **Value $17**

10

Feliz Navidad
Handcrafted • CHAD
895QX6173 • **Value $18**

11

Flik
Handcrafted • N/A
1295QXD4153 • **Value $27**

12

Forever Friends Bear
Handcrafted • PIKE
895QX6303 • **Value $17**

13

Friend of My Heart (set/2)
Handcrafted • SEAL
1495QX6723 • **Value $22**

14

Future Ballerina
Handcrafted • TAGU
795QX6756 • **Value $15**

15

Gifted Gardener
Handcrafted • CHAD
795QX6736 • **Value $15**

16

Godchild
Handcrafted • CHAD
795QX6703 • **Value $14**

17

Good Luck Dice
Handcrafted • HADD
995QX6813 • **Value $15**

18

Goofy Soccer Star
Handcrafted • CHAD
1095QXD4123 • **Value $18**

19

Granddaughter
Handcrafted • FRAN
795QX6683 • **Value $14**

20

Grandma's Memories
Handcrafted • KLIN
895QX6686 • **Value $15**

General Keepsake

	Price Paid	Value
1.		
2.		
3.		
4.		
5.		
6.		
7.		
8.		
9.		
10.		
11.		
12.		
13.		
14.		
15.		
16.		
17.		
18.		
19.		
20.		
Totals		

1998 Collection

1

Grandson
Handcrafted • FRAN
795QX6676 • **Value $14**

2

The Grinch
Handcrafted • CHAD
1395QXI6466 • **Value $58**

3

Guardian Friend
Handcrafted • LYLE
895QX6543 • **Value $18**

4

Heavenly Melody
Handcrafted • VOTR
1895QX6576 • **Value $32**

5

Holiday Camper
Handcrafted • SEAL
1295QX6783 • **Value $21**

6

Holiday Decorator
Handcrafted • WILL
1395QX6566 • **Value $20**

7

The Holy Family
(re-issued in 1999 and
2000, set/3)
Porcelain • LYLE
2500QX6523 • **Value $25**

8

Hot Wheels™
Handcrafted • CROW
1395QX6436 • **Value $23**

General Keepsake

	Price Paid	Value
1.		
2.		
3.		
4.		
5.		
6.		
7.		
8.		
9.		
10.		
11.		
12.		
13.		
14.		
15.		
16.		
17.		
18.		
19.		
20.		

9

Iago, Abu and the
Genie
Handcrafted • WILL
1295QXD4076 • **Value $21**

10

Joe Montana
Notre Dame
Handcrafted • UNRU
1495QXI6843 • **Value $22**

11

Journey To Bethlehem
Handcrafted • UNRU
1695QX6223 • **Value $30**

12

Joyful Messenger
Handcrafted/Silver-Plated • LYLE
1895QXI6733 • **Value $29**

13

King Kharoof–
Second King
Handcrafted • ANDR
1295QX6186 • **Value $27**

14

Larry, Moe, and Curly
The Three Stooges™
(set/3)
Handcrafted • LARS
2700QX6503 • **Value $52**

15

Madonna and Child
Handcrafted • RGRS
1295QX6516 • **Value $24**

16

Make-Believe Boat
Handcrafted • ESCH
1295QXD4113 • **Value $23**

17

Maxine
Handcrafted • PIKE
995QX6446 • **Value $17**

18

Memories of Christmas
Glass • LARS
595QX2406 • **Value $12**

19

Merry Chime
Handcrafted/Brass • CROW
995QX6692 • **Value $19**

20

The Mickey and
Minnie Handcar
Handcrafted • WILL
1495QXD4116 • **Value $23**

Totals

1

Mickey's Favorite Reindeer
Handcrafted • LARS
1395QXD4013 • **Value $21**

2

Miracle in Bethlehem
Handcrafted • SEAL
1295QX6513 • **Value $26**

3

Mistletoe Fairy
Handcrafted • ESCH
1295QX6216 • **Value $25**

4

Mom
Handcrafted • KLIN
895QX6656 • **Value $16**

5

Mom and Dad
Handcrafted • KLIN
995QX6653 • **Value $17**

6

Mother and Daughter
Porcelain • VOTR
895QX6696 • **Value $16**

7

Mrs. Potato Head®
Handcrafted • N/A
1095QX6886 • **Value $21**

8

Mulan, Mushu and Cri-Kee (set/2)
Handcrafted • N/A
1495QXD4156 • **Value $25**

9

Munchkinland™ Mayor and Coroner (set/2)
Handcrafted • LYLE
1395QX6463 • **Value $27**

10

National Salute
Handcrafted • RHOD
895QX6293 • **Value $15**

11

New Arrival
Porcelain • VOTR
1895QX6306 • **Value $28**

12

New Home
Handcrafted • SEAL
995QX6713 • **Value $20**

13

Nick's Wish List
Handcrafted • ANDR
895QX6863 • **Value $17**

14

Night Watch
Handcrafted • SIED
995QX6725 • **Value $19**

15

North Pole Reserve
Handcrafted • SEAL
1095QX6803 • **Value $20**

16

Our First Christmas Together
Acrylic • VOTR
795QX3193 • **Value $14**

17

Our First Christmas Together
Brass/Porcelain • VOTR
1895QX6643 • **Value $28**

18

Our First Christmas Together
Handcrafted • TAGU
895QX6636 • **Value $15**

19

OUR SONG
Ceramic • N/A
995QX6183 • **Value $16**

20

Peekaboo Bears
Handcrafted • CROW
1295QX6563 • **Value $25**

General Keepsake		
	Price Paid	Value
1.		
2.		
3.		
4.		
5.		
6.		
7.		
8.		
9.		
10.		
11.		
12.		
13.		
14.		
15.		
16.		
17.		
18.		
19.		
20.		
Totals		

1

A Perfect Match
Handcrafted • RHOD
1095QX6633 • **Value $17**

2

Polar Bowler
Handcrafted • ESCH
795QX6746 • **Value $15**

3

Princess Aurora (set/2)
Handcrafted • BRIC
1295QXD4126 • **Value $26**

4

Purr-fect Little Deer
Handcrafted • PIKE
795QX6526 • **Value $20**

5

Puttin' Around
Handcrafted • RHOD
895QX6763 • **Value $14**

6

Rocket to Success
Handcrafted • PIKE
895QX6793 • **Value $14**

7

Runaway Toboggan (set/2)
Handcrafted • N/A
1695QXD4003 • **Value $27**

8

Santa's Deer Friend
Handcrafted • CHAD
2400QX6583 • **Value $40**

General Keepsake

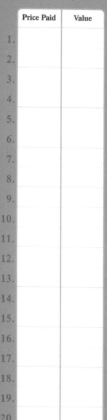

	Price Paid	Value
1.		
2.		
3.		
4.		
5.		
6.		
7.		
8.		
9.		
10.		
11.		
12.		
13.		
14.		
15.		
16.		
17.		
18.		
19.		
20.		

9

Santa's Flying Machine
Handcrafted/Tin • SEAL
1695QX6573 • **Value $27**

10

Santa's Hidden Surprise
Ceramic • N/A
1495QX6913 • **Value $24**

11

"Sew" Gifted
Handcrafted • TAGU
795QX6743 • **Value $15**

12

Simba & Nala
Handcrafted • N/A
1395QXD4073 • **Value $24**

13

Sister to Sister
Handcrafted • PIKE
895QX6693 • **Value $15**

14

Soaring With Angels
Handcrafted • SICK
1695QX6213 • **Value $32**

15

Son
Handcrafted • AUBE
895QX6666 • **Value $16**

16

Special Dog
Handcrafted • N/A
795QX6706 • **Value $14**

17

Spoonful of Love
Handcrafted • TAGU
895QX6796 • **Value $15**

18

Superman™
Pressed Tin • N/A
1295QX6423 • **Value $21**

19

Surprise Catch
Handcrafted • FRAN
795QX6753 • **Value $14**

20

Sweet Rememberings
Handcrafted • TAGU
895QX6876 • **Value $16**

1

Sweet Treat
Handcrafted • KLIN
1095QX6433 • **Value $24**

2

Tin Locomotive
Pressed Tin • SICK
2500QX6826 • **Value $47**

3

Tonka® Road Grader
Die-Cast Metal • N/A
1395QX6483 • **Value $28**

4

Treetop Choir
Handcrafted • FRAN
995QX6506 • **Value $20**

5

Warm and Cozy
Handcrafted • SICK
895QX6866 • **Value $20**

6

Watchful Shepherd
Handcrafted • KLIN
895QX6496 • **Value $19**

7

Woody the Sheriff
Handcrafted • N/A
1495QXD4163 • **Value $31**

8

Writing to Santa
Handcrafted • AUBE
795QX6533 • **Value $14**

9

1998 Corvette®
Handcrafted • PALM
2400QLX7605 • **Value $34**

10

Cinderella at the Ball
Handcrafted • N/A
2400QXD7576 • **Value $52**

11

Mickey's Comet
Handcrafted • WILL
2400QXD7586 • **Value $38**

12

St. Nicholas Circle
Thomas Kinkade,
Painter of Light™
Handcrafted • UNRU
1895QXI7556 • **Value $36**

13

Santa's Show 'n' Tell
Handcrafted • CROW
1895QLX7566 • **Value $33**

14

Santa's Spin Top
Handcrafted • TAGU
2200QLX7573 • **Value $35**

15

U.S.S. Enterprise™
NCC-1701-E
Handcrafted • NORT
2400QXI7633 • **Value $50**

16

The Washington
Monument
Handcrafted • SEAL
2400QLX7553 • **Value $45**

17

X-wing Starfighter™
Handcrafted • RHOD
2400QXI7596 • **Value $40**

18

1955 Murray® Fire Truck
Blown Glass • HADD
3500QBG6909 • **Value $48**

19

Festive Locomotive
Blown Glass • TAGU
3500QBG6903 • **Value $48**

	Price Paid	Value
General Keepsake		
1.		
2.		
3.		
4.		
5.		
6.		
7.		
8.		
General Magic		
9.		
10.		
11.		
12.		
13.		
14.		
15.		
16.		
17.		
General Crown Reflections		
18.		
19.		
Totals		

1

Frankincense
(re-issued in 1999)
Blown Glass • LARS
2200QBG6896 • **Value $30**

2

Frosty Friends (set/2)
Blown Glass • SEAL
4800QBG6907 • **Value $65**

3

Gold (re-issued in 1999)
Blown Glass • LARS
2200QBG6836 • **Value $30**

4

Myrrh
(re-issued in 1999)
Blown Glass • LARS
2200QBG6893 • **Value $30**

5

Sugarplum Cottage
Blown Glass • HADD
3500QBG6917 • **Value $55**

6

Sweet Memories (set/8)
Blown Glass • KLIN
4500QBG6933 • **Value $72**

7

Angel Chime
Die-Cast Metal • TAGU
895QXM4283 • **Value $15**

8

Betsey's Prayer
Handcrafted • KLIN
495QXM4263 • **Value $10**

9

"Coca-Cola" Time
Handcrafted • UNRU
695QXM4296 • **Value $12**

10

Ewoks™ (set/3)
Handcrafted • BRIC
1695QXI4223 • **Value $28**

11

Fishy Surprise
Handcrafted • ESCH
695QXM4276 • **Value $13**

12

Glinda, The Good Witch™
Wicked Witch of the
West™ (set/2)
Handcrafted • LYLE
1495QXM4233 • **Value $25**

13

Holly-Jolly Jig
Handcrafted • TAGU
695QXM4266 • **Value $13**

14

Peaceful Pandas
Handcrafted • SICK
595QXM4253 • **Value $14**

15

Pixie Parachute
Handcrafted • ESCH
495QXM4256 • **Value $10**

16

Sharing Joy
Handcrafted • N/A
495QXM4273 • **Value $10**

17

Singin' in the Rain™
(set/2)
Handcrafted • ANDR
1095QXM4303 • **Value $19**

18

Superman™ (set/2)
Handcrafted • CHAD
1095QXM4313 • **Value $18**

19

Tree Trimmin' Time
(set/3)
Handcrafted • N/A
1995QXD4236 • **Value $38**

20

Follow the Leader
(club edition, set/2)
Handcrafted • SIED
1695QXC4503 • **Value $38**

General
Crown Reflections

	Price Paid	Value
1.		
2.		
3.		
4.		
5.		
6.		

General Miniature

7.		
8.		
9.		
10.		
11.		
12.		
13.		
14.		
15.		
16.		
17.		
18.		
19.		

Collector's Club

20.		

Totals

1

Kringle Bells
(keepsake of
membership, miniature)
Handcrafted • BRIC
QXC4486 • **Value $17**

2

Making His Way
(keepsake of membership)
Handcrafted • SICK
QXC4523 • **Value $25**

3

New Christmas Friend
(keepsake of membership)
Handcrafted • ESCH
QXC4516 • **Value $25**

4

Our 25th Anniversary
Silver-Plated • N/A
(N/C) No stock # • **Value N/E**

5

**Santa's Merry Workshop
Musical Figurine**
Handcrafted • SEAL
3200QX6816 • **Value $52**

6

**Holiday Memories™
BARBIE™ Ornament**
Handcrafted • N/A
1495QHB6020 • **Value N/E**

7

**Holiday Memories™
BARBIE™ Porcelain
Plate (LE-24,500)**
Porcelain • N/A
3000QHB6021 • **Value N/E**

8

**Holiday Voyage™
BARBIE™ Card-Display
Figurine**
Handcrafted • N/A
4000QHB6019 • **Value N/E**

9

**Holiday Voyage™
BARBIE® Doll (2nd in
*Holiday Homecoming
Collector Series™*)**
Vinyl • N/A
5000QHB6022 • **Value N/E**

10

**Holiday Voyage™
BARBIE™ Ornament**
Handcrafted • N/A
1495QHB6016 • **Value N/E**

11

**Holiday Voyage™
BARBIE™ Porcelain
Figurine (LE-24,500)**
Porcelain • N/A
4500QHB6017 • **Value N/E**

12

**Holiday Voyage™
BARBIE™ Porcelain
Plate (LE-24,500)**
Porcelain • N/A
3000QHB6018 • **Value N/E**

13

**Collegiate Collection
(5 assorted)**
Handcrafted • HADD

1. Florida State Seminoles™
995QSR2316 • **Value N/E**
2. Michigan Wolverines™
995QSR2323 • **Value N/E**
3. North Carolina Tar Heels™
995QSR2333 • **Value N/E**
4. Notre Dame Fighting Irish™
995QSR2313 • **Value N/E**
5. Penn State Nittany Lions™
995QSR2326 • **Value N/E**

14

**1955 Murray® Tractor
and Trailer (white)**
Die-Cast Metal • PALM
(N/C) No stock # • **Value N/E**

15

**Snow Buddies
(gray rabbit)**
Handcrafted • HADD
(N/C) No stock # • **Value N/E**

16

**25th Anniversary
Gold Ball
(employee piece)**
Glass • N/A
(N/C) No stock # • **Value N/E**

17

Elf
Handcrafted • CHAD
(N/C) No stock # • **Value N/E**

Collector's Club

	Price Paid	Value
1.		
2.		
3.		
4.		

Premiere Figurines

5.		

BARBIE™ Collectibles

6.		
7.		
8.		
9.		
10.		
11.		
12.		

Collegiate Collection

13.		

Convention Pieces

14.		
15.		
16.		
17.		

Totals

1998 Collection

1

Iris Angel (white)
Handcrafted • TAGU
(N/C) No stock # • **Value N/E**

2

Joe Cool (green coat)
Handcrafted • SIED
(N/C) No stock # • **Value N/E**

3

K.C. Drummer Boy
Silver-Plated • N/A
(N/C) No stock # • **Value N/E**

4

K.C. Snowflake
Silver-Plated • UNRU
(N/C) No stock # • **Value N/E**

5

Kansas City Angel
(precious edition)
Lead Crystal/Silver-Plated • VOTR
QXC4526 • **Value N/E**

6

A Late Night Snack
(complements the
"Studio Edition Sleigh")
Handcrafted • CHAD/HADD
(N/C) No stock # • **Value N/E**

7

Mouse
Handcrafted • SIED
(N/C) No stock # • **Value N/E**

8

A Pony for Christmas
(black)
Handcrafted • SICK
(N/C) No stock # • **Value N/E**

9

Santa's Deer Friend
Handcrafted • CHAD
(N/C) No stock # • **Value N/E**

10

Snow Man
(local club piece)
Handcrafted • N/A
(N/C) No stock # • **Value N/E**

11

Studio Edition Sleigh
(artist signing piece)
Handcrafted • VARI
(N/C) No stock # • **Value N/E**

12

1926 Lionel® Catalog
Cover Tin Sign
Pressed Tin • N/A
1800QHT3701 • **Value N/E**

13

1929 Lionel® Catalog
Cover Tin Sign
Pressed Tin • N/A
1800QHT3703 • **Value N/E**

14

1952 Lionel® Catalog
Cover Tin Sign
Pressed Tin • N/A
1800QHT3702 • **Value N/E**

15

Lionel® 726 Berkshire
Steam Locomotive (1st
in *20th Century Series*)
Die-Cast Metal • N/A
($120)1QHT7801 • **Value N/E**

16

Lionel® 746 Norfolk and
Western Steam Loco-
motive (1st in *Norfolk
and Western Train Series*)
Die-Cast Metal • N/A
9000QHT7803 • **Value N/E**

17

Lionel® 2332
Pennsylvania GG1
Electric Locomotive (2nd
in *20th Century Series*)
Die-Cast Metal • N/A
9500QHT7804 • **Value N/E**

18

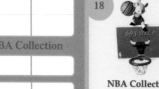

NBA Collection
(10 assorted)
Handcrafted • SIED

1. Charlotte Hornets
995QSR1033 • **Value N/E**
2. Chicago Bulls
995QSR1036 • **Value N/E**
3. Detroit Pistons
995QSR1043 • **Value N/E**
4. Houston Rockets
995QSR1046 • **Value N/E**
5. Indiana Pacers
995QSR1053 • **Value N/E**

6. Los Angeles Lakers
995QSR1056 • **Value N/E**
7. New York Knickerbockers
995QSR1063 • **Value N/E**
8. Orlando Magic
995QSR1066 • **Value N/E**
9. Seattle Supersonics
995QSR1076 • **Value N/E**
10. Utah Jazz
995QSR1083 • **Value N/E**

Convention Pieces

	Price Paid	Value
1.		
2.		
3.		
4.		
5.		
6.		
7.		
8.		
9.		
10.		
11.		

Great American Railways™

12.		
13.		
14.		
15.		
16.		
17.		

NBA Collection

18.		

Totals

VALUE GUIDE — HALLMARK KEEPSAKE ORNAMENTS

NFL Collection
(15 assorted)
Handcrafted • FRAN

1. **Carolina Panthers™**
995QSR5026 • **Value N/E**
2. **Chicago Bears™**
995QSR5033 • **Value N/E**
3. **Dallas Cowboys™**
995QSR5046 • **Value N/E**
4. **Denver Broncos™**
995QSR5053 • **Value N/E**
5. **Green Bay Packers™**
995QSR5063 • **Value N/E**

6. **Kansas City Chiefs™**
995QSR5013 • **Value N/E**
7. **Miami Dolphins™**
995QSR5096 • **Value N/E**
8. **Minnesota Vikings™**
995QSR5126 • **Value N/E**
9. **New York Giants™**
995QSR5143 • **Value N/E**
10. **Oakland Raiders™**
995QSR5086 • **Value N/E**

11. **Philadelphia Eagles™**
995QSR5153 • **Value N/E**
12. **Pittsburgh Steelers™**
995QSR5163 • **Value N/E**
13. **St. Louis Rams™**
995QSR5093 • **Value N/E**
14. **San Francisco 49ers™**
995QSR5173 • **Value N/E**
15. **Washington Redskins™**
995QSR5186 • **Value N/E**

1950s HOWDY DOODY™
Pressed Tin • N/A
1950QHM8801 • **Value N/E**

1950s Lone Ranger™
Pressed Tin • N/A
1950QHM8802 • **Value N/E**

1950s SUPERMAN™
Pressed Tin • N/A
1950QHM8803 • **Value N/E**

1970s Hot Wheels™
Pressed Tin • N/A
1950QHM8813 • **Value N/E**

Christmas Caring
Resin • BRIC
1800QHC8251 • **Value N/E**

Dreams and Wishes
Resin • VOTR
2500QHC8250 • **Value N/E**

Splendid Days
Resin • TAGU
1800QHC8216 • **Value N/E**

Thoughtful Ways
Resin • HADD/TAGU
1800QHC8215 • **Value N/E**

Together Days
Resin • BRIC
1800QHC8217 • **Value N/E**

1997

Highlights for 1997 included a new collection of Disney ornaments, as well as several ornaments based on the STAR WARS movies. The 1997 collection featured 144 Keepsake ornaments, 17 Magic ornaments and 36 Miniature ornaments. See the collectible series section for more 1997 ornaments.

1997 Corvette
Handcrafted • PALM
1395QXI6455 • **Value $28**

All-Round Sports Fan
Handcrafted • WILL
895QX6392 • **Value $29**

All-Weather Walker
Handcrafted • WILL
895QX6415 • **Value $18**

NFL Collection

	Price Paid	Value
1.		

School Days Lunch Boxes

2.		
3.		
4.		
5.		

Spoonful of Stars

6.		
7.		
8.		
9.		
10.		

General Keepsake

11.		
12.		
13.		

Totals

1

Angel Friend
Handcrafted • FRAN
1495QX6762 • **Value $27**

2

Ariel, The Little Mermaid
Handcrafted • BRIC
1295QXI4072 • **Value $23**

3

Baby's First Christmas
Handcrafted • N/A
795QX6482 • **Value $23**

4

Baby's First Christmas
Handcrafted • CROW
795QX6495 • **Value $24**

5

Baby's First Christmas
Handcrafted • VOTR
995QX6485 • **Value $23**

6

Baby's First Christmas
Handcrafted • ANDR
995QX6492 • **Value $20**

7

Baby's First Christmas
Porcelain • VOTR
1495QX6535 • **Value $25**

8

Baby's Second Christmas
Handcrafted • CROW
795QX6502 • **Value $19**

9

Biking Buddies
Handcrafted • PALM
1295QX6682 • **Value $22**

10

Book of the Year
Handcrafted • BRIC
795QX6645 • **Value $17**

11

Breezin' Along
Handcrafted • SEAL
895QX6722 • **Value $18**

12

Bucket Brigade
Handcrafted • FRAN
895QX6382 • **Value $17**

13

Catch of the Day
Handcrafted • TAGU
995QX6712 • **Value $19**

14

Child's Fifth Christmas
Handcrafted • CROW
795QX6515 • **Value $16**

15

Child's Fourth Christmas
Handcrafted • CROW
795QX6512 • **Value $16**

16

Child's Third Christmas
Handcrafted • CROW
795QX6505 • **Value $17**

17

Christmas Checkup
Handcrafted • SIED
795QX6385 • **Value $16**

18

Classic Cross
Precious Metal • VOTR
1395QX6805 • **Value $20**

19

Clever Camper
Handcrafted • CHAD
795QX6445 • **Value $18**

20

Commander Data™
Handcrafted • RGRS
1495QXI6345 • **Value $27**

1

Cycling Santa
Handcrafted • WILL
1495QX6425 • **Value $26**

2

Dad
Handcrafted • SIED
895QX6532 • **Value $18**

3

Daughter
Pressed Tin • BRIC
795QX6612 • **Value $18**

4

Downhill Run
Handcrafted • CROW
995QX6705 • **Value $20**

5

Dr. Leonard H. McCoy™
Handcrafted • RGRS
1495QXI6352 • **Value $27**

6

Elegance on Ice
Handcrafted • LYLE
995QX6432 • **Value $20**

7

Expressly for Teacher
Handcrafted • TAGU
795QX6375 • **Value $16**

8

Feliz Navidad
Handcrafted • SEAL
895QX6665 • **Value $30**

9

Friendship Blend
Handcrafted • SEAL
995QX6655 • **Value $21**

10

Garden Bouquet
Handcrafted • LYLE
1495QX6752 • **Value $30**

11

Gift of Friendship
Porcelain • N/A
1295QXE6835 • **Value $21**

12

Godchild
Handcrafted • BRIC
795QX6662 • **Value $16**

13

God's Gift of Love
Porcelain • LYLE
1695QX6792 • **Value $33**

14

Goofy's Ski Adventure
Handcrafted • CHAD
1295QXD4042 • **Value $23**

15

Granddaughter
Handcrafted • TAGU
795QX6622 • **Value $18**

16

Grandma
Handcrafted • PIKE
895QX6625 • **Value $16**

17
Grandson
Handcrafted • TAGU
795QX6615 • **Value $18**

18
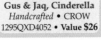
Gus & Jaq, Cinderella
Handcrafted • CROW
1295QXD4052 • **Value $26**

19

Heavenly Song
Acrylic • VOTR
1295QX6795 • **Value $24**

20

Hercules
Handcrafted • WILL
1295QXI4005 • **Value $22**

General Keepsake

	Price Paid	Value
1.		
2.		
3.		
4.		
5.		
6.		
7.		
8.		
9.		
10.		
11.		
12.		
13.		
14.		
15.		
16.		
17.		
18.		
19.		
20.		

Totals

1

Honored Guests
Handcrafted • FRAN
1495QX6745 • **Value $30**

2

Howdy Doody™
Handcrafted • LARS
1295QX6272 • **Value $29**

3

The Incredible Hulk®
Handcrafted • N/A
1295QX5471 • **Value $24**

4

**Jasmine & Aladdin,
Aladdin & the
King of Thieves**
Handcrafted • RGRS
1495QXD4062 • **Value $25**

5

Jingle Bell Jester
Handcrafted • PIKE
995QX6695 • **Value $23**

6

Juggling Stars
Handcrafted • TAGU
995QX6595 • **Value $19**

7

King Noor–First King
Handcrafted • ANDR
1295QX6552 • **Value $31**

8

Leading The Way
Handcrafted • SICK
1695QX6782 • **Value $30**

General Keepsake

	Price Paid	Value
1.		
2.		
3.		
4.		
5.		
6.		
7.		
8.		
9.		
10.		
11.		
12.		
13.		
14.		
15.		
16.		
17.		
18.		
19.		
20.		

Totals

9

Lion and Lamb
Handcrafted • WILL
795QX6602 • **Value $20**

10

The Lone Ranger™
Pressed Tin • N/A
1295QX6265 • **Value $38**

11

Love to Sew
Handcrafted • TAGU
795QX6435 • **Value $19**

12

Madonna del Rosario
Handcrafted • SICK
1295QX6545 • **Value $25**

13

Marbles Champion
Handcrafted • UNRU
1095QX6342 • **Value $22**

14

Meadow Snowman
Pressed Tin • SICK
1295QX6715 • **Value $32**

15

Megara and Pegasus
Handcrafted • CROW
1695QXI4012 • **Value $29**

16

Michigan J. Frog
Handcrafted • CHAD
995QX6332 • **Value $23**

17

Mickey's Long Shot
Handcrafted • SIED
1095QXD6412 • **Value $22**

18

Mickey's Snow Angel
Handcrafted • SIED
995QXD4035 • **Value $20**

19

Miss Gulch
Handcrafted • LYLE
1395QX6372 • **Value $28**

20

Mom
Handcrafted • SIED
895QX6525 • **Value $18**

1

Mom and Dad
Handcrafted • SIED
995QX6522 • **Value $19**

2

Mr. Potato Head®
Handcrafted • SIED
1095QX6335 • **Value $26**

3

Nativity Tree
Handcrafted • UNRU
1495QX6575 • **Value $33**

4

New Home
Handcrafted • PIKE
895QX6652 • **Value $19**

5

New Pair of Skates
Handcrafted • LARS
1395QXD4032 • **Value $25**

6

The Night Before Christmas
Handcrafted • CROW
2400QX5721 • **Value $44**

7

Our Christmas Together
Pewter • N/A
1695QX6475 • **Value $26**

8

Our First Christmas Together
Acrylic • N/A
795QX3182 • **Value $17**

9

Our First Christmas Together
Handcrafted • PIKE
895QX6472 • **Value $22**

10

Our First Christmas Together
Handcrafted • SEAL
1095QX6465 • **Value $21**

11
Phoebus & Esmeralda, The Hunchback of Notre Dame
Handcrafted • CROW
1495QXD6344 • **Value $24**

12

Playful Shepherd
Handcrafted • TAGU
995QX6592 • **Value $21**

13

Porcelain Hinged Box
Porcelain • VOTR
1495QX6772 • **Value $32**

14

Praise Him
Handcrafted • SICK
895QX6542 • **Value $19**

15

Prize Topiary
Handcrafted • SEAL
1495QX6675 • **Value $24**

16

Sailor Bear
Handcrafted • UNRU
1495QX6765 • **Value $23**

17

Santa Mail
Handcrafted • WILL
1095QX6702 • **Value $22**

18

Santa's Friend
Handcrafted • UNRU
1295QX6685 • **Value $26**

19

Santa's Magical Sleigh
Handcrafted • UNRU
2400QX6672 • **Value $42**

20
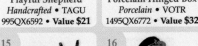
Santa's Merry Path
Handcrafted • SICK
1695QX6785 • **Value $34**

General Keepsake

	Price Paid	Value
1.		
2.		
3.		
4.		
5.		
6.		
7.		
8.		
9.		
10.		
11.		
12.		
13.		
14.		
15.		
16.		
17.		
18.		
19.		
20.		

Totals

1

Santa's Polar Friend
Handcrafted • CHAD
1695QX6755 • **Value $35**

2

Santa's Ski Adventure
Handcrafted • CHAD
1295QX6422 • **Value $25**

3

Sister to Sister
Handcrafted • PIKE
995QX6635 • **Value $20**

4

Snow Bowling
Handcrafted • WILL
695QX6395 • **Value $16**

5

Snow White, Anniversary Edition (set/2)
Handcrafted • ESCH
1695QXD4055 • **Value $33**

6

Snowgirl
Handcrafted • TAGU
795QX6562 • **Value $18**

7

Son
Pressed Tin • BRIC
795QX6605 • **Value $16**

8

Special Dog
Handcrafted • BRIC
795QX6632 • **Value $16**

9

The Spirit of Christmas
Handcrafted • LARS
995QX6585 • **Value $24**

10

Stealing a Kiss
Handcrafted • TAGU
1495QX6555 • **Value $29**

11

Sweet Discovery
Handcrafted • SICK
1195QX6325 • **Value $24**

12

Sweet Dreamer
Handcrafted • BRIC
695QX6732 • **Value $17**

13

Swinging in the Snow
Handcrafted/Glass • TAGU
1295QX6775 • **Value $22**

14

Taking A Break
Handcrafted • UNRU
1495QX6305 • **Value $29**

15

Timon & Pumbaa, The Lion King
Handcrafted • WILL
1295QXD4065 • **Value $22**

16

Tomorrow's Leader
Ceramic • N/A
995QX6452 • **Value $16**

17

Tonka® Mighty Front Loader
Die-Cast Metal • N/A
1395QX6362 • **Value $28**

18

Two-Tone, 101 Dalmatians
Handcrafted • CHAD
995QXD4015 • **Value $20**

19

Waitin' on Santa – Winnie the Pooh
Handcrafted • SIED
1295QXD6365 • **Value $26**

20

What a Deal!
Handcrafted • PIKE
895QX6442 • **Value $17**

General Keepsake

	Price Paid	Value
1.		
2.		
3.		
4.		
5.		
6.		
7.		
8.		
9.		
10.		
11.		
12.		
13.		
14.		
15.		
16.		
17.		
18.		
19.		
20.		

Totals

1

Yoda™
Handcrafted • BRIC
995QXI6355 • **Value $40**

2

Darth Vader™
Handcrafted • RHOD
2400QXI7531 • **Value $43**

3

Decorator Taz
Handcrafted • CHAD
3000QLX7502 • **Value $48**

4

Glowing Angel
Handcrafted • VOTR
1895QLX7435 • **Value $32**

5

Holiday Serenade
Handcrafted • FRAN
2400QLX7485 • **Value $39**

6

Joy to the World
Handcrafted • TAGU
1495QLX7512 • **Value $28**

7

The Lincoln Memorial
Handcrafted • SEAL
2400QLX7522 • **Value $43**

8

Madonna and Child
Handcrafted • LYLE
1995QLX7425 • **Value $38**

9

Motorcycle Chums
Handcrafted • SEAL
2400QLX7495 • **Value $44**

10

Santa's Secret Gift
Handcrafted • CHAD
2400QLX7455 • **Value $40**

11

Santa's Showboat
Handcrafted • CROW
4200QLX7465 • **Value $75**

12

SNOOPY Plays Santa
Handcrafted • RGRS
2200QLX7475 • **Value $40**

13

Teapot Party
Handcrafted • TAGU
1895QLX7482 • **Value $36**

14

U.S.S. Defiant™
Handcrafted • NORT
2400QXI7481 • **Value $42**

15

The Warmth of Home
Handcrafted • LARS
1895QXI7545 • **Value $35**

16

C-3PO™ and R2-D2™
(set/2)
Handcrafted • RHOD
1295QXI4265 • **Value $28**

17

Casablanca™ (set/3)
Handcrafted • ANDR
1995QXM4272 • **Value $33**

18

Future Star
Handcrafted • PIKE
595QXM4232 • **Value $13**

19

Gentle Giraffes
Handcrafted • SICK
595QXM4221 • **Value $14**

20

He Is Born
Handcrafted • VOTR
795QXM4235 • **Value $17**

General Keepsake	
Price Paid	Value

General Magic

1.
2.
3.
4.
5.
6.
7.
8.
9.
10.
11.
12.
13.
14.
15.

General Miniature

16.
17.
18.
19.
20.

Totals

123

1997 Collection

1

Heavenly Music
Handcrafted • TAGU
595QXM4292 • **Value $11**

2

Home Sweet Home
Handcrafted • SEAL
595QXM4222 • **Value $13**

3

Honey of a Gift–
Winnie the Pooh
Handcrafted • LARS
695QXD4255 • **Value $16**

4

Ice Cold Coca-Cola®
Handcrafted • CHAD
695QXM4252 • **Value $15**

5

King of the Forest (set/4)
Handcrafted • RGRS
2400QXM4262 • **Value $44**

6

Miniature 1997 Corvette
Handcrafted • PALM
695QXI4322 • **Value $15**

7

Our Lady of Guadalupe
Pewter • CHAD
895QXM4275 • **Value $17**

8

Peppermint Painter
Handcrafted • TAGU
495QXM4312 • **Value $13**

9

Polar Buddies
Handcrafted • FRAN
495QXM4332 • **Value $13**

10

Seeds of Joy
Handcrafted • TAGU
695QXM4242 • **Value $14**

11

Sew Talented
Handcrafted • SEAL
595QXM4195 • **Value $13**

12

Shutterbug
Handcrafted • TAGU
595QXM4212 • **Value $14**

13

Snowboard Bunny
Handcrafted • TAGU
495QXM4315 • **Value $13**

14

Tiny Home Improvers
(set/6)
Handcrafted • SEAL
2900QXM4282 • **Value $45**

15

Victorian Skater
Handcrafted • UNRU
595QXM4305 • **Value $13**

16

Away to the Window
(keepsake of membership)
Handcrafted • WILL
QXC5135 • **Value $20**

17

Farmer's Market,
Tender Touches
(club edition)
Handcrafted • SEAL
1500QXC5182 • **Value $30**

18

Happy Christmas to All!
(keepsake of membership)
Handcrafted • WILL
QXC5132 • **Value $21**

19

Jolly Old Santa
(keepsake of membership,
miniature)
Handcrafted • WILL
QXC5145 • **Value $17**

20

Ready for Santa
(keepsake of membership,
miniature)
Handcrafted • WILL
QXC5142 • **Value $13**

General Miniature

	Price Paid	Value
1.		
2.		
3.		
4.		
5.		
6.		
7.		
8.		
9.		
10.		
11.		
12.		
13.		
14.		
15.		

Collector's Club

16.		
17.		
18.		
19.		
20.		

Totals

1

The Perfect Tree,
Tender Touches
Handcrafted • SEAL
1500QX6572 • **Value $25**

2

1953 GMC (green)
Handcrafted • PALM
(N/C) No stock # • **Value N/E**

3

First Class Thank You
Handcrafted • RGRS
(N/C) No stock # • **Value N/E**

4

Mrs. Claus's Story
Handcrafted • ESCH/KLIN
($14.95) No stock # • **Value N/E**

5

Murray® Dump Truck
(orange)
Die-Cast Metal • PALM
(N/C) No stock # • **Value N/E**

6

Murray Inc.® "Pursuit"
Airplane (miniature, tan)
Die-Cast Metal • PALM
(N/C) No stock # • **Value N/E**

7

Santa's Magical Sleigh
(silver runners)
Handcrafted • UNRU
(N/C) No stock # • **Value N/E**

8

Trimming Santa's
Tree (set/2)
Handcrafted • VARI
6000QXC5175 • **Value N/E**

9

BARBIE™ Lapel Pin
(re-issued from 1996)
Handcrafted • N/A
495XLP3544 • **Value N/E**

10

Holiday BARBIE™
Stocking Hanger
(re-issued from 1996)
Handcrafted • N/A
1995XSH3101 • **Value N/E**

11

Holiday Traditions™
BARBIE® Doll (1st in
*Holiday Homecoming
Collector Series™*)
Vinyl • N/A
5000QHB3402 • **Value N/E**

12

Holiday Traditions™
BARBIE™ Ornament
Handcrafted • N/A
1495QHB6002 • **Value $23**

13

Holiday Traditions™
BARBIE™ Porcelain
Figurine
Porcelain • N/A
4500QHB6001 • **Value N/E**

14

Holiday Traditions™
BARBIE™ Porcelain Plate
Porcelain • N/A
3000QHB6003 • **Value N/E**

15

Victorian Elegance™
BARBIE™ Ornament
Handcrafted • N/A
1495QHB6004 • **Value $22**

16

Victorian Elegance™
BARBIE™ Porcelain Plate
Porcelain • N/A
3000QHB6005 • **Value N/E**

17

NBA COLLECTION
(10 assorted)
Ceramic • N/A

1. Charlotte Hornets™
995QSR1222 • **Value N/E**
2. Chicago Bulls™
995QSR1232 • **Value N/E**
3. Detroit Pistons™
995QSR1242 • **Value N/E**
4. Houston Rockets™
995QSR1245 • **Value N/E**
5. Indiana Pacers™
995QSR1252 • **Value N/E**
6. Los Angeles
Lakers™
995QSR1262 • **Value N/E**
7. New York
Knickerbockers™
995QSR1272 • **Value N/E**
8. Orlando Magic™
995QSR1282 • **Value N/E**
9. Phoenix Suns™
995QSR1292 • **Value N/E**
10. Seattle Supersonics™
995QSR1295 • **Value N/E**

Premiere Ornaments

	Price Paid	Value
1.		

Artists On Tour Pieces

2.		
3.		
4.		
5.		
6.		
7.		
8.		

BARBIE™ Collectibles

9.		
10.		
11.		
12.		
13.		
14.		
15.		
16.		

NBA Collection

17.		

Totals		

NFL COLLECTION
(30 assorted)
Handcrafted • SIED

1. **Arizona Cardinals**™
995QSR5505 • Value N/E
2. **Atlanta Falcons**™
995QSR5305 • Value N/E
3. **Baltimore Ravens**™
995QSR5352 • Value N/E
4. **Buffalo Bills**™
995QSR5312 • Value N/E
5. **Carolina Panthers**™
995QSR5315 • Value N/E
6. **Chicago Bears**™
995QSR5322 • Value N/E
7. **Cincinnati Bengals**™
995QSR5325 • Value N/E
8. **Dallas Cowboys**™
995QSR5355 • Value N/E
9. **Denver Broncos**™
995QSR5362 • Value N/E
10. **Detroit Lions**™
995QSR5365 • Value N/E

11. **Green Bay Packers**™
995QSR5372 • Value N/E
12. **Houston Oilers**™
995QSR5375 • Value N/E
13. **Indianapolis Colts**™
995QSR5411 • Value N/E
14. **Jacksonville Jaguars**™
995QSR5415 • Value N/E
15. **Kansas City Chiefs**™
995QSR5302 • Value N/E
16. **Miami Dolphins**™
995QSR5472 • Value N/E
17. **Minnesota Vikings**™
995QSR5475 • Value N/E
18. **New England Patriots**™
995QSR5482 • Value N/E
19. **New Orleans Saints**™
995QSR5485 • Value N/E
20. **New York Giants**™
995QSR5492 • Value N/E

21. **New York Jets**™
995QSR5495 • Value N/E
22. **Oakland Raiders**™
995QSR5422 • Value N/E
23. **Philadelphia Eagles**™
995QSR5502 • Value N/E
24. **Pittsburgh Steelers**™
995QSR5512 • Value N/E
25. **St. Louis Rams**™
995QSR5425 • Value N/E
26. **San Diego Chargers**™
995QSR5515 • Value N/E
27. **San Francisco 49ers**™
995QSR5522 • Value N/E
28. **Seattle Seahawks**™
995QSR5525 • Value N/E
29. **Tampa Bay Buccaneers**™
995QSR5532 • Value N/E
30. **Washington Redskins**™
995QSR5535 • Value N/E

NFL Collection

	Price Paid	Value
1.		

General Keepsake

2.		
3.		
4.		
5.		
6.		
7.		
8.		
9.		
10.		

Totals

1996

Hallmark introduced several ornaments and collectibles commemorating the Centennial Olympic Games in Atlanta, Georgia in 1996. Overall, there were 135 Keepsake ornaments in the collection, as well as 23 Magic, 13 Showcase and 34 Miniature ornaments. See the collectible series section for more 1996 ornaments.

2
101 Dalmatians
Handcrafted • N/A
1295QXI6544 • Value $22

3
Antlers Aweigh!
Handcrafted • CHAD
995QX5901 • Value $21

4
Apple for Teacher
Handcrafted • AUBE
795QX6121 • Value $13

5
Baby's First Christmas
Handcrafted • SEAL
795QX5761 • Value $22

6
Baby's First Christmas
Handcrafted • CROW
795QX5764 • Value $23

7
Baby's First Christmas
Handcrafted • ANDR
995QX5754 • Value $23

8
Baby's First Christmas
Porcelain • N/A
1095QX5751 • Value $23

9
Baby's First Christmas
Porcelain • VOTR
1895QX5744 • Value $30

10
Baby's Second Christmas
Handcrafted • CROW
795QX5771 • Value $20

1

Bounce Pass
Handcrafted • SIED
795QX6031 • **Value $15**

2

Bowl 'em Over
Handcrafted • SIED
795QX6014 • **Value $15**

3

Child Care Giver
Handcrafted • SIED
895QX6071 • **Value $16**

4

Child's Fifth Christmas
Handcrafted • RHOD
695QX5784 • **Value $17**

5

Child's Fourth Christmas
Handcrafted • CROW
795QX5781 • **Value $18**

6

Child's Third Christmas
Handcrafted • CROW
795QX5774 • **Value $19**

7

Christmas Joy
Handcrafted • UNRU
1495QX6241 • **Value $26**

8

Christmas Snowman
Handcrafted • UNRU
995QX6214 • **Value $21**

9

Close-Knit Friends
Handcrafted • BRIC
995QX5874 • **Value $18**

10

Come All Ye Faithful
Handcrafted • CROW
1295QX6244 • **Value $25**

11

Commander William T. Riker™
Handcrafted • RGRS
1495QXI5551 • **Value $30**

12

Dad
Handcrafted • SIED
795QX5831 • **Value $17**

13

Daughter
Handcrafted • PALM
895QX6077 • **Value $19**

14

Esmeralda and Djali
Handcrafted • CROW
1495QXI6351 • **Value $23**

15

Evergreen Santa
Handcrafted • LYLE
2200QX5714 • **Value $42**

16

Fan-tastic Season
Handcrafted • CHAD
995QX5924 • **Value $21**

17

Feliz Navidad
Handcrafted • SICK
995QX6304 • **Value $22**

18

Foghorn Leghorn and Henery Hawk (set/2)
Handcrafted • CHAD
1395QX5444 • **Value $23**

19

Glad Tidings
Handcrafted • LYLE
1495QX6231 • **Value $28**

20

Goal Line Glory (set/2)
Handcrafted • SEAL
1295QX6001 • **Value $25**

General Keepsake

	Price Paid	Value
1.		
2.		
3.		
4.		
5.		
6.		
7.		
8.		
9.		
10.		
11.		
12.		
13.		
14.		
15.		
16.		
17.		
18.		
19.		
20.		

Totals

1

Godchild
Handcrafted • RGRS
895QX5841 • **Value $16**

2

Granddaughter
Handcrafted • RGRS
795QX5697 • **Value $16**

3

Grandma
Handcrafted • VOTR
895QX5844 • **Value $18**

4

Grandpa
Handcrafted • VOTR
895QX5851 • **Value $18**

5

Grandson
Handcrafted • RGRS
795QX5699 • **Value $16**

6

Growth of a Leader
Ceramic • N/A
995QX5541 • **Value $17**

7

Happy Holi-doze
Handcrafted • RHOD
995QX5904 • **Value $19**

8

Hearts Full of Love
Handcrafted • RHOD
995QX5814 • **Value $20**

9

High Style
Handcrafted • CHAD
895QX6064 • **Value $19**

10

Hillside Express
Handcrafted • AUBE
1295QX6134 • **Value $23**

11

Holiday Haul
Handcrafted • SICK
1495QX6201 • **Value $32**

12

Hurrying Downstairs
Handcrafted • FRAN
895QX6074 • **Value $18**

13

I Dig Golf
Handcrafted • RHOD
1095QX5891 • **Value $20**

14

Invitation to the Games (set/2)
Ceramic • MCGE
1495QXE5511 • **Value $26**

15

It's A Wonderful Life™
Handcrafted • CROW
1495QXI6531 • **Value $36**

16

IZZY™ – The Mascot
Handcrafted • PALM
995QXE5724 • **Value $17**

17

Jackpot Jingle
Handcrafted • SIED
995QX5911 • **Value $19**

18

Jolly Wolly Ark
Handcrafted • CROW
1295QX6221 • **Value $26**

19

Kindly Shepherd
Handcrafted • ANDR
1295QX6274 • **Value $26**

20

Laverne, Victor and Hugo
Handcrafted • CROW
1295QXI6354 • **Value $21**

General Keepsake

	Price Paid	Value
1.		
2.		
3.		
4.		
5.		
6.		
7.		
8.		
9.		
10.		
11.		
12.		
13.		
14.		
15.		
16.		
17.		
18.		
19.		
20.		
Totals		

1

Lighting the Way
Handcrafted • CHAD
1295QX6124 • **Value $22**

2

A Little Song and Dance
Handcrafted • CROW
995QX6211 • **Value $19**

3

Little Spooners
Handcrafted • UNRU
1295QX5504 • **Value $24**

4

Madonna and Child
Tin • SICK
1295QX6324 • **Value $21**

5

Making His Rounds
Handcrafted • FRAN
1495QX6271 • **Value $25**

6

Marvin the Martian
Handcrafted • CHAD
1095QX5451 • **Value $24**

7

Matchless Memories
Handcrafted • CROW
995QX6061 • **Value $18**

8

Maxine
Handcrafted • PIKE
995QX6224 • **Value $26**

9

Merry Carpoolers
Handcrafted • CROW
1495QX5884 • **Value $25**

10

Mom
Handcrafted • LYLE
795QX5824 • **Value $17**

11

Mom and Dad
Handcrafted • RHOD
995QX5821 • **Value $17**

12

Mom-to-Be
Handcrafted • UNRU
795QX5791 • **Value $16**

13

Mr. Spock
Handcrafted • RGRS
1495QXI5544 • **Value $35**

14

New Home
Handcrafted • SEAL
895QX5881 • **Value $20**

15

**Olive Oyl and
Swee' Pea**
Handcrafted • CHAD
1095QX5481 • **Value $23**

16

Olympic Triumph
Handcrafted • SEAL
1095QXE5731 • **Value $19**

17

On My Way
Handcrafted • TAGU
795QX5861 • **Value $15**

18

Our Christmas Together
Handcrafted • PALM
1895QX5794 • **Value $35**

19

**Our Christmas Together
Photo Holder**
Handcrafted • CROW
895QX5804 • **Value $18**

20

**Our First Christmas
Together**
Acrylic • VOTR
695QX3051 • **Value $17**

General Keepsake

	Price Paid	Value
1.		
2.		
3.		
4.		
5.		
6.		
7.		
8.		
9.		
10.		
11.		
12.		
13.		
14.		
15.		
16.		
17.		
18.		
19.		
20.		

Totals

1996 Collection

1

Our First Christmas Together
Handcrafted • PALM
995QX5811 • **Value $22**

2

Our First Christmas Together Collector's Plate
Porcelain • N/A
1095QX5801 • **Value $22**

3

Parade of Nations
Porcelain • N/A
1095QXE5741 • **Value $19**

4

Peppermint Surprise
Handcrafted • PIKE
795QX6234 • **Value $18**

5

Percy the Small Engine – No. 6
Handcrafted • RHOD
995QX6314 • **Value $21**

6

PEZ® Snowman
Handcrafted • N/A
795QX6534 • **Value $17**

7

Polar Cycle
Handcrafted • UNRU
1295QX6034 • **Value $23**

8

Prayer for Peace
Handcrafted • LYLE
795QX6261 • **Value $17**

General Keepsake

	Price Paid	Value
1.		
2.		
3.		
4.		
5.		
6.		
7.		
8.		
9.		
10.		
11.		
12.		
13.		
14.		
15.		
16.		
17.		
18.		
19.		

9

Precious Child
Handcrafted • VOTR
895QX6251 • **Value $18**

10

Pup-Tenting
Handcrafted • PALM
795QX6011 • **Value $16**

11

Quasimodo
Handcrafted • CROW
995QXI6341 • **Value $18**

12

Regal Cardinal
Handcrafted • FRAN
995QX6204 • **Value $22**

13

Sew Sweet
Handcrafted • AUBE
895QX5921 • **Value $17**

14

Sister to Sister
Handcrafted • LYLE
995QX5834 • **Value $19**

15

Son
Handcrafted • PALM
895QX6079 • **Value $18**

16

Special Dog
Handcrafted • TAGU
795QX5864 • **Value $16**

17

SPIDER-MAN™
Handcrafted • CHAD
1295QX5757 • **Value $28**

18

Star of the Show
Handcrafted • AUBE
895QX6004 • **Value $19**

19

Tamika
Handcrafted • BRIC
795QX6301 • **Value $17**

Totals

1

Tender Lovin' Care
Handcrafted • SEAL
795QX6114 • **Value $18**

2

Thank You, Santa
Handcrafted • BRIC
795QX5854 • **Value $16**

3

This Big!
Handcrafted • SEAL
995QX5914 • **Value $18**

4

Time for a Treat
Handcrafted • SICK
1195QX5464 • **Value $23**

5

Tonka® Mighty Dump Truck
Die-Cast Metal • N/A
1395QX6321 • **Value $34**

6

A Tree for SNOOPY
Handcrafted • SIED
895QX5507 • **Value $18**

7

Welcome Guest
Handcrafted • UNRU
1495QX5394 • **Value $27**

8

Welcome Him
Handcrafted • TAGU
895QX6264 • **Value $18**

9

Winnie the Pooh and Piglet
Handcrafted • SIED
1295QX5454 • **Value $33**

10

Witch of the West
Handcrafted • LYLE
1395QX5554 • **Value $32**

11

WONDER WOMAN™
Handcrafted • RGRS
1295QX5941 • **Value $25**

12

Woodland Santa
Pressed Tin • SICK
1295QX6131 • **Value $24**

13

Yogi Bear™ and Boo Boo™
Handcrafted • RGRS
1295QX5521 • **Value $24**

14

Yuletide Cheer
Handcrafted • VOTR
795QX6054 • **Value $16**

15

Ziggy®
Handcrafted • CHAD
995QX6524 • **Value $23**

16

Baby's First Christmas
Handcrafted • FRAN
2200QLX7404 • **Value $40**

17

Chicken Coop Chorus
Handcrafted • CROW
2450QLX7491 • **Value $43**

18

Emerald City
Handcrafted • CROW
3200QLX7454 • **Value $65**

19

Father Time
Handcrafted • CHAD
2450QLX7391 • **Value $45**

20

THE JETSONS™
Handcrafted • CROW
2800QLX7411 • **Value $50**

General Keepsake

	Price Paid	Value
1.		
2.		
3.		
4.		
5.		
6.		
7.		
8.		
9.		
10.		
11.		
12.		
13.		
14.		
15.		

General Magic

16.		
17.		
18.		
19.		
20.		

Totals

1

Jukebox Party
Handcrafted • PALM
2450QLX7339 • **Value $53**

2

Let Us Adore Him
Handcrafted • LYLE
1650QLX7381 • **Value $35**

3

Lighting the Flame
Handcrafted • UNRU
2800QXE7444 • **Value $44**

4

Millennium Falcon™
Handcrafted • N/A
2400QLX7474 • **Value $50**

5

North Pole Volunteers
Handcrafted • SEAL
4200QLX7471 • **Value $84**

6

Over the Rooftops
Handcrafted • SEAL
1450QLX7374 • **Value $28**

7

PEANUTS®
Handcrafted • CHAD
1850QLX7394 • **Value $43**

8

Pinball Wonder
Handcrafted • CROW
2800QLX7451 • **Value $51**

9

Sharing a Soda
Handcrafted • CROW
2450QLX7424 • **Value $43**

10

Slippery Day
Handcrafted • SIED
2450QLX7414 • **Value $50**

11

STAR TREK®, 30 Years
(set/2, w/display base)
Handcrafted • NORT/RHOD
4500QXI7534 • **Value $82**

12

The Statue of Liberty
Handcrafted • SEAL
2450QLX7421 • **Value $45**

13

Treasured Memories
Handcrafted • SICK
1850QLX7384 • **Value $37**

14

U.S.S. Voyager™
Handcrafted • NORT
2400QXI7544 • **Value $52**

15

Video Party
Handcrafted • SIED
2800QLX7431 • **Value $48**

16

Carmen
Cookie Jar Friends
Porcelain • RGRS
1595QK1164 • **Value $24**

17

Clyde
Cookie Jar Friends
Porcelain • AUBE
1595QK1161 • **Value $21**

18

Caroling Angel
Folk Art Americana
Handcrafted/Copper • SICK
1695QK1134 • **Value $30**

19

Mrs. Claus
Folk Art Americana
Handcrafted/Copper • SICK
1895QK1204 • **Value $30**

20

Santa's Gifts
Folk Art Americana
Handcrafted/Copper • SICK
1895QK1124 • **Value $35**

General Magic

	Price Paid	Value
1.		
2.		
3.		
4.		
5.		
6.		
7.		
8.		
9.		
10.		
11.		
12.		
13.		
14.		
15.		

General Showcase

16.		
17.		
18.		
19.		
20.		

Totals

1

Balthasar (Frankincense)
Magi Bells
Porcelain • VOTR
1395QK1174 • **Value $26**

2

Caspar (Myrrh)
Magi Bells
Porcelain • VOTR
1395QK1184 • **Value $26**

3

Melchoir (Gold)
Magi Bells
Porcelain • VOTR
1395QK1181 • **Value $26**

4

The Birds' Christmas Tree
Nature's Sketchbook
Handcrafted • UNRU
1895QK1114 • **Value $30**

5

Christmas Bunny
Nature's Sketchbook
Handcrafted • FRAN
1895QK1104 • **Value $40**

6

The Holly Basket
Nature's Sketchbook
Handcrafted • LYLE
1895QK1094 • **Value $34**

7

Madonna and Child
Sacred Masterworks
Handcrafted • SICK
1595QK1144 • **Value $28**

8

Praying Madonna
Sacred Masterworks
Handcrafted • SICK
1595QK1154 • **Value $28**

9

African Elephants
Handcrafted • SICK
575QXM4224 • **Value $18**

10

Baby Sylvester
Handcrafted • PALM
575QXM4154 • **Value $16**

11

Baby Tweety
Handcrafted • PALM
575QXM4014 • **Value $26**

12

A Child's Gifts
Handcrafted • ANDR
675QXM4234 • **Value $13**

13

Christmas Bear
Handcrafted • SEAL
475QXM4241 • **Value $14**

14

Cloisonné Medallion
Cloisonné • MCGE
975QXE4041 • **Value $19**

15

Cool Delivery
Coca-Cola®
Handcrafted • PIKE
575QXM4021 • **Value $15**

16

GONE WITH THE
WIND™ (set/3)
Handcrafted • ANDR
1995QXM4211 • **Value $38**

17

Hattie Chapeau
Handcrafted • RHOD
475QXM4251 • **Value $12**

18

Joyous Angel
Handcrafted • ANDR
475QXM4231 • **Value $12**

19

Long Winter's Nap
Handcrafted • ANDR
575QXM4244 • **Value $13**

20

Message for Santa
Handcrafted • SEAL
675QXM4254 • **Value $14**

General Showcase		
	Price Paid	Value
1.		
2.		
3.		
4.		
5.		
6.		
7.		
8.		
General Miniature		
9.		
10.		
11.		
12.		
13.		
14.		
15.		
16.		
17.		
18.		
19.		
20.		
Totals		

133

1996 Collection

1

O Holy Night (set/4)
Handcrafted • RHOD
2450QXM4204 • **Value $34**

2

Peaceful Christmas
Handcrafted • UNRU
475QXM4214 • **Value $13**

3

Sparkling Crystal Angel
Lead Crystal/Silver • VOTR
975QXM4264 • **Value $22**

4

Tiny Christmas Helpers (set/6)
Handcrafted • SEAL
2900QXM4261 • **Value $50**

5

A Tree for WOODSTOCK
Handcrafted • SIED
575QXM4767 • **Value $18**

6

The Vehicles of STAR WARS™ (set/3)
Handcrafted • RHOD
1995QXM4024 • **Value $42**

7

Winnie the Pooh and Tigger
Handcrafted • SIED
975QXM4044 • **Value $24**

8

Airmail for Santa (gift membership bonus)
Handcrafted • RGRS
QXC4194 • **Value $22**

General Miniature

	Price Paid	Value
1.		
2.		
3.		
4.		
5.		
6.		
7.		

Collector's Club

8.		
9.		
10.		
11.		
12.		
13.		

Premiere Ornaments

14.		
15.		

Artists On Tour Pieces

16.		
17.		
18.		
19.		
20.		

Totals

9

Holiday Bunny (early renewal piece, miniature)
Handcrafted • FRAN
QXC4191 • **Value $16**

10

Rudolph the Red-Nosed Reindeer® (keepsake of membership, magic)
Handcrafted • SIED
QXC7341 • **Value $25**

11

Rudolph®'s Helper (keepsake of membership, miniature)
Handcrafted • SIED
QXC4171 • **Value $17**

12

Santa (keepsake of membership)
Handcrafted • SIED
QXC4164 • **Value $22**

13

The Wizard of OZ™ (club edition)
Handcrafted • RGRS
1295QXC4161 • **Value $60**

14

"Get Hooked On Collecting" Starter Set (book with "Filled With Memories" ornament)
Handcrafted • N/A
799XPR837 • **Value N/E**

15

Welcome Sign, Tender Touches
Handcrafted • SEAL
1500QX6331 • **Value $25**

16

1955 Chevrolet Cameo (red)
Handcrafted • PALM
(N/C) No stock # • **Value N/E**

17

Gold Rocking Horse (miniature)
Handcrafted • SICK
($12.95) No stock # • **Value $48**

18

Murray® Airplane (tan)
Die-Cast Metal • PALM
(N/C) No stock # • **Value N/E**

19

Murray® Fire Truck (miniature, white)
Die-Cast Metal • PALM
(N/C) No stock # • **Value N/E**

20

Santa's Toy Shop (set/2, artist signing piece)
Handcrafted • VARI
6000QXC4201 • **Value $124**

1
Toy Shop Santa
Handcrafted • UNRU
($14.95) No stock # • **Value $38**

2
BARBIE™ Lapel Pin
(re-issued in 1997)
Handcrafted • N/A
495XLP3544 • **Value N/E**

3
Holiday BARBIE™
Stocking Hanger
(re-issued in 1997)
Handcrafted • N/A
1995XSH3101 • **Value N/E**

4
Yuletide Romance™
BARBIE® Doll
(3rd & final in series)
Vinyl • N/A
5000QHX3401 • **Value $100**

5
Reindeer Rooters
Handcrafted • CROW
(N/C) No stock # • **Value N/E**

6
Golden Age
Batman and Robin™
"The Dynamic Duo™"
Handcrafted • UNRU
7000QHF3103 • **Value N/E**

7
Golden Age
Superman™ "Man of
Steel™" (LE-14,500)
Handcrafted • N/A
8000QHF3101 • **Value N/E**

8
Golden Age Wonder
Woman™ "Champion
of Freedom"
Handcrafted • RGRS
3500QHF3107 • **Value N/E**

9
Modern Era Batman™
"Guardian of
Gotham City™"
Handcrafted • CHAD
5500QHF3104 • **Value N/E**

10
Modern Era Robin™
"World's Bravest
Teenager"
Handcrafted • CHAD
4000QHF3105 • **Value N/E**

11
Modern Era
Superman™ "In A
Single Bound"
Handcrafted • N/A
6000QHF3102 • **Value N/E**

12
Modern Era Wonder
Woman™ "Warrior of
Strength and Wisdom"
Handcrafted • RGRS
3500QHF3106 • **Value N/E**

13
NFL COLLECTION
(14 assorted)
Glass • N/A

1. **Buffalo Bills™**
595BIL2035 • **Value $10**
2. **Carolina Panthers™**
(re-issued from 1995)
595PNA2035 • **Value $10**
3. **Chicago Bears™**
(re-issued from 1995)
595BRS2035 • **Value $10**
4. **Dallas Cowboys™**
(re-issued from 1995)
595COW2035 • **Value $10**
5. **Green Bay Packers™**
595PKR2035 • **Value $10**
6. **Kansas City Chiefs™**
(re-issued from 1995)
595CHF2035 • **Value $10**
7. **Los Angeles Raiders™**
(re-issued from 1995)
595RDR2035 • **Value $10**
8. **Minnesota Vikings™**
(re-issued from 1995)
595VIK2035 • **Value $10**
9. **New England Patriots™**
(re-issued from 1995)
595NEP2035 • **Value $10**
10. **Philadelphia Eagles™**
(re-issued from 1995)
595EAG2035 • **Value $10**
11. **Pittsburgh Steelers™**
595PIT2035 • **Value $10**
12. **St. Louis Rams™**
595RAM2035 • **Value $10**
13. **San Francisco 49ers™**
(re-issued from 1995)
595FOR2035 • **Value $10**
14. **Washington Redskins™**
(re-issued from 1995)
595RSK2035 • **Value $10**

14
NFL COLLECTION
(30 assorted)
Handcrafted • UNRU

1. **Arizona Cardinals™**
995QSR6484 • **Value $15**
2. **Atlanta Falcons™**
995QSR6364 • **Value $15**
3. **Browns™**
995QSR6391 • **Value $15**
4. **Buffalo Bills™**
995QSR6371 • **Value $15**
5. **Carolina Panthers™**
995QSR6374 • **Value $15**
6. **Chicago Bears™**
995QSR6381 • **Value $15**
7. **Cincinnati Bengals™**
995QSR6384 • **Value $15**
8. **Dallas Cowboys™**
995QSR6394 • **Value $18**
9. **Denver Broncos™**
995QSR6411 • **Value $15**
10. **Detroit Lions™**
995QSR6414 • **Value $15**
11. **Green Bay Packers™**
995QSR6421 • **Value $20**
12. **Indianapolis Colts™**
995QSR6431 • **Value $15**

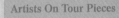

Artists On Tour Pieces

	Price Paid	Value
1.		

BARBIE™ Collectibles

2.		
3.		
4.		

Club Tour Ornaments

5.		

D.C. Super Heroes Figurines

6.		
7.		
8.		
9.		
10.		
11.		
12.		

NFL Collection

13.		
14.		

1996 / 1995 Collection

13. Jacksonville Jaguars™
995QSR6434 • Value **$15**
14. Kansas City Chiefs™
995QSR6361 • Value **$15**
15. Miami Dolphins™
995QSR6451 • Value **$15**
16. Minnesota Vikings™
995QSR6454 • Value **$15**
17. New England Patriots™
995QSR6461 • Value **$15**
18. New Orleans Saints™
995QSR6464 • Value **$15**

19. New York Giants™
995QSR6471 • Value **$15**
20. New York Jets™
995QSR6474 • Value **$15**
21. Oakland Raiders™
995QSR6441 • Value **$15**
22. Oilers™
995QSR6424 • Value **$15**
23. Philadelphia Eagles™
995QSR6481 • Value **$15**
24. Pittsburgh Steelers™
995QSR6491 • Value **$15**

25. St. Louis Rams™
995QSR6444 • Value **$15**
26. San Diego Chargers™
995QSR6494 • Value **$15**
27. San Francisco 49ers™
995QSR6501 • Value **$15**
28. Seattle Seahawks™
995QSR6504 • Value **$15**
29. Tampa Bay Buccaneers™
995QSR6511 • Value **$15**
30. Washington Redskins™
995QSR6514 • Value **$15**

1

Gymnastics Figurine
Handcrafted • LYLE
1750QHC8204 • **Value N/E**

2

Olympic Triumph Figurine (LE-24,500)
Handcrafted • UNRU
5000QHC8191 • **Value N/E**

3

Parade of Nations Plate
Porcelain • N/A
3000QHC8194 • **Value N/E**

4

Swimming Figurine
Handcrafted • CHAD
1750QHC8211 • **Value N/E**

5

Track and Field Figurine
Handcrafted • N/A
1750QHC8201 • **Value N/E**

Olympic Collectibles

	Price Paid	Value
1.		
2.		
3.		
4.		
5.		

General Keepsake

6.		
7.		
8.		
9.		
10.		
11.		
12.		
13.		
14.		

Totals

1995

More great BARBIE™, STAR TREK™ and sports ornaments were released in 1995, as well as a record number of Showcase ornaments. In the 1995 line, there were 146 Keepsake, 20 Magic, 20 Showcase and 36 Miniature ornaments. See the collectible series section for more 1995 ornaments.

6

Acorn 500
Handcrafted • SIED
1095QX5929 • **Value $21**

7

Across the Miles
Handcrafted • FRAN
895QX5847 • **Value $20**

8

Air Express
Handcrafted • SEAL
795QX5977 • **Value $18**

9

Anniversary Year
Handcrafted • UNRU
895QX5819 • **Value $18**

10

Baby's First Christmas
Handcrafted • VOTR
795QX5549 • **Value $19**

11

Baby's First Christmas
Handcrafted • CROW
795QX5559 • **Value $23**

12

Baby's First Christmas
Handcrafted • ANDR
995QX5557 • **Value $20**

13

Baby's First Christmas
Handcrafted • ANDR
1895QX5547 • **Value $45**

14

Baby's First Christmas – Baby Boy
Glass • N/A
500QX2319 • **Value $17**

1
Baby's First Christmas – Baby Girl
Glass • N/A
500QX2317 • **Value $17**

2
Baby's Second Christmas
Handcrafted • CROW
795QX5567 • **Value $24**

3
Barrel-Back Rider
Handcrafted • FRAN
995QX5189 • **Value $24**

4
Batmobile
Handcrafted • PALM
1495QX5739 • **Value $26**

5
Betty and Wilma
Handcrafted • RHOD
1495QX5417 • **Value $23**

6
Beverly and Teddy
Handcrafted • UNRU
2175QX5259 • **Value $34**

7
Bingo Bear
Handcrafted • VOTR
795QX5919 • **Value $18**

8
Bobbin' Along
Handcrafted • CROW
895QX5879 • **Value $30**

9
Brother
Handcrafted • LYLE
695QX5679 • **Value $14**

10
Bugs Bunny
Handcrafted • CHAD
895QX5019 • **Value $22**

11
Captain James T. Kirk
Handcrafted • RGRS
1395QXI5539 • **Value $27**

12
Captain Jean-Luc Picard
Handcrafted • RGRS
1395QXI5737 • **Value $28**

13
Captain John Smith and Meeko
Handcrafted • CROW
1295QXI6169 • **Value $21**

14
Catch the Spirit
Handcrafted • SIED
795QX5899 • **Value $19**

15
Child's Fifth Christmas
Handcrafted • RHOD
695QX5637 • **Value $17**

16
Child's Fourth Christmas
Handcrafted • FRAN
695QX5629 • **Value $19**

17
Child's Third Christmas
Handcrafted • CROW
795QX5627 • **Value $19**

18
Christmas Fever
Handcrafted • AUBE
795QX5967 • **Value $18**

19
Christmas Morning
Handcrafted • FRAN
1095QX5997 • **Value $19**

20
Christmas Patrol
Handcrafted • ANDR
795QX5959 • **Value $19**

General Keepsake

	Price Paid	Value
1.		
2.		
3.		
4.		
5.		
6.		
7.		
8.		
9.		
10.		
11.		
12.		
13.		
14.		
15.		
16.		
17.		
18.		
19.		
20.		
Totals		

1

Colorful World
Handcrafted • CROW
1095QX5519 • **Value $26**

2

Cows of Bali
Handcrafted • ANDR
895QX5999 • **Value $18**

3

Dad
Handcrafted • SIED
795QX5649 • **Value $16**

4

Dad-to-Be
Handcrafted • RHOD
795QX5667 • **Value $14**

5

Daughter
Handcrafted • PALM
695QX5677 • **Value $18**

6

Delivering Kisses
Handcrafted • SICK
1095QX4107 • **Value $24**

7

Dream On
Handcrafted • FRAN
1095QX6007 • **Value $22**

8

Dudley the Dragon
Handcrafted • PIKE
1095QX6209 • **Value $21**

9

Faithful Fan
Handcrafted • SIED
895QX5897 • **Value $18**

10

Feliz Navidad
Handcrafted • RHOD
795QX5869 • **Value $20**

11

For My Grandma
Handcrafted • PALM
695QX5729 • **Value $15**

12

Forever Friends Bear
Handcrafted • BRWN
895QX5258 • **Value $22**

13

Friendly Boost
Handcrafted • PALM
895QX5827 • **Value $21**

14

GARFIELD®
Handcrafted • N/A
1095QX5007 • **Value $26**

15

Glinda, Witch of the North
Handcrafted • LYLE
1395QX5749 • **Value $39**

16

Godchild
Handcrafted/Brass • PALM
795QX5707 • **Value $20**

17

Godparent
Glass • VOTR
500QX2417 • **Value $14**

18

Gopher Fun
Handcrafted • SIED
995QX5887 • **Value $19**

19

Grandchild's First Christmas
Handcrafted • FRAN
795QX5777 • **Value $16**

20

Granddaughter
Handcrafted • RGRS
695QX5779 • **Value $18**

General Keepsake

	Price Paid	Value
1.		
2.		
3.		
4.		
5.		
6.		
7.		
8.		
9.		
10.		
11.		
12.		
13.		
14.		
15.		
16.		
17.		
18.		
19.		
20.		
Totals		

1

Grandmother
Handcrafted • ANDR
795QX5767 • Value **$21**

2

Grandpa
Handcrafted • CROW
895QX5769 • Value **$17**

3

Grandparents
Glass • LYLE
500QX2419 • Value **$13**

4

Grandson
Handcrafted • RGRS
695QX5787 • Value **$18**

5

Happy Wrappers (set/2)
Handcrafted • CROW
1095QX6037 • Value **$21**

6

Heaven's Gift (set/2)
Handcrafted • ANDR
2000QX6057 • Value **$47**

7

Hockey Pup
Handcrafted • CROW
995QX5917 • Value **$23**

8

Important Memo
Handcrafted • SICK
895QX5947 • Value **$17**

9

In a Heartbeat
Handcrafted • ANDR
895QX5817 • Value **$20**

10

In Time With Christmas
Handcrafted • CROW
1295QX6049 • Value **$27**

11

Joy to the World
Handcrafted • ANDR
895QX5867 • Value **$21**

12

**LEGO® Fireplace
With Santa**
Handcrafted • CROW
1095QX4769 • Value **$26**

13

Lou Rankin Bear
Handcrafted • SIED
995QX4069 • Value **$22**

14

The Magic School Bus™
Handcrafted • RHOD
1095QX5849 • Value **$21**

15

Mary Engelbreit
Glass • N/A
500QX2409 • Value **$16**

16

Merry RV
Handcrafted • PALM
1295QX6027 • Value **$25**

17

Mom
Handcrafted • SIED
795QX5647 • Value **$18**

18

Mom and Dad
Handcrafted • RGRS
995QX5657 • Value **$26**

19

Mom-to-Be
Handcrafted • RHOD
795QX5659 • Value **$16**

20

Muletide Greetings
Handcrafted • CHAD
795QX6009 • Value **$16**

General Keepsake

	Price Paid	Value
1.		
2.		
3.		
4.		
5.		
6.		
7.		
8.		
9.		
10.		
11.		
12.		
13.		
14.		
15.		
16.		
17.		
18.		
19.		
20.		
Totals		

1
New Home
Handcrafted • ANDR
895QX5839 • **Value $18**

2
North Pole 911
Handcrafted • SEAL
1095QX5957 • **Value $23**

3
Number One Teacher
Handcrafted • SEAL
795QX5949 • **Value $17**

4
The Olympic Spirit Centennial Games Atlanta 1996
Acrylic • N/A
795QX3169 • **Value $20**

5
On the Ice
Handcrafted • CROW
795QX6047 • **Value $21**

6
Our Christmas Together
Handcrafted • LYLE
995QX5809 • **Value $19**

7
Our Family
Handcrafted • CHAD
795QX5709 • **Value $17**

8
Our First Christmas
Handcrafted • LYLE
1695QX5797 • **Value $30**

9
Our First Christmas Together
Acrylic • LYLE
695QX3177 • **Value $17**

10
Our First Christmas Together
Handcrafted • SIED
895QX5799 • **Value $22**

11
Our First Christmas Together
Handcrafted • SEAL
895QX5807 • **Value $20**

12
Our Little Blessings
Handcrafted • CROW
1295QX5209 • **Value $27**

13
Packed With Memories
Handcrafted • SEAL
795QX5639 • **Value $20**

14
Percy, Flit and Meeko
Handcrafted • CROW
995QXI6179 • **Value $22**

15
Perfect Balance
Handcrafted • SIED
795QX5927 • **Value $18**

16
PEZ® Santa
Handcrafted • FRAN
795QX5267 • **Value $20**

17
Pocahontas
Handcrafted • CROW
1295QXI6177 • **Value $23**

18
Pocahontas and Captain John Smith
Handcrafted • CROW
1495QXI6197 • **Value $25**

19
Polar Coaster
Handcrafted • CROW
895QX6117 • **Value $24**

20
Popeye®
Handcrafted • CHAD
1095QX5257 • **Value $27**

General Keepsake

	Price Paid	Value
1.		
2.		
3.		
4.		
5.		
6.		
7.		
8.		
9.		
10.		
11.		
12.		
13.		
14.		
15.		
16.		
17.		
18.		
19.		
20.		
Totals		

1

Refreshing Gift
Handcrafted • UNRU
1495QX4067 • **Value $30**

2

Rejoice!
Handcrafted • LYLE
1095QX5987 • **Value $24**

3

Roller Whiz
Handcrafted • SEAL
795QX5937 • **Value $19**

4

Santa In Paris
Handcrafted • SICK
895QX5877 • **Value $26**

5

Santa's Serenade
Handcrafted • CROW
895QX6017 • **Value $19**

6

Santa's Visitors
Glass • N/A
500QX2407 • **Value $18**

7

**Simba, Pumbaa
and Timon**
Handcrafted • CROW
1295QX6159 • **Value $21**

8

Sister
Handcrafted • LYLE
695QX5687 • **Value $15**

9

Sister to Sister
Handcrafted • VOTR
895QX5689 • **Value $18**

10

Ski Hound
Handcrafted • RHOD
895QX5909 • **Value $20**

11

Son
Handcrafted • PALM
695QX5669 • **Value $18**

12

Special Cat
Handcrafted • CHAD
795QX5717 • **Value $17**

13

Special Dog
Handcrafted • CHAD
795QX5719 • **Value $17**

14

Surfin' Santa
Handcrafted • CROW
995QX6019 • **Value $26**

15

**Sylvester and
Tweety (set/2)**
Handcrafted • CHAD
1395QX5017 • **Value $25**

16

Takin' a Hike
Handcrafted • FRAN
795QX6029 • **Value $19**

17

Tennis, Anyone?
Handcrafted • AUBE
795QX5907 • **Value $19**

18

**Thomas the Tank
Engine – No. 1**
Handcrafted • RHOD
995QX5857 • **Value $33**

19

Three Wishes
Handcrafted • ANDR
795QX5979 • **Value $21**

20

Two for Tea
Handcrafted • JLEE
995QX5829 • **Value $30**

General Keepsake		
	Price Paid	Value
1.		
2.		
3.		
4.		
5.		
6.		
7.		
8.		
9.		
10.		
11.		
12.		
13.		
14.		
15.		
16.		
17.		
18.		
19.		
20.		
Totals		

1

Vera the Mouse
Porcelain • N/A
895QX5537 • **Value $18**

2

Waiting Up for Santa
Handcrafted • PALM
895QX6106 • **Value $17**

3

Water Sports (set/2)
Handcrafted • SIED
1495QX6039 • **Value $37**

4

Wheel of Fortune®
Handcrafted • SICK
1295QX6187 • **Value $25**

5

**Winnie the Pooh
and Tigger**
Handcrafted • SIED
1295QX5009 • **Value $34**

6

The Winning Play
Handcrafted • SIED
795QX5889 • **Value $22**

7

Baby's First Christmas
Handcrafted • CROW
2200QLX7317 • **Value $39**

8

Coming to See Santa
Handcrafted • PALM
3200QLX7369 • **Value $64**

9

Fred and Dino
Handcrafted • RHOD
2800QLX7289 • **Value $53**

10

Friends Share Fun
Handcrafted • RGRS
1650QLX7349 • **Value $35**

11

Goody Gumballs!
Handcrafted • SIED
1250QLX7367 • **Value $32**

12

Headin' Home
Handcrafted • JLEE
2200QLX7327 • **Value $46**

13

Holiday Swim
Handcrafted • RGRS
1850QLX7319 • **Value $37**

14

Jumping for Joy
Handcrafted • FRAN
2800QLX7347 • **Value $52**

15

**My First HOT
WHEELS™**
Handcrafted • CROW
2800QLX7279 • **Value $52**

16

Romulan Warbird™
Handcrafted • NORT
2400QXI7267 • **Value $43**

17

Santa's Diner
Handcrafted • VOTR
2450QLX7337 • **Value $37**

18

Space Shuttle
Handcrafted • CROW
2450QLX7396 • **Value $46**

19

Superman™
Handcrafted • CHAD
2800QLX7309 • **Value $50**

20

Victorian Toy Box
Handcrafted • LYLE
4200QLX7357 • **Value $64**

General Keepsake	Price Paid	Value
1.		
2.		
3.		
4.		
5.		
6.		
General Magic		
7.		
8.		
9.		
10.		
11.		
12.		
13.		
14.		
15.		
16.		
17.		
18.		
19.		
20.		
Totals		

1

Wee Little Christmas
Handcrafted • CROW
2200QLX7329 • **Value $44**

2

Winnie the Pooh
Too Much Hunny
Handcrafted • SIED
2450QLX7297 • **Value $53**

3

Angel of Light
All Is Bright
Handcrafted • ANDR
1195QK1159 • **Value $23**

4

Gentle Lullaby
All Is Bright
Handcrafted • ANDR
1195QK1157 • **Value $23**

5

Carole
Angel Bells
Porcelain • VOTR
1295QK1147 • **Value $28**

6
Joy
Angel Bells
Porcelain • VOTR
1295QK1137 • **Value $31**

7

Noelle
Angel Bells
Porcelain • VOTR
1295QK1139 • **Value $25**

8

Fetching the Firewood
Folk Art Americana
Handcrafted • SICK
1595QK1057 • **Value $35**

9

Fishing Party
Folk Art Americana
Handcrafted • SICK
1595QK1039 • **Value $35**

10
Guiding Santa
Folk Art Americana
Handcrafted • SICK
1895QK1037 • **Value $46**

11

Learning to Skate
Folk Art Americana
Handcrafted • SICK
1495QK1047 • **Value $38**

12

Away in a Manger
Holiday Enchantment
Porcelain • N/A
1395QK1097 • **Value $27**

13

Following the Star
Holiday Enchantment
Porcelain • VOTR
1395QK1099 • **Value $27**

14

Cozy Cottage Teapot
Invitation To Tea
Handcrafted • ANDR
1595QK1127 • **Value $29**

15

European Castle Teapot
Invitation To Tea
Handcrafted • ANDR
1595QK1129 • **Value $29**

16

Victorian Home Teapot
Invitation To Tea
Handcrafted • ANDR
1595QK1119 • **Value $33**

17

Backyard Orchard
Nature's Sketchbook
Handcrafted • FRAN
1895QK1069 • **Value $32**

18

Christmas Cardinal
Nature's Sketchbook
Handcrafted • LYLE
1895QK1077 • **Value $42**

19

Raising a Family
Nature's Sketchbook
Handcrafted • LYLE
1895QK1067 • **Value $32**

20

Violets and Butterflies
Nature's Sketchbook
Handcrafted • LYLE
1695QK1079 • **Value $32**

General Magic

	Price Paid	Value
1.		
2.		

General Showcase

3.		
4.		
5.		
6.		
7.		
8.		
9.		
10.		
11.		
12.		
13.		
14.		
15.		
16.		
17.		
18.		
19.		
20.		

Totals

1995 Collection

1

Jolly Santa
Symbols Of Christmas
Handcrafted • ANDR
1595QK1087 • **Value $27**

2

Sweet Song
Symbols Of Christmas
Handcrafted • ANDR
1595QK1089 • **Value $27**

3

Baby's First Christmas
Handcrafted • SEAL
475QXM4027 • **Value $13**

4

Calamity Coyote
Handcrafted • RGRS
675QXM4467 • **Value $16**

5

Christmas Wishes
Handcrafted • SEAL
375QXM4087 • **Value $16**

6

Cloisonné Partridge
Cloisonné • VOTR
975QXM4017 • **Value $19**

7

Downhill Double
Handcrafted • PALM
475QXM4837 • **Value $12**

8

Friendship Duet
Handcrafted • UNRU
475QXM4019 • **Value $13**

9

Furrball
Handcrafted • RGRS
575QXM4459 • **Value $16**

10

Grandpa's Gift
Handcrafted • RGRS
575QXM4829 • **Value $13**

11

Heavenly Praises
Handcrafted • ANDR
575QXM4037 • **Value $13**

12

Joyful Santa
Handcrafted • UNRU
475QXM4089 • **Value $13**

13

Little Beeper
Handcrafted • RGRS
575QXM4469 • **Value $16**

14

Merry Walruses
Handcrafted • SICK
575QXM4057 • **Value $22**

15

**A Moustershire
Christmas (set/4)**
Handcrafted • RHOD
2450QXM4839 • **Value $43**

16

**Pebbles and
Bamm-Bamm**
Handcrafted • RHOD
975QXM4757 • **Value $18**

17

Playful Penguins
Handcrafted • SICK
575QXM4059 • **Value $24**

18

Precious Creations
Handcrafted • SICK
975QXM4077 • **Value $19**

19

Santa's Visit
Handcrafted • CROW
775QXM4047 • **Value $18**

20

**The Ships of STAR
TREK® (set/3)**
Handcrafted • N/A
1995QXI4109 • **Value $29**

General Showcase	Price Paid	Value
1.		
2.		
General Miniature		
3.		
4.		
5.		
6.		
7.		
8.		
9.		
10.		
11.		
12.		
13.		
14.		
15.		
16.		
17.		
18.		
19.		
20.		

Totals

1

Starlit Nativity
Handcrafted • UNRU
775QXM4039 • **Value $19**

2

Sugarplum Dreams
Handcrafted • CROW
475QXM4099 • **Value $14**

3

Tiny Treasures (set/6)
Handcrafted • SEAL
2900QXM4009 • **Value $47**

4

Tunnel of Love
Handcrafted • CROW
475QXM4029 • **Value $13**

5

Cinderella's Stepsisters
(gift membership bonus,
Merry Miniature)
Handcrafted • PIKE
375QXC4159 • **Value N/E**

6

Collecting Memories
(keepsake of membership)
Handcrafted • SIED
QXC4117 • **Value $22**

7

Cool Santa (keepsake of
membership, miniature)
Handcrafted • FRAN
QXC4457 • **Value $16**

8

Cozy Christmas (early
renewal gift, miniature)
Handcrafted • FRAN
QXC4119 • **Value $19**

9

Fishing For Fun
(keepsake of membership)
Handcrafted • SEAL
QXC5207 • **Value $22**

10

A Gift From Rodney
(keepsake of
membership, miniature)
Handcrafted • SICK
QXC4129 • **Value $16**

11

Home From The Woods
(club edition)
Handcrafted • SICK
1595QXC1059 • **Value $55**

12

May Flower (club edi-
tion, Easter sidekick)
Handcrafted • SIED
495QXC8246 • **Value $48**

13

Happy Holidays
Handcrafted • VOTR
295QX6307 • **Value $14**

14

Hooked On Collecting –
1995 – Ornament Premiere
Handcrafted • PALM
(N/C) No stock # • **Value $10**

15

Wish List
Handcrafted • SEAL
1500QX5859 • **Value $24**

16

Charlie Brown
A Charlie Brown Christmas
Handcrafted • SIED
395QRP4207 • **Value $25**

17

Linus
A Charlie Brown Christmas
Handcrafted • RGRS
395QRP4217 • **Value $20**

18

Lucy
A Charlie Brown Christmas
Handcrafted • SIED
395QRP4209 • **Value $20**

19

SNOOPY
A Charlie Brown Christmas
Handcrafted • RGRS
395QRP4219 • **Value $27**

20

WOODSTOCK w/tree
and snowbase
A Charlie Brown Christmas
Handcrafted • RGRS
395QRP4227 • **Value $18**

General Miniature		
	Price Paid	Value
1.		
2.		
3.		
4.		
Collector's Club		
5.		
6.		
7.		
8.		
9.		
10.		
11.		
12.		
Premiere Ornaments		
13.		
14.		
15.		
Reach Ornaments		
16.		
17.		
18.		
19.		
20.		
Totals		

1995 Collection

1

Happy Holidays® BARBIE™ Stocking Hanger
Handcrafted • N/A
1995XSH3119 • **Value $16**

2

Holiday BARBIE™ Lapel Pin
Handcrafted • N/A
495XLP3547 • **Value N/E**

3

Holiday Memories™ BARBIE® Doll (2nd in series)
Vinyl • N/A
4500XPF3407 • **Value $110**

4

1956 Ford Truck (black)
Handcrafted • PALM
(N/C) No stock # • **Value N/E**

5

Artists' Caricature Ball Ornament
Glass • N/A
($7.95) No stock # • **Value $25**

6

Christmas Eve Bake-Off
Handcrafted • VARI
6000QXC4049 • **Value $115**

7

Cookie Time
Handcrafted • VOTR
($12.95) No stock # • **Value $24**

8

Murray® Champion (red)
Die-Cast Metal • PALM
(N/C) No stock # • **Value N/E**

BARBIE™ Collectibles

	Price Paid	Value
1.		
2.		
3.		

Expo Ornaments

4.		
5.		
6.		
7.		
8.		
9.		
10.		

NFL Collection

11.		
12.		

Personalized Ornaments

13.		
14.		
15.		

Totals

9

Murray® Fire Truck (white)
Die-Cast Metal • PALM
(N/C) No stock # • **Value N/E**

10

Pewter Rocking Horse (miniature)
Pewter • N/A
($7.95) No stock # • **Value $55**

11

NFL COLLECTION (10 assorted, re-issued in 1996)
Glass • N/A

1. Carolina Panthers™
595PNA2035 • **Value $10**
2. Chicago Bears™
595BRS2035 • **Value $10**
3. Dallas Cowboys™
595COW2035 • **Value $10**
4. Kansas City Chiefs™
595CHF2035 • **Value $10**
5. Los Angeles Raiders™
595RDR2035 • **Value $10**
6. Minnesota Vikings™
595VIK2035 • **Value $10**
7. New England Patriots™
595NEP2035 • **Value $10**
8. Philadelphia Eagles™
595EAG2035 • **Value $10**
9. San Francisco 49ers™
595FOR2035 • **Value $10**
10. Washington Redskins™
595RSK2035 • **Value $10**

12

NFL COLLECTION (10 assorted)
Handcrafted • SIED

1. Carolina Panthers™
995QSR6227 • **Value $30**
2. Chicago Bears™
995QSR6237 • **Value $30**
3. Dallas Cowboys™
995QSR6217 • **Value $30**
4. Kansas City Chiefs™
995QSR6257 • **Value $30**
5. Los Angeles Raiders™
995QSR6249 • **Value $30**
6. Minnesota Vikings™
995QSR6267 • **Value $30**
7. New England Patriots™
995QSR6228 • **Value $30**
8. Philadelphia Eagles™
995QSR6259 • **Value $30**
9. San Francisco 49ers™
995QSR6239 • **Value $30**
10. Washington Redskins™
995QSR6247 • **Value $30**

13

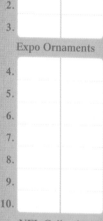

Baby Bear
Handcrafted • ANDR
1295QP6157 • **Value N/E**

14

The Champ
Handcrafted • VOTR
1295QP6127 • **Value N/E**

15

Computer Cat 'n' Mouse (re-issued from 1994)
Handcrafted • SEAL
1295QP6046 • **Value N/E**

1

Cookie Time
(re-issued from 1994)
Handcrafted • VOTR
1295QP6073 • **Value N/E**

2

Etch-A-Sketch®
(re-issued from 1994)
Handcrafted • CROW
1295QP6015 • **Value N/E**

3

From The Heart
(re-issued from 1994)
Handcrafted • RHOD
1495QP6036 • **Value N/E**

4

Key Note
Handcrafted • SEAL
1295QP6149 • **Value N/E**

5

Mailbox Delivery
(re-issued from 1993)
Handcrafted • CROW
1495QP6015 • **Value N/E**

6

Novel Idea
(re-issued from 1994)
Handcrafted • VOTR
1295QP6066 • **Value N/E**

7

On the Billboard
(re-issued from 1993)
Handcrafted • CROW
1295QP6022 • **Value N/E**

8

Playing Ball
(re-issued from 1993)
Handcrafted • FRAN
1295QP6032 • **Value N/E**

9

Reindeer Rooters
(re-issued from 1994)
Handcrafted • CROW
1295QP6056 • **Value N/E**

1994

Hallmark created a sensation in 1994 with the release of "The Beatles Gift Set," as well as several new ornaments featuring LOONEY TUNES™ and Wizard of OZ™ characters. The 1994 collection featured 149 Keepsake, 24 Magic, 18 Showcase and 38 Miniature ornaments. See the collectible series section for more 1994 ornaments.

10

Across the Miles
Handcrafted • ANDR
895QX5656 • **Value $20**

11

All Pumped Up
Handcrafted • RHOD
895QX5923 • **Value $20**

12

Angel Hare
Handcrafted/Brass • SICK
895QX5896 • **Value $23**

13

Anniversary Year
Brass/Chrome • BISH
1095QX5683 • **Value $23**

14

Baby's First Christmas
Handcrafted • VOTR
795QX5636 • **Value $24**

15

Baby's First Christmas
Handcrafted • N/A
795QX5713 • **Value $30**

Personalized Ornaments

	Price Paid	Value
1.		
2.		
3.		
4.		
5.		
6.		
7.		
8.		
9.		

General Keepsake

10.		
11.		
12.		
13.		
14.		
15.		

Totals

1994 Collection

1

Baby's First Christmas
Handcrafted • SEAL
1295QX5743 • **Value $28**

2

Baby's First Christmas
Porcelain/Brass • UNRU
1895QX5633 • **Value $33**

3

Baby's First Christmas – Baby Boy
Glass • N/A
500QX2436 • **Value $18**

4

Baby's First Christmas – Baby Girl
Glass • N/A
500QX2433 • **Value $18**

5

Baby's Second Christmas
Handcrafted • CROW
795QX5716 • **Value $23**

6

Barney™
Handcrafted • RHOD
995QX5966 • **Value $25**

7

Batman
Handcrafted • CHAD
1295QX5853 • **Value $28**

8

The Beatles Gift Set
Handcrafted • RGRS
4800QX5373 • **Value $100**

9

Big Shot
Handcrafted • SIED
795QX5873 • **Value $19**

10

Brother
Handcrafted • PIKE
695QX5516 • **Value $17**

11

Busy Batter
Handcrafted • SIED
795QX5876 • **Value $20**

12

Candy Caper
Handcrafted • ANDR
895QX5776 • **Value $22**

13

Caring Doctor
Handcrafted • RGRS
895QX5823 • **Value $18**

14

Champion Teacher
Handcrafted • SIED
695QX5836 • **Value $17**

15

Cheers To You!
Handcrafted/Brass • CROW
1095QX5796 • **Value $27**

16

Cheery Cyclists
Handcrafted • CROW
1295QX5786 • **Value $27**

17

Child Care Giver
Handcrafted • VOTR
795QX5906 • **Value $16**

18

Child's Fifth Christmas
Handcrafted • RHOD
695QX5733 • **Value $19**

19

Child's Fourth Christmas
Handcrafted • FRAN
695QX5726 • **Value $20**

20

Child's Third Christmas
Handcrafted • FRAN
695QX5723 • **Value $21**

General Keepsake

	Price Paid	Value
1.		
2.		
3.		
4.		
5.		
6.		
7.		
8.		
9.		
10.		
11.		
12.		
13.		
14.		
15.		
16.		
17.		
18.		
19.		
20.		

Totals

1
Coach
Handcrafted • UNRU
795QX5933 • **Value $17**

2
Cock-a-Doodle Christmas
Handcrafted • VOTR
895QX5396 • **Value $27**

3
Colors of Joy
Handcrafted • SEAL
795QX5893 • **Value $20**

4
The Cowardly Lion
Handcrafted • ANDR
995QX5446 • **Value $47**

5
Dad
Handcrafted • RGRS
795QX5463 • **Value $17**

6
Dad-to-Be
Handcrafted • PIKE
795QX5473 • **Value $18**

7
Daffy Duck
Handcrafted • PALM
895QX5415 • **Value $23**

8
Daisy Days
Handcrafted • CHAD
995QX5986 • **Value $21**

9
Daughter
Handcrafted • ANDR
695QX5623 • **Value $19**

10
Dear Santa Mouse (set/2)
Handcrafted • CROW
1495QX5806 • **Value $30**

11
Dorothy and Toto
Handcrafted • LYLE
1095QX5433 • **Value $83**

12
Extra-Special Delivery
Handcrafted • CROW
795QX5833 • **Value $19**

13
Feelin' Groovy
Handcrafted • N/A
795QX5953 • **Value $26**

14
A Feline of Christmas
Handcrafted • ANDR
895QX5816 • **Value $30**

15
Feliz Navidad
Handcrafted • RGRS
895QX5793 • **Value $24**

16
Follow the Sun
Handcrafted • CROW
895QX5846 • **Value $19**

17
For My Grandma
Handcrafted • DLEE
695QX5613 • **Value $17**

18
Fred and Barney
Handcrafted • RHOD
1495QX5003 • **Value $32**

19
Friendly Push
Handcrafted • SIED
895QX5686 • **Value $20**

20
Friendship Sundae
Handcrafted • SICK
1095QX4766 • **Value $26**

General Keepsake

	Price Paid	Value
1.		
2.		
3.		
4.		
5.		
6.		
7.		
8.		
9.		
10.		
11.		
12.		
13.		
14.		
15.		
16.		
17.		
18.		
19.		
20.		

Totals

1

GARFIELD
Handcrafted • N/A
1295QX5753 • **Value $32**

2

Gentle Nurse
Handcrafted • LYLE
695QX5973 • **Value $21**

3

Godchild
Handcrafted • RGRS
895QX4453 • **Value $24**

4

Godparent
Glass • N/A
500QX2423 • **Value $21**

5

Grandchild's First Christmas
Handcrafted • UNRU
795QX5676 • **Value $19**

6

Granddaughter
Handcrafted • PIKE
695QX5523 • **Value $18**

7

Grandmother
Handcrafted • ANDR
795QX5673 • **Value $18**

8

Grandpa
Handcrafted • UNRU
795QX5616 • **Value $21**

9

Grandparents
Glass • N/A
500QX2426 • **Value $17**

10

Grandson
Handcrafted • PIKE
695QX5526 • **Value $18**

11

Happy Birthday, Jesus
Handcrafted • LYLE
1295QX5423 • **Value $30**

12

Harvest Joy
Handcrafted • CHAD
995QX5993 • **Value $20**

13

Hearts in Harmony
Porcelain • ANDR
1095QX4406 • **Value $25**

14

Helpful Shepherd
Handcrafted • CHAD
895QX5536 • **Value $22**

15

Holiday Patrol
Handcrafted • RHOD
895QX5826 • **Value $18**

16

Ice Show
Handcrafted • ANDR
795QX5946 • **Value $20**

17

In the Pink
Handcrafted • ANDR
995QX5763 • **Value $23**

18
It's a Strike
Handcrafted • SIED
895QX5856 • **Value $21**

19
Jingle Bell Band
Handcrafted • CROW
1095QX5783 • **Value $31**

20
Joyous Song
Handcrafted • ANDR
895QX4473 • **Value $20**

General Keepsake

	Price Paid	Value
1.		
2.		
3.		
4.		
5.		
6.		
7.		
8.		
9.		
10.		
11.		
12.		
13.		
14.		
15.		
16.		
17.		
18.		
19.		
20.		
Totals		

1

Jump-along Jackalope
Handcrafted • FRAN
895QX5756 • **Value $18**

2

Keep on Mowin'
Handcrafted • SIED
895QX5413 • **Value $18**

3

Kickin' Roo
Handcrafted • SIED
795QX5916 • **Value $18**

4

Kitty's Catamaran
Handcrafted • SEAL
1095QX5416 • **Value $23**

5

Kringle's Kayak
Handcrafted • SEAL
795QX5886 • **Value $22**

6

Lou Rankin Seal
Handcrafted • BISH
995QX5456 • **Value $22**

7

Lucinda and Teddy
Handcrafted/Fabric • UNRU
2175QX4813 • **Value $40**

8

Magic Carpet Ride
Handcrafted • SEAL
795QX5883 • **Value $24**

9

Making It Bright
Handcrafted • RHOD
895QX5403 • **Value $20**

10

Mary Engelbreit
Glass • N/A
500QX2416 • **Value $19**

11

Merry Fishmas
Handcrafted • PALM
895QX5913 • **Value $22**

12

Mistletoe Surprise (set/2)
Handcrafted • SEAL
1295QX5996 • **Value $32**

13

Mom
Handcrafted • RGRS
795QX5466 • **Value $18**

14

Mom and Dad
Handcrafted • SIED
995QX5666 • **Value $24**

15

Mom-to-Be
Handcrafted • PIKE
795QX5506 • **Value $18**

16

Mufasa and Simba
Handcrafted • CROW
1495QX5406 • **Value $29**

17

Nephew
Handcrafted • FRAN
795QX5546 • **Value $17**

18

New Home
Handcrafted • ANDR
895QX5663 • **Value $22**

19

Niece
Handcrafted • FRAN
795QX5543 • **Value $17**

20

Norman Rockwell Art
Glass • LYLE
500QX2413 • **Value $18**

General Keepsake

	Price Paid	Value
1.		
2.		
3.		
4.		
5.		
6.		
7.		
8.		
9.		
10.		
11.		
12.		
13.		
14.		
15.		
16.		
17.		
18.		
19.		
20.		

Totals

1994 Collection

1

Open-and-Shut Holiday
Handcrafted • SIED
995QX5696 • **Value $23**

2

Our Christmas Together
Handcrafted • RGRS
995QX4816 • **Value $22**

3

Our Family
Handcrafted • ANDR
795QX5576 • **Value $19**

4

Our First Christmas Together
Acrylic • VOTR
695QX3186 • **Value $17**

5

Our First Christmas Together
Brass/Fabric • ANDR
1895QX5706 • **Value $31**

6

Our First Christmas Together
Handcrafted • PALM
895QX5653 • **Value $22**

7

Our First Christmas Together
Handcrafted • BISH
995QX5643 • **Value $25**

8

Out of This World Teacher
Handcrafted • UNRU
795QX5766 • **Value $20**

General Keepsake

	Price Paid	Value
1.		
2.		
3.		
4.		
5.		
6.		
7.		
8.		
9.		
10.		
11.		
12.		
13.		
14.		
15.		
16.		
17.		
18.		
19.		
20.		

9

Practice Makes Perfect
Handcrafted • PALM
895QX5863 • **Value $19**

10

Red Hot Holiday
Handcrafted • RGRS
795QX5843 • **Value $18**

11

Reindeer Pro
Handcrafted • RHOD
795QX5926 • **Value $20**

12

Relaxing Moment
Handcrafted • FRAN
1495QX5356 • **Value $32**

13

Road Runner and Wile E. Coyote
Handcrafted • CHAD
1295QX5602 • **Value $30**

14

Santa's LEGO® Sleigh
Handcrafted • CROW
1095QX5453 • **Value $33**

15

The Scarecrow
Handcrafted • UNRU
995QX5436 • **Value $50**

16

Secret Santa
Handcrafted • UNRU
795QX5736 • **Value $19**

17

A Sharp Flat
Handcrafted • CROW
1095QX5773 • **Value $25**

18

Simba and Nala (set/2)
Handcrafted • CROW
1295QX5303 • **Value $30**

19

Sister
Handcrafted • PIKE
695QX5513 • **Value $19**

20

Sister to Sister
Handcrafted • RHOD
995QX5533 • **Value $26**

Totals

VALUE GUIDE — HALLMARK KEEPSAKE ORNAMENTS

1

Son
Handcrafted • ANDR
695QX5626 • **Value $17**

2

Special Cat
Acrylic • RHOD
795QX5606 • **Value $17**

3

Special Dog
Handcrafted • RHOD
795QX5603 • **Value $17**

4

Speedy Gonzales
Handcrafted • PALM
895QX5343 • **Value $22**

5

Stamp of Approval
Handcrafted • SICK
795QX5703 • **Value $18**

6

Sweet Greeting (set/2)
Handcrafted • PALM
1095QX5803 • **Value $25**

7

The Tale of Peter Rabbit
BEATRIX POTTER
Glass • N/A
500QX2443 • **Value $21**

8

Tasmanian Devil
Handcrafted • PALM
895QX5605 • **Value $57**

9

Thick 'n' Thin
Handcrafted • RGRS
1095QX5693 • **Value $22**

10

Thrill a Minute
Handcrafted • SIED
895QX5866 • **Value $21**

11

Time of Peace
Handcrafted • ANDR
795QX5813 • **Value $18**

12

Timon and Pumbaa
Handcrafted • CROW
895QX5366 • **Value $24**

13

The Tin Man
Handcrafted • UNRU
995QX5443 • **Value $52**

14

Tou Can Love
Handcrafted • RGRS
895QX5646 • **Value $21**

15

Tulip Time
Handcrafted • CHAD
995QX5983 • **Value $20**

16

**Winnie the Pooh
and Tigger**
Handcrafted • SIED
1295QX5746 • **Value $37**

17

Yosemite Sam
Handcrafted • PALM
895QX5346 • **Value $20**

18

Yuletide Cheer
Handcrafted • CHAD
995QX5976 • **Value $21**

19

Away in a Manger
Handcrafted • LYLE
1600QLX7383 • **Value $38**

20

Baby's First Christmas
Handcrafted • FRAN
2000QLX7466 • **Value $44**

General Keepsake

	Price Paid	Value
1.		
2.		
3.		
4.		
5.		
6.		
7.		
8.		
9.		
10.		
11.		
12.		
13.		
14.		
15.		
16.		
17.		
18.		

General Magic

19.		
20.		

Totals

153

1994 Collection

1

Barney™
Handcrafted • N/A
2400QLX7506 • **Value $48**

2

Candy Cane Lookout
Handcrafted • FRAN
1800QLX7376 • **Value $77**

3

Conversations With Santa
Handcrafted • SEAL
2800QLX7426 • **Value $60**

4

Country Showtime
Handcrafted • SICK
2200QLX7416 • **Value $49**

5

The Eagle Has Landed
Handcrafted • SEAL
2400QLX7486 • **Value $54**

6

Feliz Navidad
Handcrafted • CROW
2800QLX7433 • **Value $64**

7

Gingerbread Fantasy
Handcrafted • PALM
4400QLX7382 • **Value $95**

8

Klingon Bird of Prey™
Handcrafted • NORT
2400QLX7386 • **Value $50**

9

Kringle Trolley
Handcrafted • CROW
2000QLX7413 • **Value $46**

10

Maxine
Handcrafted • SICK
2000QLX7503 • **Value $51**

11

Peekaboo Pup
Handcrafted • RGRS
2000QLX7423 • **Value $45**

12

Rock Candy Miner
Handcrafted • SIED
2000QLX7403 • **Value $38**

13

Santa's Sing-Along
Handcrafted • CROW
2400QLX7473 • **Value $56**

14

Simba, Sarabi and Mufasa
Handcrafted • CROW
2000QLX7516 • **Value $40**

15

Simba, Sarabi and Mufasa (recalled due to defective sound)
Handcrafted • CROW
3200QLX7513 • **Value $76**

16

Very Merry Minutes
Handcrafted • VOTR
2400QLX7443 • **Value $49**

17

White Christmas
Handcrafted • DLEE
2800QLX7463 • **Value $65**

18

Winnie the Pooh Parade
Handcrafted • CROW
3200QLX7493 • **Value $72**

19

Home for the Holidays
Christmas Lights
Porcelain • PALM
1575QK1123 • **Value $22**

20

Moonbeams
Christmas Lights
Porcelain • ANDR
1575QK1116 • **Value $20**

General Magic

	Price Paid	Value
1.		
2.		
3.		
4.		
5.		
6.		
7.		
8.		
9.		
10.		
11.		
12.		
13.		
14.		
15.		
16.		
17.		
18.		

General Showcase

19.		
20.		

Totals

1
Mother and Child
Christmas Lights
Porcelain • RGRS
1575QK1126 • **Value $20**

2
Peaceful Village
Christmas Lights
Porcelain • CHAD
1575QK1106 • **Value $20**

3
Catching 40 Winks
Folk Art Americana
Handcrafted • SICK
1675QK1183 • **Value $36**

4
Going to Town
Folk Art Americana
Handcrafted • SICK
1575QK1166 • **Value $35**

5
Racing Through the Snow
Folk Art Americana
Handcrafted • SICK
1575QK1173 • **Value $48**

6
Rarin' to Go
Folk Art Americana
Handcrafted • SICK
1575QK1193 • **Value $38**

7
Roundup Time
Folk Art Americana
Handcrafted • SICK
1675QK1176 • **Value $35**

8
Dapper Snowman
Holiday Favorites
Porcelain • VOTR
1375QK1053 • **Value $20**

9
Graceful Fawn
Holiday Favorites
Porcelain • VOTR
1175QK1033 • **Value $20**

10
Jolly Santa
Holiday Favorites
Porcelain • VOTR
1375QK1046 • **Value $26**

11
Joyful Lamb
Holiday Favorites
Porcelain • VOTR
1175QK1036 • **Value $20**

12
Peaceful Dove
Holiday Favorites
Porcelain • VOTR
1175QK1043 • **Value $20**

13
Silver Bells
Old-World Silver
Silver-Plated • UNRU
2475QK1026 • **Value $32**

14
Silver Bows
Old-World Silver
Silver-Plated • PALM
2475QK1023 • **Value $32**

15
Silver Poinsettia
Old-World Silver
Silver-Plated • UNRU
2475QK1006 • **Value $33**

16
Silver Snowflakes
Old-World Silver
Silver-Plated • UNRU
2475QK1016 • **Value $32**

17
Babs Bunny
Handcrafted • PALM
575QXM4116 • **Value $16**

18
Baby's First Christmas
Handcrafted • LYLE
575QXM4003 • **Value $16**

19
Baking Tiny Treats (set/6)
Handcrafted • SEAL
2900QXM4033 • **Value $65**

20
Beary Perfect Tree
Handcrafted • BISH
475QXM4076 • **Value $14**

1994 Collection

1

Buster Bunny
Handcrafted • PALM
575QXM5163 • **Value $15**

2

Corny Elf
Handcrafted • RHOD
450QXM4063 • **Value $13**

3

Cute as a Button
Handcrafted • CROW
375QXM4103 • **Value $15**

4

Dazzling Reindeer
Handcrafted • VOTR
975QXM4026 • **Value $23**

5

Dizzy Devil
Handcrafted • PALM
575QXM4133 • **Value $16**

6

Friends Need Hugs
Handcrafted • LYLE
450QXM4016 • **Value $15**

7

Graceful Carousel Horse
Pewter • BISH
775QXM4056 • **Value $19**

8

Hamton
Handcrafted • PALM
575QXM4126 • **Value $15**

9

Have a Cookie
Handcrafted • DLEE
575QXM5166 • **Value $15**

10

Hearts A-Sail
Handcrafted • BISH
575QXM4006 • **Value $14**

11

Jolly Visitor
Handcrafted • SICK
575QXM4053 • **Value $15**

12

Jolly Wolly Snowman
Handcrafted • VOTR
375QXM4093 • **Value $14**

13

Journey to Bethlehem
Handcrafted • LYLE
575QXM4036 • **Value $19**

14

Just My Size
Handcrafted • BISH
375QXM4086 • **Value $12**

15

Love Was Born
Handcrafted • SICK
450QXM4043 • **Value $15**

16

Melodic Cherub
Handcrafted • RGRS
375QXM4066 • **Value $11**

17
A Merry Flight
Handcrafted • CROW
575QXM4073 • **Value $14**

18

Mom
Handcrafted • RGRS
450QXM4013 • **Value $14**

19

Noah's Ark (set/3)
Handcrafted • SICK
2450QXM4106 • **Value $60**

20

Plucky Duck
Handcrafted • PALM
575QXM4123 • **Value $15**

General Miniature

	Price Paid	Value
1.		
2.		
3.		
4.		
5.		
6.		
7.		
8.		
9.		
10.		
11.		
12.		
13.		
14.		
15.		
16.		
17.		
18.		
19.		
20.		

1
Pour Some More
Handcrafted • CHAD
575QXM5156 • **Value $14**

2
Scooting Along
Handcrafted • FRAN
675QXM5173 • **Value $17**

3
Sweet Dreams
Handcrafted • CROW
300QXM4096 • **Value $13**

4
Tea With Teddy
Handcrafted • RGRS
725QXM4046 • **Value $18**

5
First Hello
(gift membership bonus)
Handcrafted • RGRS
QXC4846 • **Value $34**

6
Happy Collecting
(early renewal piece, Merry Miniature)
Handcrafted • N/A
QXC4803 • **Value $36**

7
Holiday Pursuit
(keepsake of membership)
Handcrafted • FRAN
QXC4823 • **Value $30**

8
Jolly Holly Santa
(club edition)
Handcrafted • LYLE
2200QXC4833 • **Value $52**

9
Majestic Deer
(club edition)
Porcelain/Pewter • UNRU
2500QXC4836 • **Value $55**

10
On Cloud Nine
(club edition)
Handcrafted • DLEE
1200QXC4853 • **Value $35**

11
Sweet Bouquet
(keepsake of membership, miniature)
Handcrafted • N/A
QXC4806 • **Value $32**

12
Tilling Time
(Easter sidekick gift)
Handcrafted • SEAL
QXC8256 • **Value $58**

13
Collector's Survival Kit Premiere '94
Handcrafted • RGRS
(N/C) No stock # • **Value $23**

14
Eager for Christmas
Handcrafted • SEAL
1500QX5336 • **Value $30**

15
The Country Church
Sarah, Plain and Tall
Handcrafted • BAUR
795XPR9450 • **Value $22**

16
The Hays Train Station
Sarah, Plain and Tall
Handcrafted • BAUR
795XPR9452 • **Value $22**

17
Mrs. Parkley's General Store
Sarah, Plain and Tall
Handcrafted • BAUR
795XPR9451 • **Value $22**

18
Sarah's Maine Home
Sarah, Plain and Tall
Handcrafted • BAUR
795XPR9454 • **Value $24**

19
Sarah's Prairie Home
Sarah, Plain and Tall
Handcrafted • BAUR
795XPR9453 • **Value $24**

20
Victorian Elegance™ BARBIE® Doll
(1st in series)
Vinyl • N/A
4000XPF3546 • **Value $95**

General Miniature	
	Price Paid	Value
1.		
2.		
3.		
4.		

Collector's Club	
5.		
6.		
7.		
8.		
9.		
10.		
11.		
12.		

Premiere Ornaments	
13.		
14.		

Reach Figurines	
15.		
16.		
17.		
18.		
19.		

BARBIE™ Collectibles	
20.		

Totals

1994 Collection

1

Golden Bows
Gold-Plated • PALM
($10.00) No stock # • **Value $20**

2

Golden Dove of Peace
Gold-Plated • PALM
($10.00) No stock # • **Value $20**

3

Golden Poinsettia
Gold-Plated • UNRU
($10.00) No stock # • **Value $20**

4

Golden Santa
Gold-Plated • UNRU
($10.00) No stock # • **Value $20**

5

Golden Sleigh
Gold-Plated • PALM
($10.00) No stock # • **Value $20**

6

Golden Stars and Holly
Gold-Plated • PALM
($10.00) No stock # • **Value $20**

7

Mrs. Claus' Cupboard
(w/ miniature ornaments)
Handcrafted • N/A
5500QXC4843 • **Value N/E**

8

Baby Block Photoholder
(re-issued from 1993)
Handcrafted • FRAN
1495QP6035 • **Value N/E**

9

Computer Cat 'n' Mouse
(re-issued in 1995)
Handcrafted • SEAL
1295QP6046 • **Value N/E**

10

Cookie Time
(re-issued in 1995)
Handcrafted • VOTR
1295QP6073 • **Value N/E**

11

Etch-A-Sketch®
(re-issued in 1995)
Handcrafted • CROW
1295QP6006 • **Value N/E**

12

Festive Album Photoholder
(re-issued from 1993)
Handcrafted • VOTR
1295QP6025 • **Value N/E**

13

From The Heart
(re-issued in 1995)
Handcrafted • RHOD
1495QP6036 • **Value N/E**

14

Goin' Fishin'
Handcrafted • PALM
1495QP6023 • **Value N/E**

15

Going Golfin'
(re-issued from 1993)
Handcrafted • PALM
1295QP6012 • **Value N/E**

16

Holiday Hello
Handcrafted • SIED
2495QXR6116 • **Value $42**

17

Mailbox Delivery
(re-issued from 1993)
Handcrafted • CROW
1495QP6015 • **Value N/E**

18

Novel Idea
(re-issued in 1995)
Handcrafted • VOTR
1295QP6066 • **Value N/E**

19

On the Billboard
(re-issued from 1993)
Handcrafted • CROW
1295QP6022 • **Value N/E**

20

Playing Ball
(re-issued from 1993)
Handcrafted • FRAN
1295QP6032 • **Value N/E**

Expo Ornaments

	Price Paid	Value
1.		
2.		
3.		
4.		
5.		
6.		
7.		

Personalized Ornaments

8.		
9.		
10.		
11.		
12.		
13.		
14.		
15.		
16.		
17.		
18.		
19.		
20.		

1

Reindeer Rooters
(re-issued in 1995)
Handcrafted • CROW
1295QP6056 • **Value N/E**

2

Santa Says
(re-issued from 1993)
Handcrafted • SEAL
1495QP6005 • **Value N/E**

1993

The 20th anniversary of Keepsake Ornaments was celebrated in 1993 with four special ornaments, including "Glowing Pewter Wreath" and pieces to complement three popular collectible series. Overall, there were 141 Keepsake, 21 Magic, 19 Showcase and 36 Miniature ornaments. See the collectible series section for more 1993 ornaments.

3

Across the Miles
Handcrafted • FRAN
875QX5912 • **Value $21**

4

Anniversary Year Photoholder
Brass/Chrome • LYLE
975QX5972 • **Value $21**

5

Apple for Teacher
Handcrafted • SEAL
775QX5902 • **Value $16**

6

Baby's First Christmas
Handcrafted • CROW
775QX5525 • **Value $32**

7

Baby's First Christmas
Handcrafted • ANDR
1075QX5515 • **Value $23**

8

Baby's First Christmas
Silver-Plated • PALM
1875QX5512 • **Value $40**

9

Baby's First Christmas – Baby Boy
Glass • VOTR
475QX2105 • **Value $17**

10

Baby's First Christmas – Baby Girl
Glass • VOTR
475QX2092 • **Value $17**

11

Baby's First Christmas Photoholder
Handcrafted/Lace • RGRS
775QX5522 • **Value $22**

12

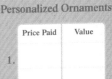

Baby's Second Christmas
Handcrafted • FRAN
675QX5992 • **Value $25**

13

Beary Gifted
Handcrafted • CROW
775QX5762 • **Value $19**

14

Big on Gardening
Handcrafted • VOTR
975QX5842 • **Value $17**

15

Big Roller
Handcrafted • SIED
875QX5352 • **Value $19**

Personalized Ornaments

	Price Paid	Value
1.		
2.		

General Keepsake

3.		
4.		
5.		
6.		
7.		
8.		
9.		
10.		
11.		
12.		
13.		
14.		
15.		

Totals

1

Bird-Watcher
Handcrafted • JLEE
975QX5252 • **Value $18**

2

Bowling for ZZZs
Handcrafted • FRAN
775QX5565 • **Value $17**

3

Brother
Handcrafted • RGRS
675QX5542 • **Value $14**

4

Bugs Bunny
Handcrafted • SICK
875QX5412 • **Value $28**

5

Caring Nurse
Handcrafted • FRAN
675QX5785 • **Value $19**

6

A Child's Christmas
Handcrafted • FRAN
975QX5882 • **Value $23**

7

Child's Fifth Christmas
Handcrafted • RHOD
675QX5222 • **Value $16**

8

Child's Fourth Christmas
Handcrafted • FRAN
675QX5215 • **Value $16**

9

Child's Third Christmas
Handcrafted • FRAN
675QX5995 • **Value $17**

10

Christmas Break
Handcrafted • SEAL
775QX5825 • **Value $24**

11

Clever Cookie
Handcrafted/Tin • SICK
775QX5662 • **Value $26**

12

Coach
Handcrafted • PALM
675QX5935 • **Value $16**

13

Curly 'n' Kingly
Handcrafted/Brass • CROW
1075QX5285 • **Value $23**

14

Dad
Handcrafted • JLEE
775QX5855 • **Value $19**

15

Dad-to-Be
Handcrafted • JLEE
675QX5532 • **Value $15**

16

Daughter
Handcrafted • VOTR
675QX5872 • **Value $22**

17

Dickens Caroler Bell – Lady Daphne
Porcelain • CHAD
2175QX5505 • **Value $42**

18

Dunkin' Roo
Handcrafted • SIED
775QX5575 • **Value $17**

19

Eeyore
Handcrafted • SIED
975QX5712 • **Value $24**

20

Elmer Fudd
Handcrafted • LYLE
875QX5495 • **Value $20**

1

Faithful Fire Fighter
Handcrafted • VOTR
775QX5782 • **Value $18**

2

Feliz Navidad
Handcrafted/Brass • DLEE
875QX5365 • **Value $21**

3

Fills the Bill
Handcrafted • SIED
875QX5572 • **Value $19**

4

Glowing Pewter Wreath
Pewter • UNRU
1875QX5302 • **Value $38**

5

Godchild
Handcrafted • CHAD
875QX5875 • **Value $20**

6

Grandchild's First
Christmas
Handcrafted • FRAN
675QX5552 • **Value $16**

7

Granddaughter
Handcrafted • CHAD
675QX5635 • **Value $17**

8

Grandmother
Handcrafted • ANDR
675QX5665 • **Value $16**

9

Grandparents
Glass • VOTR
475QX2085 • **Value $17**

10

Grandson
Handcrafted • CHAD
675QX5632 • **Value $17**

11

Great Connections (set/2)
Handcrafted • RGRS
1075QX5402 • **Value $27**

12

He Is Born
Handcrafted • LYLE
975QX5362 • **Value $39**

13

High Top-Purr
Handcrafted • SEAL
875QX5332 • **Value $27**

14

Home for Christmas
Handcrafted • SIED
775QX5562 • **Value $17**

15

Howling Good Time
Handcrafted • RGRS
975QX5255 • **Value $21**

16

Icicle Bicycle
Handcrafted • JLEE
975QX5835 • **Value $21**

17

Julianne and Teddy
Handcrafted • UNRU
2175QX5295 • **Value $46**

18

Kanga and Roo
Handcrafted • SIED
975QX5672 • **Value $22**

19

Little Drummer Boy
Handcrafted • PALM
875QX5372 • **Value $20**

20

Look for the Wonder
Handcrafted • DLEE
1275QX5685 • **Value $25**

General Keepsake

	Price Paid	Value
1.		
2.		
3.		
4.		
5.		
6.		
7.		
8.		
9.		
10.		
11.		
12.		
13.		
14.		
15.		
16.		
17.		
18.		
19.		
20.		

Totals

1

Lou Rankin Polar Bear
Handcrafted • RHOD
975QX5745 • **Value $28**

2

Makin' Music
Handcrafted/Brass • SEAL
975QX5325 • **Value $19**

3

Making Waves
Handcrafted • PALM
975QX5775 • **Value $29**

4

Mary Engelbreit
Glass • N/A
500QX2075 • **Value $18**

5

Maxine
Handcrafted • SICK
875QX5385 • **Value $26**

6

Mom
Handcrafted • JLEE
775QX5852 • **Value $19**

7

Mom and Dad
Handcrafted • PALM
975QX5845 • **Value $19**

8

Mom-to-Be
Handcrafted • JLEE
675QX5535 • **Value $17**

9

Nephew
Handcrafted • RGRS
675QX5735 • **Value $13**

10

New Home
Enamel/Metal • PALM
775QX5905 • **Value $32**

11

Niece
Handcrafted • RGRS
675QX5732 • **Value $13**

12

On Her Toes
Handcrafted • ANDR
875QX5265 • **Value $23**

13

One-Elf Marching Band
Handcrafted/Brass • CHAD
1275QX5342 • **Value $28**

14

Our Christmas Together
Handcrafted • DLEE
1075QX5942 • **Value $24**

15

Our Family Photoholder
Handcrafted • UNRU
775QX5892 • **Value $19**

16

**Our First Christmas
Together**
Acrylic • ANDR
675QX3015 • **Value $18**

17

**Our First Christmas
Together**
Brass/Silver-Plated • RGRS
1875QX5955 • **Value $40**

18

**Our First Christmas
Together**
Handcrafted • LYLE
975QX5642 • **Value $18**

19

**Our First Christmas
Together Photoholder**
Handcrafted • UNRU
875QX5952 • **Value $18**

20

Owl
Handcrafted • SIED
975QX5695 • **Value $21**

1

PEANUTS®
Glass • N/A
500QX2072 • **Value $27**

2

Peek-a-Boo Tree
Handcrafted • CROW
1075QX5245 • **Value $25**

3

Peep Inside
Handcrafted • DLEE
1375QX5322 • **Value $27**

4

People Friendly
Handcrafted • SEAL
875QX5932 • **Value $19**

5

Perfect Match
Handcrafted • SIED
875QX5772 • **Value $19**

6

The Pink Panther
Handcrafted • PALM
1275QX5755 • **Value $24**

7

Playful Pals
Handcrafted • RGRS
1475QX5742 • **Value $30**

8

Popping Good Times
(set/2)
Handcrafted • CHAD
1475QX5392 • **Value $30**

9

Porky Pig
Handcrafted • ANDR
875QX5652 • **Value $20**

10

Putt-Putt Penguin
Handcrafted • JLEE
975QX5795 • **Value $22**

11

Quick as a Fox
Handcrafted • CROW
875QX5792 • **Value $19**

12

Rabbit
Handcrafted • SIED
975QX5702 • **Value $22**

13

Ready for Fun
Handcrafted/Tin • LYLE
775QX5124 • **Value $18**

14

Room for One More
Handcrafted • CROW
875QX5382 • **Value $48**

15

Silvery Noel
Silver-Plated • LYLE
1275QX5305 • **Value $35**

16

Sister
Handcrafted • RGRS
675QX5545 • **Value $20**

17

Sister to Sister
Handcrafted • SEAL
975QX5885 • **Value $54**

18

Smile! It's Christmas
Photoholder
Handcrafted • SEAL
975QX5335 • **Value $21**

19

Snow Bear Angel
Handcrafted • JLEE
775QX5355 • **Value $19**

20

Snowbird
Handcrafted • JLEE
775QX5765 • **Value $19**

General Keepsake		
	Price Paid	Value
1.		
2.		
3.		
4.		
5.		
6.		
7.		
8.		
9.		
10.		
11.		
12.		
13.		
14.		
15.		
16.		
17.		
18.		
19.		
20.		
Totals		

1

Snowy Hideaway
Handcrafted • FRAN
975QX5312 • **Value $22**

2

Son
Handcrafted • VOTR
675QX5865 • **Value $20**

3

Special Cat Photoholder
Handcrafted/Brass • VOTR
775QX5235 • **Value $14**

4

Special Dog Photoholder
Handcrafted/Brass • VOTR
775QX5962 • **Value $14**

5

Star of Wonder
Handcrafted • LYLE
675QX5982 • **Value $38**

6

**Star Teacher
Photoholder**
Handcrafted • ANDR
575QX5645 • **Value $13**

7

**Strange and
Wonderful Love**
Handcrafted • SICK
875QX5965 • **Value $18**

8

Superman™
Handcrafted • CHAD
1275QX5752 • **Value $48**

General Keepsake

	Price Paid	Value
1.		
2.		
3.		
4.		
5.		
6.		
7.		
8.		
9.		
10.		
11.		
12.		
13.		
14.		
15.		
16.		
17.		
18.		
19.		
20.		

Totals

9

The Swat Team (set/2)
Handcrafted/Yarn • ANDR
1275QX5395 • **Value $31**

10

Sylvester and Tweety
Handcrafted • PALM
975QX5405 • **Value $33**

11

That's Entertainment
Handcrafted • SIED
875QX5345 • **Value $20**

12

Tigger and Piglet
Handcrafted • SIED
975QX5705 • **Value $47**

13

Tin Airplane
Pressed Tin • SICK
775QX5622 • **Value $28**

14

Tin Blimp
Pressed Tin • SICK
775QX5625 • **Value $18**

15

Tin Hot Air Balloon
Pressed Tin • SICK
775QX5615 • **Value $21**

16

**To My Grandma
Photoholder**
Handcrafted • DLEE
775QX5555 • **Value $17**

17

Top Banana
Handcrafted • RGRS
775QX5925 • **Value $18**

18

Wake-Up Call
Handcrafted • UNRU
875QX5262 • **Value $20**

19

**Warm and Special
Friends**
Handcrafted/Metal • VOTR
1075QX5895 • **Value $26**

20

Water Bed Snooze
Handcrafted • JLEE
975QX5375 • **Value $22**

1

Winnie the Pooh
Handcrafted • SIED
975QX5715 • **Value $36**

2

Baby's First Christmas
Handcrafted • FRAN
2200QLX7365 • **Value $46**

3

Bells Are Ringing
Handcrafted • CROW
2800QLX7402 • **Value $64**

4

Dog's Best Friend
Handcrafted • JLEE
1200QLX7172 • **Value $25**

5

Dollhouse Dreams
Handcrafted • CROW
2200QLX7372 • **Value $48**

6

Home on the Range
Handcrafted • SICK
3200QLX7395 • **Value $68**

7

The Lamplighter
Handcrafted • PALM
1800QLX7192 • **Value $43**

8

Last Minute Shopping
Handcrafted • VOTR
2800QLX7385 • **Value $64**

9

Messages of Christmas
Handcrafted • SIED
3500QLX7476 • **Value $48**

10

North Pole Merrython
Handcrafted • SEAL
2500QLX7392 • **Value $57**

11

Our First Christmas Together
Handcrafted • CHAD
2000QLX7355 • **Value $45**

12

Radio News Flash
Handcrafted • DLEE
2200QLX7362 • **Value $48**

13

Raiding the Fridge
Handcrafted • RGRS
1600QLX7185 • **Value $38**

14

Road Runner and Wile E. Coyote™
Handcrafted • CHAD
3000QLX7415 • **Value $75**

15

Santa's Snow-Getter
Handcrafted • CROW
1800QLX7352 • **Value $42**

16

Santa's Workshop
Handcrafted • SIED
2800QLX7375 • **Value $62**

17

Song of the Chimes
Handcrafted/Brass • ANDR
2500QLX7405 • **Value $58**

18

U.S.S. Enterprise™ THE NEXT GENERATION™
Handcrafted • NORT
2400QLX7412 • **Value $55**

19

Winnie the Pooh
Handcrafted • SIED
2400QLX7422 • **Value $50**

General Keepsake	
Price Paid	**Value**
1.	

General Magic	
2.	
3.	
4.	
5.	
6.	
7.	
8.	
9.	
10.	
11.	
12.	
13.	
14.	
15.	
16.	
17.	
18.	
19.	
Totals	

1

Angel in Flight
Folk Art Americana
Handcrafted • SICK
1575QK1052 • **Value $52**

2

Polar Bear Adventure
Folk Art Americana
Handcrafted • SICK
1500QK1055 • **Value $66**

3

Riding in the Woods
Folk Art Americana
Handcrafted • SICK
1575QK1065 • **Value $70**

4

Riding the Wind
Folk Art Americana
Handcrafted • SICK
1575QK1045 • **Value $60**

5

Santa Claus
Folk Art Americana
Handcrafted • SICK
1675QK1072 • **Value $220**

6

Angelic Messengers
Holiday Enchantment
Porcelain • VOTR
1375QK1032 • **Value $35**

7

Bringing Home the Tree
Holiday Enchantment
Porcelain • CHAD
1375QK1042 • **Value $32**

8

Journey to the Forest
Holiday Enchantment
Porcelain • N/A
1375QK1012 • **Value $30**

9

The Magi
Holiday Enchantment
Porcelain • N/A
1375QK1025 • **Value $32**

10

Visions of Sugarplums
Holiday Enchantment
Porcelain • N/A
1375QK1005 • **Value $32**

11

Silver Dove of Peace
Old-World Silver
Silver-Plated • PALM
2475QK1075 • **Value $37**

12

Silver Santa
Old-World Silver
Silver-Plated • UNRU
2475QK1092 • **Value $52**

13

Silver Sleigh
Old-World Silver
Silver-Plated • PALM
2475QK1082 • **Value $40**

14

Silver Stars and Holly
Old-World Silver
Silver-Plated • PALM
2475QK1085 • **Value $36**

15

Christmas Feast
Portraits in Bisque
Porcelain • PIKE
1575QK1152 • **Value $33**

16

Joy of Sharing
Portraits in Bisque
Porcelain • LYLE
1575QK1142 • **Value $33**

17

Mistletoe Kiss
Portraits in Bisque
Porcelain • PIKE
1575QK1145 • **Value $31**

18

**Norman Rockwell
– Filling the Stockings**
Portraits in Bisque
Porcelain • DUTK
1575QK1155 • **Value $35**

19

**Norman Rockwell
– Jolly Postman**
Portraits in Bisque
Porcelain • DUTK
1575QK1162 • **Value $35**

General Showcase

	Price Paid	Value
1.		
2.		
3.		
4.		
5.		
6.		
7.		
8.		
9.		
10.		
11.		
12.		
13.		
14.		
15.		
16.		
17.		
18.		
19.		

Totals

1

Baby's First Christmas
Handcrafted • VOTR
575QXM5145 • **Value $13**

2

Cheese Please
Handcrafted • SIED
375QXM4072 • **Value $10**

3

Christmas Castle
Handcrafted • SEAL
575QXM4085 • **Value $14**

4

Cloisonné Snowflake
Cloisonné/Brass • VOTR
975QXM4012 • **Value $21**

5

Country Fiddling
Handcrafted • FRAN
375QXM4062 • **Value $12**

6

Crystal Angel
Crystal/Gold-Plated • PALM
975QXM4015 • **Value $55**

7

Ears to Pals
Handcrafted • ANDR
375QXM4075 • **Value $9**

8

Grandma
Handcrafted • SEAL
450QXM5162 • **Value $13**

9

I Dream of Santa
Handcrafted • SICK
375QXM4055 • **Value $12**

10

Into the Woods
Handcrafted • SEAL
375QXM4045 • **Value $10**

11

Learning to Skate
Handcrafted • CHAD
300QXM4122 • **Value $10**

12

Lighting a Path
Handcrafted • CHAD
300QXM4115 • **Value $10**

13

Merry Mascot
Handcrafted • SIED
375QXM4042 • **Value $11**

14

Mom
Handcrafted • ANDR
450QXM5155 • **Value $14**

15

Monkey Melody
Handcrafted • SICK
575QXM4092 • **Value $15**

16

North Pole Fire Truck
Handcrafted • PALM
475QXM4105 • **Value $14**

17

Pear-Shaped Tones
Handcrafted • LYLE
375QXM4052 • **Value $10**

18

Pull Out a Plum
Handcrafted • FRAN
575QXM4095 • **Value $15**

19

Refreshing Flight
Handcrafted • CHAD
575QXM4112 • **Value $15**

20

'Round the Mountain
Handcrafted • CROW
725QXM4025 • **Value $19**

General Miniature	Price Paid	Value
1.		
2.		
3.		
4.		
5.		
6.		
7.		
8.		
9.		
10.		
11.		
12.		
13.		
14.		
15.		
16.		
17.		
18.		
19.		
20.		
Totals		

1

Secret Pal
Handcrafted • RGRS
375QXM5172 • **Value $11**

2

Snuggle Birds
Handcrafted • ANDR
575QXM5182 • **Value $16**

3

Special Friends
Handcrafted • FRAN
450QXM5165 • **Value $11**

4

Tiny Green Thumbs
(set/6)
Handcrafted • SEAL
2900QXM4032 • **Value $50**

5

Visions of Sugarplums
Pewter • PALM
725QXM4022 • **Value $18**

6

Circle of Friendship
(gift membership bonus)
Glass • N/A
QXC2112 • **Value $280**

7

Forty Winks
(keepsake of
membership, miniature)
Handcrafted • FRAN
QXC5294 • **Value $34**

8

Gentle Tidings
(club edition, LE-17,500)
Porcelain • ANDR
2500QXC5442 • **Value $53**

9

It's in the Mail
(keepsake of membership)
Handcrafted • SEAL
QXC5272 • **Value $26**

10

Sharing Christmas
(club edition, LE-16,500)
Handcrafted • LYLE
2000QXC5435 • **Value $52**

11

**Trimmed With
Memories** (club edition)
Handcrafted • SICK
1200QXC5432 • **Value $46**

12

You're Always Welcome
Handcrafted • SEAL
975QX5692 • **Value $62**

13

Abearnathy
*The Bearingers of
Victoria Circle*
Handcrafted • N/A
495XPR9747 • **Value $11**

14

Bearnadette
*The Bearingers of
Victoria Circle*
Handcrafted • N/A
495XPR9748 • **Value $11**

15

Fireplace Base
*The Bearingers of
Victoria Circle*
Handcrafted • N/A
495XPR9749 • **Value $13**

16

Mama Bearinger
*The Bearingers of
Victoria Circle*
Handcrafted • N/A
495XPR9745 • **Value $11**

17

Papa Bearinger
*The Bearingers of
Victoria Circle*
Handcrafted • N/A
495XPR9746 • **Value $11**

18

25 Years Together
Porcelain • N/A
800AGA7687 • **Value $20**

19

50 Years Together
Porcelain • N/A
800AGA7788 • **Value $20**

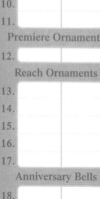

1

Our First Anniversary
Porcelain • N/A
1000AGA7865 • **Value $20**

2

Our Fifth Anniversary
Porcelain • N/A
1000AGA7866 • **Value $20**

3

Our Tenth Anniversary
Porcelain • N/A
1000AGA7867 • **Value $20**

4

25 Years Together
Porcelain • N/A
1000AGA7686 • **Value $20**

5

40 Years Together
Porcelain • N/A
1000AGA7868 • **Value $20**

6

50 Years Together
Porcelain • N/A
1000AGA7787 • **Value $20**

7

Santa's Favorite Stop
Handcrafted • VARI
5500QXC4125 • **Value $350**

8

Baby's Christening
Handcrafted • N/A
1200BBY2917 • **Value $18**

9

**Baby's Christening
Photoholder**
Silver-Plated • N/A
1000BBY1335 • **Value $15**

10

Baby's First Christmas
Handcrafted • N/A
1200BBY2918 • **Value $17**

11

Baby's First Christmas
Handcrafted • N/A
1400BBY2919 • **Value $20**

12

**Baby's First Christmas
Photoholder**
Silver-Plated • N/A
1000BBY1470 • **Value $15**

13

**Granddaughter's First
Christmas**
Handcrafted • N/A
1400BBY2802 • **Value $18**

14

**Grandson's First
Christmas**
Handcrafted • N/A
1400BBY2801 • **Value $18**

15

K.C. Angel
Silver-Plated • N/A
(N/C) No stock # • **Value $575**

16

**Baby Block Photoholder
(re-issued in 1994)**
Handcrafted • FRAN
1475QP6035 • **Value N/E**

17

Cool Snowman
Glass • N/A
875QP6052 • **Value N/E**

18

**Festive Album
Photoholder
(re-issued in 1994)**
Handcrafted • VOTR
1275QP6025 • **Value N/E**

19

Filled With Cookies
Handcrafted • RGRS
1275QP6042 • **Value N/E**

20

**Going Golfin'
(re-issued in 1994)**
Handcrafted • PALM
1275QP6012 • **Value N/E**

Anniversary Ornaments

	Price Paid	Value
1.		
2.		
3.		
4.		
5.		
6.		

Artists On Tour Pieces

7.		

Baby Ornaments

8.		
9.		
10.		
11.		
12.		
13.		
14.		

Convention Ornaments

15.		

Personalized Ornaments

16.		
17.		
18.		
19.		
20.		

Totals

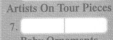

1

Here's Your Fortune
Handcrafted • SEAL
1075QP6002 • **Value N/E**

2

Mailbox Delivery
(re-issued in 1994 and 1995)
Handcrafted • CROW
1475QP6015 • **Value N/E**

3

On the Billboard
(re-issued in 1994 and 1995)
Handcrafted • CROW
1275QP6022 • **Value N/E**

4

PEANUTS®
Glass • N/A
900QP6045 • **Value N/E**

5

Playing Ball
(re-issued in 1994 and 1995)
Handcrafted • FRAN
1275QP6032 • **Value N/E**

6

Reindeer in the Sky
Glass • N/A
875QP6055 • **Value N/E**

7

Santa Says
(re-issued in 1994)
Handcrafted • SEAL
1475QP6005 • **Value N/E**

Personalized Ornaments

	Price Paid	Value
1.		
2.		
3.		
4.		
5.		
6.		
7.		

General Keepsake

8.		
9.		
10.		
11.		
12.		
13.		
14.		
15.		
16.		

1992

Of note in the 1992 collection was the debut of the "unofficial series" of handcrafted Coca-Cola® Santa ornaments in the Keepsake and Miniature lines. For 1992, there were 126 Keepsake ornaments, 21 Magic ornaments and 48 Miniature ornaments. See the collectible series section for more 1992 ornaments.

8

Across The Miles
Acrylic • RHOD
675QX3044 • **Value $15**

9

Anniversary Year Photoholder
Chrome/Brass • UNRU
975QX4851 • **Value $28**

10

Baby's First Christmas
Handcrafted • FRAN
775QX4644 • **Value $39**

11

Baby's First Christmas
Porcelain • ANDR
1875QX4581 • **Value $36**

12

Baby's First Christmas – Baby Boy
Satin • VOTR
475QX2191 • **Value $19**

13

Baby's First Christmas – Baby Girl
Satin • VOTR
475QX2204 • **Value $19**

14

Baby's First Christmas Photoholder
Fabric • VOTR
775QX4641 • **Value $26**

15

Baby's Second Christmas
Handcrafted • FRAN
675QX4651 • **Value $24**

16

Bear Bell Champ
Handcrafted/Brass • SEAL
775QX5071 • **Value $27**

Totals

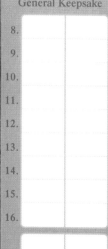

1

Brother
Handcrafted • CROW
675QX4684 • **Value $16**

2

Cheerful Santa
Handcrafted • UNRU
975QX5154 • **Value $32**

3

A Child's Christmas
Handcrafted • FRAN
975QX4574 • **Value $19**

4

Child's Fifth Christmas
Handcrafted • RHOD
675QX4664 • **Value $20**

5

Child's Fourth Christmas
Handcrafted • FRAN
675QX4661 • **Value $23**

6

Child's Third Christmas
Handcrafted • FRAN
675QX4654 • **Value $21**

7

Cool Fliers (set/2)
Handcrafted • JLEE
1075QX5474 • **Value $26**

8

Dad
Handcrafted • SIED
775QX4674 • **Value $21**

9

Dad-to-Be
Handcrafted • JLEE
675QX4611 • **Value $18**

10

Daughter
Handcrafted • FRAN
675QX5031 • **Value $28**

11

Deck the Hogs
Handcrafted • FRAN
875QX5204 • **Value $26**

General Keepsake

	Price Paid	Value
1.		
2.		
3.		
4.		
5.		
6.		
7.		
8.		
9.		
10.		
11.		
12.		
13.		
14.		
15.		
16.		
17.		
18.		
19.		
20.		

12

Dickens Caroler Bell – Lord Chadwick
Porcelain • CHAD
2175QX4554 • **Value $44**

13

Down-Under Holiday
Handcrafted • CROW
775QX5144 • **Value $22**

14

Egg Nog Nest
Handcrafted • N/A
775QX5121 • **Value $18**

15

Elfin Marionette
Handcrafted • CHAD
1175QX5931 • **Value $25**

16

Elvis
Brass-Plated • RHOD/LYLE
1475QX5624 • **Value $27**

17

Eric the Baker
Handcrafted • SICK
875QX5244 • **Value $22**

18

Feliz Navidad
Handcrafted • ANDR
675QX5181 • **Value $24**

19

For My Grandma Photoholder
Fabric • N/A
775QX5184 • **Value $18**

20

For The One I Love
Porcelain • LYLE
975QX4844 • **Value $24**

Totals

1

Franz the Artist
Handcrafted • SICK
875QX5261 • **Value $27**

2

Frieda the Animals' Friend
Handcrafted • SICK
875QX5264 • **Value $25**

3

Friendly Greetings
Handcrafted • CHAD
775QX5041 • **Value $17**

4

Friendship Line
Handcrafted • SEAL
975QX5034 • **Value $32**

5

From Our Home to Yours
Glass • VOTR
475QX2131 • **Value $17**

6

Fun on a Big Scale
Handcrafted • CROW
1075QX5134 • **Value $25**

7

GARFIELD
Handcrafted • PALM
775QX5374 • **Value $22**

8

Genius at Work
Handcrafted • CROW
1075QX5371 • **Value $24**

9

Godchild
Handcrafted • UNRU
675QX5941 • **Value $22**

10

Golf's a Ball
Handcrafted • SCHU
675QX5984 • **Value $30**

11

Gone Wishin'
Handcrafted • DLEE
875QX5171 • **Value $19**

12

Granddaughter
Handcrafted • SEAL
675QX5604 • **Value $22**

13

Granddaughter's First Christmas
Handcrafted • SIED
675QX4634 • **Value $19**

14

Grandmother
Glass • N/A
475QX2011 • **Value $19**

15

Grandparents
Glass • N/A
475QX2004 • **Value $17**

16

Grandson
Handcrafted • SEAL
675QX5611 • **Value $19**

17

Grandson's First Christmas
Handcrafted • SIED
675QX4621 • **Value $19**

18

Green Thumb Santa
Handcrafted • PALM
775QX5101 • **Value $19**

19

Hello-Ho-Ho
Handcrafted • CROW
975QX5141 • **Value $25**

20

Holiday Memo
Handcrafted • RGRS
775QX5044 • **Value $18**

General Keepsake

	Price Paid	Value
1.		
2.		
3.		
4.		
5.		
6.		
7.		
8.		
9.		
10.		
11.		
12.		
13.		
14.		
15.		
16.		
17.		
18.		
19.		
20.		

Totals

1
Holiday Teatime (set/2)
Handcrafted • RGRS
1475QX5431 • **Value $30**

2
Holiday Wishes
Handcrafted • PIKE
775QX5131 • **Value $18**

3
Honest George
Handcrafted • JLEE
775QX5064 • **Value $17**

4
Jesus Loves Me
Cameo • ANDR
775QX3024 • **Value $18**

5
Love to Skate
Handcrafted • RGRS
875QX4841 • **Value $22**

6
Loving Shepherd
Handcrafted/Brass • ANDR
775QX5151 • **Value $19**

7
Ludwig the Musician
Handcrafted • SICK
875QX5281 • **Value $22**

8
Max the Tailor
Handcrafted • SICK
875QX5251 • **Value $24**

9
**Memories to Cherish
Photoholder**
Porcelain • ANDR
1075QX5161 • **Value $24**

10
Merry "Swiss" Mouse
Handcrafted • SEAL
775QX5114 • **Value $16**

11
Mom
Handcrafted • RGRS
775QX5164 • **Value $20**

12
Mom and Dad
Handcrafted • SIED
975QX4671 • **Value $39**

13
Mom-to-Be
Handcrafted • JLEE
675QX4614 • **Value $18**

14
Mother Goose
Handcrafted • CROW
1375QX4984 • **Value $31**

15
New Home
Handcrafted • PIKE
875QX5191 • **Value $18**

16
Norman Rockwell Art
Glass • LYLE
500QX2224 • **Value $24**

17
North Pole Fire Fighter
Handcrafted/Brass • SEAL
975QX5104 • **Value $22**

18
Otto the Carpenter
Handcrafted • SICK
875QX5254 • **Value $24**

19
**Our First Christmas
Together**
Acrylic • VOTR
675QX3011 • **Value $20**

20
**Our First Christmas
Together**
Handcrafted • JLEE
975QX5061 • **Value $21**

General Keepsake

	Price Paid	Value
1.		
2.		
3.		
4.		
5.		
6.		
7.		
8.		
9.		
10.		
11.		
12.		
13.		
14.		
15.		
16.		
17.		
18.		
19.		
20.		
Totals		

1

Our First Christmas Together Photoholder
Handcrafted • SEAL
875QX4694 • **Value $27**

2

Owl
Handcrafted • SIED
975QX5614 • **Value $28**

3

Partridge IN a Pear Tree
Handcrafted • SIED
875QX5234 • **Value $22**

4

PEANUTS®
Glass • N/A
500QX2244 • **Value $28**

5

Please Pause Here
Handcrafted • DLEE
1475QX5291 • **Value $36**

6

Polar Post
Handcrafted • SEAL
875QX4914 • **Value $22**

7

Rapid Delivery
Handcrafted • PALM
875QX5094 • **Value $23**

8

A Santa-Full!
Handcrafted • FRAN
975QX5991 • **Value $44**

	Price Paid	Value
1.		
2.		
3.		
4.		
5.		
6.		
7.		
8.		
9.		
10.		
11.		
12.		
13.		
14.		
15.		
16.		
17.		
18.		
19.		
20.		

Totals

9

Santa Maria
Handcrafted • CROW
1275QX5074 • **Value $24**

10

Santa's Hook Shot (set/2)
Handcrafted • SEAL
1275QX5434 • **Value $30**

11

Santa's Roundup
Handcrafted • JLEE
875QX5084 • **Value $27**

12

Secret Pal
Handcrafted • RGRS
775QX5424 • **Value $16**

13

Silver Star Train Set (set/3)
Die-Cast Metal • SICK
2800QX5324 • **Value $60**

14

Sister
Handcrafted • CROW
675QX4681 • **Value $17**

15

Skiing 'Round
Handcrafted • JLEE
875QX5214 • **Value $19**

16

Sky Line Caboose
Die-Cast Metal • SICK
975QX5321 • **Value $26**

17

Sky Line Coal Car
Die-Cast Metal • SICK
975QX5401 • **Value $22**

18

Sky Line Locomotive
Die-Cast Metal • SICK
975QX5311 • **Value $45**

19

Sky Line Stock Car
Die-Cast Metal • SICK
975QX5314 • **Value $22**

20

SNOOPY® and WOODSTOCK
Handcrafted • RGRS
875QX5954 • **Value $40**

1

Son
Handcrafted • FRAN
675QX5024 • **Value $25**

2

Special Cat Photoholder
Handcrafted • CHAD
775QX5414 • **Value $19**

3

Special Dog Photoholder
Handcrafted • CHAD
775QX5421 • **Value $28**

4

Spirit of Christmas Stress
Handcrafted • CHAD
875QX5231 • **Value $22**

5

Stocked With Joy
Pressed Tin • SICK
775QX5934 • **Value $22**

6

Tasty Christmas
Handcrafted • FRAN
975QX5994 • **Value $27**

7

Teacher
Glass • N/A
475QX2264 • **Value $18**

8

Toboggan Tail
Handcrafted • ANDR
775QX5459 • **Value $18**

9

Tread Bear
Handcrafted • SEAL
875QX5091 • **Value $25**

10

Turtle Dreams
Handcrafted • JLEE
875QX4991 • **Value $25**

11

Uncle Art's Ice Cream
Handcrafted • SIED
875QX5001 • **Value $26**

12

V.P. of Important Stuff
Handcrafted • SIED
675QX5051 • **Value $16**

13

World-Class Teacher
Handcrafted • SIED
775QX5054 • **Value $19**

14

Baby's First Christmas
Handcrafted • CROW
2200QLX7281 • **Value $100**

15

Christmas Parade
Handcrafted • SICK
3000QLX7271 • **Value $66**

16

Continental Express
Handcrafted • SICK
3200QLX7264 • **Value $78**

17

The Dancing Nutcracker
Handcrafted • VOTR
3000QLX7261 • **Value $60**

18

Enchanted Clock
Handcrafted • CROW
3000QLX7274 • **Value $64**

19

Feathered Friends
Handcrafted • SICK
1400QLX7091 • **Value $33**

20

Good Sledding Ahead
Handcrafted • PALM
2800QLX7244 • **Value $58**

General Keepsake		
	Price Paid	Value
1.		
2.		
3.		
4.		
5.		
6.		
7.		
8.		
9.		
10.		
11.		
12.		
13.		
General Magic		
14.		
15.		
16.		
17.		
18.		
19.		
20.		
Totals		

1

Lighting the Way
Handcrafted • ANDR
1800QLX7231 • **Value $48**

2

Look! It's Santa
Handcrafted • DLEE
1400QLX7094 • **Value $45**

3

Nut Sweet Nut
Handcrafted • CROW
1000QLX7081 • **Value $24**

4

Our First Christmas Together
Panorama Ball • CHAD
2000QLX7221 • **Value $45**

5

Santa Special
(re-issued from 1991)
Handcrafted • SEAL
4000QLX7167 • **Value $80**

6

Santa Sub
Handcrafted • CROW
1800QLX7321 • **Value $40**

7

Santa's Answering Machine
Handcrafted • JLEE
2200QLX7241 • **Value $42**

8

Shuttlecraft Galileo™ From the Starship Enterprise™
Handcrafted • RHOD
2400QLX7331 • **Value $48**

General Magic

	Price Paid	Value
1.		
2.		
3.		
4.		
5.		
6.		
7.		
8.		
9.		
10.		
11.		

General Miniature

12.		
13.		
14.		
15.		
16.		
17.		
18.		
19.		
20.		

9

Under Construction
Handcrafted • PALM
1800QLX7324 • **Value $42**

10

Watch Owls
Porcelain • FRAN
1200QLX7084 • **Value $30**

11

Yuletide Rider
Handcrafted • SEAL
2800QLX7314 • **Value $60**

12

A+ Teacher
Handcrafted • UNRU
375QXM5511 • **Value $11**

13

Angelic Harpist
Handcrafted • LYLE
450QXM5524 • **Value $17**

14

Baby's First Christmas
Handcrafted/Brass • LYLE
450QXM5494 • **Value $21**

15

Black-Capped Chickadee
Handcrafted • FRAN
300QXM5484 • **Value $18**

16

Bright Stringers
Handcrafted • SEAL
375QXM5841 • **Value $18**

17

Buck-A-Roo
Handcrafted • CROW
450QXM5814 • **Value $16**

18

Christmas Bonus
Handcrafted • PALM
300QXM5811 • **Value $9**

19

Christmas Copter
Handcrafted • FRAN
575QXM5844 • **Value $15**

20

Coca-Cola® Santa
Handcrafted • UNRU
575QXM5884 • **Value $18**

Totals

1

Cool Uncle Sam
Handcrafted • JLEE
300QXM5561 • **Value $16**

2

Cozy Kayak
Handcrafted • JLEE
375QXM5551 • **Value $14**

3

Fast Finish
Handcrafted • RHOD
375QXM5301 • **Value $13**

4

Feeding Time
Handcrafted • CROW
575QXM5481 • **Value $16**

5

Friendly Tin Soldier
Pressed Tin • SICK
450QXM5874 • **Value $18**

6

Friends Are Tops
Handcrafted • CROW
450QXM5521 • **Value $12**

7

Gerbil Inc.
Handcrafted • SIED
375QXM5924 • **Value $12**

8

Going Places
Handcrafted • ANDR
375QXM5871 • **Value $11**

9

Grandchild's First Christmas
Handcrafted • FRAN
575QXM5501 • **Value $15**

10

Grandma
Handcrafted • UNRU
450QXM5514 • **Value $15**

11

Harmony Trio (set/3)
Handcrafted • VOTR
1175QXM5471 • **Value $23**

12

Hickory, Dickory, Dock
Handcrafted • CHAD
375QXM5861 • **Value $14**

13

Holiday Holly
Gold-Plated • N/A
975QXM5364 • **Value $17**

14

Holiday Splash
Handcrafted • FRAN
575QXM5834 • **Value $15**

15

Hoop It Up
Handcrafted • CROW
450QXM5831 • **Value $13**

16

Inside Story
Handcrafted • SEAL
725QXM5881 • **Value $22**

17

Little Town of Bethlehem
Handcrafted • SICK
300QXM5864 • **Value $24**

18

Minted for Santa
Copper • UNRU
375QXM5854 • **Value $15**

19

Mom
Handcrafted • ANDR
450QXM5504 • **Value $16**

20

Perfect Balance
Handcrafted • RGRS
300QXM5571 • **Value $13**

General Miniature	
Price Paid	**Value**
1.	
2.	
3.	
4.	
5.	
6.	
7.	
8.	
9.	
10.	
11.	
12.	
13.	
14.	
15.	
16.	
17.	
18.	
19.	
20.	
Totals	

1

Polar Polka
Handcrafted • SEAL
450QXM5534 • **Value $15**

2

Puppet Show
Handcrafted • SIED
300QXM5574 • **Value $13**

3

Sew, Sew Tiny (set/6)
Handcrafted • SEAL
2900QXM5794 • **Value $58**

4

Ski for Two
Handcrafted • ANDR
450QXM5821 • **Value $14**

5

Snowshoe Bunny
Handcrafted • VOTR
375QXM5564 • **Value $13**

6

Snug Kitty
Handcrafted • PIKE
375QXM5554 • **Value $13**

7

Spunky Monkey
Handcrafted • CHAD
300QXM5921 • **Value $16**

8

Visions of Acorns
Handcrafted • ANDR
450QXM5851 • **Value $16**

9

Wee Three Kings
Handcrafted • PALM
575QXM5531 • **Value $20**

10

**Chipmunk Parcel
Service (early renewal
piece, miniature)**
Handcrafted • SEAL
QXC5194 • **Value $27**

11

**Christmas Treasures
(set/4, club edition,
LE-15,500, miniature)**
Handcrafted • CHAD
2200QXC5464 • **Value $165**

12

**Rodney Takes Flight
(keepsake of membership)**
Handcrafted • DLEE
QXC5081 • **Value $30**

13

**Santa's Club List
(club edition, magic)**
Handcrafted • SEAL
1500QXC7291 • **Value $44**

14

**Victorian Skater
(club edition, LE-14,700)**
Porcelain • UNRU
2500QXC4067 • **Value $67**

15

O Christmas Tree
Porcelain • VOTR
1075QX5411 • **Value $30**

16

Comet and Cupid
Santa and His Reindeer
Handcrafted/Brass • CROW
495XPR9737 • **Value $23**

17

Dasher and Dancer
Santa and His Reindeer
Handcrafted/Brass • CROW
495XPR9735 • **Value $45**

18

Donder and Blitzen
Santa and His Reindeer
Handcrafted/Brass • CROW
495XPR9738 • **Value $38**

19

Prancer and Vixen
Santa and His Reindeer
Handcrafted/Brass • CROW
495XPR9736 • **Value $23**

20

Santa Claus
Santa and His Reindeer
Handcrafted/Brass • CROW
495XPR9739 • **Value $30**

General Miniature

	Price Paid	Value
1.		
2.		
3.		
4.		
5.		
6.		
7.		
8.		
9.		

Collector's Club

10.		
11.		
12.		
13.		
14.		

Premiere Ornaments

15.		

Reach Ornaments

16.		
17.		
18.		
19.		
20.		

Totals

1

25 Years Together
Porcelain • N/A
800AGA7134 • **Value $17**

2

50 Years Together
Porcelain • N/A
800AGA7235 • **Value $17**

3

Our First Anniversary
Porcelain • N/A
1000AGA7318 • **Value $19**

4

Our Fifth Anniversary
Porcelain • N/A
1000AGA7319 • **Value $19**

5

Our Tenth Anniversary
Porcelain • N/A
1000AGA7317 • **Value $19**

6

25 Years Together
Porcelain • N/A
1000AGA7113 • **Value $19**

7

40 Years Together
Porcelain • N/A
1000AGA7316 • **Value $20**

8

50 Years Together
Porcelain • N/A
1000AGA7214 • **Value $20**

9

Baby's Christening
Fabric • N/A
850BBY1331 • **Value $15**

10

Baby's First Christmas
Fabric • N/A
850BBY1456 • **Value $15**

11

Baby's First Christmas
Plush • N/A
850BBY1557 • **Value $15**

1991

In 1991 an exciting Magic ornament depicting the "Starship Enterprise™" (the first of many STAR TREK® ornaments) was issued and quickly became a collectors' favorite. This year's collection featured 128 Keepsake, 23 Magic and 47 Miniature ornaments. See the collectible series section for more 1991 ornaments.

12

Across the Miles
Acrylic • LYLE
675QX3157 • **Value $16**

13

All-Star
Handcrafted • SIED
675QX5329 • **Value $22**

14

Baby's First Christmas
Handcrafted • FRAN
775QX4889 • **Value $36**

15

Baby's First Christmas
Silver-Plated • FRAN
1775QX5107 • **Value $46**

16

Baby's First Christmas – Baby Boy
Satin • HAMI
475QX2217 • **Value $21**

17

Baby's First Christmas – Baby Girl
Satin • HAMI
475QX2227 • **Value $21**

Anniversary Bells	Price Paid	Value
1.		
2.		
Anniversary Ornaments		
3.		
4.		
5.		
6.		
7.		
8.		
Baby Ornaments		
9.		
10.		
11.		
General Keepsake		
12.		
13.		
14.		
15.		
16.		
17.		
Totals		

1991 Collection

1

Baby's First Christmas
Photoholder
Fabric • VOTR
775QX4869 • **Value $30**

2

Baby's Second
Christmas
Handcrafted • FRAN
675QX4897 • **Value $33**

3

Basket Bell Players
Handcrafted/Wicker • SEAL
775QX5377 • **Value $28**

4

The Big Cheese
Handcrafted • SIED
675QX5327 • **Value $20**

5

Bob Cratchit
Porcelain • UNRU
1375QX4997 • **Value $37**

6

Brother
Handcrafted • SIED
675QX5479 • **Value $21**

7

A Child's Christmas
Handcrafted • FRAN
975QX4887 • **Value $17**

8

Child's Fifth Christmas
Handcrafted • RHOD
675QX4909 • **Value $19**

9

Child's Fourth
Christmas
Handcrafted • FRAN
675QX4907 • **Value $20**

10

Child's Third Christmas
Handcrafted • FRAN
675QX4899 • **Value $29**

11

Chilly Chap
Handcrafted • DLEE
675QX5339 • **Value $18**

12

Christmas Welcome
Handcrafted • SICK
975QX5299 • **Value $24**

13

Christopher Robin
Handcrafted • SIED
975QX5579 • **Value $40**

14

Cuddly Lamb
Handcrafted • RGRS
675QX5199 • **Value $22**

15

Dad
Handcrafted • JLEE
775QX5127 • **Value $20**

16

Dad-to-Be
Handcrafted • JLEE
575QX4879 • **Value $17**

17

Daughter
Handcrafted • SIED
575QX5477 • **Value $42**

18

Dickens Caroler Bell
– Mrs. Beaumont
Porcelain • CHAD
2175QX5039 • **Value $42**

19

Dinoclaus
Handcrafted • CHAD
775QX5277 • **Value $24**

20

Ebenezer Scrooge
Porcelain • UNRU
1375QX4989 • **Value $48**

General Keepsake		
	Price Paid	**Value**
1.		
2.		
3.		
4.		
5.		
6.		
7.		
8.		
9.		
10.		
11.		
12.		
13.		
14.		
15.		
16.		
17.		
18.		
19.		
20.		
Totals		

1

Evergreen Inn
Handcrafted • SEAL
875QX5389 • **Value $18**

2

Extra-Special Friends
Glass • N/A
475QX2279 • **Value $16**

3

Fanfare Bear
Handcrafted • SEAL
875QX5337 • **Value $20**

4

Feliz Navidad
Handcrafted • JLEE
675QX5279 • **Value $27**

5

Fiddlin' Around
Handcrafted • VOTR
775QX4387 • **Value $19**

6

Fifty Years Together Photoholder
Handcrafted/Brass • VOTR
875QX4947 • **Value $19**

7

First Christmas Together
Acrylic • PIKE
675QX3139 • **Value $26**

8

First Christmas Together
Glass • N/A
475QX2229 • **Value $22**

9

First Christmas Together
Handcrafted • SICK
875QX4919 • **Value $29**

10

First Christmas Together Photoholder
Handcrafted/Brass • VOTR
875QX4917 • **Value $28**

11

Five Years Together
Faceted Glass • N/A
775QX4927 • **Value $18**

12

Flag of Liberty
Handcrafted • DLEE
675QX5249 • **Value $18**

13

Folk Art Reindeer
Wood/Brass • VOTR
875QX5359 • **Value $20**

14

Forty Years Together
Faceted Glass • N/A
775QX4939 • **Value $18**

15

Friends Are Fun
Handcrafted • CROW
975QX5289 • **Value $23**

16

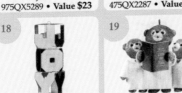

From Our Home to Yours
Glass • VOTR
475QX2287 • **Value $22**

17

GARFIELD®
Handcrafted • RHOD
775QX5177 • **Value $32**

18

Gift of Joy
Brass/Chrome/Copper • MCGE
875QX5319 • **Value $26**

19

Glee Club Bears
Handcrafted • SEAL
875QX4969 • **Value $22**

20

Godchild
Handcrafted • BISH
675QX5489 • **Value $23**

General Keepsake	
Price Paid	**Value**
1.	
2.	
3.	
4.	
5.	
6.	
7.	
8.	
9.	
10.	
11.	
12.	
13.	
14.	
15.	
16.	
17.	
18.	
19.	
20.	
Totals	

1991 Collection

1

Granddaughter
Glass • PYDA
475QX2299 • **Value $27**

2

Granddaughter's First Christmas
Handcrafted • CHAD
675QX5119 • **Value $23**

3

Grandmother
Glass • N/A
475QX2307 • **Value $20**

4

Grandparents
Glass • PYDA
475QX2309 • **Value $15**

5

Grandson
Glass • PYDA
475QX2297 • **Value $24**

6

Grandson's First Christmas
Handcrafted • CHAD
675QX5117 • **Value $23**

7

Holiday Cafe
Handcrafted • SEAL
875QX5399 • **Value $17**

8

Hooked on Santa
Handcrafted • JLEE
775QX4109 • **Value $28**

9
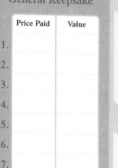
Jesus Loves Me
Cameo • RHOD
775QX3147 • **Value $18**

10

Jolly Wolly Santa
Pressed Tin • SICK
775QX5419 • **Value $28**

11

Jolly Wolly Snowman
Pressed Tin • SICK
775QX5427 • **Value $28**

12

Jolly Wolly Soldier
Pressed Tin • SICK
775QX5429 • **Value $22**

13

Joyous Memories Photoholder
Handcrafted • VOTR
675QX5369 • **Value $27**

14

Kanga and Roo
Handcrafted • SIED
975QX5617 • **Value $50**

15

Look Out Below
Handcrafted • SEAL
875QX4959 • **Value $22**

16

Loving Stitches
Handcrafted • SEAL
875QX4987 • **Value $33**

17

Mary Engelbreit
Glass • N/A
475QX2237 • **Value $30**

18

Merry Carolers
Porcelain • UNRU
2975QX4799 • **Value $96**

19

Mom and Dad
Handcrafted • N/A
975QX5467 • **Value $26**

20

Mom-to-Be
Handcrafted • JLEE
575QX4877 • **Value $22**

General Keepsake

	Price Paid	Value
1.		
2.		
3.		
4.		
5.		
6.		
7.		
8.		
9.		
10.		
11.		
12.		
13.		
14.		
15.		
16.		
17.		
18.		
19.		
20.		

Totals

VALUE GUIDE — HALLMARK KEEPSAKE ORNAMENTS

1

Mother
Porcelain/Tin • N/A
975QX5457 • **Value $37**

2

Mrs. Cratchit
Porcelain • UNRU
1375QX4999 • **Value $35**

3

New Home
Handcrafted • BISH
675QX5449 • **Value $32**

4

Night Before Christmas
Handcrafted • SICK
975QX5307 • **Value $24**

5

Noah's Ark
Handcrafted • CROW
1375QX4867 • **Value $50**

6

Norman Rockwell Art
Glass • LYLE
500QX2259 • **Value $30**

7

Notes of Cheer
Handcrafted • SIED
575QX5357 • **Value $14**

8

Nutshell Nativity
Handcrafted • RGRS
675QX5176 • **Value $27**

9

Nutty Squirrel
Handcrafted • PIKE
575QX4833 • **Value $16**

10

Old-Fashioned Sled
Handcrafted • SICK
875QX4317 • **Value $21**

11

On a Roll
Handcrafted • CROW
675QX5347 • **Value $21**

12

Partridge in a Pear Tree
Handcrafted • SICK
975QX5297 • **Value $19**

13

PEANUTS®
Glass • N/A
500QX2257 • **Value $28**

14

Piglet and Eeyore
Handcrafted • SIED
975QX5577 • **Value $57**

15

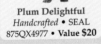

Plum Delightful
Handcrafted • SEAL
875QX4977 • **Value $20**

16

Polar Circus Wagon
Handcrafted • SICK
1375QX4399 • **Value $27**

17

Polar Classic
Handcrafted • SIED
675QX5287 • **Value $22**

18

Rabbit
Handcrafted • SIED
975QX5607 • **Value $37**

19

Santa Sailor
Handcrafted/Metal • SEAL
975QX4389 • **Value $27**

20

Santa's Studio
Handcrafted • SEAL
875QX5397 • **Value $19**

General Keepsake

	Price Paid	Value
1.		
2.		
3.		
4.		
5.		
6.		
7.		
8.		
9.		
10.		
11.		
12.		
13.		
14.		
15.		
16.		
17.		
18.		
19.		
20.		

Totals

1991 Collection

1

Sister
Handcrafted • LYLE
675QX5487 • **Value $20**

2

Ski Lift Bunny
Handcrafted • JLEE
675QX5447 • **Value $21**

3

SNOOPY® and WOODSTOCK
Handcrafted • RHOD
675QX5197 • **Value $37**

4

Snow Twins
Handcrafted • SEAL
875QX4979 • **Value $22**

5

Snowy Owl
Handcrafted • SICK
775QX5269 • **Value $20**

6

Son
Handcrafted • SIED
575QX5469 • **Value $20**

7

Sweet Talk
Handcrafted • UNRU
875QX5367 • **Value $28**

8

Sweetheart
Porcelain • N/A
975QX4957 • **Value $27**

9

Teacher
Glass • RGRS
475QX2289 • **Value $13**

10

Ten Years Together
Faceted Glass • N/A
775QX4929 • **Value $19**

11

Terrific Teacher
Handcrafted • SICK
675QX5309 • **Value $18**

12

Tigger
Handcrafted • SIED
975QX5609 • **Value $125**

13

Tiny Tim
Porcelain • UNRU
1075QX5037 • **Value $43**

14

Tramp and Laddie
Handcrafted • FRAN
775QX4397 • **Value $47**

15

Twenty-Five Years Together Photoholder
Handcrafted/Chrome • VOTR
875QX4937 • **Value $17**

16

Under the Mistletoe
Handcrafted • PIKE
875QX4949 • **Value $22**

17

Up 'N' Down Journey
Handcrafted • CROW
975QX5047 • **Value $30**

18

Winnie-the-Pooh
Handcrafted • SIED
975QX5569 • **Value $59**

19

Yule Logger
Handcrafted • SEAL
875QX4967 • **Value $24**

20

Arctic Dome
Handcrafted • CROW
2500QLX7117 • **Value $58**

General Keepsake

	Price Paid	Value
1.		
2.		
3.		
4.		
5.		
6.		
7.		
8.		
9.		
10.		
11.		
12.		
13.		
14.		
15.		
16.		
17.		
18.		
19.		

General Magic

20.		

Totals

1

Baby's First Christmas
Handcrafted • SEAL
3000QLX7247 • **Value $100**

2

Bringing Home the Tree
Handcrafted • UNRU
2800QLX7249 • **Value $65**

3

Elfin Engineer
Handcrafted • CHAD
1000QLX7209 • **Value $27**

4

Father Christmas
Handcrafted • UNRU
1400QLX7147 • **Value $40**

5

Festive Brass Church
Brass • MCGE
1400QLX7179 • **Value $35**

6

First Christmas Together
Handcrafted • SICK
2500QLX7137 • **Value $57**

7

Friendship Tree
Handcrafted • DUTK
1000QLX7169 • **Value $27**

8

Holiday Glow
Panorama Ball • PIKE
1400QLX7177 • **Value $32**

9

It's a Wonderful Life
Handcrafted • DLEE
2000QLX7237 • **Value $75**

10

Jingle Bears
Handcrafted • JLEE
2500QLX7323 • **Value $56**

11

Kringle's Bumper Cars
Handcrafted • SICK
2500QLX7119 • **Value $58**

12

Mole Family Home
Handcrafted • JLEE
2000QLX7149 • **Value $48**

13

Salvation Army Band
Handcrafted • UNRU
3000QLX7273 • **Value $77**

14

Santa Special
(re-issued in 1992)
Handcrafted • SEAL
4000QLX7167 • **Value $80**

15

Santa's Hot Line
Handcrafted • CROW
1800QLX7159 • **Value $42**

16

Ski Trip
Handcrafted • SEAL
2800QLX7266 • **Value $63**

17

Sparkling Angel
Handcrafted • CHAD
1800QLX7157 • **Value $40**

18

Starship Enterprise™
Handcrafted • NORT
2000QLX7199 • **Value $395**

19

Toyland Tower
Handcrafted • CROW
2000QLX7129 • **Value $47**

20

All Aboard
Handcrafted • CHAD
450QXM5869 • **Value $18**

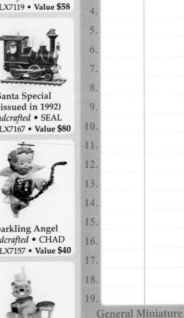

	General Magic	
	Price Paid	Value
1.		
2.		
3.		
4.		
5.		
6.		
7.		
8.		
9.		
10.		
11.		
12.		
13.		
14.		
15.		
16.		
17.		
18.		
19.		
	General Miniature	
20.		

Totals

1

Baby's First Christmas
Handcrafted • FRAN
600QXM5799 • **Value $22**

2

Brass Bells
Brass • ANDR
300QXM5977 • **Value $11**

3

Brass Church
Brass • N/A
300QXM5979 • **Value $10**

4

Brass Soldier
Brass • N/A
300QXM5987 • **Value $10**

5

Bright Boxers
Handcrafted • RHOD
450QXM5877 • **Value $16**

6

Busy Bear
Wood • RHOD
450QXM5939 • **Value $12**

7

Cardinal Cameo
Handcrafted • LYLE
600QXM5957 • **Value $19**

8

Caring Shepherd
Porcelain • FRAN
600QXM5949 • **Value $18**

9

Cool 'n Sweet
Porcelain • PIKE
450QXM5867 • **Value $24**

10

Country Sleigh
Enamel • VOTR
450QXM5999 • **Value $16**

11

Courier Turtle
Handcrafted • PIKE
450QXM5857 • **Value $14**

12

Fancy Wreath
Handcrafted • LYLE
450QXM5917 • **Value $13**

13

Feliz Navidad
Handcrafted/Straw • RGRS
600QXM5887 • **Value $18**

14

First Christmas Together
Handcrafted/Brass • UNRU
600QXM5819 • **Value $17**

15

Fly By
Handcrafted • CROW
450QXM5859 • **Value $17**

16

Friendly Fawn
Handcrafted • JLEE
600QXM5947 • **Value $18**

17

Grandchild's First Christmas
Porcelain • RGRS
450QXM5697 • **Value $14**

18

Heavenly Minstrel
Handcrafted • DLEE
975QXM5687 • **Value $26**

19

Holiday Snowflake
Acrylic • RHOD
300QXM5997 • **Value $14**

20

Key to Love
Handcrafted • CROW
450QXM5689 • **Value $17**

General Miniature

	Price Paid	Value
1.		
2.		
3.		
4.		
5.		
6.		
7.		
8.		
9.		
10.		
11.		
12.		
13.		
14.		
15.		
16.		
17.		
18.		
19.		
20.		

Totals

1

Kitty in a Mitty
Handcrafted • ANDR
450QXM5879 • **Value $13**

2

Li'l Popper
Handcrafted • SICK
450QXM5897 • **Value $22**

3

Love Is Born
Porcelain • VOTR
600QXM5959 • **Value $21**

4

Lulu & Family
Handcrafted • RGRS
600QXM5677 • **Value $23**

5

Mom
Handcrafted • SIED
600QXM5699 • **Value $18**

6

N. Pole Buddy
Handcrafted • PALM
450QXM5927 • **Value $18**

7

Noel
Acrylic • N/A
300QXM5989 • **Value $14**

8

Ring-A-Ding Elf
Handcrafted/Brass • CHAD
850QXM5669 • **Value $21**

9

Seaside Otter
Handcrafted • SIED
450QXM5909 • **Value $14**

10

Silvery Santa
Silver-Plated • JLEE
975QXM5679 • **Value $23**

11

Special Friends
Handcrafted/Wicker • JLEE
850QXM5797 • **Value $21**

12

Tiny Tea Party Set (set/6)
Handcrafted/Porcelain • SEAL
2900QXM5827 • **Value $165**

13

Top Hatter
Handcrafted • SEAL
600QXM5889 • **Value $18**

14

Treeland Trio
Handcrafted • CHAD
850QXM5899 • **Value $19**

15

Upbeat Bear
Handcrafted/Metal • FRAN
600QXM5907 • **Value $17**

16

Vision of Santa
Handcrafted • CHAD
450QXM5937 • **Value $14**

17

Wee Toymaker
Handcrafted • BISH
850QXM5967 • **Value $17**

18

Beary Artistic
(club edition, magic)
Handcrafted/Acrylic • SIED
1000QXC7259 • **Value $38**

19

Five Years Together
(charter member gift)
Acrylic • N/A
QXC3159 • **Value $58**

20

Galloping Into Christmas
(club edition, LE-28,400)
Pressed Tin • SICK
1975QXC4779 • **Value $115**

General Miniature		
	Price Paid	Value
1.		
2.		
3.		
4.		
5.		
6.		
7.		
8.		
9.		
10.		
11.		
12.		
13.		
14.		
15.		
16.		
17.		

Collector's Club		
18.		
19.		
20.		

Totals

187

1991 / 1990 Collection

1

Hidden Treasure & Li'l Keeper (set/2, keepsake of membership)
Handcrafted • CROW
QXC4769 • **Value $45**

2

Secrets for Santa (club edition, LE-28,700)
Handcrafted • RGRS
2375QXC4797 • **Value $55**

3

Santa's Premiere
Porcelain • N/A
1075QX5237 • **Value $38**

4

Caboose
Claus & Co. R.R.
Handcrafted • PALM
($3.95)411XPR9733 • **Value $18**

5

Claus & Co. R.R. Trestle Display Stand
Claus & Co. R.R.
Handcrafted • PALM
($2.95)411XPR9734 • **Value $12**

6

Gift Car
Claus & Co. R.R.
Handcrafted • PALM
($3.95)411XPR9731 • **Value $15**

7

Locomotive
Claus & Co. R.R.
Handcrafted • PALM
($3.95)411XPR9730 • **Value $34**

8

Passenger Car
Claus & Co. R.R.
Handcrafted • PALM
($3.95)411XPR9732 • **Value $15**

9

Baby's Christening 1991
Porcelain • JLEE
1000BBY1317 • **Value $18**

10

Baby's First Christmas 1991
Porcelain • JLEE
1000BBY1416 • **Value $18**

11

Baby's First Christmas 1991
Porcelain • RGRS
1000BBY1514 • **Value $18**

12

Kansas City Santa
Silver-Plated • N/A
(N/C) No stock # • **Value $975**

1990

The 1990 collection included an adorable group of six "polar penguins" as well as the first of four porcelain ornaments in the "Dickens Caroler Bell" collection. In all, there were 128 Keepsake ornaments, 21 Magic ornaments and a whopping 54 Miniature ornaments in the 1990 line. See the collectible series section for more 1990 ornaments.

13

Across the Miles
Acrylic • VOTR
675QX3173 • **Value $17**

14

Angel Kitty
Handcrafted • PYDA
875QX4746 • **Value $26**

15

Baby Unicorn
Porcelain • RGRS
975QX5486 • **Value $24**

Collector's Club

	Price Paid	Value
1.		
2.		

Premiere Ornaments

3.		

Reach Ornaments

4.		
5.		
6.		
7.		
8.		

Baby Celebrations

9.		
10.		
11.		

Convention Ornaments

12.		

General Keepsake

13.		
14.		
15.		

Totals

1

Baby's First Christmas
Acrylic • RGRS
675QX3036 • **Value $23**

2

Baby's First Christmas
Handcrafted • FRAN
775QX4856 • **Value $40**

3

Baby's First Christmas
Handcrafted • FRAN
975QX4853 • **Value $23**

4

Baby's First Christmas – Baby Boy
Satin • N/A
475QX2063 • **Value $24**

5

Baby's First Christmas – Baby Girl
Satin • N/A
475QX2066 • **Value $24**

6

Baby's First Christmas Photoholder
Fabric • N/A
775QX4843 • **Value $30**

7

Baby's Second Christmas
Handcrafted • FRAN
675QX4863 • **Value $38**

8

Bearback Rider
Handcrafted • CROW
975QX5483 • **Value $31**

9

Beary Good Deal
Handcrafted • SIED
675QX4733 • **Value $16**

10

Billboard Bunny
Handcrafted • JLEE
775QX5196 • **Value $22**

11

Born to Dance
Handcrafted • PIKE
775QX5043 • **Value $24**

12

Brother
Handcrafted • SIED
575QX4493 • **Value $14**

13

Child Care Giver
Acrylic • N/A
675QX3166 • **Value $13**

14

Child's Fifth Christmas
Handcrafted • RHOD
675QX4876 • **Value $20**

15

Child's Fourth Christmas
Handcrafted • FRAN
675QX4873 • **Value $20**

16

Child's Third Christmas
Handcrafted • FRAN
675QX4866 • **Value $24**

17

Chiming In
Handcrafted/Brass • PIKE
975QX4366 • **Value $24**

18

Christmas Croc
Handcrafted • PYDA
775QX4373 • **Value $25**

19

Christmas Partridge
Dimensional Brass • SICK
775QX5246 • **Value $23**

20

Claus Construction
(re-issued from 1989)
Handcrafted • SEAL
775QX4885 • **Value $35**

General Keepsake

	Price Paid	Value
1.		
2.		
3.		
4.		
5.		
6.		
7.		
8.		
9.		
10.		
11.		
12.		
13.		
14.		
15.		
16.		
17.		
18.		
19.		
20.		

Totals

1

Copy of Cheer
Handcrafted • SIED
775QX4486 • **Value $18**

2

Country Angel
(cancelled after
limited production)
Handcrafted • N/A
675QX5046 • **Value $195**

3

Coyote Carols
Handcrafted • JLEE
875QX4993 • **Value $27**

4

Cozy Goose
Handcrafted • PIKE
575QX4966 • **Value $15**

5

Dad
Handcrafted • JLEE
675QX4533 • **Value $17**

6

Dad-to-Be
Handcrafted • SIED
575QX4913 • **Value $22**

7

Daughter
Handcrafted • SIED
575QX4496 • **Value $23**

8

Dickens Caroler Bell
– Mr. Ashbourne
Porcelain • CHAD
2175QX5056 • **Value $49**

General Keepsake

	Price Paid	Value
1.		
2.		
3.		
4.		
5.		
6.		
7.		
8.		
9.		
10.		
11.		
12.		
13.		
14.		
15.		
16.		
17.		
18.		
19.		
20.		

9

Donder's Diner
Handcrafted • DLEE
1375QX4823 • **Value $22**

10

Feliz Navidad
Handcrafted • N/A
675QX5173 • **Value $30**

11

Fifty Years Together
Faceted Glass • PATT
975QX4906 • **Value $20**

12

First Christmas
Together
Acrylic • VOTR
675QX3146 • **Value $27**

13

First Christmas
Together
Glass • VOTR
475QX2136 • **Value $25**

14

First Christmas
Together
Handcrafted • PYDA
975QX4883 • **Value $28**

15

First Christmas
Together – Photoholder
Fabric • VOTR
775QX4886 • **Value $20**

16

Five Years Together
Glass • VOTR
475QX2103 • **Value $18**

17

Forty Years Together
Faceted Glass • PATT
975QX4903 • **Value $19**

18

Friendship Kitten
Handcrafted • RHOD
675QX4143 • **Value $25**

19

From Our
Home to Yours
Glass • N/A
475QX2166 • **Value $22**

20

GARFIELD®
Glass • N/A
475QX2303 • **Value $25**

Totals

1

Gentle Dreamers
Handcrafted • FRAN
875QX4756 • **Value $33**

2

Gingerbread Elf
Handcrafted • N/A
575QX5033 • **Value $21**

3

Godchild
Acrylic • FRAN
675QX3176 • **Value $19**

4

Golf's My Bag
Handcrafted • JLEE
775QX4963 • **Value $30**

5

Goose Cart
Handcrafted • N/A
775QX5236 • **Value $16**

6

Granddaughter
Glass • LYLE
475QX2286 • **Value $26**

7

**Granddaughter's
First Christmas**
Acrylic • FRAN
675QX3106 • **Value $22**

8

Grandmother
Glass • VOTR
475QX2236 • **Value $19**

9

Grandparents
Glass • N/A
475QX2253 • **Value $19**

10

Grandson
Glass • VOTR
475QX2293 • **Value $21**

11

**Grandson's
First Christmas**
Acrylic • FRAN
675QX3063 • **Value $21**

12

Hang in There
Handcrafted • SEAL
675QX4713 • **Value $24**

13

Happy Voices
Wood • VOTR
675QX4645 • **Value $16**

14

Happy Woodcutter
Handcrafted • JLEE
975QX4763 • **Value $23**

15

Holiday Cardinals
Dimensional Brass • LYLE
775QX5243 • **Value $25**

16

Home for the Owlidays
Handcrafted • N/A
675QX5183 • **Value $17**

17

Hot Dogger
Handcrafted • CROW
775QX4976 • **Value $19**

18

Jesus Loves Me
Acrylic • PATT
675QX3156 • **Value $16**

19

Jolly Dolphin
Handcrafted • RGRS
675QX4683 • **Value $34**

20

Joy is in the Air
Handcrafted • CROW
775QX5503 • **Value $27**

General Keepsake		
	Price Paid	Value
1.		
2.		
3.		
4.		
5.		
6.		
7.		
8.		
9.		
10.		
11.		
12.		
13.		
14.		
15.		
16.		
17.		
18.		
19.		
20.		
Totals		

1990 Collection

1

King Klaus
Handcrafted • SEAL
775QX4106 • **Value $21**

2

Kitty's Best Pal
Handcrafted • FRAN
675QX4716 • **Value $24**

3

Little Drummer Boy
Handcrafted • UNRU
775QX5233 • **Value $22**

4

Long Winter's Nap
Handcrafted • RGRS
675QX4703 • **Value $26**

5

Loveable Dears
Handcrafted • UNRU
875QX5476 • **Value $21**

6

Meow Mart
Handcrafted • PIKE
775QX4446 • **Value $30**

7

Mom and Dad
Handcrafted • CHAD
875QX4593 • **Value $27**

8

Mom-to-Be
Handcrafted • SIED
575QX4916 • **Value $33**

9

Mooy Christmas
Handcrafted • N/A
675QX4933 • **Value $32**

10

Mother
Ceramic/Bisque • VOTR
875QX4536 • **Value $25**

11

Mouseboat
Handcrafted • SEAL
775QX4753 • **Value $18**

12

New Home
Handcrafted • PYDA
675QX4343 • **Value $29**

13

Norman Rockwell Art
Glass • LYLE
475QX2296 • **Value $26**

14

Nutshell Chat
Handcrafted • N/A
675QX5193 • **Value $27**

15

Nutshell Holiday
(re-issued from 1989)
Handcrafted • RGRS
575QX4652 • **Value $27**

16

Peaceful Kingdom
Glass • N/A
475QX2106 • **Value $24**

17

PEANUTS®
Glass • N/A
475QX2233 • **Value $28**

18

Pepperoni Mouse
Handcrafted • SIED
675QX4973 • **Value $20**

19

Perfect Catch
Handcrafted • SIED
775QX4693 • **Value $21**

20

Polar Jogger
Handcrafted • SIED
575QX4666 • **Value $19**

General Keepsake

	Price Paid	Value
1.		
2.		
3.		
4.		
5.		
6.		
7.		
8.		
9.		
10.		
11.		
12.		
13.		
14.		
15.		
16.		
17.		
18.		
19.		
20.		
	Totals	

1

Polar Pair
Handcrafted • SIED
575QX4626 • **Value $26**

2

Polar Sport
Handcrafted • SIED
775QX5156 • **Value $24**

3

Polar TV
Handcrafted • SIED
775QX5166 • **Value $19**

4

Polar V.I.P.
Handcrafted • SIED
575QX4663 • **Value $18**

5

Polar Video
Handcrafted • SIED
575QX4633 • **Value $18**

6

Poolside Walrus
Handcrafted • JLEE
775QX4986 • **Value $24**

7

S. Claus Taxi
Handcrafted • DUTK
1175QX4686 • **Value $28**

8

Santa Schnoz
Handcrafted • CROW
675QX4983 • **Value $34**

9

Sister
Glass • N/A
475QX2273 • **Value $23**

10

SNOOPY and WOODSTOCK
Handcrafted • RHOD
675QX4723 • **Value $38**

11

Son
Handcrafted • SIED
575QX4516 • **Value $27**

12

Spencer® Sparrow, Esq.
(re-issued from 1989)
Handcrafted • PIKE
675QX4312 • **Value $25**

13

Spoon Rider
Handcrafted • ANDR
975QX5496 • **Value $20**

14

Stitches of Joy
Handcrafted • JLEE
775QX5186 • **Value $26**

15

Stocking Kitten
(re-issued from 1989)
Handcrafted • PIKE
675QX4565 • **Value $21**

16

Stocking Pals
Handcrafted • SEAL
1075QX5493 • **Value $26**

17

Sweetheart
Handcrafted • RHOD
1175QX4893 • **Value $30**

18

Teacher
Handcrafted • SEAL
775QX4483 • **Value $15**

19

Ten Years Together
Glass • LYLE
475QX2153 • **Value $22**

20

Three Little Piggies
Handcrafted • CROW
775QX4996 • **Value $27**

General Keepsake		
	Price Paid	Value
1.		
2.		
3.		
4.		
5.		
6.		
7.		
8.		
9.		
10.		
11.		
12.		
13.		
14.		
15.		
16.		
17.		
18.		
19.		
20.		
Totals		

1

Time for Love
Glass • LYLE
475QX2133 • **Value $26**

2

Twenty-Five Years Together
Faceted Glass • PATT
975QX4896 • **Value $20**

3

Two Peas in a Pod
Handcrafted • ANDR
475QX4926 • **Value $35**

4

Welcome, Santa
Handcrafted • CROW
1175QX4773 • **Value $27**

5

Baby's First Christmas
Handcrafted • PALM
2800QLX7246 • **Value $62**

6

Beary Short Nap
Handcrafted • SIED
1000QLX7326 • **Value $31**

7

Blessings of Love
Panorama Ball • N/A
1400QLX7363 • **Value $52**

8

Children's Express
Handcrafted • SICK
2800QLX7243 • **Value $77**

General Keepsake

	Price Paid	Value
1.		
2.		
3.		
4.		

General Magic

5.		
6.		
7.		
8.		
9.		
10.		
11.		
12.		
13.		
14.		
15.		
16.		
17.		
18.		
19.		
20.		

9

Christmas Memories
Handcrafted • UNRU
2500QLX7276 • **Value $56**

10

Deer Crossing
Handcrafted • SIED
1800QLX7213 • **Value $48**

11

Elf of the Year
Handcrafted • ANDR
1000QLX7356 • **Value $24**

12

Elfin Whittler
Handcrafted • CROW
2000QLX7265 • **Value $52**

13

First Christmas Together
Handcrafted • DLEE
1800QLX7255 • **Value $48**

14

Holiday Flash
Handcrafted • CHAD
1800QLX7333 • **Value $39**

15

Hop 'N Pop Popper
Handcrafted • SIED
2000QLX7353 • **Value $95**

16

Letter to Santa
Handcrafted • RGRS
1400QLX7226 • **Value $35**

17

Mrs. Santa's Kitchen
Handcrafted • RHOD
2500QLX7263 • **Value $72**

18

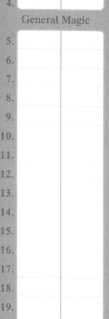

Partridges in a Pear
Dimensional Brass • LYLE
1400QLX7212 • **Value $35**

19

Santa's Ho-Ho-Hoedown
Handcrafted • CROW
2500QLX7256 • **Value $90**

20

Song and Dance
Handcrafted • RGRS
2000QLX7253 • **Value $94**

Totals

1

Starlight Angel
Handcrafted • RGRS
1400QLX7306 • **Value $38**

2

Starship Christmas
Handcrafted • SIED
1800QLX7336 • **Value $50**

3

Acorn Squirrel
(re-issued from 1989)
Handcrafted • PIKE
450QXM5682 • **Value $13**

4

Acorn Wreath
Handcrafted • CROW
600QXM5686 • **Value $13**

5

Air Santa
Handcrafted • N/A
450QXM5656 • **Value $15**

6

Baby's First Christmas
Handcrafted • FRAN
850QXM5703 • **Value $17**

7

Basket Buddy
Handcrafted/Wicker • RGRS
600QXM5696 • **Value $13**

8

Bear Hug
Handcrafted • PALM
600QXM5633 • **Value $14**

9

Brass Bouquet
Brass • LYLE
600QXM5776 • **Value $7**

10

Brass Horn
Brass • N/A
300QXM5793 • **Value $9**

11

Brass Peace
Brass • N/A
300QXM5796 • **Value $9**

12

Brass Santa
Brass • PATT
300QXM5786 • **Value $8**

13

Brass Year
Brass • N/A
300QXM5833 • **Value $8**

14

Busy Carver
Handcrafted • CROW
450QXM5673 • **Value $10**

15

Christmas Dove
Handcrafted • SIED
450QXM5636 • **Value $16**

16

Cloisonné Poinsettia
Cloisonné • VOTR
1050QXM5533 • **Value $24**

17

Country Heart
Handcrafted • RGRS
450QXM5693 • **Value $10**

18

Cozy Skater
(re-issued from 1989)
Handcrafted • LYLE
450QXM5735 • **Value $14**

19

First Christmas Together
Porcelain • ANDR
600QXM5536 • **Value $13**

20

Going Sledding
Handcrafted • JLEE
450QXM5683 • **Value $17**

General Magic

	Price Paid	Value
1.		
2.		

General Miniature

3.		
4.		
5.		
6.		
7.		
8.		
9.		
10.		
11.		
12.		
13.		
14.		
15.		
16.		
17.		
18.		
19.		
20.		

Totals

1990 Collection

1

Grandchild's First Christmas
Handcrafted • SIED
600QXM5723 • **Value $12**

2
Happy Bluebird
(re-issued from 1989)
Handcrafted • RGRS
450QXM5662 • **Value $16**

3
Holiday Cardinal
Acrylic • FRAN
300QXM5526 • **Value $13**

4
Lion and Lamb
Wood • SICK
450QXM5676 • **Value $11**

5
Little Soldier
(re-issued from 1989)
Handcrafted • SICK
450QXM5675 • **Value $12**

6

Loving Hearts
Acrylic • N/A
300QXM5523 • **Value $13**

7
Madonna and Child
Handcrafted • RGRS
600QXM5643 • **Value $13**

8
Mother
Cameo • LYLE
450QXM5716 • **Value $17**

General Miniature

	Price Paid	Value
1.		
2.		
3.		
4.		
5.		
6.		
7.		
8.		
9.		
10.		
11.		
12.		
13.		
14.		
15.		
16.		
17.		
18.		
19.		
20.		

9
Nativity
Handcrafted • UNRU
450QXM5706 • **Value $21**

10

Old-World Santa
(re-issued from 1989)
Handcrafted • SIED
300QXM5695 • **Value $11**

11

Panda's Surprise
Handcrafted • FRAN
450QXM5616 • **Value $13**

12
Perfect Fit
Handcrafted • CHAD
450QXM5516 • **Value $15**

13

Puppy Love
Handcrafted • PALM
600QXM5666 • **Value $14**

14

Roly-Poly Pig
(re-issued from 1989)
Handcrafted • PIKE
300QXM5712 • **Value $19**

15
Ruby Reindeer
Glass • PATT
600QXM5816 • **Value $13**

16

Santa's Journey
Handcrafted • SICK
850QXM5826 • **Value $22**

17

Santa's Streetcar
Handcrafted • DLEE
850QXM5766 • **Value $19**

18

Snow Angel
Handcrafted • JLEE
600QXM5773 • **Value $14**

19

Special Friends
Handcrafted • PIKE
600QXM5726 • **Value $15**

20

Stamp Collector
Handcrafted • CROW
450QXM5623 • **Value $11**

1

Stocking Pal
(re-issued from 1989)
Handcrafted • JLEE
450QXM5672 • **Value $12**

2

Stringing Along
Handcrafted • SEAL
850QXM5606 • **Value $17**

3

Sweet Slumber
Handcrafted • SIED
450QXM5663 • **Value $12**

4

Teacher
Handcrafted • PIKE
450QXM5653 • **Value $10**

5

Type of Joy
Handcrafted • CHAD
450QXM5646 • **Value $11**

6

Warm Memories
Handcrafted • SEAL
450QXM5713 • **Value $10**

7

Wee Nutcracker
Handcrafted • SIED
850QXM5843 • **Value $16**

8

Armful of Joy
(members only ornament)
Handcrafted • FRAN
975QXC4453 • **Value $46**

9

Christmas Limited
(club edition, LE-38,700)
Die-Cast Metal • SICK
1975QXC4766 • **Value $110**

10

Club Hollow
(keepsake of membership)
Handcrafted • CROW
QXC4456 • **Value $38**

11

Crown Prince
(keepsake of
membership, miniature)
Handcrafted • RGRS
QXC5603 • **Value $37**

12

Dove of Peace
(club edition, LE-25,400)
Porcelain/Brass • SICK
2475QXC4476 • **Value $77**

13

Sugar Plum Fairy
(club edition, LE-25,400)
Porcelain • ANDR
2775QXC4473 • **Value $60**

14

Little Bear (miniature)
Handcrafted • SIED
($2.95)620XPR9723 • **Value $10**

15

Little Frosty (miniature)
Handcrafted • SIED
($2.95)620XPR9720 • **Value $11**

16

Little Husky (miniature)
Handcrafted • SEAL
($2.95)620XPR9722 • **Value $12**

17

Little Seal (miniature)
Handcrafted • JLEE
($2.95)620XPR9721 • **Value $10**

18

Memory Wreath
(miniature)
Handcrafted • DLEE
($2.95)620XPR9724 • **Value $10**

19

Baby's Christening 1990
Porcelain • JLEE
1000BBY1326 • **Value $27**

20

Baby's First
Christmas 1990
Handcrafted • JLEE
1000BBY1454 • **Value $27**

General Miniature

	Price Paid	Value
1.		
2.		
3.		
4.		
5.		
6.		
7.		

Collector's Club

8.		
9.		
10.		
11.		
12.		
13.		

Reach Ornaments

14.		
15.		
16.		
17.		
18.		

Baby Celebrations

19.		
20.		

Totals

1990 / 1989 Collection

1

Baby's First Christmas 1990
Porcelain • RGRS
1000BBY1554 • **Value $27**

1989

In 1989 Hallmark debuted a popular collection of dated teddy bear ornaments celebrating a child's first five Christmases. In the 1989 collection, there were a total of 123 Keepsake ornaments, 19 Magic ornaments and 41 Miniature ornaments. See the collectibles series section for more 1989 ornaments.

2

Baby Partridge
Handcrafted • FRAN
675QX4525 • **Value $16**

3

Baby's First Christmas
Acrylic • FRAN
675QX3815 • **Value $20**

4

Baby's First Christmas
Handcrafted • CHAD
725QX4492 • **Value $90**

5

Baby's First Christmas – Baby Boy
Satin • VOTR
475QX2725 • **Value $20**

Baby Celebrations

	Price Paid	Value
1.		

General Keepsake

2.		
3.		
4.		
5.		
6.		
7.		
8.		
9.		
10.		
11.		
12.		
13.		
14.		
15.		
16.		
17.		

Totals

6

Baby's First Christmas – Baby Girl
Satin • VOTR
475QX2722 • **Value $20**

7

Baby's First Christmas Photoholder
Handcrafted • VOTR
625QX4682 • **Value $52**

8

Baby's Second Christmas
Handcrafted • FRAN
675QX4495 • **Value $32**

9

Balancing Elf
Handcrafted • CHAD
675QX4895 • **Value $24**

10

Bear-i-Tone
Handcrafted • SIED
475QX4542 • **Value $20**

11

Brother
Handcrafted • LYLE
725QX4452 • **Value $20**

12

Cactus Cowboy
Handcrafted • DUTK
675QX4112 • **Value $45**

13

Camera Claus
Handcrafted • SIED
575QX5465 • **Value $22**

14

Carousel Zebra
Handcrafted • SICK
925QX4515 • **Value $23**

15

Cherry Jubilee
Handcrafted • SICK
500QX4532 • **Value $27**

16

Child's Fifth Christmas
Handcrafted • RHOD
675QX5435 • **Value $20**

17

Child's Fourth Christmas
Handcrafted • FRAN
675QX5432 • **Value $20**

1

Child's Third Christmas
Handcrafted • FRAN
675QX4695 • **Value $22**

2

Claus Construction
(re-issued in 1990)
Handcrafted • SEAL
775QX4885 • **Value $35**

3

Cool Swing
Handcrafted • CROW
625QX4875 • **Value $35**

4

Country Cat
Handcrafted • PYDA
625QX4672 • **Value $21**

5

Cranberry Bunny
Handcrafted • RGRS
575QX4262 • **Value $18**

6

Dad
Handcrafted • N/A
725QX4412 • **Value $16**

7

Daughter
Handcrafted • SICK
625QX4432 • **Value $21**

8

Deer Disguise
Handcrafted • SIED
575QX4265 • **Value $24**

9

Feliz Navidad
Handcrafted • PYDA
675QX4392 • **Value $30**

10

Festive Angel
Dimensional Brass • N/A
675QX4635 • **Value $27**

11

Festive Year
Acrylic • VOTR
775QX3842 • **Value $23**

12

Fifty Years Together
Photoholder
Porcelain • RGRS
875QX4862 • **Value $17**

13

The First Christmas
Cameo • N/A
775QX5475 • **Value $20**

14
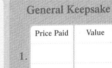
First Christmas Together
Acrylic • RHOD
675QX3832 • **Value $24**

15
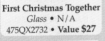
First Christmas Together
Glass • N/A
475QX2732 • **Value $27**

16

First Christmas Together
Handcrafted • RGRS
975QX4852 • **Value $24**

17

Five Years Together
Glass • N/A
475QX2735 • **Value $18**

18

Forty Years Together
Photoholder
Porcelain • RGRS
875QX5452 • **Value $17**

19

Friendship Time
Handcrafted • N/A
975QX4132 • **Value $35**

20

From Our
Home to Yours
Acrylic • N/A
625QX3845 • **Value $22**

1989 Collection

1

Gentle Fawn
Handcrafted • RGRS
775QX5485 • **Value $22**

2

George Washington Bicentennial
Acrylic • N/A
625QX3862 • **Value $19**

3

Godchild
Acrylic • FRAN
625QX3112 • **Value $17**

4

Goin' South
Handcrafted • CROW
425QX4105 • **Value $24**

5

Gone Fishing
(re-issued from 1988)
Handcrafted • SIED
575QX4794 • **Value $24**

6

Graceful Swan
Dimensional Brass • N/A
675QX4642 • **Value $21**

7

Granddaughter
Glass • N/A
475QX2782 • **Value $25**

8

Granddaughter's First Christmas
Acrylic • FRAN
675QX3822 • **Value $22**

9

Grandmother
Glass • LYLE
475QX2775 • **Value $18**

10

Grandparents
Glass • LYLE
475QX2772 • **Value $18**

11

Grandson
Glass • N/A
475QX2785 • **Value $22**

12

Grandson's First Christmas
Acrylic • FRAN
675QX3825 • **Value $18**

13

Gratitude
Acrylic • VOTR
675QX3852 • **Value $15**

14

Gym Dandy
Handcrafted • SIED
575QX4185 • **Value $20**

15

Hang in There
Handcrafted • CROW
525QX4305 • **Value $35**

16

Here's the Pitch
Handcrafted • SIED
575QX5455 • **Value $22**

17

Hoppy Holidays
Handcrafted • SIED
775QX4692 • **Value $24**

18

Horse Weathervane
Handcrafted • SICK
575QX4632 • **Value $18**

19

Joyful Trio
Handcrafted • FRAN
975QX4372 • **Value $17**

20

A KISS™ From Santa
(re-issued from 1988)
Handcrafted • UNRU
450QX4821 • **Value $30**

General Keepsake

	Price Paid	Value
1.		
2.		
3.		
4.		
5.		
6.		
7.		
8.		
9.		
10.		
11.		
12.		
13.		
14.		
15.		
16.		
17.		
18.		
19.		
20.		
Totals		

1

Kristy Claus
Handcrafted • SIED
575QX4245 • **Value $15**

2

Language of Love
Acrylic • N/A
625QX3835 • **Value $25**

3

Let's Play
Handcrafted • CROW
725QX4882 • **Value $29**

4

Mail Call
Handcrafted • SEAL
875QX4522 • **Value $21**

5

Merry-Go-Round Unicorn
Porcelain • RGRS
1075QX4472 • **Value $24**

6

Mom and Dad
Handcrafted • PIKE
975QX4425 • **Value $22**

7

Mother
Porcelain • N/A
975QX4405 • **Value $30**

8

New Home
Glass • VOTR
475QX2755 • **Value $23**

9

Norman Rockwell
Glass • LYLE
475QX2762 • **Value $22**

10

North Pole Jogger
Handcrafted • SIED
575QX5462 • **Value $23**

11

Nostalgic Lamb
Handcrafted • PYDA
675QX4665 • **Value $15**

12

Nutshell Dreams
Handcrafted • CHAD
575QX4655 • **Value $24**

13

**Nutshell Holiday
(re-issued in 1990)**
Handcrafted • RGRS
575QX4652 • **Value $27**

14

Nutshell Workshop
Handcrafted • CHAD
575QX4872 • **Value $24**

15

Old-World Gnome
Handcrafted • N/A
775QX4345 • **Value $24**

16

On the Links
Handcrafted • SIED
575QX4192 • **Value $24**

17

**OREO® Chocolate
Sandwich Cookies
(re-issued from 1988)**
Handcrafted • UNRU
400QX4814 • **Value $22**

18

**The Ornament
Express (set/3)**
Handcrafted • SICK
2200QX5805 • **Value $44**

19

Owliday Greetings
Handcrafted • PIKE
400QX4365 • **Value $21**

20

Paddington™ Bear
Handcrafted • FRAN
575QX4292 • **Value $23**

General Keepsake		
	Price Paid	Value
1.		
2.		
3.		
4.		
5.		
6.		
7.		
8.		
9.		
10.		
11.		
12.		
13.		
14.		
15.		
16.		
17.		
18.		
19.		
20.		
Totals		

1

Party Line
(re-issued from 1988)
Handcrafted • PIKE
875QX4761 • **Value $31**

2

PEANUTS® – A Charlie
Brown Christmas
Glass • N/A
475QX2765 • **Value $47**

3

Peek-a-Boo Kitties
(re-issued from 1988)
Handcrafted • CROW
750QX4871 • **Value $25**

4

Peppermint Clown
Porcelain • DUTK
2475QX4505 • **Value $44**

5

Playful Angel
Handcrafted • DLEE
675QX4535 • **Value $24**

6

Polar Bowler
(re-issued from 1988)
Handcrafted • SIED
575QX4784 • **Value $19**

7

Rodney Reindeer
Handcrafted • SIED
675QX4072 • **Value $17**

8

Rooster Weathervane
Handcrafted • SICK
575QX4675 • **Value $18**

9

Sea Santa
Handcrafted • SIED
575QX4152 • **Value $29**

10

Sister
Glass • N/A
475QX2792 • **Value $21**

11

SNOOPY and
WOODSTOCK
Handcrafted • RHOD
675QX4332 • **Value $40**

12

Snowplow Santa
Handcrafted • SIED
575QX4205 • **Value $23**

13

Son
Handcrafted • SICK
625QX4445 • **Value $21**

14

Sparkling Snowflake
Brass • LYLE
775QX5472 • **Value $24**

15

Special Delivery
Handcrafted • RGRS
525QX4325 • **Value $24**

16

Spencer® Sparrow, Esq.
(re-issued in 1990)
Handcrafted • PIKE
675QX4312 • **Value $25**

17

Stocking Kitten
(re-issued in 1990)
Handcrafted • PIKE
675QX4565 • **Value $21**

18

Sweet Memories
Photoholder
Handcrafted • N/A
675QX4385 • **Value $25**

19

Sweetheart
Handcrafted • SICK
975QX4865 • **Value $36**

20

Teacher
Handcrafted • SIED
575QX4125 • **Value $24**

General Keepsake

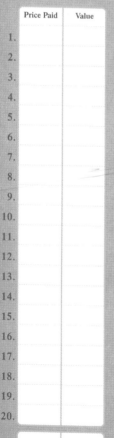

	Price Paid	Value
1.		
2.		
3.		
4.		
5.		
6.		
7.		
8.		
9.		
10.		
11.		
12.		
13.		
14.		
15.		
16.		
17.		
18.		
19.		
20.		

Totals

1

Teeny Taster
(re-issued from 1988)
Handcrafted • SEAL
475QX4181 • **Value $31**

2

Ten Years Together
Glass • LYLE
475QX2742 • **Value $27**

3

TV Break
Handcrafted • DLEE
625QX4092 • **Value $20**

4

Twenty-Five Years
Together Photoholder
Porcelain • RGRS
875QX4855 • **Value $17**

5

Wiggly Snowman
Handcrafted • RHOD
675QX4892 • **Value $29**

6

World of Love
Glass • N/A
475QX2745 • **Value $36**

7

Angel Melody
Acrylic • VOTR
950QLX7202 • **Value $24**

8

The Animals Speak
Panorama Ball • FRAN
1350QLX7232 • **Value $122**

9

Baby's First Christmas
Handcrafted • SEAL
3000QLX7272 • **Value $62**

10

Backstage Bear
Handcrafted • SIED
1350QLX7215 • **Value $37**

11

Busy Beaver
Handcrafted • DLEE
1750QLX7245 • **Value $48**

12

First Christmas Together
Handcrafted • DLEE
1750QLX7342 • **Value $45**

13

Holiday Bell
Lead Crystal • N/A
1750QLX7222 • **Value $36**

14

Joyous Carolers
Handcrafted • UNRU
3000QLX7295 • **Value $72**

15

Kringle's Toy Shop
(re-issued from 1988)
Handcrafted • SEAL
2450QLX7017 • **Value $54**

16

Loving Spoonful
Handcrafted • SIED
1950QLX7262 • **Value $40**

17

Metro Express
Handcrafted • SICK
2800QLX7275 • **Value $84**

18

Moonlit Nap
(re-issued from 1988)
Handcrafted • CHAD
875QLX7134 • **Value $29**

19

Rudolph the
Red-Nosed Reindeer®
Handcrafted • CHAD
1950QLX7252 • **Value $62**

20

Spirit of St. Nick
Handcrafted • SEAL
2450QLX7285 • **Value $68**

	Price Paid	Value
General Keepsake		
1.		
2.		
3.		
4.		
5.		
6.		
General Magic		
7.		
8.		
9.		
10.		
11.		
12.		
13.		
14.		
15.		
16.		
17.		
18.		
19.		
20.		
Totals		

1

Tiny Tinker
Handcrafted • CROW
1950QLX7174 • **Value $57**

2

Unicorn Fantasy
Handcrafted • RHOD
950QLX7235 • **Value $23**

3

Acorn Squirrel
(re-issued in 1990)
Handcrafted • PIKE
450QXM5682 • **Value $13**

4

Baby's First Christmas
Handcrafted • PIKE
600QXM5732 • **Value $14**

5

Brass Partridge
Brass • LYLE
300QXM5725 • **Value $13**

6

Brass Snowflake
Dimensional Brass • LYLE
450QXM5702 • **Value $14**

7

Bunny Hug
Acrylic • VOTR
300QXM5775 • **Value $11**

8

Country Wreath
(re-issued from 1988)
Handcrafted • RGRS
450QXM5731 • **Value $12**

9

Cozy Skater
(re-issued in 1990)
Handcrafted • LYLE
450QXM5735 • **Value $14**

10

First Christmas Together
Ceramic • VOTR
850QXM5642 • **Value $12**

11

Folk Art Bunny
Handcrafted • PATT
450QXM5692 • **Value $12**

12

Happy Bluebird
(re-issued in 1990)
Handcrafted • RGRS
450QXM5662 • **Value $16**

13

Holiday Deer
Acrylic • VOTR
300QXM5772 • **Value $12**

14

Holy Family
(re-issued from 1988)
Handcrafted • UNRU
850QXM5611 • **Value $16**

15

Kitty Cart
Wood • PATT
300QXM5722 • **Value $10**

16

Little Soldier
(re-issued in 1990)
Handcrafted • SICK
450QXM5675 • **Value $12**

17

Little Star Bringer
Handcrafted • LYLE
600QXM5622 • **Value $21**

18

Load of Cheer
Handcrafted • RHOD
600QXM5745 • **Value $19**

19

Lovebirds
Handcrafted/Brass • PIKE
600QXM5635 • **Value $14**

20

Merry Seal
Porcelain • FRAN
600QXM5755 • **Value $16**

General Magic

	Price Paid	Value
1.		
2.		

General Miniature

3.		
4.		
5.		
6.		
7.		
8.		
9.		
10.		
11.		
12.		
13.		
14.		
15.		
16.		
17.		
18.		
19.		
20.		

1

Mother
Cameo • N/A
600QXM5645 • **Value $13**

2

Old-World Santa
(re-issued in 1990)
Handcrafted • SIED
300QXM5695 • **Value $11**

3

Pinecone Basket
Handcrafted • RHOD
450QXM5734 • **Value $9**

4

Puppy Cart
Wood • SICK
300QXM5715 • **Value $10**

5

Rejoice
Acrylic • VOTR
300QXM5782 • **Value $10**

6

Roly-Poly Pig
(re-issued in 1990)
Handcrafted • PIKE
300QXM5712 • **Value $19**

7

Roly-Poly Ram
Handcrafted • N/A
300QXM5705 • **Value $16**

8

Santa's Magic Ride
Handcrafted • RGRS
850QXM5632 • **Value $21**

9

Santa's Roadster
Handcrafted • CROW
600QXM5665 • **Value $20**

10

Scrimshaw Reindeer
Handcrafted • VOTR
450QXM5685 • **Value $12**

11

Sharing a Ride
Handcrafted • DUTK
850QXM5765 • **Value $18**

12

Slow Motion
Handcrafted • SIED
600QXM5752 • **Value $17**

13

Special Friend
Handcrafted/Willow • N/A
450QXM5652 • **Value $14**

14

Starlit Mouse
Handcrafted • RHOD
450QXM5655 • **Value $18**

15

Stocking Pal
(re-issued in 1990)
Handcrafted • JLEE
450QXM5672 • **Value $12**

16

Strollin' Snowman
Porcelain • SIED
450QXM5742 • **Value $17**

17

Three Little Kitties
(re-issued from 1988)
Handcrafted/Willow • PIKE
600QXM5694 • **Value $18**

18

Christmas is Peaceful
(club edition, LE-49,900)
Bone China • SEAL
1850QXC4512 • **Value $47**

19

Collect a Dream
(club edition)
Handcrafted • PIKE
900QXC4285 • **Value $70**

20

Noelle
(club edition, LE-49,900)
Porcelain • UNRU
1975QXC4483 • **Value $58**

General Miniature	Price Paid	Value
1.		
2.		
3.		
4.		
5.		
6.		
7.		
8.		
9.		
10.		
11.		
12.		
13.		
14.		
15.		
16.		
17.		
Collector's Club		
18.		
19.		
20.		
Totals		

1

Sitting Purrty
(keepsake of
membership, miniature)
Handcrafted • DUTK
QXC5812 • **Value $50**

2

Visit From Santa
(keepsake of membership)
Handcrafted • CROW
QXC5802 • **Value $56**

3

Carousel Display Stand
Handcrafted/Brass • N/A
($1.00)629XPR9723 • **Value $10**

4

Ginger
Handcrafted/Brass • JLEE
($3.95)629XPR9721 • **Value $20**

5

Holly
Handcrafted/Brass • JLEE
($3.95)629XPR9722 • **Value $20**

6

Snow
Handcrafted/Brass • JLEE
($3.95)629XPR9719 • **Value $35**

7

Star
Handcrafted/Brass • JLEE
($3.95)629XPR9720 • **Value $20**

8

**Baby's Christening
Keepsake**
Acrylic • N/A
700BBY1325 • **Value $30**

Collector's Club

	Price Paid	Value
1.		
2.		

Reach Ornaments

3.		
4.		
5.		
6.		
7.		

Baby Celebrations

8.		
9.		
10.		
11.		

General Keepsake

12.		
13.		
14.		
15.		
16.		
17.		

9

Baby's First Birthday
Acrylic • N/A
550BBY1729 • **Value $30**

10

**Baby's First
Christmas – Baby Boy**
(same as #475QX2725)
Satin • VOTR
475BBY1453 • **Value $20**

11

**Baby's First
Christmas – Baby Girl**
(same as #475QX2722)
Satin • VOTR
475BBY1553 • **Value $20**

1988

1988 was the year Hallmark introduced its famous collection of
Miniature ornaments to the
Keepsake family. In its debut year, the Miniature line featured
27 ornaments, while the Keepsake line included 118 and Magic
included 20. See the collectible series section for more 1988
ornaments.

12

Americana Drum
Tin • SICK
775QX4881 • **Value $34**

13

Arctic Tenor
Handcrafted • SIED
400QX4721 • **Value $18**

14

Baby Redbird
Handcrafted • CHAD
500QX4101 • **Value $22**

15

Baby's First Christmas
Acrylic • PIKE
600QX3721 • **Value $23**

16

Baby's First Christmas
Handcrafted • CROW
975QX4701 • **Value $40**

17

**Baby's First Christmas
– Baby Boy**
Satin • N/A
475QX2721 • **Value $25**

Totals

1

Baby's First Christmas – Baby Girl
Satin • N/A
475QX2724 • **Value $25**

2

Baby's First Christmas Photoholder
Fabric • N/A
750QX4704 • **Value $31**

3

Baby's Second Christmas
Handcrafted • PIKE
600QX4711 • **Value $35**

4

Babysitter
Glass • SICK
475QX2791 • **Value $12**

5

Child's Third Christmas
Handcrafted • CHAD
600QX4714 • **Value $29**

6

Christmas Cardinal
Handcrafted • RGRS
475QX4941 • **Value $21**

7

Christmas Cuckoo
Handcrafted • CROW
800QX4801 • **Value $33**

8

Christmas Memories Photoholder
Acrylic • PATT
650QX3724 • **Value $26**

9

Cool Juggler
Handcrafted • CROW
650QX4874 • **Value $23**

10

Cymbals of Christmas
Handcrafted/Acrylic • DLEE
550QX4111 • **Value $30**

11

Dad
Handcrafted • SIED
700QX4141 • **Value $26**

12

Daughter
Handcrafted • PATT
575QX4151 • **Value $60**

13

Feliz Navidad
Handcrafted • UNRU
675QX4161 • **Value $36**

14

Fifty Years Together
Acrylic • N/A
675QX3741 • **Value $19**

15

Filled With Fudge
Handcrafted • SEAL
475QX4191 • **Value $34**

16

First Christmas Together
Acrylic • VOTR
675QX3731 • **Value $26**

17

First Christmas Together
Glass • N/A
475QX2741 • **Value $25**

18

First Christmas Together
Handcrafted • PIKE
900QX4894 • **Value $34**

19

Five Years Together
Glass • MCGE
475QX2744 • **Value $19**

20

From Our Home to Yours
Glass • PATT
475QX2794 • **Value $18**

General Keepsake

	Price Paid	Value
1.		
2.		
3.		
4.		
5.		
6.		
7.		
8.		
9.		
10.		
11.		
12.		
13.		
14.		
15.		
16.		
17.		
18.		
19.		
20.		

Totals

1

Glowing Wreath
Dimensional Brass • PATT
600QX4921 • **Value $15**

2

Go for the Gold
Handcrafted • SIED
800QX4174 • **Value $29**

3

Godchild
Glass • N/A
475QX2784 • **Value $21**

4

Goin' Cross Country
Handcrafted • SICK
850QX4764 • **Value $26**

5

Gone Fishing
(re-issued in 1989)
Handcrafted • SIED
500QX4794 • **Value $24**

6

Granddaughter
Glass • VOTR
475QX2774 • **Value $35**

7

Grandmother
Glass • N/A
475QX2764 • **Value $21**

8

Grandparents
Glass • PATT
475QX2771 • **Value $22**

9

Grandson
Glass • VOTR
475QX2781 • **Value $33**

10

Gratitude
Acrylic • PATT
600QX3754 • **Value $14**

11

Happy Holidata
(re-issued from 1987)
Handcrafted • SIED
650QX4717 • **Value $32**

12

Hoe-Hoe-Hoe!
Handcrafted • SIED
500QX4221 • **Value $18**

13

Holiday Hero
Handcrafted • SIED
500QX4231 • **Value $22**

14

In a Nutshell
(re-issued from 1987)
Handcrafted • UNRU
550QX4697 • **Value $33**

15

Jingle Bell Clown
Handcrafted • N/A
1500QX4774 • **Value $34**

16

Jolly Walrus
Handcrafted • RGRS
450QX4731 • **Value $27**

17

A KISS™ From Santa
(re-issued in 1989)
Handcrafted • UNRU
450QX4821 • **Value $30**

18

Kiss the Claus
Handcrafted • SIED
500QX4861 • **Value $17**

19

Kringle Moon
Handcrafted • RGRS
550QX4951 • **Value $36**

20

Kringle Portrait
Handcrafted • N/A
750QX4961 • **Value $35**

General Keepsake

	Price Paid	Value
1.		
2.		
3.		
4.		
5.		
6.		
7.		
8.		
9.		
10.		
11.		
12.		
13.		
14.		
15.		
16.		
17.		
18.		
19.		
20.		

Totals

1

Kringle Tree
Handcrafted • N/A
650QX4954 • **Value $42**

2

Little Jack Horner
Handcrafted • SIED
800QX4081 • **Value $27**

3

Love Fills the Heart
Acrylic • VOTR
600QX3744 • **Value $26**

4

Love Grows
Glass • VOTR
475QX2754 • **Value $35**

5

Love Santa
Handcrafted • SIED
500QX4864 • **Value $19**

6

Loving Bear
Handcrafted • RGRS
475QX4934 • **Value $21**

7

Merry-Mint Unicorn
Porcelain • RGRS
850QX4234 • **Value $24**

8

Midnight Snack
Handcrafted • SIED
600QX4104 • **Value $23**

9

Mistletoad
(re-issued from 1987)
Handcrafted • CROW
700QX4687 • **Value $32**

10

Mother
Acrylic • N/A
650QX3751 • **Value $20**

11

Mother and Dad
Porcelain • LYLE
800QX4144 • **Value $21**

12

New Home
Acrylic • VOTR
600QX3761 • **Value $24**

13

Nick the Kick
Handcrafted • SIED
500QX4224 • **Value $26**

14

Night Before Christmas
(re-issued from 1987)
Handcrafted • CROW
650QX4517 • **Value $36**

15

Noah's Ark
Pressed Tin • SICK
850QX4904 • **Value $45**

16

Norman Rockwell:
Christmas Scenes
Glass • LYLE
475QX2731 • **Value $27**

17

Old-Fashioned Church
Wood • SICK
400QX4981 • **Value $25**

18

Old-Fashioned
Schoolhouse
Wood • SICK
400QX4971 • **Value $25**

19

OREO® Chocolate
Sandwich Cookies
(re-issued in 1989)
Handcrafted • UNRU
400QX4814 • **Value $22**

20

"Owliday" Wish
(re-issued from 1987)
Handcrafted • PIKE
650QX4559 • **Value $21**

General Keepsake

	Price Paid	Value
1.		
2.		
3.		
4.		
5.		
6.		
7.		
8.		
9.		
10.		
11.		
12.		
13.		
14.		
15.		
16.		
17.		
18.		
19.		
20.		

Totals

1

Par for Santa
Handcrafted • SIED
500QX4791 • **Value $22**

2

Party Line
(re-issued in 1989)
Handcrafted • PIKE
875QX4761 • **Value $31**

3

PEANUTS®
Glass • N/A
475QX2801 • **Value $53**

4

Peek-a-Boo Kitties
(re-issued in 1989)
Handcrafted • CROW
750QX4871 • **Value $25**

5

Polar Bowler
(re-issued in 1989)
Handcrafted • SIED
500QX4784 • **Value $19**

6

Purrfect Snuggle
Handcrafted • RGRS
625QX4744 • **Value $30**

7

Reindoggy
(re-issued from 1987)
Handcrafted • SIED
575QX4527 • **Value $39**

8

Sailing! Sailing!
Pressed Tin • SICK
850QX4911 • **Value $27**

General Keepsake

	Price Paid	Value
1.		
2.		
3.		
4.		
5.		
6.		
7.		
8.		
9.		
10.		
11.		
12.		
13.		
14.		
15.		
16.		
17.		
18.		
19.		
20.		

9

St. Louie Nick
(re-issued from 1987)
Handcrafted • DUTK
775QX4539 • **Value $33**

10

Santa Flamingo
Handcrafted • PYDA
475QX4834 • **Value $37**

11

Shiny Sleigh
Dimensional Brass • PATT
575QX4924 • **Value $19**

12

Sister
Porcelain • VOTR
800QX4994 • **Value $32**

13

Slipper Spaniel
Handcrafted • CROW
425QX4724 • **Value $20**

14

SNOOPY® and
WOODSTOCK
Handcrafted • UNRU
600QX4741 • **Value $48**

15

Soft Landing
Handcrafted • CHAD
700QX4751 • **Value $26**

16

Son
Handcrafted • PATT
575QX4154 • **Value $41**

17

Sparkling Tree
Dimensional Brass • PATT
600QX4931 • **Value $20**

18

Spirit of Christmas
Glass • LYLE
475QX2761 • **Value $25**

19

Squeaky Clean
Handcrafted • PIKE
675QX4754 • **Value $23**

20

Starry Angel
Handcrafted • RGRS
475QX4944 • **Value $21**

Totals

1

Sweet Star
Handcrafted • SEAL
500QX4184 • **Value $33**

2

Sweetheart
Handcrafted • UNRU
975QX4901 • **Value $25**

3

Teacher
Handcrafted • PIKE
625QX4171 • **Value $21**

4

Teeny Taster
(re-issued in 1989)
Handcrafted • SEAL
475QX4181 • **Value $31**

5

Ten Years Together
Glass • N/A
475QX2751 • **Value $22**

6

The Town Crier
Handcrafted • SEAL
550QX4734 • **Value $22**

7

Travels with Santa
Handcrafted • DLEE
1000QX4771 • **Value $40**

8

Treetop Dreams
(re-issued from 1987)
Handcrafted • SEAL
675QX4597 • **Value $32**

9

**Twenty-Five
Years Together**
Acrylic • PATT
675QX3734 • **Value $18**

10

Uncle Sam Nutcracker
Handcrafted • DLEE
700QX4884 • **Value $36**

11

Very Strawbeary
Handcrafted • DUTK
475QX4091 • **Value $23**

12

Winter Fun
Handcrafted • CHAD
850QX4781 • **Value $22**

13

**The Wonderful
Santacycle**
Handcrafted • SEAL
2250QX4114 • **Value $47**

14

Year to Remember
Ceramic • N/A
700QX4164 • **Value $25**

15

Baby's First Christmas
Handcrafted • SEAL
2400QLX7184 • **Value $60**

16

Bearly Reaching
Handcrafted • SICK
950QLX7151 • **Value $37**

17

Christmas Is Magic
Handcrafted • CROW
1200QLX7171 • **Value $58**

18

Christmas Morning
(re-issued from 1987)
Handcrafted • CROW
2450QLX7013 • **Value $48**

19

Circling the Globe
Handcrafted • CROW
1050QLX7124 • **Value $44**

20

Country Express
Handcrafted • SICK
2450QLX7211 • **Value $72**

General Keepsake

	Price Paid	Value
1.		
2.		
3.		
4.		
5.		
6.		
7.		
8.		
9.		
10.		
11.		
12.		
13.		
14.		

General Magic

15.		
16.		
17.		
18.		
19.		
20.		

Totals

1988 Collection

1

Festive Feeder
Handcrafted • SICK
1150QLX7204 • **Value $50**

2

First Christmas Together
Handcrafted • SICK
1200QLX7027 • **Value $40**

3

Heavenly Glow
Brass • PYDA
1175QLX7114 • **Value $28**

4

Kitty Capers
Handcrafted • PIKE
1300QLX7164 • **Value $44**

5

Last-Minute Hug
Handcrafted • UNRU
2200QLX7181 • **Value $48**

6

Moonlit Nap
(re-issued in 1989)
Handcrafted • CHAD
875QLX7134 • **Value $29**

7

Parade of the Toys
Handcrafted • SICK
2450QLX7194 • **Value $53**

8

Radiant Tree
Brass • LYLE
1175QLX7121 • **Value $27**

General Magic

	Price Paid	Value
1.		
2.		
3.		
4.		
5.		
6.		
7.		
8.		
9.		
10.		
11.		

General Miniature

12.		
13.		
14.		
15.		
16.		
17.		
18.		
19.		
20.		

9

Skater's Waltz
Handcrafted • UNRU
2450QLX7201 • **Value $55**

10

Song of Christmas
Acrylic • N/A
850QLX7111 • **Value $28**

11

Tree of Friendship
Acrylic • N/A
850QLX7104 • **Value $27**

12

Baby's First Christmas
Handcrafted • DLEE
600QXM5744 • **Value $12**

13

Brass Angel
Brass • LYLE
150QXM5671 • **Value $20**

14

Brass Star
Brass • LYLE
150QXM5664 • **Value $20**

15

Brass Tree
Brass • LYLE
150QXM5674 • **Value $20**

16

Candy Cane Elf
Handcrafted • SIED
300QXM5701 • **Value $19**

17

Country Wreath
(re-issued in 1989)
Handcrafted • RGRS
400QXM5731 • **Value $12**

18

First Christmas Together
Wood/Straw • MCGE
400QXM5741 • **Value $13**

19

Folk Art Lamb
Wood • PATT
275QXM5681 • **Value $24**

20

Folk Art Reindeer
Wood • PATT
300QXM5684 • **Value $20**

Totals

1

Friends Share Joy
Acrylic • PATT
200QXM5764 • **Value $15**

2

Gentle Angel
Acrylic • VOTR
200QXM5771 • **Value $20**

3

Happy Santa
Glass • PATT
450QXM5614 • **Value $22**

4

Holy Family
(re-issued in 1989)
Handcrafted • UNRU
850QXM5611 • **Value $16**

5

Jolly St. Nick
Handcrafted • UNRU
800QXM5721 • **Value $32**

6

Joyous Heart
Wood • MCGE
350QXM5691 • **Value $30**

7

Little Drummer Boy
Handcrafted • SIED
450QXM5784 • **Value $28**

8

Love Is Forever
Acrylic • PATT
200QXM5774 • **Value $16**

9

Mother
Handcrafted • PIKE
300QXM5724 • **Value $13**

10

Skater's Waltz
Handcrafted • UNRU
700QXM5601 • **Value $20**

11

Sneaker Mouse
Handcrafted • N/A
400QXM5711 • **Value $21**

12

Snuggly Skater
Handcrafted • SIED
450QXM5714 • **Value $27**

13

Sweet Dreams
Handcrafted • N/A
700QXM5604 • **Value $22**

14

Three Little Kitties
(re-issued in 1989)
Handcrafted/Willow • PIKE
600QXM5694 • **Value $18**

15

Angelic Minstrel
(club edition, LE-49,900)
Porcelain • DLEE
2950QX4084 • **Value $52**

16

Christmas is Sharing
(club edition, LE-49,900)
Bone China • SEAL
1750QX4071 • **Value $48**

17

Hold on Tight
(early renewal piece,
miniature)
Handcrafted • SIED
QXC5704 • **Value $75**

18

Our Clubhouse
(keepsake of membership)
Handcrafted • SIED
QXC5804 • **Value $46**

19

Seal of Friendship
(gift membership bonus,
Merry Miniature)
Handcrafted • VOTR
QXC5104 • **Value $60**

20

Sleighful of Dreams
(club edition)
Handcrafted • SICK
800QXC5801 • **Value $70**

General Miniature

	Price Paid	Value
1.		
2.		
3.		
4.		
5.		
6.		
7.		
8.		
9.		
10.		
11.		
12.		
13.		
14.		

Collector's Club

15.		
16.		
17.		
18.		
19.		
20.		

Totals

1

Kringle's Toy Shop
(re-issued in 1989, magic)
Handcrafted • SEAL
2450QLX7017 • **Value $54**

1987

Among the most sought-after ornaments from 1987 is "Bright Christmas Dreams," which is coveted by collectors of the "CRAYOLA® Crayon" collectible series, although it is not officially a part of that series. Overall, there were 122 Keepsake ornaments and 18 Magic ornaments. See the collectible series section for more 1987 ornaments.

2

Baby Locket
Textured Metal • N/A
1500QX4617 • **Value $30**

3

Baby's First Christmas
Acrylic • N/A
600QX3729 • **Value $21**

4

Baby's First Christmas
Handcrafted • DLEE
975QX4113 • **Value $28**

5

Baby's First Christmas – Baby Boy
Satin • PATT
475QX2749 • **Value $30**

6

Baby's First Christmas – Baby Girl
Satin • PATT
475QX2747 • **Value $27**

7

Baby's First Christmas Photoholder
Fabric • N/A
750QX4619 • **Value $31**

8

Baby's Second Christmas
Handcrafted • DLEE
575QX4607 • **Value $33**

9

Babysitter
Glass • PIKE
475QX2797 • **Value $22**

10

Beary Special
Handcrafted • SIED
475QX4557 • **Value $28**

11

Bright Christmas Dreams
Handcrafted • SIED
725QX4737 • **Value $92**

12

Child's Third Christmas
Handcrafted • CROW
575QX4599 • **Value $28**

13

Chocolate Chipmunk
Handcrafted • SEAL
600QX4567 • **Value $55**

14

Christmas Cuddle
Handcrafted • N/A
575QX4537 • **Value $35**

15

Christmas Fun Puzzle
Handcrafted • DLEE
800QX4679 • **Value $30**

16

Christmas is Gentle
(LE-24,700)
Bone China • SEAL
1750QX4449 • **Value $82**

17

Christmas Keys
Handcrafted • UNRU
575QX4739 • **Value $34**

VALUE GUIDE — HALLMARK KEEPSAKE ORNAMENTS

1

Christmas Time Mime
(LE-24,700)
Porcelain • UNRU
2750QX4429 • **Value $62**

2

The Constitution
Acrylic • PATT
650QX3777 • **Value $28**

3

Country Wreath
Wood/Straw • PYDA
575QX4709 • **Value $31**

4

Currier & Ives:
American Farm Scene
Glass • LYLE
475QX2829 • **Value $32**

5

Dad
Handcrafted • SIED
600QX4629 • **Value $40**

6

Daughter
Handcrafted • SICK
575QX4637 • **Value $30**

7

December Showers
Handcrafted • DLEE
550QX4487 • **Value $37**

8

Doc Holiday
Handcrafted • SEAL
800QX4677 • **Value $46**

9

Dr. Seuss: The
Grinch's Christmas
Glass • N/A
475QX2783 • **Value $105**

10

Favorite Santa
Porcelain • DUTK
2250QX4457 • **Value $50**

11

Fifty Years Together
Porcelain • SEAL
800QX4437 • **Value $28**

12

First Christmas
Together
Acrylic • N/A
650QX3719 • **Value $25**

13

First Christmas
Together
Glass • LYLE
475QX2729 • **Value $24**

14

First Christmas
Together
Handcrafted • N/A
800QX4459 • **Value $38**

15

First Christmas
Together
Handcrafted • DLEE
950QX4467 • **Value $29**

16

First Christmas
Together
Textured Brass • N/A
1500QX4469 • **Value $30**

17

Folk Art Santa
Handcrafted • SICK
525QX4749 • **Value $36**

18

From Our
Home to Yours
Glass • PYDA
475QX2799 • **Value $47**

19

Fudge Forever
Handcrafted • DUTK
500QX4497 • **Value $38**

20

Godchild
Glass • PYDA
475QX2767 • **Value $23**

General Keepsake	Price Paid	Value
1.		
2.		
3.		
4.		
5.		
6.		
7.		
8.		
9.		
10.		
11.		
12.		
13.		
14.		
15.		
16.		
17.		
18.		
19.		
20.		
Totals		

1

Goldfinch
Porcelain • SICK
700QX4649 • **Value $85**

2

**Grandchild's
First Christmas**
Handcrafted • SEAL
900QX4609 • **Value $25**

3

Granddaughter
Bezeled Satin • VOTR
600QX3747 • **Value $25**

4

Grandmother
Glass • N/A
475QX2779 • **Value $18**

5

Grandparents
Glass • PIKE
475QX2777 • **Value $19**

6

Grandson
Glass • VOTR
475QX2769 • **Value $28**

7

Happy Holidata
(re-issued in 1988)
Handcrafted • SIED
650QX4717 • **Value $32**

8

Happy Santa
Handcrafted • CROW
475QX4569 • **Value $32**

9

Heart in Blossom
Acrylic • VOTR
600QX3727 • **Value $23**

10

Heavenly Harmony
Handcrafted • CROW
1500QX4659 • **Value $34**

11

Holiday Greetings
Bezeled Foil • N/A
600QX3757 • **Value $13**

12

Holiday Hourglass
Handcrafted • UNRU
800QX4707 • **Value $28**

13

Hot Dogger
Handcrafted • UNRU
650QX4719 • **Value $28**

14

Husband
Cameo • VOTR
700QX3739 • **Value $11**

15

I Remember Santa
Glass • LYLE
475QX278-9 • **Value $37**

16

Icy Treat
Handcrafted • SIED
450QX4509 • **Value $29**

17

In a Nutshell
(re-issued in 1988)
Handcrafted • UNRU
550QX4697 • **Value $33**

18

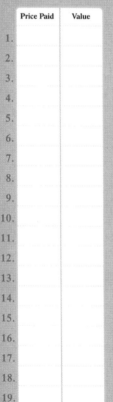

Jack Frosting
Handcrafted • SEAL
700QX4499 • **Value $54**

19

Jammie Pies™
Glass • N/A
475QX2839 • **Value $21**

20

**Jogging
Through the Snow**
Handcrafted • DUTK
725QX4577 • **Value $40**

General Keepsake

	Price Paid	Value
1.		
2.		
3.		
4.		
5.		
6.		
7.		
8.		
9.		
10.		
11.		
12.		
13.		
14.		
15.		
16.		
17.		
18.		
19.		
20.		

Totals

1

Jolly Follies
Handcrafted • CROW
850QX4669 • **Value $36**

2

Jolly Hiker
(re-issued from 1986)
Handcrafted • SIED
500QX4832 • **Value $30**

3

Joy Ride
Handcrafted • SEAL
1150QX4407 • **Value $77**

4

Joyous Angels
Handcrafted • SEAL
775QX4657 • **Value $27**

5

Let It Snow
Handcrafted • N/A
650QX4589 • **Value $25**

6

L'il Jingler
(re-issued from 1986)
Handcrafted • SEAL
675QX4193 • **Value $42**

7

Little Whittler
Handcrafted • DUTK
600QX4699 • **Value $35**

8

Love Is Everywhere
Glass • LYLE
475QX2787 • **Value $26**

9

Merry Koala
(re-issued from 1986)
Handcrafted • SICK
500QX4153 • **Value $25**

10

Mistletoad
(re-issued in 1988)
Handcrafted • CROW
700QX4687 • **Value $32**

11

Mother
Acrylic • PIKE
650QX3737 • **Value $18**

12

Mother and Dad
Porcelain • PIKE
700QX4627 • **Value $26**

13

Mouse in the Moon
(re-issued from 1986)
Handcrafted • SEAL
550QX4166 • **Value $24**

14

Nature's Decorations
Glass • VOTR
475QX2739 • **Value $36**

15

New Home
Acrylic • PATT
600QX3767 • **Value $29**

16

Niece
Glass • N/A
475QX2759 • **Value $13**

17

Night Before Christmas
(re-issued in 1988)
Handcrafted • CROW
650QX4517 • **Value $36**

18

Norman Rockwell:
Christmas Scenes
Glass • LYLE
475QX2827 • **Value $27**

19

Nostalgic Rocker
Wood • SICK
650QX4689 • **Value $32**

20

"Owliday" Wish
(re-issued in 1988)
Handcrafted • PIKE
650QX4559 • **Value $21**

General Keepsake

	Price Paid	Value
1.		
2.		
3.		
4.		
5.		
6.		
7.		
8.		
9.		
10.		
11.		
12.		
13.		
14.		
15.		
16.		
17.		
18.		
19.		
20.		

Totals

1987 Collection

1

Paddington™ Bear
Handcrafted • PIKE
550QX4727 • **Value $34**

2

PEANUTS®
Glass • N/A
475QX2819 • **Value $40**

3

Pretty Kitty
Handcrafted/Glass • CROW
1100QX4489 • **Value $34**

4

Promise of Peace
Acrylic • PIKE
650QX3749 • **Value $27**

5

Raccoon Biker
Handcrafted • SIED
700QX4587 • **Value $32**

6

Reindoggy
(re-issued in 1988)
Handcrafted • SIED
575QX4527 • **Value $39**

7

St. Louie Nick
(re-issued in 1988)
Handcrafted • DUTK
775QX4539 • **Value $33**

8

Santa at the Bat
Handcrafted • SIED
775QX4579 • **Value $29**

9

Seasoned Greetings
Handcrafted • SEAL
625QX4549 • **Value $30**

10

Sister
Wood • SICK
600QX4747 • **Value $16**

11

Sleepy Santa
Handcrafted • CROW
625QX4507 • **Value $40**

12

SNOOPY and WOODSTOCK
Handcrafted • SIED
725QX4729 • **Value $52**

13

Son
Handcrafted • SICK
575QX4639 • **Value $44**

14

Special Memories Photoholder
Fabric • N/A
675QX4647 • **Value $27**

15

Spots 'n Stripes
Handcrafted • N/A
550QX4529 • **Value $28**

16

Sweetheart
Handcrafted • SICK
1100QX4479 • **Value $30**

17

Teacher
Handcrafted • SIED
575QX4667 • **Value $23**

18

Ten Years Together
Porcelain • VOTR
700QX4447 • **Value $24**

19

Three Men in a Tub
Handcrafted • DLEE
800QX4547 • **Value $27**

20

Time for Friends
Glass • VOTR
475QX2807 • **Value $24**

General Keepsake

	Price Paid	Value
1.		
2.		
3.		
4.		
5.		
6.		
7.		
8.		
9.		
10.		
11.		
12.		
13.		
14.		
15.		
16.		
17.		
18.		
19.		
20.		
Totals		

Value Guide — Hallmark Keepsake Ornaments

1

Treetop Dreams
(re-issued in 1988)
Handcrafted • SEAL
675QX4597 • **Value $32**

2

Treetop Trio
(re-issued from 1986)
Handcrafted • DLEE
1100QX4256 • **Value $35**

3

**Twenty-Five
Years Together**
Porcelain • N/A
750QX4439 • **Value $27**

4

Walnut Shell Rider
(re-issued from 1986)
Handcrafted • SEAL
600QX4196 • **Value $28**

5

Warmth of Friendship
Acrylic • N/A
600QX3759 • **Value $12**

6

Wee Chimney Sweep
Handcrafted • SEAL
625QX4519 • **Value $27**

7

Word of Love
Porcelain • N/A
800QX4477 • **Value $25**

8

Angelic Messengers
Panorama Ball • UNRU
1875QLX7113 • **Value $58**

9

Baby's First Christmas
Handcrafted • N/A
1350QLX7049 • **Value $37**

10

Bright Noel
Acrylic • VOTR
700QLX7059 • **Value $33**

11

Christmas Morning
(re-issued in 1988)
Handcrafted • CROW
2450QLX7013 • **Value $48**

12

**First Christmas
Together**
Handcrafted • N/A
1150QLX7087 • **Value $50**

13

Good Cheer Blimp
Handcrafted • SICK
1600QLX7046 • **Value $58**

14

Keep on Glowin'!
(re-issued from 1986)
Handcrafted • CROW
1000QLX7076 • **Value $48**

15

Keeping Cozy
Handcrafted • CROW
1175QLX7047 • **Value $37**

16

Lacy Brass Snowflake
Brass • N/A
1150QLX7097 • **Value $26**

17

Loving Holiday
Handcrafted • SEAL
2200QLX7016 • **Value $55**

18

**Memories Are Forever
Photoholder**
Handcrafted • SEAL
850QLX7067 • **Value $37**

19

Meowy Christmas!
Handcrafted • PIKE
1000QLX7089 • **Value $62**

20

Season for Friendship
Acrylic • N/A
850QLX7069 • **Value $23**

1

Train Station
Handcrafted • DLEE
1275QLX7039 • **Value $52**

2

Village Express
(re-issued from 1986)
Handcrafted • SICK
2450QLX7072 • **Value $118**

3

Carousel Reindeer
(club edition)
Handcrafted • SICK
800QXC5817 • **Value $68**

4

Wreath of Memories
(keepsake of membership)
Handcrafted • UNRU
QXC5809 • **Value $57**

5

**North Pole Power
& Light**
Handcrafted • CROW
($2.95)627XPR9333 • **Value $27**

1986

One of the biggest stories among Hallmark collectors in 1986 was the hard-to-find porcelain "Magical Unicorn" ornament which was limited to 24,700 pieces. The 1986 collection featured 120 Keepsake ornaments and 16 Magic ornaments. See the collectible series section for more 1986 ornaments.

General Magic

	Price Paid	Value
1.		
2.		

Collector's Club

3.		
4.		

Open House Ornaments

5.		

General Keepsake

6.		
7.		
8.		
9.		
10.		
11.		
12.		
13.		
14.		
15.		
16.		
17.		

6

Acorn Inn
Handcrafted • UNRU
850QX4243 • **Value $31**

7

Baby Locket
Textured Brass • MCGE
1600QX4123 • **Value $29**

8

Baby's First Christmas
Acrylic • PALM
600QX3803 • **Value $25**

9

Baby's First Christmas
Handcrafted • SICK
900QX4126 • **Value $42**

10

Baby's First Christmas
Satin • PATT
550QX2713 • **Value $27**

11

**Baby's First Christmas
Photoholder**
Fabric • PATT
800QX3792 • **Value $26**

12

**Baby's Second
Christmas**
Handcrafted • SIED
650QX4133 • **Value $29**

13

Baby-Sitter
Glass • N/A
475QX2756 • **Value $13**

14

Beary Smooth Ride
(re-issued from 1985)
Handcrafted • SICK
650QX4805 • **Value $24**

15

Bluebird
Porcelain • SICK
725QX4283 • **Value $57**

16

Chatty Penguin
Plush • CROW
575QX4176 • **Value $26**

17

Child's Third Christmas
Fabric • VOTR
650QX4136 • **Value $24**

1

Christmas Beauty
Lacquer • PATT
600QX3223 • **Value $12**

2

Christmas Guitar
Handcrafted • UNRU
700QX5126 • **Value $23**

3

Cookies for Santa
Handcrafted • MCGE
450QX4146 • **Value $31**

4

Country Sleigh
Handcrafted • SICK
1000QX5113 • **Value $28**

5

Daughter
Handcrafted • SEAL
575QX4306 • **Value $50**

6

Do Not Disturb Bear
(re-issued from 1985)
Handcrafted • SEAL
775QX4812 • **Value $34**

7

Father
Wood • VOTR
650QX4313 • **Value $14**

8

Favorite Tin Drum
Tin • SICK
850QX5143 • **Value $32**

9

Festive Treble Clef
Handcrafted • SIED
875QX5133 • **Value $25**

10

Fifty Years Together
Porcelain • PIKE
1000QX4006 • **Value $19**

11

First Christmas Together
Acrylic • MCGE
700QX3793 • **Value $20**

12

First Christmas Together
Glass • N/A
475QX2703 • **Value $20**

13

First Christmas Together
Handcrafted • SICK
1200QX4096 • **Value $30**

14

First Christmas Together
Textured Brass • N/A
1600QX4003 • **Value $23**

15

Friends Are Fun
Glass • CROW
475QX2723 • **Value $45**

16

Friendship Greeting
Fabric • N/A
800QX4273 • **Value $16**

17

Friendship's Gift
Acrylic • N/A
600QX3816 • **Value $17**

18

From Our Home to Yours
Acrylic • N/A
600QX3833 • **Value $16**

19

Glowing Christmas Tree
Acrylic • PATT
700QX4286 • **Value $16**

20

Godchild
Satin • N/A
475QX2716 • **Value $19**

	Price Paid	Value
1.		
2.		
3.		
4.		
5.		
6.		
7.		
8.		
9.		
10.		
11.		
12.		
13.		
14.		
15.		
16.		
17.		
18.		
19.		
20.		

General Keepsake

Totals

1986 Collection

1

Grandchild's
First Christmas
Handcrafted • N/A
1000QX4116 • **Value $17**

2

Granddaughter
Glass • LYLE
475QX2736 • **Value $25**

3

Grandmother
Satin • PATT
475QX2743 • **Value $16**

4

Grandparents
Porcelain • PATT
750QX4323 • **Value $23**

5

Grandson
Glass • VOTR
475QX2733 • **Value $32**

6

Gratitude
Satin/Wood • PIKE
600QX4326 • **Value $13**

7

Happy
Christmas to Owl
Handcrafted • UNRU
600QX4183 • **Value $26**

8

Heathcliff
Handcrafted • SEAL
750QX4363 • **Value $27**

General Keepsake

	Price Paid	Value
1.		
2.		
3.		
4.		
5.		
6.		
7.		
8.		
9.		
10.		
11.		
12.		
13.		
14.		
15.		
16.		
17.		
18.		
19.		
20.		

Totals

9

Heavenly Dreamer
Handcrafted • DLEE
575QX4173 • **Value $34**

10

Heirloom Snowflake
Fabric • PATT
675QX5153 • **Value $21**

11

Holiday Horn
Porcelain • UNRU
800QX5146 • **Value $35**

12

Holiday Jingle Bell
Handcrafted • N/A
1600QX4046 • **Value $56**

13

Husband
Cameo • PIKE
800QX3836 • **Value $13**

14

Jolly Hiker
(re-issued in 1987)
Handcrafted • SIED
500QX4832 • **Value $30**

15

Jolly St. Nick
Porcelain • UNRU
2250QX4296 • **Value $72**

16

Joy of Friends
Bezeled Satin • PATT
675QX3823 • **Value $16**

17

Joyful Carolers
Handcrafted • SICK
975QX5136 • **Value $38**

18

Katybeth
Porcelain • N/A
700QX4353 • **Value $27**

19

Kitty Mischief
(re-issued from 1985)
Handcrafted • DUTK
500QX4745 • **Value $25**

20

Li'l Jingler
(re-issued in 1987)
Handcrafted • SEAL
675QX4193 • **Value $42**

1

Little Drummers
Handcrafted • CROW
1250QX5116 • **Value $35**

2

Loving Memories
Handcrafted • SEAL
900QX4093 • **Value $36**

3

The Magi
Glass • PIKE
475QX2726 • **Value $23**

4

Magical Unicorn
(LE-24,700)
Porcelain • UNRU
2750QX4293 • **Value $110**

5

Marionette Angel
(cancelled after limited production)
Handcrafted • N/A
850QX4023 • **Value $400**

6

Mary Emmerling: American Country Collection
Glass • N/A
795QX2752 • **Value $27**

7

Memories to Cherish
Ceramic • VOTR
750QX4276 • **Value $31**

8

Merry Koala
(re-issued in 1987)
Handcrafted • SICK
500QX4153 • **Value $25**

9

Merry Mouse
(re-issued from 1985)
Handcrafted • DUTK
450QX4032 • **Value $33**

10

Mother
Acrylic • N/A
700QX3826 • **Value $20**

11

Mother and Dad
Porcelain • PYDA
750QX4316 • **Value $22**

12

Mouse in the Moon
(re-issued in 1987)
Handcrafted • SEAL
550QX4166 • **Value $24**

13

Nephew
Bezeled Lacquer • N/A
625QX3813 • **Value $15**

14

New Home
Glass • CROW
475QX2746 • **Value $62**

15

Niece
Fabric/Wood • N/A
600QX4266 • **Value $13**

16

Norman Rockwell
Glass • PIKE
475QX2763 • **Value $30**

17

Nutcracker Santa
Handcrafted • UNRU
1000QX5123 • **Value $50**

18

Open Me First
Handcrafted • N/A
725QX4226 • **Value $34**

19

Paddington™ Bear
Handcrafted • SIED
600QX4356 • **Value $42**

20

PEANUTS®
Glass • N/A
475QX2766 • **Value $46**

General Keepsake

	Price Paid	Value
1.		
2.		
3.		
4.		
5.		
6.		
7.		
8.		
9.		
10.		
11.		
12.		
13.		
14.		
15.		
16.		
17.		
18.		
19.		
20.		

Totals

223

1

Playful Possum
Handcrafted/Glass • CROW
1100QX4253 • **Value $31**

2

Popcorn Mouse
Handcrafted • SICK
675QX4213 • **Value $52**

3

Puppy's Best Friend
Handcrafted • UNRU
650QX4203 • **Value $28**

4

Rah Rah Rabbit
Handcrafted • CROW
700QX4216 • **Value $36**

5

Remembering Christmas
Porcelain • N/A
875QX5106 • **Value $29**

6

Santa's Hot Tub
Handcrafted • SEAL
1200QX4263 • **Value $60**

7

Season of the Heart
Glass • PATT
475QX2706 • **Value $18**

8

Shirt Tales™ Parade
Glass • N/A
475QX2773 • **Value $17**

9

Sister
Bezeled Satin • VOTR
675QX3806 • **Value $15**

10

Skateboard Raccoon
(re-issued from 1985)
Handcrafted • DUTK
650QX4732 • **Value $42**

11

Ski Tripper
Handcrafted • SIED
675QX4206 • **Value $23**

12

SNOOPY® and WOODSTOCK
Handcrafted • SIED
800QX4346 • **Value $57**

13

Snow Buddies
Handcrafted • DUTK
800QX4236 • **Value $42**

14

Snow-Pitching Snowman
(re-issued from 1985)
Handcrafted • DLEE
450QX4702 • **Value $23**

15

Soccer Beaver
(re-issued from 1985)
Handcrafted • DUTK
650QX4775 • **Value $27**

16

Son
Handcrafted • SEAL
575QX4303 • **Value $38**

17

Special Delivery
Handcrafted • SIED
500QX4156 • **Value $28**

18

Star Brighteners
Acrylic • VOTR
600QX3226 • **Value $19**

19

The Statue of Liberty
Acrylic • PYDA
600QX3843 • **Value $27**

20

Sweetheart
Handcrafted • SEAL
1100QX4086 • **Value $72**

General Keepsake

	Price Paid	Value
1.		
2.		
3.		
4.		
5.		
6.		
7.		
8.		
9.		
10.		
11.		
12.		
13.		
14.		
15.		
16.		
17.		
18.		
19.		
20.		

Totals

1.
Teacher
Glass • N/A
475QX2753 • **Value $12**

2.
Ten Years Together
Porcelain • N/A
750QX4013 • **Value $23**

3.
Timeless Love
Acrylic • VOTR
600QX3796 • **Value $32**

4.
Tipping the Scales
Handcrafted • DUTK
675QX4186 • **Value $26**

5.
Touchdown Santa
Handcrafted • DUTK
800QX4233 • **Value $45**

6.
Treetop Trio
(re-issued in 1987)
Handcrafted • DLEE
1100QX4256 • **Value $35**

7.
**Twenty-Five
Years Together**
Porcelain • VOTR
800QX4103 • **Value $23**

8.
Walnut Shell Rider
(re-issued in 1987)
Handcrafted • SEAL
600QX4196 • **Value $28**

9.
Welcome, Christmas
Handcrafted • CROW
825QX5103 • **Value $32**

10.
**Wynken,
Blynken and Nod**
Handcrafted • DLEE
975QX4246 • **Value $45**

11.
Baby's First Christmas
Panorama Ball • CROW
1950QLX7103 • **Value $48**

12.
Christmas Sleigh Ride
Handcrafted • SEAL
2450QLX7012 • **Value $137**

13.
**First Christmas
Together**
Handcrafted • SEAL
1400QLX7073 • **Value $45**

14.
General Store
Handcrafted • DLEE
1575QLX7053 • **Value $62**

15.
Gentle Blessings
Panorama Ball • SICK
1500QLX7083 • **Value $170**

16.
Keep on Glowin'!
(re-issued in 1987)
Handcrafted • CROW
1000QLX7076 • **Value $48**

17.
Merry Christmas Bell
Acrylic • VOTR
850QLX7093 • **Value $24**

18.
Mr. and Mrs. Santa
(re-issued from 1985)
Handcrafted • N/A
1450QLX7052 • **Value $88**

19.
Santa's On His Way
Panorama Ball • UNRU
1500QLX7115 • **Value $74**

20.
Santa's Snack
Handcrafted • CROW
1000QLX7066 • **Value $60**

	Price Paid	Value
General Keepsake		
1.		
2.		
3.		
4.		
5.		
6.		
7.		
8.		
9.		
10.		
General Magic		
11.		
12.		
13.		
14.		
15.		
16.		
17.		
18.		
19.		
20.		
Totals		

1986 / 1985 Collection

Sharing Friendship
Acrylic • VOTR
850QLX7063 • **Value $24**

Sugarplum Cottage
(re-issued from 1984)
Handcrafted • N/A
1100QLX7011 • **Value $42**

Village Express
(re-issued in 1987)
Handcrafted • SICK
2450QLX7072 • **Value $118**

On the Right Track
Porcelain • DUTK
1500QSP4201 • **Value $48**

Coca-Cola® Santa
Glass • N/A
475QXO2796 • **Value $24**

Old-Fashioned Santa
Handcrafted • SICK
1275QXO4403 • **Value $60**

Santa and His Reindeer
Handcrafted • N/A
975QXO4406 • **Value $38**

Santa's Panda Pal
Handcrafted • N/A
500QXO4413 • **Value $30**

General Magic

	Price Paid	Value
1.		
2.		
3.		

Gold Crown Ornaments

4.		

Open House Ornaments

5.		
6.		
7.		
8.		

General Keepsake

9.		
10.		
11.		
12.		
13.		
14.		
15.		
16.		
17.		

Totals

1985

Some of the most popular pieces in 1985 were based on favorite themes such as Santa Claus, SNOOPY® and the nostalgic artwork of Norman Rockwell. For 1985, there were a total of 114 Keepsake ornament designs and 14 Magic ornaments. See the collectible series section for more 1985 ornaments.

Baby Locket
Textured Brass • MCGE
1600QX4012 • **Value $32**

Baby's First Christmas
Acrylic • N/A
575QX3702 • **Value $19**

Baby's First Christmas
Embroidered Fabric • N/A
700QX4782 • **Value $17**

Baby's First Christmas
Fabric • N/A
1600QX4995 • **Value $43**

Baby's First Christmas
Handcrafted • DLEE
1500QX4992 • **Value $58**

Baby's First Christmas
Satin • VOTR
500QX2602 • **Value $24**

Baby's Second Christmas
Handcrafted • N/A
600QX4785 • **Value $39**

Babysitter
Glass • PYDA
475QX2642 • **Value $14**

Baker Elf
Handcrafted • SEAL
575QX4912 • **Value $33**

VALUE GUIDE — HALLMARK KEEPSAKE ORNAMENTS

1

Beary Smooth Ride
(re-issued in 1986)
Handcrafted • SICK
650QX4805 • **Value $24**

2

Betsey Clark
Porcelain • N/A
850QX5085 • **Value $34**

3

Bottlecap Fun Bunnies
Handcrafted • SIED
775QX4815 • **Value $36**

4

Candle Cameo
Bezeled Cameo • PIKE
675QX3742 • **Value $15**

5

Candy Apple Mouse
Handcrafted • SICK
650QX4705 • **Value $66**

6

Charming Angel
Fabric • PYDA
975QX5125 • **Value $26**

7

Children in the Shoe
Handcrafted • SEAL
950QX4905 • **Value $52**

8

Child's Third Christmas
Handcrafted • SEAL
600QX4755 • **Value $30**

9

Christmas Treats
Bezeled Glass • N/A
550QX5075 • **Value $18**

10

Country Goose
Wood • PYDA
775QX5185 • **Value $16**

11

Dapper Penguin
Handcrafted • SEAL
500QX4772 • **Value $33**

12

Daughter
Wood • N/A
550QX5032 • **Value $21**

13

A DISNEY Christmas
Glass • N/A
475QX2712 • **Value $36**

14

Do Not Disturb Bear
(re-issued in 1986)
Handcrafted • SEAL
775QX4812 • **Value $34**

15

Doggy in a Stocking
Handcrafted • N/A
550QX4742 • **Value $43**

16

Engineering Mouse
Handcrafted • SIED
550QX4735 • **Value $28**

17

Father
Wood • VOTR
650QX3762 • **Value $13**

18

First Christmas Together
Acrylic • N/A
675QX3705 • **Value $20**

19

First Christmas Together
Brass • SEAL
1675QX4005 • **Value $26**

20
First Christmas Together
Fabric/Wood • N/A
800QX5072 • **Value $15**

General Keepsake

	Price Paid	Value
1.		
2.		
3.		
4.		
5.		
6.		
7.		
8.		
9.		
10.		
11.		
12.		
13.		
14.		
15.		
16.		
17.		
18.		
19.		
20.		

Totals

227

1985 Collection

1

First Christmas
Together
Glass • N/A
475QX2612 • **Value $20**

2

First Christmas
Together
Porcelain • SICK
1300QX4935 • **Value $25**

3

FRAGGLE
ROCK™ Holiday
Glass • N/A
475QX2655 • **Value $30**

4

Friendship
Bezeled Satin • PYDA
675QX3785 • **Value $18**

5

Friendship
Embroidered Satin • PATT
775QX5062 • **Value $16**

6

From Our
House to Yours
Needlepoint Fabric • PATT
775QX5202 • **Value $13**

7

Godchild
Bezeled Satin • MCGE
675QX3802 • **Value $15**

8

Good Friends
Glass • N/A
475QX2652 • **Value $31**

9

Grandchild's
First Christmas
Handcrafted • N/A
1100QX4955 • **Value $23**

10

Grandchild's
First Christmas
Satin • VOTR
500QX2605 • **Value $15**

11

Granddaughter
Glass • N/A
475QX2635 • **Value $28**

12

Grandmother
Glass • PATT
475QX2625 • **Value $18**

13

Grandparents
Bezeled Lacquer • PIKE
700QX3805 • **Value $14**

14

Grandson
Glass • VOTR
475QX2622 • **Value $28**

15

Heart Full of Love
Bezeled Satin • N/A
675QX3782 • **Value $21**

16

Heavenly Trumpeter
(LE-24,700)
Porcelain • DLEE
2750QX4052 • **Value $105**

17

Holiday Heart
Porcelain • N/A
800QX4982 • **Value $26**

18

Hugga Bunch™
Glass • N/A
500QX2715 • **Value $30**

19

Ice Skating Owl
Handcrafted • SIED
500QX4765 • **Value $24**

20

Keepsake Basket
Fabric • PIKE
1500QX5145 • **Value $23**

General Keepsake

	Price Paid	Value
1.		
2.		
3.		
4.		
5.		
6.		
7.		
8.		
9.		
10.		
11.		
12.		
13.		
14.		
15.		
16.		
17.		
18.		
19.		
20.		
	Totals	

1

Kit the Shepherd
Handcrafted • SIED
575QX4845 • **Value $26**

2

Kitty Mischief
(re-issued in 1986)
Handcrafted • DUTK
500QX4745 • **Value $25**

3

Lacy Heart
Fabric • N/A
875QX5112 • **Value $27**

4

Lamb in Legwarmers
Handcrafted • N/A
700QX4802 • **Value $25**

5

Love at Christmas
Acrylic • MCGE
575QX3715 • **Value $40**

6

Merry Mouse
(re-issued in 1986)
Handcrafted • DUTK
450QX4032 • **Value $33**

7

Merry Shirt Tales™
Glass • N/A
475QX2672 • **Value $23**

8

Mother
Acrylic • PIKE
675QX3722 • **Value $15**

9

Mother and Dad
Porcelain • VOTR
775QX5092 • **Value $23**

10

Mouse Wagon
Handcrafted • N/A
575QX4762 • **Value $63**

11

Muffin the Angel
Handcrafted • SIED
575QX4835 • **Value $27**

12

Nativity Scene
Glass • N/A
475QX2645 • **Value $35**

13

New Home
Glass • PYDA
475QX2695 • **Value $30**

14

Niece
Acrylic • N/A
575QX5205 • **Value $13**

15

Night Before Christmas
Panorama Ball • SEAL
1300QX4494 • **Value $45**

16

Norman Rockwell
Glass • MCGE
475QX2662 • **Value $43**

17

Nostalgic Sled
(re-issued from 1984)
Handcrafted • SICK
600QX4424 • **Value $28**

18

Old-Fashioned Doll
Fabric/Porcelain • N/A
1450QX5195 • **Value $41**

19

Old-Fashioned Wreath
Brass/Acrylic • N/A
750QX3735 • **Value $26**

20

Peaceful Kingdom
Acrylic • PIKE
575QX3732 • **Value $32**

General Keepsake

	Price Paid	Value
1.		
2.		
3.		
4.		
5.		
6.		
7.		
8.		
9.		
10.		
11.		
12.		
13.		
14.		
15.		
16.		
17.		
18.		
19.		
20.		
Totals		

1

PEANUTS®
Glass • N/A
475QX2665 • **Value $38**

2

Porcelain Bird
Porcelain • SICK
650QX4795 • **Value $35**

3

Rainbow Brite™
and Friends
Glass • N/A
475QX2682 • **Value $26**

4

Rocking Horse
Memories
Fabric/Wood • VOTR
1000QX5182 • **Value $18**

5

Roller Skating Rabbit
(re-issued from 1984)
Handcrafted • SEAL
500QX4571 • **Value $32**

6

Santa Pipe
Handcrafted • DUTK
950QX4942 • **Value $26**

7

Santa's Ski Trip
Handcrafted • SEAL
1200QX4962 • **Value $62**

8

Sewn Photoholder
Embroidered Fabric • PIKE
700QX3795 • **Value $36**

General Keepsake

	Price Paid	Value
1.		
2.		
3.		
4.		
5.		
6.		
7.		
8.		
9.		
10.		
11.		
12.		
13.		
14.		
15.		
16.		
17.		
18.		
19.		
20.		

9

Sheep at Christmas
Handcrafted • SICK
825QX5175 • **Value $28**

10

Sister
Porcelain • PATT
725QX5065 • **Value $24**

11

Skateboard Raccoon
(re-issued in 1986)
Handcrafted • DUTK
650QX4732 • **Value $42**

12

SNOOPY® and
WOODSTOCK
Handcrafted • SIED
750QX4915 • **Value $84**

13

Snowflake
Fabric • PATT
650QX5105 • **Value $22**

14

Snow-Pitching Snowman
(re-issued in 1986)
Handcrafted • DLEE
450QX4702 • **Value $23**

15

Snowy Seal
(re-issued from 1984)
Handcrafted • SEAL
400QX4501 • **Value $22**

16

Soccer Beaver
(re-issued in 1986)
Handcrafted • DUTK
650QX4775 • **Value $27**

17

Son
Handcrafted • SIED
550QX5025 • **Value $48**

18

Special Friends
Arylic • PALM
575QX3725 • **Value $12**

19

The Spirit of
Santa Claus
Handcrafted • DLEE
2250QX4985 • **Value $107**

20

Stardust Angel
Handcrafted • DLEE
575QX4752 • **Value $38**

Totals

1

Sun and Fun Santa
Handcrafted • SIED
775QX4922 • **Value $42**

2

Swinging Angel Bell
Handcrafted/Glass • SIED
1100QX4925 • **Value $36**

3

Teacher
Handcrafted • N/A
600QX5052 • **Value $20**

4

**Three Kittens
in a Mitten
(re-issued from 1984)**
Handcrafted • DLEE
800QX4311 • **Value $56**

5

Trumpet Panda
Handcrafted • SEAL
450QX4712 • **Value $26**

6

**Twenty-Five
Years Together**
Porcelain • N/A
800QX5005 • **Value $17**

7

Victorian Lady
Porcelain/Fabric • N/A
950QX5132 • **Value $25**

8

Whirligig Santa
Wood • N/A
1250QX5192 • **Value $27**

9

With Appreciation
Acrylic • N/A
675QX3752 • **Value $14**

10

**All Are Precious
(re-issued from 1984)**
Acrylic • N/A
800QLX7044 • **Value $28**

11

Baby's First Christmas
Handcrafted • SEAL
1650QLX7005 • **Value $42**

12

Christmas Eve Visit
Etched Brass • N/A
1200QLX7105 • **Value $34**

13

Katybeth
Acrylic • N/A
1075QLX7102 • **Value $44**

14

Little Red Schoolhouse
Handcrafted • DLEE
1575QLX7112 • **Value $92**

15

Love Wreath
Acrylic • VOTR
850QLX7025 • **Value $30**

16

**Mr. and Mrs. Santa
(re-issued in 1986)**
Handcrafted • N/A
1450QLX7052 • **Value $88**

17

**Nativity
(re-issued from 1984)**
Panorama Ball • SEAL
1200QLX7001 • **Value $32**

18

**Santa's Workshop
(re-issued from 1984)**
Panorama Ball • N/A
1300QLX7004 • **Value $65**

19

Season of Beauty
Classic Shape • LYLE
800QLX7122 • **Value $27**

20

**Sugarplum Cottage
(re-issued from 1984)**
Handcrafted • N/A
1100QLX7011 • **Value $42**

General Keepsake	Price Paid	Value
1.		
2.		
3.		
4.		
5.		
6.		
7.		
8.		
9.		

General Magic		
10.		
11.		
12.		
13.		
14.		
15.		
16.		
17.		
18.		
19.		
20.		
Totals		

1985 / 1984 Collection

1

Swiss Cheese Lane
Handcrafted • N/A
1300QLX7065 • **Value $49**

2

Village Church
(re-issued from 1984)
Handcrafted • DLEE
1500QLX7021 • **Value $53**

3

Santa Claus
Lacquer • N/A
675QX3005 • **Value $12**

4

Santa's Village
Lacquer • N/A
675QX3002 • **Value $12**

1984

1984 was a landmark year for Hallmark ornaments with the debut of lighted Magic ornaments (then called "Lighted Ornaments"). In later years, these ornaments would also incorporate motion and sound. There were 10 Magic ornaments issued in 1984, as well as 110 Keepsake designs. See the collectible series section for more 1984 ornaments.

5

Alpine Elf
Handcrafted • SEAL
600QX4521 • **Value $40**

General Magic

Price Paid	Value
1.	
2.	

Santa Claus – The Movie

3.	
4.	

General Keepsake

5.	
6.	
7.	
8.	
9.	
10.	
11.	
12.	
13.	
14.	
15.	
16.	
17.	

Totals

6

Amanda
Fabric/Porcelain • N/A
900QX4321 • **Value $33**

7
Baby's First Christmas
Acrylic • N/A
600QX3401 • **Value $41**

8
Baby's First Christmas
Classic Shape • DLEE
1600QX9041 • **Value $49**

9

Baby's First Christmas
Handcrafted • N/A
1400QX4381 • **Value $49**

10

Baby's First
Christmas – Boy
Satin • N/A
450QX2404 • **Value $30**

11
Baby's First
Christmas – Girl
Satin • N/A
450QX2401 • **Value $29**

12

Baby's First Christmas
– Photoholder
Fabric • N/A
700QX3001 • **Value $20**

13

Baby's Second
Christmas
Satin • N/A
450QX2411 • **Value $40**

14
Baby-sitter
Glass • N/A
450QX2531 • **Value $15**

15

Bell Ringer Squirrel
Handcrafted/Glass • SEAL
1000QX4431 • **Value $40**

16

Betsey Clark Angel
Porcelain • N/A
900QX4624 • **Value $36**

17

Chickadee
Porcelain • SICK
600QX4514 • **Value $42**

1

Child's Third Christmas
Satin • N/A
450QX2611 • **Value $25**

2

Christmas Memories Photoholder
Fabric • N/A
650QX3004 • **Value $28**

3

Christmas Owl
Handcrafted/Acrylic • SEAL
600QX4441 • **Value $33**

4

A Christmas Prayer
Satin • N/A
450QX2461 • **Value $24**

5

Classical Angel
(LE-24,700)
Porcelain • DLEE
2750QX4591 • **Value $100**

6

Cuckoo Clock
Handcrafted • DLEE
1000QX4551 • **Value $54**

7

Currier & Ives
Glass • N/A
450QX2501 • **Value $26**

8

Daughter
Glass • N/A
450QX2444 • **Value $37**

9

DISNEY
Glass • N/A
450QX2504 • **Value $42**

10

Embroidered Heart
(re-issued from 1983)
Fabric • N/A
650QX4217 • **Value $27**

11

Embroidered Stocking
(re-issued from 1983)
Fabric • SICK
650QX4796 • **Value $24**

12

Father
Acrylic • N/A
600QX2571 • **Value $20**

13

First Christmas Together
Acrylic • N/A
600QX3421 • **Value $22**

14

First Christmas Together
Brushed Brass • SEAL
1500QX4364 • **Value $37**

15

First Christmas Together
Cameo • MCGE
750QX3404 • **Value $25**

16

First Christmas Together
Classic Shape • MCGE
1600QX9044 • **Value $43**

17

First Christmas Together
Glass • N/A
450QX2451 • **Value $30**

18

Flights of Fantasy
Glass • N/A
450QX2564 • **Value $23**

19

Fortune Cookie Elf
Handcrafted • SICK
450QX4524 • **Value $42**

20

Friendship
Glass • N/A
450QX2481 • **Value $22**

General Keepsake

	Price Paid	Value
1.		
2.		
3.		
4.		
5.		
6.		
7.		
8.		
9.		
10.		
11.		
12.		
13.		
14.		
15.		
16.		
17.		
18.		
19.		
20.		

Totals

1

Frisbee® Puppy
Handcrafted • N/A
500QX4444 • **Value $56**

2

From Our Home to Yours
Glass • N/A
450QX2484 • **Value $54**

3

The Fun of Friendship
Acrylic • N/A
600QX3431 • **Value $36**

4

A Gift of Friendship
Glass • N/A
450QX2604 • **Value $25**

5

Gift of Music
Handcrafted • SEAL
1500QX4511 • **Value $100**

6

Godchild
Glass • N/A
450QX2421 • **Value $20**

7

Grandchild's First Christmas
Handcrafted • N/A
1100QX4601 • **Value $27**

8

Grandchild's First Christmas
Satin • N/A
450QX2574 • **Value $18**

9

Granddaughter
Glass • N/A
450QX2431 • **Value $27**

10

Grandmother
Glass • N/A
450QX2441 • **Value $19**

11

Grandparents
Glass • N/A
450QX2561 • **Value $19**

12

Grandson
Glass • N/A
450QX2424 • **Value $27**

13

Gratitude
Acrylic • N/A
600QX3444 • **Value $14**

14

Heartful of Love
Bone China • N/A
1000QX4434 • **Value $49**

15

Holiday Friendship
Panorama Ball • N/A
1300QX4451 • **Value $32**

16

Holiday Jester
Handcrafted • SICK
1100QX4374 • **Value $35**

17

Holiday Starburst
Glass • N/A
500QX2534 • **Value $23**

18

Katybeth
Porcelain • N/A
900QX4631 • **Value $30**

19

Kit
Handcrafted • N/A
550QX4534 • **Value $31**

20
Love
Glass • N/A
450QX2554 • **Value $28**

1

Love . . . the Spirit of Christmas
Glass • N/A
450QX2474 • **Value $44**

2

Madonna and Child
Acrylic • PALM
600QX3441 • **Value $50**

3

Marathon Santa
Handcrafted • SEAL
800QX4564 • **Value $43**

4

The Miracle of Love
Acrylic • N/A
600QX3424 • **Value $35**

5

Mother
Acrylic • N/A
600QX3434 • **Value $18**

6

Mother and Dad
Bone China • N/A
650QX2581 • **Value $29**

7

Mountain Climbing Santa
(re-issued from 1983)
Handcrafted • SEAL
650QX4077 • **Value $38**

8

Muffin
Handcrafted • DLEE
550QX4421 • **Value $32**

9

The MUPPETS™
Glass • N/A
450QX2514 • **Value $37**

10

Musical Angel
Handcrafted • DLEE
550QX4344 • **Value $73**

11

Napping Mouse
Handcrafted • N/A
550QX4351 • **Value $52**

12

Needlepoint Wreath
Fabric • PIKE
650QX4594 • **Value $17**

13

New Home
Glass • N/A
450QX2454 • **Value $83**

14

Norman Rockwell
Glass • MCGE
450QX2511 • **Value $32**

15

Nostalgic Sled
(re-issued in 1985)
Handcrafted • SICK
600QX4424 • **Value $28**

16

Old Fashioned Rocking Horse
Acrylic/Brass • N/A
750QX3464 • **Value $23**

17

Peace on Earth
Cameo • N/A
750QX3414 • **Value $31**

18

PEANUTS®
Satin • N/A
450QX2521 • **Value $42**

19

Peppermint 1984
Handcrafted • DLEE
450QX4561 • **Value $54**

20

Polar Bear Drummer
Handcrafted • SEAL
450QX4301 • **Value $32**

General Keepsake

	Price Paid	Value
1.		
2.		
3.		
4.		
5.		
6.		
7.		
8.		
9.		
10.		
11.		
12.		
13.		
14.		
15.		
16.		
17.		
18.		
19.		
20.		
Totals		

1984 Collection

1

Raccoon's Christmas
Handcrafted • SEAL
900QX4474 • **Value $55**

2

Reindeer Racetrack
Glass • N/A
450QX2544 • **Value $26**

3

Roller Skating Rabbit
(re-issued in 1985)
Handcrafted • SEAL
500QX4571 • **Value $32**

4

Santa
Fabric • N/A
750QX4584 • **Value $22**

5

Santa Mouse
Handcrafted • SIED
450QX4334 • **Value $52**

6

Santa Star
Handcrafted • N/A
550QX4504 • **Value $39**

7

Santa Sulky Driver
Etched Brass • N/A
900QX4361 • **Value $35**

8

A Savior is Born
Glass • N/A
450QX2541 • **Value $34**

9

Shirt Tales™
Satin • N/A
450QX2524 • **Value $21**

10

Sister
Bone China • N/A
650QX2594 • **Value $30**

11

**SNOOPY® and
WOODSTOCK**
Handcrafted • SEAL
750QX4391 • **Value $97**

12

Snowmobile Santa
Handcrafted • N/A
650QX4314 • **Value $36**

13

Snowshoe Penguin
Handcrafted • SICK
650QX4531 • **Value $48**

14

Snowy Seal
(re-issued in 1985)
Handcrafted • SEAL
400QX4501 • **Value $22**

15

Son
Glass • N/A
450QX2434 • **Value $32**

16

Teacher
Glass • N/A
450QX2491 • **Value $15**

17

Ten Years Together
Bone China • N/A
650QX2584 • **Value $16**

18

**Three Kittens in a
Mitten (re-issued in 1985)**
Handcrafted • DLEE
800QX4311 • **Value $56**

19

**Twelve Days
of Christmas**
Handcrafted • SEAL
1500QX4159 • **Value $115**

20

**Twenty-Five Years
Together**
Bone China • N/A
650QX2591 • **Value $22**

General Keepsake		
	Price Paid	Value
1.		
2.		
3.		
4.		
5.		
6.		
7.		
8.		
9.		
10.		
11.		
12.		
13.		
14.		
15.		
16.		
17.		
18.		
19.		
20.		
Totals		

1

Uncle Sam
Pressed Tin • SICK
600QX4491 • **Value $52**

2

White Christmas
Classic Shape • N/A
1600QX9051 • **Value $95**

3

All Are Precious
(re-issued in 1985)
Acrylic • N/A
800QLX7044 • **Value $28**

4

Brass Carousel
Etched Brass • N/A
900QLX7071 • **Value $88**

5

Christmas in the Forest
Classic Shape • N/A
800QLX7034 • **Value $22**

6

City Lights
Handcrafted • SIED
1000QLX7014 • **Value $55**

7

Nativity
(re-issued in 1985)
Panorama Ball • SEAL
1200QLX7001 • **Value $32**

8

Santa's Arrival
Panorama Ball • DLEE
1300QLX7024 • **Value $64**

9

Santa's Workshop
(re-issued in 1985)
Panorama Ball • N/A
1300QLX7004 • **Value $65**

10

Stained Glass
Classic Shape • N/A
800QLX7031 • **Value $22**

11

Sugarplum Cottage
(re-issued in
1985 and 1986)
Handcrafted • N/A
1100QLX7011 • **Value $42**

12

Village Church
(re-issued in 1985)
Handcrafted • DLEE
1500QLX7021 • **Value $53**

1983

1983 marked the 10th anniversary of Keepsake ornaments. Among the popular pieces from 1983 were a pair of angel ornaments, "Baroque Angels" and "Rainbow Angel," as well as three ornaments featuring Muppets™ characters. The 1983 line featured 111 Keepsake ornaments. See the collectible series section for more 1983 ornaments.

13

25th Christmas Together
Glass • N/A
450QX2247 • **Value $23**

14

1983
Glass • N/A
450QX2209 • **Value $30**

15

Angel Messenger
Handcrafted • SEAL
650QX4087 • **Value $99**

General Keepsake		
	Price Paid	Value
1.		
2.		
General Magic		
3.		
4.		
5.		
6.		
7.		
8.		
9.		
10.		
11.		
12.		
General Keepsake		
13.		
14.		
15.		
Totals		

1

Angels
Glass • N/A
500QX2197 • **Value $26**

2

The Annunciation
Glass • N/A
450QX2167 • **Value $32**

3

Baby's First Christmas
Acrylic • N/A
700QX3029 • **Value $24**

4

Baby's First Christmas
Cameo • SICK
750QX3019 • **Value $18**

5

Baby's First Christmas
Handcrafted • DLEE
1400QX4027 • **Value $38**

6

Baby's First
Christmas – Boy
Satin • N/A
450QX2009 • **Value $28**

7

Baby's First
Christmas – Girl
Satin • N/A
450QX2007 • **Value $29**

8

Baby's Second
Christmas
Satin • N/A
450QX2267 • **Value $36**

9

Baroque Angels
Handcrafted • DLEE
1300QX4229 • **Value $128**

10

Bell Wreath
Brass • SICK
650QX4209 • **Value $35**

11

Betsey Clark
Handcrafted • SEAL
650QX4047 • **Value $34**

12

Betsey Clark
Porcelain • N/A
900QX4401 • **Value $35**

13

Brass Santa
Brass • SEAL
900QX4239 • **Value $25**

14

Caroling Owl
Handcrafted • SEAL
450QX4117 • **Value $41**

15

Child's Third Christmas
Satin Piqué • N/A
450QX2269 • **Value $27**

16

Christmas Joy
Satin • N/A
450QX2169 • **Value $33**

17

Christmas Kitten
(re-issued from 1982)
Handcrafted • N/A
400QX4543 • **Value $40**

18

Christmas Koala
Handcrafted • SEAL
400QX4199 • **Value $34**

19

Christmas Stocking
Acrylic • N/A
600QX3039 • **Value $42**

20

Christmas Wonderland
Glass • N/A
450QX2219 • **Value $127**

General Keepsake

	Price Paid	Value
1.		
2.		
3.		
4.		
5.		
6.		
7.		
8.		
9.		
10.		
11.		
12.		
13.		
14.		
15.		
16.		
17.		
18.		
19.		
20.		
	Totals	

1
Currier & Ives
Glass • N/A
450QX2159 • **Value $26**

2
Cycling Santa
(re-issued from 1982)
Handcrafted • N/A
2000QX4355 • **Value $155**

3
Daughter
Glass • N/A
450QX2037 • **Value $46**

4
DISNEY
Glass • N/A
450QX2129 • **Value $56**

5
Embroidered Heart
(re-issued in 1984)
Fabric • N/A
650QX4217 • **Value $27**

6
Embroidered Stocking
(re-issued in 1984)
Fabric • SICK
650QX4796 • **Value $24**

7
Enameled Christmas Wreath
Enameled • N/A
900QX3119 • **Value $15**

8
First Christmas Together
Acrylic • N/A
600QX3069 • **Value $25**

9
First Christmas Together
Cameo • N/A
750QX3017 • **Value $23**

10
First Christmas Together
Classic Shape • N/A
600QX3107 • **Value $38**

11
First Christmas Together
Glass • SICK
450QX2089 • **Value $32**

12
First Christmas Together – Brass Locket
Brass • SEAL
1500QX4329 • **Value $36**

13
Friendship
Acrylic • N/A
600QX3059 • **Value $21**

14
Friendship
Glass • N/A
450QX2077 • **Value $22**

15
Godchild
Glass • N/A
450QX2017 • **Value $19**

16
Grandchild's First Christmas
Classic Shape • N/A
600QX3129 • **Value $24**

17
Grandchild's First Christmas
Handcrafted • N/A
1400QX4309 • **Value $37**

18
Granddaughter
Glass • N/A
450QX2027 • **Value $30**

19
Grandmother
Glass • N/A
450QX2057 • **Value $23**

20
Grandparents
Ceramic • N/A
650QX4299 • **Value $23**

General Keepsake

	Price Paid	Value
1.		
2.		
3.		
4.		
5.		
6.		
7.		
8.		
9.		
10.		
11.		
12.		
13.		
14.		
15.		
16.		
17.		
18.		
19.		
20.		

Totals

1

Grandson
Satin • N/A
450QX2019 • **Value $30**

2

Heart
Acrylic • SICK
400QX3079 • **Value $52**

3

Here Comes Santa
Glass • N/A
450QX2177 • **Value $42**

4

Hitchhiking Santa
Handcrafted • SEAL
800QX4247 • **Value $42**

5

Holiday Puppy
Handcrafted • N/A
350QX4127 • **Value $30**

6

Jack Frost
Handcrafted • N/A
900QX4079 • **Value $62**

7

Jolly Santa
Handcrafted • N/A
350QX4259 • **Value $36**

8

KERMIT the FROG™
(re-issued from 1982)
Handcrafted • DLEE
1100QX4956 • **Value $110**

9

Love
Acrylic • N/A
600QX3057 • **Value $20**

10

Love
Classic Shape • N/A
600QX3109 • **Value $40**

11

Love
Glass • N/A
450QX2079 • **Value $56**

12

Love
Porcelain • SICK
1300QX4227 • **Value $38**

13

Love Is a Song
Glass • N/A
450QX2239 • **Value $32**

14

Madonna and Child
Porcelain • N/A
1200QX4287 • **Value $45**

15

Mailbox Kitten
Handcrafted • N/A
650QX4157 • **Value $64**

16

Mary Hamilton
Glass • N/A
450QX2137 • **Value $46**

17

Memories to Treasure
Acrylic • N/A
700QX3037 • **Value $32**

18

MISS PIGGY™
Handcrafted • N/A
1300QX4057 • **Value $225**

19

Mom and Dad
Ceramic • PIKE
650QX4297 • **Value $26**

20

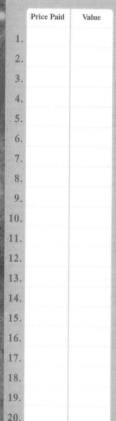

Mother
Acrylic • N/A
600QX3067 • **Value $21**

1
Mother and Child
Cameo • N/A
750QX3027 • **Value $40**

2
Mountain Climbing Santa
(re-issued in 1984)
Handcrafted • SEAL
650QX4077 • **Value $38**

3
Mouse in Bell
Handcrafted/Glass • N/A
1000QX4197 • **Value $67**

4
Mouse on Cheese
Handcrafted • SICK
650QX4137 • **Value $50**

5
The MUPPETS™
Satin • N/A
450QX2147 • **Value $52**

6
New Home
Satin • N/A
450QX2107 • **Value $36**

7
Norman Rockwell
Glass • N/A
450QX2157 • **Value $55**

8
An Old Fashioned Christmas
Glass • N/A
450QX2179 • **Value $32**

9
Old-Fashioned Santa
Handcrafted • SICK
1100QX4099 • **Value $69**

10
Oriental Butterflies
Glass • N/A
450QX2187 • **Value $32**

11
PEANUTS®
Satin • N/A
450QX2127 • **Value $40**

12
Peppermint Penguin
Handcrafted • N/A
650QX4089 • **Value $47**

13
Porcelain Doll, Diana
Porcelain/Fabric • DLEE
900QX4237 • **Value $33**

14
Rainbow Angel
Handcrafted • DLEE
550QX4167 • **Value $112**

15
Santa
Acrylic • N/A
400QX3087 • **Value $35**

16
Santa's Many Faces
Classic Shape • N/A
600QX3117 • **Value $33**

17
Santa's on His Way
Handcrafted • N/A
1000QX4269 • **Value $38**

18
Santa's Workshop
(re-issued from 1982)
Handcrafted • DLEE
1000QX4503 • **Value $85**

19
Scrimshaw Reindeer
Handcrafted • SEAL
800QX4249 • **Value $35**

20
Season's Greetings
Glass • N/A
450QX2199 • **Value $26**

General Keepsake

	Price Paid	Value
1.		
2.		
3.		
4.		
5.		
6.		
7.		
8.		
9.		
10.		
11.		
12.		
13.		
14.		
15.		
16.		
17.		
18.		
19.		
20.		

Totals

1
SHIRT TALES™
Glass • N/A
450QX2149 • **Value $28**

2
Sister
Glass • N/A
450QX2069 • **Value $26**

3
Skating Rabbit
Handcrafted • N/A
800QX4097 • **Value $55**

4
Ski Lift Santa
Handcrafted/Brass • N/A
800QX4187 • **Value $73**

5
Skiing Fox
Handcrafted • DLEE
800QX4207 • **Value $40**

6
Sneaker Mouse
Handcrafted • SEAL
450QX4009 • **Value $42**

7
Son
Satin • N/A
450QX2029 • **Value $40**

8
Star of Peace
Acrylic • SEAL
600QX3047 • **Value $20**

General Keepsake

	Price Paid	Value
1.		
2.		
3.		
4.		
5.		
6.		
7.		
8.		
9.		
10.		
11.		
12.		
13.		
14.		
15.		

Musical Ornaments

16.		
17.		
18.		
19.		

9
Teacher
Acrylic • N/A
600QX3049 • **Value $15**

10
Teacher
Glass • N/A
450QX2249 • **Value $16**

11
Tenth Christmas Together
Ceramic • N/A
650QX4307 • **Value $27**

12
Time for Sharing
Acrylic • N/A
600QX3077 • **Value $38**

13
Tin Rocking Horse
Pressed Tin • SICK
650QX4149 • **Value $53**

14
Unicorn
Porcelain • N/A
1000QX4267 • **Value $66**

15
The Wise Men
Glass • N/A
450QX2207 • **Value $55**

16
Baby's First Christmas
Classic Shape • N/A
1600QMB9039 • **Value $87**

17
Friendship
Classic Shape • N/A
1600QMB9047 • **Value $115**

18
Nativity
Classic Shape • N/A
1600QMB9049 • **Value $125**

19
Twelve Days of Christmas
Handcrafted • SEAL
1500QMB4159 • **Value $100**

Totals

1982

The 1982 collection was highlighted by the always-popular creations of Hallmark artist, Donna Lee. Among her sought-after 1982 designs were "Baroque Angel," "Pinecone Home" and "Raccoon Surprises." Overall, there were 104 Keepsake ornaments issued in 1982. See the collectible series section for more 1982 ornaments.

1
25th Christmas Together
Glass • N/A
450QX2116 • **Value $21**

2
50th Christmas Together
Glass • N/A
450QX2123 • **Value $21**

3
Angel
Acrylic • N/A
550QX3096 • **Value $34**

4
Angel Chimes
Chrome-Plated Brass • N/A
550QX5026 • **Value $37**

5
Arctic Penguin
Acrylic • N/A
400QX3003 • **Value $22**

6
Baby's First Christmas
Acrylic • SEAL
550QX3023 • **Value $38**

7
Baby's First Christmas
Handcrafted • SEAL
1300QX4553 • **Value $48**

8
Baby's First Christmas – Boy
Satin • N/A
450QX2163 • **Value $27**

9
Baby's First Christmas – Girl
Satin • N/A
450QX2073 • **Value $27**

10
Baby's First Christmas – Photoholder
Acrylic • N/A
650QX3126 • **Value $30**

11
Baroque Angel
Handcrafted/Brass • DLEE
1500QX4566 • **Value $175**

12
Bell Chimes
Chrome-Plated Brass • SICK
550QX4943 • **Value $29**

13
Betsey Clark
Cameo • N/A
850QX3056 • **Value $28**

14
Brass Bell
Brass • DLEE
1200QX4606 • **Value $29**

15
Christmas Angel
Glass • N/A
450QX2206 • **Value $27**

16
Christmas Fantasy
(re-issued from 1981)
Handcrafted/Brass • N/A
1300QX1554 • **Value $90**

17
Christmas Kitten
(re-issued in 1983)
Handcrafted • N/A
400QX4543 • **Value $40**

General Keepsake

	Price Paid	Value
1.		
2.		
3.		
4.		
5.		
6.		
7.		
8.		
9.		
10.		
11.		
12.		
13.		
14.		
15.		
16.		
17.		
Totals		

243

1

Christmas Magic
Acrylic • N/A
550QX3113 • **Value $30**

2

Christmas Memories – Photoholder
Acrylic • SICK
650QX3116 • **Value $25**

3

Christmas Owl
(re-issued from 1980)
Handcrafted • N/A
400QX1314 • **Value $49**

4

Christmas Sleigh
Acrylic • N/A
550QX3093 • **Value $72**

5

Cloisonné Angel
Cloisonné • N/A
1200QX1454 • **Value $97**

6

Cookie Mouse
Handcrafted • SICK
450QX4546 • **Value $60**

7

Cowboy Snowman
Handcrafted • N/A
800QX4806 • **Value $56**

8

Currier & Ives
Glass • N/A
450QX2013 • **Value $24**

	Price Paid	Value
1.		
2.		
3.		
4.		
5.		
6.		
7.		
8.		
9.		
10.		
11.		
12.		
13.		
14.		
15.		
16.		
17.		
18.		
19.		
20.		

9

Cycling Santa
(re-issued in 1983)
Handcrafted • N/A
2000QX4355 • **Value $155**

10

Daughter
Satin • N/A
450QX2046 • **Value $35**

11

DISNEY
Satin • N/A
450QX2173 • **Value $37**

12

THE DIVINE MISS PIGGY™
(re-issued from 1981)
Handcrafted • FRAN
1200QX4255 • **Value $94**

13

Dove Love
Acrylic • SICK
450QX4623 • **Value $52**

14

Elfin Artist
Handcrafted • SICK
900QX4573 • **Value $50**

15

Embroidered Tree
Fabric • N/A
650QX4946 • **Value $39**

16

Father
Satin • SICK
450QX2056 • **Value $21**

17

First Christmas Together
Acrylic • SEAL
550QX3026 • **Value $20**

18

First Christmas Together
Cameo • N/A
850QX3066 • **Value $45**

19

First Christmas Together
Glass • N/A
450QX2113 • **Value $36**

20

First Christmas Together – Locket
Brass • SEAL
1500QX4563 • **Value $26**

Totals

1

Friendship
Acrylic • N/A
550QX3046 • **Value $24**

2

Friendship
Satin • N/A
450QX2086 • **Value $21**

3

Godchild
Glass • N/A
450QX2226 • **Value $23**

4

Granddaughter
Glass • N/A
450QX2243 • **Value $26**

5

Grandfather
Satin • N/A
450QX2076 • **Value $20**

6

Grandmother
Satin • N/A
450QX2003 • **Value $19**

7

Grandparents
Glass • N/A
450QX2146 • **Value $18**

8

Grandson
Satin • N/A
450QX2246 • **Value $27**

9

Ice Sculptor
(re-issued from 1981)
Handcrafted • DLEE
800QX4322 • **Value $97**

10

Jingling Teddy
Brass • SEAL
400QX4776 • **Value $40**

11

Joan Walsh Anglund
Satin • N/A
450QX2193 • **Value $23**

12

Jogging Santa
Handcrafted • N/A
800QX4576 • **Value $50**

13

Jolly Christmas Tree
Handcrafted • N/A
650QX4653 • **Value $83**

14

KERMIT the FROG™
(re-issued in 1983)
Handcrafted • DLEE
1100QX4956 • **Value $110**

15

Love
Acrylic • N/A
550QX3043 • **Value $30**

16

Love
Satin • N/A
450QX2096 • **Value $18**

17

Mary Hamilton
Satin • N/A
450QX2176 • **Value $26**

18

Merry Christmas
Glass • N/A
450QX2256 • **Value $24**

19

Merry Moose
Handcrafted • N/A
550QX4155 • **Value $60**

20
MISS PIGGY™ and
KERMIT™
Satin • N/A
450QX2183 • **Value $42**

General Keepsake

	Price Paid	Value
1.		
2.		
3.		
4.		
5.		
6.		
7.		
8.		
9.		
10.		
11.		
12.		
13.		
14.		
15.		
16.		
17.		
18.		
19.		
20.		

Totals

245

1982 Collection

1

Moments of Love
Satin • N/A
450QX2093 • **Value $20**

2
Mother
Glass • N/A
450QX2053 • **Value $20**

3
Mother and Dad
Glass • N/A
450QX2223 • **Value $17**

4

MUPPETS™ Party
Satin • N/A
450QX2186 • **Value $42**

5

Musical Angel
Handcrafted • DLEE
550QX4596 • **Value $130**

6
Nativity
Acrylic • N/A
450QX3083 • **Value $50**

7
New Home
Satin • N/A
450QX2126 • **Value $23**

8

Norman Rockwell
Satin • N/A
450QX2023 • **Value $28**

9

Old Fashioned Christmas
Glass • N/A
450QX2276 • **Value $48**

10
Old World Angels
Glass • N/A
450QX2263 • **Value $27**

11

Patterns of Christmas
Glass • N/A
450QX2266 • **Value $23**

12

PEANUTS®
Satin • N/A
450QX2006 • **Value $40**

13

Peeking Elf
Handcrafted • N/A
650QX4195 • **Value $40**

14

Perky Penguin
(re-issued from 1981)
Handcrafted • N/A
400QX4095 • **Value $60**

15

Pinecone Home
Handcrafted • DLEE
800QX4613 • **Value $173**

16

Raccoon Surprises
Handcrafted • DLEE
900QX4793 • **Value $164**

17

Santa
Glass • BLAC
450QX2216 • **Value $23**

18

Santa and Reindeer
Handcrafted/Brass • SICK
900QX4676 • **Value $52**

19

Santa Bell
Porcelain • N/A
1500QX1487 • **Value $60**

20

Santa's Flight
Acrylic • N/A
450QX3086 • **Value $47**

General Keepsake

	Price Paid	Value
1.		
2.		
3.		
4.		
5.		
6.		
7.		
8.		
9.		
10.		
11.		
12.		
13.		
14.		
15.		
16.		
17.		
18.		
19.		
20.		

Totals

1

Santa's Sleigh
Brass • SEAL
900QX4786 • **Value $35**

2

Santa's Workshop
(re-issued in 1983)
Handcrafted • DLEE
1000QX4503 • **Value $85**

3

Season for Caring
Satin • N/A
450QX2213 • **Value $26**

4

Sister
Glass • N/A
450QX2083 • **Value $32**

5

Snowy Seal
Acrylic • N/A
400QX3006 • **Value $22**

6

Son
Satin • N/A
450QX2043 • **Value $32**

7

The Spirit of Christmas
Handcrafted • SICK
1000QX4526 • **Value $130**

8

Stained Glass
Glass • N/A
450QX2283 • **Value $26**

9

Teacher
Acrylic • SICK
650QX3123 • **Value $19**

10

Teacher
Glass • N/A
450QX2143 • **Value $14**

11

Teacher – Apple
Acrylic • SEAL
550QX3016 • **Value $16**

12

Three Kings
Cameo • BLAC
850QX3073 • **Value $27**

13

Tin Soldier
Pressed Tin • SICK
650QX4836 • **Value $48**

14

Tree Chimes
Stamped Brass • SEAL
550QX4846 • **Value $42**

15

**Twelve Days
of Christmas**
Glass • N/A
450QX2036 • **Value $32**

16

Dimensional Ornament
Dimensional Brass • N/A
($3.50) No stock # • **Value $42**

17

Baby's First Christmas
Classic Shape • N/A
1600QMB9007 • **Value $88**

18

First Christmas Together
Classic Shape • N/A
1600QMB9019 • **Value $85**

19

Love
Classic Shape • N/A
1600QMB9009 • **Value $88**

General Keepsake	Price Paid	Value
1.		
2.		
3.		
4.		
5.		
6.		
7.		
8.		
9.		
10.		
11.		
12.		
13.		
14.		
15.		
Early Promotional Ornaments		
16.		
Musical Ornaments		
17.		
18.		
19.		
Totals		

1981

Santa Claus was well-represented in Hallmark's collection for 1981 with several coveted designs, including the handcrafted ornaments "Sailing Santa" and "Space Santa," as well as the ball ornament "Traditional (Black Santa)." The 1981 line featured 99 Keepsake ornaments. See the collectible series section for more 1981 ornaments.

1

25th Christmas Together
Acrylic • N/A
550QX5042 • **Value $23**

2

25th Christmas Together
Glass • N/A
450QX7075 • **Value $23**

3

50th Christmas
Glass • N/A
450QX7082 • **Value $18**

4

Angel
Acrylic • N/A
400QX5095 • **Value $68**

5

Angel
Acrylic • N/A
450QX5075 • **Value $27**

6

Angel
(re-issued from 1980)
Yarn • N/A
300QX1621 • **Value $12**

7

Baby's First Christmas
Acrylic • N/A
550QX5162 • **Value $34**

8

Baby's First Christmas
Cameo • N/A
850QX5135 • **Value $20**

9

Baby's First Christmas
Handcrafted • N/A
1300QX4402 • **Value $53**

10

Baby's First
Christmas – Black
Satin • N/A
450QX6022 • **Value $28**

11

Baby's First
Christmas – Boy
Satin • N/A
450QX6015 • **Value $25**

12

Baby's First
Christmas – Girl
Satin • N/A
450QX6002 • **Value $25**

13

Betsey Clark
Cameo • N/A
850QX5122 • **Value $32**

14

Betsey Clark
Handcrafted • FRAN
900QX4235 • **Value $77**

15

Calico Kitty
Fabric • N/A
300QX4035 • **Value $20**

16

Candyville Express
Handcrafted • N/A
750QX4182 • **Value $105**

17

Cardinal Cutie
Fabric • N/A
300QX4002 • **Value $23**

General Keepsake

	Price Paid	Value
1.		
2.		
3.		
4.		
5.		
6.		
7.		
8.		
9.		
10.		
11.		
12.		
13.		
14.		
15.		
16.		
17.		

Totals

1

Checking It Twice
(re-issued from 1980)
Handcrafted • BLAC
2250QX1584 • **Value $200**

2

**Christmas 1981 –
Schneeberg**
Satin • N/A
450QX8095 • **Value $27**

3

Christmas Dreams
Handcrafted • DLEE
1200QX4375 • **Value $220**

4

Christmas Fantasy
(re-issued in 1982)
Handcrafted • N/A
1300QX1554 • **Value $90**

5

Christmas in the Forest
Glass • N/A
450QX8135 • **Value $142**

6

Christmas Magic
Satin • N/A
450QX8102 • **Value $27**

7

Christmas Star
Acrylic • N/A
550QX5015 • **Value $30**

8

Christmas Teddy
Plush • N/A
550QX4042 • **Value $23**

9

**Clothespin
Drummer Boy**
Handcrafted • N/A
450QX4082 • **Value $47**

10

Daughter
Satin • N/A
450QX6075 • **Value $41**

11

DISNEY
Satin • N/A
450QX8055 • **Value $33**

12

**THE DIVINE MISS
PIGGY™**
(re-issued in 1982)
Handcrafted • FRAN
1200QX4255 • **Value $94**

13

Dough Angel
(re-issued from 1978)
Handcrafted • DLEE
550QX1396 • **Value $90**

14

Drummer Boy
Wood • N/A
250QX1481 • **Value $47**

15

Father
Satin • N/A
450QX6095 • **Value $20**

16

First Christmas Together
Acrylic • N/A
550QX5055 • **Value $24**

17

First Christmas Together
Glass • N/A
450QX7062 • **Value $26**

18

The Friendly Fiddler
Handcrafted • DLEE
800QX4342 • **Value $80**

19

Friendship
Acrylic • N/A
550QX5035 • **Value $34**

20

Friendship
Satin • N/A
450QX7042 • **Value $28**

General Keepsake		
	Price Paid	Value
1.		
2.		
3.		
4.		
5.		
6.		
7.		
8.		
9.		
10.		
11.		
12.		
13.		
14.		
15.		
16.		
17.		
18.		
19.		
20.		
Totals		

1

The Gift of Love
Glass • N/A
450QX7055 • **Value $27**

2

Gingham Dog
Fabric • N/A
300QX4022 • **Value $23**

3

Godchild
Satin • N/A
450QX6035 • **Value $24**

4

Granddaughter
Satin • N/A
450QX6055 • **Value $25**

5

Grandfather
Glass • N/A
450QX7015 • **Value $23**

6

Grandmother
Satin • N/A
450QX7022 • **Value $22**

7

Grandparents
Glass • N/A
450QX7035 • **Value $21**

8

Grandson
Satin • N/A
450QX6042 • **Value $25**

General Keepsake

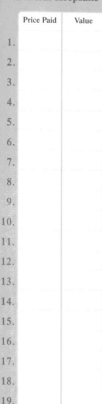

	Price Paid	Value
1.		
2.		
3.		
4.		
5.		
6.		
7.		
8.		
9.		
10.		
11.		
12.		
13.		
14.		
15.		
16.		
17.		
18.		
19.		
20.		

Totals

9

A Heavenly Nap
(re-issued from 1980)
Handcrafted • DLEE
650QX1394 • **Value $48**

10

Home
Satin • N/A
450QX7095 • **Value $22**

11

Ice Fairy
Handcrafted • DLEE
650QX4315 • **Value $110**

12

The Ice Sculptor
(re-issued in 1982)
Handcrafted • DLEE
800QX4322 • **Value $97**

13

Joan Walsh Anglund
Satin • N/A
450QX8042 • **Value $27**

14

Jolly Snowman
Handcrafted • N/A
350QX4075 • **Value $60**

15

KERMIT the FROG™
Handcrafted • FRAN
900QX4242 • **Value $100**

16

Let Us Adore Him
Glass • N/A
450QX8115 • **Value $65**

17

Love
Acrylic • N/A
550QX5022 • **Value $50**

18

Love and Joy
(Porcelain Chimes)
Porcelain • N/A
900QX4252 • **Value $98**

19

Marty Links™
Satin • N/A
450QX8082 • **Value $25**

20

Mary Hamilton
Glass • N/A
450QX8062 • **Value $21**

VALUE GUIDE — HALLMARK KEEPSAKE ORNAMENTS

1

Merry Christmas
Glass • N/A
450QX8142 • **Value $27**

2

Mother
Satin • N/A
450QX6082 • **Value $20**

3

Mother and Dad
Satin • N/A
450QX7002 • **Value $17**

4

Mouse
Acrylic • N/A
400QX5082 • **Value $30**

5

Mr. & Mrs. Claus (set/2, re-issued from 1975)
Handcrafted • N/A
1200QX4485 • **Value $130**

6

MUPPETS™
Satin • N/A
450QX8075 • **Value $36**

7

PEANUTS®
Satin • N/A
450QX8035 • **Value $38**

8

Peppermint Mouse
Fabric • N/A
300QX4015 • **Value $42**

9

Perky Penguin (re-issued in 1982)
Handcrafted • N/A
350QX4095 • **Value $60**

10

Puppy Love
Handcrafted • N/A
350QX4062 • **Value $35**

11

Raccoon Tunes
Plush • N/A
550QX4055 • **Value $27**

12

Sailing Santa
Handcrafted • N/A
1300QX4395 • **Value $295**

13

St. Nicholas
Pressed Tin • SICK
550QX4462 • **Value $55**

14

Santa (re-issued from 1980)
Yarn • N/A
300QX1614 • **Value $11**

15

Santa Mobile (re-issued from 1980)
Chrome Plate • N/A
550QX1361 • **Value $48**

16

Santa's Coming
Satin • N/A
450QX8122 • **Value $30**

17

Santa's Surprise
Satin • N/A
450QX8155 • **Value $27**

18

Shepherd Scene
Acrylic • N/A
550QX5002 • **Value $31**

19

Snowflake Chimes (re-issued from 1980)
Chrome Plate • SICK
550QX1654 • **Value $34**

20

Snowman
Acrylic • N/A
400QX5102 • **Value $29**

General Keepsake

	Price Paid	Value
1.		
2.		
3.		
4.		
5.		
6.		
7.		
8.		
9.		
10.		
11.		
12.		
13.		
14.		
15.		
16.		
17.		
18.		
19.		
20.		

Totals

1

Snowman
(re-issued from 1980)
Yarn • N/A
300QX1634 • **Value $10**

2

Snowman Chimes
Chrome Plate • N/A
550QX4455 • **Value $32**

3

Soldier
(re-issued from 1980)
Yarn • N/A
300QX1641 • **Value $11**

4

Son
Satin • N/A
450QX6062 • **Value $30**

5

Space Santa
Handcrafted • N/A
650QX4302 • **Value $118**

6

Star Swing
Handcrafted/Brass • SICK
550QX4215 • **Value $44**

7

The Stocking Mouse
Handcrafted • N/A
450QX4122 • **Value $92**

8

Teacher
Satin • N/A
450QX8002 • **Value $15**

9

Topsy-Turvy Tunes
Handcrafted • DLEE
750QX4295 • **Value $75**

10

Traditional (Black Santa)
Satin • N/A
450QX8015 • **Value $100**

11

Tree Photoholder
Acrylic • N/A
550QX5155 • **Value $30**

12

Unicorn
Cameo • N/A
850QX5165 • **Value $25**

13

A Well-Stocked Stocking
Handcrafted • N/A
900QX1547 • **Value $77**

1980

Teddy bear lovers have always been able to find great Hallmark bear ornaments and in 1980 Hallmark offered up two special treats in "Caroling Bear" and "Christmas Teddy." In the collection for 1980 there were a total of 85 Keepsake ornaments. See the collectible series section for more 1980 ornaments.

14

25th Christmas Together
Glass • N/A
400QX2061 • **Value $22**

15

Angel
(re-issued in 1981)
Yarn • N/A
300QX1621 • **Value $12**

16

Angel Music
(re-issued from 1979)
Fabric • N/A
200QX3439 • **Value $25**

General Keepsake

	Price Paid	Value
1.		
2.		
3.		
4.		
5.		
6.		
7.		
8.		
9.		
10.		
11.		
12.		
13.		

General Keepsake

14.		
15.		
16.		

Totals

1

The Animals' Christmas
Handcrafted • DLEE
800QX1501 • **Value $59**

2

Baby's First Christmas
Handcrafted • SICK
12QX1561 • **Value $48**

3
Baby's First Christmas
Satin • N/A
400QX2001 • **Value $28**

4

Beauty of Friendship
Acrylic • N/A
400QX3034 • **Value $67**

5
Betsey Clark
Cameo • N/A
650QX3074 • **Value $53**

6

Betsey Clark's Christmas
Handcrafted • N/A
750X1494 • **Value $38**

7

Black Baby's First Christmas
Satin • N/A
400QX2294 • **Value $31**

8

Caroling Bear
Handcrafted • DLEE
750QX1401 • **Value $150**

9

Checking It Twice
(re-issued in 1981)
Handcrafted • BLAC
2000QX1584 • **Value $200**

10

Christmas at Home
Glass • N/A
400QX2101 • **Value $40**

11

Christmas Cardinals
Glass • N/A
400QX2241 • **Value $32**

12

Christmas Choir
Glass • N/A
400QX2281 • **Value $83**

13

Christmas is for Children
(re-issued from 1979)
Handcrafted • N/A
550QX1359 • **Value $92**

14

Christmas Love
Glass • N/A
400QX2074 • **Value $52**

15

Christmas Owl
(re-issued in 1982)
Handcrafted • N/A
400QX1314 • **Value $49**

16

Christmas Teddy
Handcrafted • N/A
250QX1354 • **Value $132**

17

Christmas Time
Satin • N/A
400QX2261 • **Value $33**

18

A Christmas Treat
(re-issued from 1979)
Handcrafted • N/A
550QX1347 • **Value $84**

19

A Christmas Vigil
Handcrafted • DLEE
900QX1441 • **Value $130**

20

Clothespin Soldier
Handcrafted • N/A
350QX1341 • **Value $42**

	General Keepsake	
	Price Paid	Value
1.		
2.		
3.		
4.		
5.		
6.		
7.		
8.		
9.		
10.		
11.		
12.		
13.		
14.		
15.		
16.		
17.		
18.		
19.		
20.		
Totals		

1

Dad
Glass • N/A
400QX2141 • **Value $18**

2

Daughter
Glass • N/A
400QX2121 • **Value $42**

3

DISNEY
Satin • N/A
400QX2181 • **Value $35**

4

Dove
Acrylic • N/A
400QX3081 • **Value $42**

5

Drummer Boy
Acrylic • N/A
400QX3094 • **Value $29**

6

Drummer Boy
Handcrafted • DLEE
550QX1474 • **Value $95**

7

Elfin Antics
Handcrafted • N/A
900QX1421 • **Value $220**

8

**First
Christmas Together**
Acrylic • N/A
400QX3054 • **Value $48**

9

**First
Christmas Together**
Glass • N/A
400QX2054 • **Value $40**

10

Friendship
Glass • N/A
400QX2081 • **Value $23**

11

Granddaughter
Satin • N/A
400QX2021 • **Value $36**

12

Grandfather
Glass • N/A
400QX2314 • **Value $20**

13

Grandmother
Glass • N/A
400QX2041 • **Value $20**

14

Grandparents
Glass • N/A
400QX2134 • **Value $42**

15

Grandson
Satin • N/A
400QX2014 • **Value $35**

16

Happy Christmas
Satin • N/A
400QX2221 • **Value $27**

17
Heavenly Minstrel
Handcrafted • DLEE
1500QX1567 • **Value $340**

18

**A Heavenly Nap
(re-issued in 1981)**
Handcrafted • DLEE
650QX1394 • **Value $48**

19

Heavenly Sounds
Handcrafted • N/A
750QX1521 • **Value $98**

20

Joan Walsh Anglund
Satin • N/A
400QX2174 • **Value $24**

1

Jolly Santa
Glass • N/A
400QX2274 • **Value $29**

2

Joy
Acrylic • N/A
400QX3501 • **Value $29**

3

Love
Acrylic • N/A
400QX3021 • **Value $66**

4

Marty Links™
Satin • N/A
400QX2214 • **Value $21**

5

Mary Hamilton
Glass • N/A
400QX2194 • **Value $23**

6

Merry Redbird
Handcrafted • N/A
350QX1601 • **Value $70**

7

Merry Santa
(re-issued from 1979)
Fabric • N/A
200QX3427 • **Value $19**

8

Mother
Acrylic • N/A
400QX3041 • **Value $37**

9

Mother
Satin • N/A
400QX2034 • **Value $22**

10

Mother and Dad
Glass • N/A
400QX2301 • **Value $24**

11

MUPPETS™
Satin • N/A
400QX2201 • **Value $39**

12

Nativity
Glass • N/A
400QX2254 • **Value $90**

13

PEANUTS®
Satin • N/A
400QX2161 • **Value $42**

14

Reindeer Chimes
(re-issued from 1978)
Chrome Plate • SICK
550QX3203 • **Value $48**

15

Rocking Horse
(re-issued from 1979)
Fabric • N/A
200QX3407 • **Value $22**

16

Santa
Acrylic • N/A
400QX3101 • **Value $26**

17

Santa
(re-issued in 1981)
Yarn • N/A
300QX1614 • **Value $11**

18

Santa 1980
Handcrafted • N/A
550QX1461 • **Value $98**

19

Santa Mobile
(re-issued in 1981)
Chrome Plate • N/A
550QX1361 • **Value $48**

20

Santa's Flight
Pressed Tin • SICK
550QX1381 • **Value $118**

General Keepsake

	Price Paid	Value
1.		
2.		
3.		
4.		
5.		
6.		
7.		
8.		
9.		
10.		
11.		
12.		
13.		
14.		
15.		
16.		
17.		
18.		
19.		
20.		

Totals

1

Santa's Workshop
Satin • N/A
400QX2234 • **Value $32**

2

Skating Snowman
(re-issued from 1979)
Handcrafted • DLEE
550QX1399 • **Value $85**

3

Snowflake Chimes
(re-issued in 1981)
Chrome Plate • SICK
550QX1654 • **Value $34**

4

The Snowflake Swing
Handcrafted • N/A
400QX1334 • **Value $45**

5

Snowman
(re-issued in 1981)
Yarn • N/A
300QX1634 • **Value $10**

6

Soldier
(re-issued in 1981)
Yarn • N/A
300QX1641 • **Value $11**

7

Son
Glass • N/A
400QX2114 • **Value $35**

8

**A Spot of
Christmas Cheer**
Handcrafted • DLEE
800QX1534 • **Value $152**

9

Stuffed Full Stocking
(re-issued from 1979)
Fabric • N/A
200QX3419 • **Value $26**

10

Swingin' on a Star
Handcrafted • N/A
400QX1301 • **Value $80**

11

Teacher
Satin • N/A
400QX2094 • **Value $18**

12

Three Wise Men
Acrylic • N/A
400QX3001 • **Value $34**

13

Wreath
Acrylic • N/A
400QX3014 • **Value $82**

1979

Among the most popular Hallmark ornaments in the early years were the ball ornaments commemorating "Baby's First Christmas." In 1979, Hallmark released its first handcrafted ornament with this theme. Overall, there were 65 Keepsake ornaments in 1979. See the collectible series section for more 1979 ornaments.

14

Angel Delight
Handcrafted • N/A
300QX1307 • **Value $98**

15

Angel Music
(re-issued in 1980)
Fabric • N/A
200QX3439 • **Value $25**

16

Baby's First Christmas
Handcrafted • N/A
800QX1547 • **Value $130**

General Keepsake

	Price Paid	Value
1.		
2.		
3.		
4.		
5.		
6.		
7.		
8.		
9.		
10.		
11.		
12.		
13.		

General Keepsake

14.		
15.		
16.		

Totals

1
Baby's First Christmas
Satin • N/A
350QX2087 • **Value $33**

2
Behold the Star
Satin • N/A
350QX2559 • **Value $39**

3
Black Angel
Glass • BLAC
350QX2079 • **Value $27**

4
Christmas Angel
Acrylic • N/A
350QX3007 • **Value $138**

5
Christmas Cheer
Acrylic • N/A
350QX3039 • **Value $83**

6
Christmas Chickadees
Glass • N/A
350QX2047 • **Value $35**

7
Christmas Collage
Glass • N/A
350QX2579 • **Value $37**

8
Christmas Eve Surprise
Handcrafted • N/A
650QX1579 • **Value $70**

9
Christmas Heart
Handcrafted • SICK
650QX1407 • **Value $105**

10
Christmas is for Children
(re-issued in 1980)
Handcrafted • N/A
500QX1359 • **Value $92**

11
Christmas Traditions
Glass • SICK
350QX2539 • **Value $39**

12
A Christmas Treat
(re-issued in 1980)
Handcrafted • N/A
500QX1347 • **Value $84**

13
Christmas Tree
Acrylic • N/A
350QX3027 • **Value $78**

14
The Downhill Run
Handcrafted • DLEE
650QX1459 • **Value $175**

15
The Drummer Boy
Handcrafted • N/A
800QX1439 • **Value $130**

16
Friendship
Glass • N/A
350QX2039 • **Value $25**

17
Granddaughter
Satin • N/A
350QX2119 • **Value $38**

18
Grandmother
Glass • N/A
350QX2527 • **Value $28**

19
Grandson
Satin • N/A
350QX2107 • **Value $38**

20
Green Boy
(re-issued from 1978)
Yarn • N/A
200QX1231 • **Value $28**

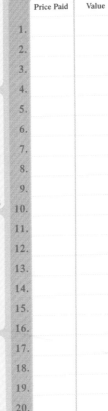

General Keepsake

	Price Paid	Value
1.		
2.		
3.		
4.		
5.		
6.		
7.		
8.		
9.		
10.		
11.		
12.		
13.		
14.		
15.		
16.		
17.		
18.		
19.		
20.		

Totals

1

Green Girl
(re-issued from 1978)
Yarn • N/A
200QX1261 • **Value $24**

2

Holiday Scrimshaw
Handcrafted • N/A
400QX1527 • **Value $220**

3

Holiday Wreath
Acrylic • N/A
350QX3539 • **Value $44**

4

Joan Walsh Anglund
Satin • N/A
350QX2059 • **Value $37**

5

The Light of Christmas
Glass • N/A
350QX2567 • **Value $33**

6

Love
Acrylic • N/A
350QX3047 • **Value $95**

7

Love
Glass • N/A
350QX2587 • **Value $80**

8

Mary Hamilton
Satin • N/A
350QX2547 • **Value $28**

General Keepsake

	Price Paid	Value
1.		
2.		
3.		
4.		
5.		
6.		
7.		
8.		
9.		
10.		
11.		
12.		
13.		
14.		
15.		
16.		
17.		
18.		
19.		
20.		

9

A Matchless Christmas
Handcrafted • N/A
400QX1327 • **Value $88**

10

Merry Santa
(re-issued in 1980)
Fabric • N/A
200QX3427 • **Value $19**

11

Mother
Glass • N/A
350QX2519 • **Value $27**

12

Mr. Claus
(re-issued from 1978)
Yarn • N/A
200QX3403 • **Value $24**

13

Mrs. Claus
(re-issued from 1978)
Yarn • N/A
200QX1251 • **Value $23**

14

New Home
Satin • N/A
350QX2127 • **Value $46**

15

Night Before Christmas
Satin • N/A
350QX2147 • **Value $40**

16

Our First
Christmas Together
Glass • N/A
350QX2099 • **Value $70**

17

Our Twenty-Fifth
Anniversary
Glass • N/A
350QX2507 • **Value $27**

18

Outdoor Fun
Handcrafted • SICK
800QX1507 • **Value $142**

19

Partridge in a Pear Tree
Acrylic • N/A
350QX3519 • **Value $43**

20

PEANUTS®
(Time to Trim)
Satin • N/A
350QX2027 • **Value $46**

Totals

1

Raccoon
(re-issued from 1978)
Handcrafted • DLEE
650QX1423 • **Value $99**

2

Ready for Christmas
Handcrafted • DLEE
650QX1339 • **Value $152**

3

Reindeer Chimes
(re-issued from 1978)
Chrome Plate • SICK
450QX3203 • **Value $48**

4

Rocking Horse
(re-issued in 1980)
Fabric • N/A
200QX3407 • **Value $22**

5

Santa
(re-issued from 1978)
Handcrafted • N/A
300QX1356 • **Value $70**

6

Santa's Here
Handcrafted • SICK
500QX1387 • **Value $70**

7

The Skating Snowman
(re-issued in 1980)
Handcrafted • DLEE
500QX1399 • **Value $85**

8

Snowflake
Acrylic • N/A
350QX3019 • **Value $43**

9

Spencer® Sparrow, Esq.
Satin • N/A
350QX2007 • **Value $46**

10

Star Chimes
Chrome Plate • SICK
450QX1379 • **Value $73**

11

Star Over Bethlehem
Acrylic • SICK
350QX3527 • **Value $72**

12

Stuffed Full Stocking
(re-issued in 1980)
Fabric • N/A
200QX3419 • **Value $26**

13

Teacher
Satin • N/A
350QX2139 • **Value $17**

14

Winnie-the-Pooh
Satin • N/A
350QX2067 • **Value $47**

15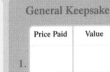

Words of Christmas
Acrylic • N/A
350QX3507 • **Value $78**

General Keepsake	Price Paid	Value
1.		
2.		
3.		
4.		
5.		
6.		
7.		
8.		
9.		
10.		
11.		
12.		
13.		
14.		
15.		
Totals		

1978

In the 6th year of Hallmark ornaments several unique handcrafted ornaments proved to be the most popular, including "Angels," "Animal Home," "Calico Mouse," "Red Cardinal" and "Schneeberg Bell." The 1978 collection featured 54 Keepsake ornaments. See the collectible series section for more 1978 ornaments.

1
25th Christmas Together
Glass • N/A
350QX2696 • **Value $34**

2
Angel
Acrylic • N/A
350QX3543 • **Value $47**

3
Angel
(re-issued in 1981)
Handcrafted • DLEE
450QX1396 • **Value $90**

4
Angels
Handcrafted • N/A
800QX1503 • **Value $385**

5
Animal Home
Handcrafted • DLEE
600QX1496 • **Value $190**

General Keepsake		
	Price Paid	Value
1.		
2.		
3.		
4.		
5.		
6.		
7.		
8.		
9.		
10.		
11.		
12.		
13.		
14.		
15.		
16.		
17.		
Totals		

6
Baby's First Christmas
Satin • N/A
350QX2003 • **Value $96**

7
Calico Mouse
Handcrafted • N/A
450QX1376 • **Value $182**

8
Candle
Acrylic • N/A
350QX3576 • **Value $85**

9
DISNEY
Satin • N/A
350QX2076 • **Value $120**

10
Dove
Acrylic • PALM
350QX3103 • **Value $110**

11
Dove
Handcrafted • SICK
450QX1903 • **Value $88**

12
Drummer Boy
Glass • N/A
350QX2523 • **Value $45**

13
Drummer Boy
Handcrafted • N/A
250QX1363 • **Value $77**

14
First Christmas Together
Satin • N/A
350QX2183 • **Value $48**

15
For Your New Home
Satin • N/A
350QX2176 • **Value $26**

16
Granddaughter
Satin • N/A
350QX2163 • **Value $45**

17
Grandmother
Satin • N/A
350QX2676 • **Value $44**

1

Grandson
Satin • N/A
350QX2156 • **Value $48**

2

Green Boy
(re-issued in 1979)
Yarn • N/A
200QX1231 • **Value $28**

3

Green Girl
(re-issued in 1979)
Yarn • N/A
200QX1261 • **Value $24**

4

Hallmark's Antique
Card Collection Design
Satin • N/A
350QX2203 • **Value $45**

5

Holly and
Poinsettia Ball
Handcrafted • SICK
600QX1476 • **Value $89**

6

Joan Walsh Anglund
Satin • N/A
350QX2216 • **Value $65**

7

Joy
Glass • N/A
350QX2543 • **Value $50**

8

Joy
Handcrafted • N/A
450QX1383 • **Value $92**

9

Locomotive
Acrylic • N/A
350QX3563 • **Value $60**

10

Love
Glass • N/A
350QX2683 • **Value $60**

11

Merry Christmas
Acrylic • PALM
350QX3556 • **Value $57**

12

Merry Christmas (Santa)
Satin • N/A
350QX2023 • **Value $53**

13

Mother
Glass • N/A
350QX2663 • **Value $44**

14

Mr. Claus
(re-issued in 1979)
Yarn • N/A
200QX3403 • **Value $24**

15

Mrs. Claus
(re-issued in 1979)
Yarn • N/A
200QX1251 • **Value $23**

16

Nativity
Acrylic • PALM
350QX3096 • **Value N/E**

17

Nativity
Glass • N/A
350QX2536 • **Value N/E**

18

Panorama Ball
Handcrafted • N/A
600QX1456 • **Value $145**

19

PEANUTS®
Satin • N/A
250QX2036 • **Value $63**

General Keepsake

	Price Paid	Value
1.		
2.		
3.		
4.		
5.		
6.		
7.		
8.		
9.		
10.		
11.		
12.		
13.		
14.		
15.		
16.		
17.		
18.		
19.		

Totals

1978 Collection

1

PEANUTS®
Satin • N/A
250QX2043 • **Value $72**

2

PEANUTS®
Satin • N/A
350QX2056 • **Value $73**

3

PEANUTS®
Satin • N/A
350QX2063 • **Value $63**

4

Praying Angel
Handcrafted • DLEE
250QX1343 • **Value $85**

5

The Quail
Glass • N/A
350QX2516 • **Value $42**

6

Red Cardinal
Handcrafted • UNRU
450QX1443 • **Value $172**

7

Reindeer Chimes
(re-issued in 1979 and 1980)
Chrome Plate • SICK
450QX3203 • **Value $48**

8

Rocking Horse
Handcrafted • N/A
600QX1483 • **Value $95**

9

Santa
Acrylic • PALM
350QX3076 • **Value $86**

10

Santa
(re-issued in 1979)
Handcrafted • N/A
250QX1356 • **Value $70**

11

Schneeberg Bell
Handcrafted • N/A
800QX1523 • **Value $195**

12

Skating Raccoon
(re-issued in 1979)
Handcrafted • DLEE
600QX1423 • **Value $99**

13

Snowflake
Acrylic • PALM
350QX3083 • **Value $68**

14

Spencer® Sparrow, Esq.
Satin • N/A
350QX2196 • **Value $49**

15

Yesterday's Toys
Glass • N/A
350QX2503 • **Value $42**

General Keepsake

	Price Paid	Value
1.		
2.		
3.		
4.		
5.		
6.		
7.		
8.		
9.		
10.		
11.		
12.		
13.		
14.		
15.		
Totals		

1977

The 1977 collection was highlighted by a group of handcrafted ornaments designed to have an antique wooden appearance. Called the "Nostalgia Collection," these ornaments were "Angel," "Antique Car," "Nativity," and "Toys." In 1977, there were 53 Keepsake ornaments. See the collectible series section for more 1977 ornaments.

1

Angel
Cloth • N/A
175QX2202 • **Value $47**

2

Angel
Handcrafted • DLEE
500QX1822 • **Value $133**

3

Angel
Handcrafted • N/A
600QX1722 • **Value $135**

4

Antique Car
Handcrafted • SICK
500QX1802 • **Value $72**

5

Baby's First Christmas
Satin • N/A
350QX1315 • **Value $86**

6

Bell
Acrylic • SICK
350QX2002 • **Value $50**

7

Bell
Glass • N/A
350QX1542 • **Value $39**

8

Bellringer
Handcrafted • N/A
600QX1922 • **Value $63**

9

Candle
Acrylic • N/A
350QX2035 • **Value $60**

10

Charmers
Glass • N/A
350QX1535 • **Value $62**

11

Christmas Mouse
Satin • N/A
350QX1342 • **Value $58**

12

Currier & Ives
Satin • N/A
350QX1302 • **Value $57**

13

Della Robia Wreath
Handcrafted • DLEE
450QX1935 • **Value $115**

14

Desert
Glass • N/A
250QX1595 • **Value $43**

15

DISNEY
Satin • N/A
350QX1335 • **Value $72**

16

DISNEY (set/2)
Satin • N/A
400QX1375 • **Value $58**

17

Drummer Boy
Acrylic • N/A
350QX3122 • **Value $64**

General Keepsake

	Price Paid	Value
1.		
2.		
3.		
4.		
5.		
6.		
7.		
8.		
9.		
10.		
11.		
12.		
13.		
14.		
15.		
16.		
17.		

Totals

1
First Christmas Together
Satin • N/A
350QX1322 • **Value $76**

2
For Your New Home
Glass • N/A
350QX2635 • **Value $37**

3
Granddaughter
Satin • N/A
350QX2082 • **Value $38**

4
Grandma Moses
Glass • N/A
350QX1502 • **Value $72**

5
Grandmother
Glass • N/A
350QX2602 • **Value $48**

6
Grandson
Satin • N/A
350QX2095 • **Value $36**

7
House
Handcrafted • N/A
600QX1702 • **Value $135**

8
Jack-in-the-Box
Handcrafted • N/A
600QX1715 • **Value $130**

General Keepsake

	Price Paid	Value
1.		
2.		
3.		
4.		
5.		
6.		
7.		
8.		
9.		
10.		
11.		
12.		
13.		
14.		
15.		
16.		
17.		
18.		
19.		
20.		
	Totals	

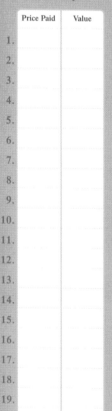

9
Joy
Acrylic • N/A
350QX2015 • **Value $52**

10
Joy
Acrylic • N/A
350QX3102 • **Value $48**

11
Love
Glass • N/A
350QX2622 • **Value $30**

12
Mandolin
Glass • N/A
350QX1575 • **Value $40**

13
Mother
Glass • N/A
350QX2615 • **Value $38**

14
Mountains
Glass • N/A
250QX1582 • **Value $35**

15
Nativity
Handcrafted • N/A
500QX1815 • **Value $160**

16
Norman Rockwell
Glass • N/A
350QX1515 • **Value $68**

17
Ornaments
Glass • N/A
350QX1555 • **Value $47**

18
Peace on Earth
Acrylic • N/A
350QX3115 • **Value $62**

19
PEANUTS®
Glass • N/A
250QX1622 • **Value $79**

20
PEANUTS® (set/2)
Glass • N/A
400QX1635 • **Value $94**

1

PEANUTS®
Satin • N/A
350QX1355 • **Value $82**

2

Rabbit
Satin • N/A
250QX1395 • **Value $92**

3

Reindeer
Handcrafted • N/A
600QX1735 • **Value $125**

4

Santa
Cloth • N/A
175QX2215 • **Value $68**

5

Seashore
Glass • N/A
250QX1602 • **Value $48**

6

**Snowflake
Collection (set/4)**
Chrome-Plated Zinc • SICK
500QX2102 • **Value $90**

7

Snowman
Handcrafted • SICK
450QX1902 • **Value $79**

8

Squirrel
Satin • N/A
250QX1382 • **Value $98**

9

Stained Glass
Glass • N/A
350QX1522 • **Value $61**

10

Star
Acrylic • N/A
350QX3135 • **Value $54**

11

Toys
Handcrafted • SICK
500QX1835 • **Value $154**

12

Weather House
Handcrafted • N/A
600QX1915 • **Value $102**

13

Wharf
Glass • N/A
250QX1615 • **Value $39**

14

Wreath
Acrylic • N/A
350QX2022 • **Value $60**

15

Wreath
Glass • N/A
350QX1562 • **Value $43**

General Keepsake

	Price Paid	Value
1.		
2.		
3.		
4.		
5.		
6.		
7.		
8.		
9.		
10.		
11.		
12.		
13.		
14.		
15.		

Totals

1976

The 1976 collection of ornaments featured popular themes such as Santa Claus, locomotives, partridges and drummer boys, all in a variety of different handcrafted styles. For the Bicentennial year, Hallmark issued a total of 39 Keepsake ornaments. See the collectible series section for more 1976 ornaments.

1

Angel
Handcrafted • N/A
300QX1761 • **Value $170**

2

Angel
Handcrafted • SICK
450QX1711 • **Value $170**

3

Baby's First Christmas
Satin • N/A
250QX2111 • **Value $155**

4

Betsey Clark
Satin • N/A
250QX2101 • **Value $63**

5

Betsey Clark (set/3)
Satin • N/A
450QX2181 • **Value $60**

6

Bicentennial '76 Commemorative
Satin • N/A
250QX2031 • **Value $58**

7

Bicentennial Charmers
Glass • N/A
300QX1981 • **Value $72**

8

Cardinals
Glass • N/A
225QX2051 • **Value $62**

9

Caroler
(re-issued from 1975)
Yarn • N/A
175QX1261 • **Value $22**

10

Charmers (set/2)
Satin • N/A
350QX2151 • **Value $76**

11

Chickadees
Glass • N/A
225QX2041 • **Value $62**

12

Colonial Children (set/2)
Glass • N/A
400QX2081 • **Value $77**

13

Currier & Ives
Glass • N/A
300QX1971 • **Value $49**

14

Currier & Ives
Satin • N/A
250QX2091 • **Value $49**

15

Drummer Boy
(re-issued from 1975)
Handcrafted • SICK
400QX1301 • **Value $160**

16

Drummer Boy
Handcrafted • N/A
500QX1841 • **Value $150**

17

Drummer Boy
(re-issued from 1975)
Yarn • N/A
175QX1231 • **Value $25**

General Keepsake

	Price Paid	Value
1.		
2.		
3.		
4.		
5.		
6.		
7.		
8.		
9.		
10.		
11.		
12.		
13.		
14.		
15.		
16.		
17.		
Totals		

1

Happy the Snowman (set/2)
Satin • N/A
350QX2161 • **Value $53**

2

Locomotive (re-issued from 1975)
Handcrafted • SICK
400QX2221 • **Value $190**

3

Marty Links™ (set/2)
Glass • N/A
400QX2071 • **Value $55**

4

Mrs. Santa (re-issued from 1975)
Yarn • N/A
175QX1251 • **Value $23**

5

Norman Rockwell
Glass • N/A
300QX1961 • **Value $80**

6

Partridge
Handcrafted • SICK
450QX1741 • **Value $195**

7

Partridge
Handcrafted • N/A
500QX1831 • **Value $118**

8

Peace on Earth (re-issued from 1975)
Handcrafted • SICK
400QX2231 • **Value $160**

9

Raggedy Andy™ (re-issued from 1975)
Yarn • N/A
175QX1221 • **Value $47**

10

Raggedy Ann™
Satin • N/A
250X2121 • **Value $60**

11

Raggedy Ann™ (re-issued from 1975)
Yarn • N/A
175QX1211 • **Value $45**

12

Reindeer
Handcrafted • N/A
300QX1781 • **Value $112**

13

Rocking Horse (re-issued from 1975)
Handcrafted • SICK
400QX1281 • **Value $170**

14

Rudolph and Santa
Satin • N/A
250QX2131 • **Value $92**

15

Santa
Handcrafted • N/A
300QX1771 • **Value $215**

16

Santa
Handcrafted • SICK
450QX1721 • **Value $110**

17

Santa
Handcrafted • N/A
500QX1821 • **Value $170**

18

Santa (re-issued from 1975)
Yarn • N/A
175QX1241 • **Value $24**

19

Shepherd
Handcrafted • N/A
300QX1751 • **Value $135**

20

Soldier
Handcrafted • SICK
450QX1731 • **Value $100**

General Keepsake

	Price Paid	Value
1.		
2.		
3.		
4.		
5.		
6.		
7.		
8.		
9.		
10.		
11.		
12.		
13.		
14.		
15.		
16.		
17.		
18.		
19.		
20.		
Totals		

1

Train
Handcrafted • N/A
500QX1811 • **Value $145**

1975

A whole new era of Christmas ornaments began when Hallmark debuted
12 handcrafted ornaments in 1975.
These early handcrafted designs are highly sought-after by collectors. Overall, there were 32 Keepsake ornaments issued in
1975, double the total of the previous year. See the collectible
series section for more 1975 ornaments.

2

Betsey Clark
Handcrafted • DLEE
250QX1571 • **Value $235**

3

Betsey Clark
Satin • N/A
250QX1631 • **Value $46**

4

Betsey Clark (set/2)
Satin • N/A
350QX1671 • **Value $48**

5

Betsey Clark (set/4)
Satin • N/A
450QX1681 • **Value $55**

General Keepsake		
	Price Paid	Value
1.		

General Keepsake

2.
3.
4.
5.
6.
7.
8.
9.
10.
11.
12.
13.
14.
15.
16.
17.

Totals

6

Buttons & Bo (set/4)
Glass • N/A
500QX1391 • **Value $55**

7

Charmers
Glass • N/A
300QX1351 • **Value $49**

8

Currier & Ives (set/2)
Glass • N/A
400QX1371 • **Value $40**

9

Currier & Ives
Satin • N/A
250QX1641 • **Value $40**

10

Drummer Boy
Handcrafted • DLEE
250QX1611 • **Value $245**

11

Drummer Boy
(re-issued in 1976)
Handcrafted • SICK
350QX1301 • **Value $160**

12

Drummer Boy
(re-issued in 1976)
Yarn • N/A
175QX1231 • **Value $25**

13

Joy
Handcrafted • SICK
350QX1321 • **Value $215**

14

Little Girl
(re-issued in 1976)
Yarn • N/A
175QX1261 • **Value $22**

15

Little Miracles (set/4)
Glass • N/A
500QX1401 • **Value $42**

16

Locomotive
(re-issued in 1976)
Handcrafted • SICK
350QX1271 • **Value $190**

17

Marty Links™
Glass • N/A
300QX1361 • **Value $50**

VALUE GUIDE — HALLMARK KEEPSAKE ORNAMENTS

1
Mrs. Santa
(re-issued in 1981)
Handcrafted • DLEE
250QX1561 • **Value $230**

2
Mrs. Santa
(re-issued in 1976)
Yarn • N/A
175QX1251 • **Value $23**

3
Norman Rockwell
Glass • N/A
300QX1341 • **Value $65**

4
Norman Rockwell
Satin • N/A
250QX1661 • **Value $63**

5
Peace On Earth
(re-issued in 1976)
Handcrafted • SICK
350QX1311 • **Value $160**

6
Raggedy Andy™
Handcrafted • DLEE
250QX1601 • **Value $355**

7
Raggedy Andy™
(re-issued in 1976)
Yarn • N/A
175QX1221 • **Value $47**

8
Raggedy Ann™
Handcrafted • DLEE
250QX1591 • **Value $305**

9
Raggedy Ann™
Satin • N/A
250QX1651 • **Value $52**

10
Raggedy Ann™
(re-issued in 1976)
Yarn • N/A
175QX1211 • **Value $45**

11
Raggedy Ann™ and
Raggedy Andy™ (set/2)
Glass • N/A
400QX1381 • **Value $68**

12
Rocking Horse
(re-issued in 1976)
Handcrafted • SICK
350QX1281 • **Value $170**

13
Santa
(re-issued in 1981)
Handcrafted • DLEE
250QX1551 • **Value $230**

14
Santa
(re-issued in 1976)
Yarn • N/A
175QX1241 • **Value $24**

15
Santa & Sleigh
Handcrafted • SICK
350QX1291 • **Value $235**

General Keepsake

	Price Paid	Value
1.		
2.		
3.		
4.		
5.		
6.		
7.		
8.		
9.		
10.		
11.		
12.		
13.		
14.		
15.		

Totals

269

1974

In the second year of Keepsake ornaments, the collection featured popular Christmas scenes from Norman Rockwell, Betsey Clark and Currier & Ives. Of the 16 Keepsake designs or sets offered in 1974, 10 were ball ornaments and 6 were made from yarn. See the collectible series section for more 1974 ornaments.

1

Angel
Glass • N/A
250QX1101 • **Value $77**

2

Angel
Yarn • N/A
150QX1031 • **Value $29**

3

Buttons & Bo (set/2)
Glass • N/A
350QX1131 • **Value $50**

4

Charmers
Glass • N/A
250QX1091 • **Value $52**

5

Currier & Ives (set/2)
Glass • N/A
350QX1121 • **Value $60**

6

Elf
Yarn • N/A
150QX1011 • **Value $26**

7

Little Miracles (set/4)
Glass • N/A
450QX1151 • **Value $62**

8

Mrs. Santa
Yarn • N/A
150QX1001 • **Value $24**

9

Norman Rockwell
Glass • N/A
250QX1061 • **Value $98**

10

Norman Rockwell
Glass • N/A
250QX1111 • **Value $86**

11

Raggedy Ann™ and Raggedy Andy™ (set/4)
Glass • N/A
450QX1141 • **Value $90**

12

Santa
Yarn • N/A
150QX1051 • **Value $26**

13

Snowgoose
Glass • N/A
250QX1071 • **Value $72**

14

Snowman
Yarn • N/A
150QX1041 • **Value $24**

15

Soldier
Yarn • N/A
150QX1021 • **Value $25**

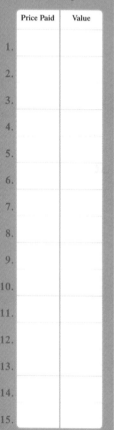

1974 Collection

General Keepsake

	Price Paid	Value
1.		
2.		
3.		
4.		
5.		
6.		
7.		
8.		
9.		
10.		
11.		
12.		
13.		
14.		
15.		
Totals		

1973

The very first year of Hallmark Keepsake Ornaments was 1973. This year's debut offering consisted of 6 ball ornaments and 12 yarn ornaments, making a total of 18 Keepsake designs. The first Keepsake series, "Betsey Clark," began this year. See the collectible series section for more 1973 ornaments.

1

Angel
Yarn • N/A
125XHD785 • **Value $28**

2

Betsey Clark
Glass • N/A
250XHD1002 • **Value $94**

3

Blue Girl
Yarn • N/A
125XHD852 • **Value $24**

4

Boy Caroler
Yarn • N/A
125XHD832 • **Value $26**

5

Choir Boy
Yarn • N/A
125XHD805 • **Value $27**

6

Christmas Is Love
Glass • N/A
250XHD1062 • **Value $78**

7

Elf
Yarn • N/A
125XHD792 • **Value $26**

8

Elves
Glass • N/A
250XHD1035 • **Value $87**

9

Green Girl
Yarn • N/A
125XHD845 • **Value $26**

10

Little Girl
Yarn • N/A
125XHD825 • **Value $26**

11

Manger Scene
Glass • N/A
250XHD1022 • **Value $93**

12
Mr. Santa
Yarn • N/A
125XHD745 • **Value $26**

13

Mrs. Santa
Yarn • N/A
125XHD752 • **Value $26**

14
Mr. Snowman
Yarn • N/A
125XHD765 • **Value $25**

15

Mrs. Snowman
Yarn • N/A
125XHD772 • **Value $24**

16

Santa with Elves
Glass • N/A
250XHD1015 • **Value $82**

17

Soldier
Yarn • N/A
100XHD812 • **Value $24**

General Keepsake

	Price Paid	Value
1.		
2.		
3.		
4.		
5.		
6.		
7.		
8.		
9.		
10.		
11.		
12.		
13.		
14.		
15.		
16.		
17.		

Totals

Spring Ornaments

Spring Ornaments

Eighteen new pieces were added to the Spring ornaments collection this year, including eight ornaments which are part of a collectible series. Only one new series has been introduced for 2000 ("Spring Is in the Air") while two series ("Beatrix Potter™" and "Cottontail Express") celebrate their final editions.

Collectible Series

1

Apple Blossom Lane
(1st, 1995)
Handcrafted • FRAN
895QEO8207 • **Value $22**

2

Apple Blossom Lane
(2nd, 1996)
Handcrafted • FRAN
895QEO8084 • **Value $18**

3

Apple Blossom Lane
(3rd & final, 1997)
Handcrafted • FRAN
895QEO8662 • **Value $19**

4

Peter Rabbit™
(1st, 1996)
Handcrafted • VOTR
895QEO8071 • **Value $80**

Apple Blossom Lane

	Price Paid	Value
1.		
2.		
3.		

Beatrix Potter™

4.		
5.		
6.		
7.	17.00	
8.		

Children's Collector BARBIE™ Ornament

9.		
10.		
11.		

Collector's Plate

12.		
13.		
14.		
15.		

Cottontail Express

16.		

Totals

5

Jemima Puddle-duck™
(2nd, 1997)
Handcrafted • VOTR
895QEO8645 • **Value $25**

6

Benjamin Bunny™
Beatrix Potter™
(3rd, 1998)
Handcrafted • VOTR
895QEO8383 • **Value $20**

7

Tom Kitten™
(4th, 1999)
Handcrafted • VOTR
895QEO8329 • **Value $17**

8
New!

Mr. Jeremy Fisher™
Beatrix Potter™
(5th & final, 2000)
Handcrafted • VOTR
895QEO8441 • **Value $8.95**

9

Based on the BARBIE® as Rapunzel Doll (1st, 1997)
Handcrafted • RGRS
1495QEO8635 • **Value $33**

10

Based on the BARBIE® as Little Bo Peep Doll
(2nd, 1998)
Handcrafted • RGRS
1495QEO8373 • **Value $25**

11

Based on the BARBIE™ as Cinderella Doll
(3rd & final, 1999)
Handcrafted • RGRS
1495QEO8327 • **Value $24**

12

"Gathering Sunny Memories" (1st, 1994)
Porcelain • VOTR
775QEO8233 • **Value $33**

13

"Catching the Breeze"
(2nd, 1995)
Porcelain • VOTR
795QEO8219 • **Value $20**

14

"Keeping a Secret"
(3rd, 1996)
Porcelain • VOTR
795QEO8221 • **Value $17**

15

"Sunny Sunday Best"
(4th & final, 1997)
Porcelain • VOTR
795QEO8675 • **Value $16**

16

Locomotive (1st, 1996)
Handcrafted • CROW
895QEO8074 • **Value $43**

1

Colorful Coal Car
(2nd, 1997)
Handcrafted • CROW
895QEO8652 • **Value $20**

2

Passenger Car (3rd, 1998)
Handcrafted • CROW
995QEO8376 • **Value $19**

3

Flatbed Car (4th, 1999)
Handcrafted • CROW
995QEO8387 • **Value $18**

4

New!

Caboose
(5th & final, 2000)
Handcrafted • CROW
995QEO8464 • **Value $9.95**

5

Easter Egg Surprise
(1st, 1999)
Porcelain • VOTR
1495QEO8377 • **Value $26**

6

New!

Rabbit (2nd, 2000)
Porcelain • VOTR
1495QEO8461 • **Value $14.95**

7

Easter Parade (1st, 1992)
Handcrafted • CROW
675QEO9301 • **Value $28**

8

Easter Parade (2nd, 1993)
Handcrafted • JLEE
675QEO8325 • **Value $21**

9

Easter Parade
(3rd & final, 1994)
Handcrafted • RHOD
675QEO8136 • **Value $20**

10

Eggs in Sports
(1st, 1992)
Handcrafted • SIED
675QEO9341 • **Value $33**

11

Eggs in Sports
(2nd, 1993)
Handcrafted • SIED
675QEO8332 • **Value $21**

12

Eggs in Sports
(3rd & final, 1994)
Handcrafted • SIED
675QEO8133 • **Value $20**

13

Strawberry (1st, 1999)
Handcrafted • TAGU
995QEO8369 • **Value $18**

14

New!

Blueberry (2nd, 2000)
Handcrafted • TAGU
995QEO8454 • **Value $9.95**

15

Garden Club (1st, 1995)
Handcrafted • SICK
795QEO8209 • **Value $20**

16

Garden Club (2nd, 1996)
Handcrafted • PALM
795QEO8091 • **Value $17**

17

Garden Club (3rd, 1997)
Handcrafted • BRIC
795QEO8665 • **Value $16**

18

Garden Club
(4th & final, 1998)
Handcrafted • PIKE
795QEO8426 • **Value $16**

Cottontail Express	Price Paid	Value
1.		
2.		
3.		
4.		
Easter Egg Surprise		
5.		
6.		
Easter Parade		
7.		
8.		
9.		
Eggs In Sports		
10.		
11.		
12.		
Fairy Berry Bears		
13.		
14.		
Garden Club		
15.		
16.		
17.		
18.		
Totals		

Spring Ornaments

1

Here Comes Easter
(1st, 1994)
Handcrafted • CROW
775QEO8093 • **Value $36**

2

Here Comes Easter
(2nd, 1995)
Handcrafted • CROW
795QEO8217 • **Value $20**

3

Here Comes Easter
(3rd, 1996)
Handcrafted • CROW
795QEO8094 • **Value $18**

4

Here Comes Easter
(4th & final, 1997)
Handcrafted • CROW
795QEO8682 • **Value $17**

5

Joyful Angels (1st, 1996)
Handcrafted • LYLE
995QEO8184 • **Value $28**

6

Joyful Angels (2nd, 1997)
Handcrafted • LYLE
1095QEO8655 • **Value $22**

7

Joyful Angels
(3rd & final, 1998)
Handcrafted • LYLE
1095QEO8386 • **Value $19**

8

1935 Steelcraft
Streamline Velocipede
by Murray® (1st, 1997)
Die-Cast Metal • RHOD
1295QEO8632 • **Value $27**

9

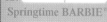

1939 Mobo Horse
(2nd, 1998)
Die-Cast Metal • N/A
1295QEO8393 • **Value $26**

10

1950 GARTON®
Delivery Cycle
(3rd, 1999)
Die-Cast Metal • N/A
1295QEO8367 • **Value $23**

11

New!

Hopalong Cassidy™
Velocipede (4th, 2000)
Die-Cast Metal • N/A
1295QEO8411 • **Value $12.95**

12

New!

Eastern Bluebird
(1st, 2000)
Handcrafted • CROW
995QEO8451 • **Value $9.95**

13

Springtime BARBIE™
(1st, 1995)
Handcrafted • ANDR
1295QEO8069 • **Value $34**

14

Springtime BARBIE™
(2nd, 1996)
Handcrafted • ANDR
1295QEO8081 • **Value $27**

15

Springtime BARBIE™
(3rd & final, 1997)
Handcrafted • ANDR
1295QEO8642 • **Value $25**

16

Springtime Bonnets
(1st, 1993)
Handcrafted • DLEE
775QEO8322 • **Value $30**

17

Springtime Bonnets
(2nd, 1994)
Handcrafted • BISH
775QEO8096 • **Value $26**

18

Springtime Bonnets
(3rd, 1995)
Handcrafted • UNRU
795QEO8227 • **Value $20**

Here Comes Easter

	Price Paid	Value
1.		
2.		
3.		
4.		

Joyful Angels

5.		
6.		
7.		

Sidewalk Cruisers

8.		
9.		
10.		
11.		

Spring Is in the Air

12.		

Springtime BARBIE™

13.		
14.		
15.		

Springtime Bonnets

16.		
17.		
18.		

Totals

1

Springtime Bonnets
(4th, 1996)
Handcrafted • PIKE
795QEO8134 • **Value $26**

2

Springtime Bonnets
(5th & final, 1997)
Handcrafted • PIKE
795QEO8672 • **Value $16**

3

1931 Ford Model A
Roadster (1st, 1998)
Die-Cast Metal • PALM
1495QEO8416 • **Value $29**

4

1932 Chevrolet®
Standard Sports Roadster
(2nd, 1999)
Die-Cast Metal • PALM
1495QEO8379 • **Value $26**

5
New!

1935 Auburn Speedster
(3rd, 2000)
Die-Cast Metal • PALM
1495QEO8401 • **Value $14.95**

6

1956 GARTON® Hot
Rod Racer (1st, 1999)
Die-Cast Metal • UNRU
1395QEO8479 • **Value $24**

7
New!

1940 GARTON®
"Red Hot" Roadster
(2nd, 2000)
Die-Cast Metal • PALM
1395QEO8404 • **Value $13.95**

2000

8

Alice in Wonderland,
Madame Alexander®
Handcrafted • FRAN
1495QEO8421 • **Value $14.95**

9

Ballerina BARBIE™
Handcrafted • ANDR
1295QEO8471 • **Value $12.95**

10

Bar and Shield
Harley-Davidson®
Die-Cast Metal • RHOD
1395QEO8544 • **Value $13.95**

	Price Paid	Value
1.		
2.		

3.		
4.		
5.		

6.		
7.		

11
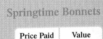
Bugs Bunny
Looney Tunes™
Pressed Tin • N/A
1095QEO8524 • **Value $10.95**

12

Frolicking Friends
Bambi, Thumper and
Flower (set/3)
Handcrafted • N/A
1495QEO8434 • **Value $14.95**

13

Happy Diploma Day!
Handcrafted • N/A
1095QEO8431 • **Value $10.95**

14

Peanuts® Lunch Box Set
(set/2)
Pressed Tin • N/A
1495QEO8444 • **Value $14.95**

15

A Snug Hug
Handcrafted • PIKE
995QEO8424 • **Value $9.95**

16

A Swing With Friends
Handcrafted • N/A
1495QEO8414 • **Value $14.95**

8.		
9.		
10.		
11.		
12.		
13.		
14.		
15.		
16.		
17.		

17

Time in the Garden
Handcrafted/Cast Metal • SEAL
1095QEO8511 • **Value $10.95**

Totals

1999

1

40th Anniversary
Edition BARBIE™
Lunch Box
Pressed Tin • N/A
1295QEO8399 • **Value $23**

2

Batter Up! Charlie
Brown and Snoopy,
PEANUTS® (set/2)
Handcrafted • RHOD
1295QEO8389 • **Value $24**

3

Birthday Celebration
Handcrafted • AUBE
895QEO8409 • **Value $16**

4

Cross of Faith
Precious Metal • VOTR
1395QEO8467 • **Value $25**

5

Easter Egg Nest
Pressed Tin • SICK
795QEO8427 • **Value $16**

6

Final Putt,
Minnie Mouse
Handcrafted • N/A
1095QEO8349 • **Value $19**

7

Friendly Delivery,
Mary's Bears
Handcrafted • KLIN
1295QEO8419 • **Value $23**

8

Happy Bubble Blower
Handcrafted • TAGU
795QEO8437 • **Value $13**

9

Happy Diploma Day!
Handcrafted • N/A
1095QEO8357 • **Value $20**

10

Inspirational Angel
Handcrafted • LYLE
1295QEO8347 • **Value $23**

11

Mop Top Billy,
Madame Alexander®
(complements Mop Top
Wendy, 1998)
Handcrafted • FRAN
1495QEO8337 • **Value $25**

12

Precious Baby,
Commemorative
Handcrafted • LYLE
995QEO8417 • **Value $17**

13

Spring Chick
Handcrafted • AUBE
2200QEO8469 • **Value $37**

14

Springtime Harvest
Handcrafted • SICK
795QEO8429 • **Value $14**

15

The Tale of Peter
Rabbit™, Beatrix
Potter™ (set/3)
Handcrafted • VOTR
1995QEO8397 • **Value $35**

16

Tiggerific Easter
Delivery
Handcrafted • N/A
1095QEO8359 • **Value $20**

17

Wedding Memories
Porcelain • UNRU
995QEO8407 • **Value $18**

1999 Collection

	Price Paid	Value
1.		
2.		
3.		
4.		
5.		
6.		
7.		
8.		
9.		
10.		
11.		
12.		
13.		
14.		
15.		
16.		
17.		
Totals		

1998

1

Bashful Gift (set/2)
Handcrafted • AUBE
1195QEO8446 • **Value $22**

2

Bouquet of Memories
Handcrafted • TAGU
795QEO8456 • **Value $16**

3

Forever Friends
The Andrew
Brownsword Collection
Handcrafted • PIKE
995QEO8423 • **Value $19**

4

The Garden of Piglet
and Pooh (set/2)
Handcrafted • N/A
1295QEO8403 • **Value $25**

5

Going Up? Charlie
Brown – PEANUTS®
Handcrafted • PIKE
995QEO8433 • **Value $20**

6

Happy Diploma Day!
Handcrafted • HADD
795QEO8476 • **Value $17**

7

Midge™ – 35th
Anniversary
Handcrafted • ANDR
1495QEO8413 • **Value $26**

8

Practice Swing –
Donald Duck
Handcrafted • N/A
1095QEO8396 • **Value $21**

9

Precious Baby
Handcrafted • TAGU
995QEO8463 • **Value $18**

10

Special Friends
Handcrafted • VOTR
1295QEO8523 • **Value $20**

11

STAR WARS™
Pressed Tin • N/A
1295QEO8406 • **Value $25**

12

Sweet Birthday
Handcrafted • KLIN
795QEO8473 • **Value $16**

13

Tigger in the Garden
(Spring Preview)
Handcrafted • N/A
995QEO8436 • **Value $19**

14

Victorian Cross
Pewter • UNRU
895QEO8453 • **Value $18**

15

Wedding Memories
Porcelain • VOTR
995QEO8466 • **Value $19**

16

What's Your Name?
Handcrafted • KLIN
795QEO8443 • **Value $17**

17

Fair Valentine™
BARBIE® Doll
(3rd & final in *Be My
Valentine Collector Series™*)
Vinyl • N/A
5000QHV8743 • **Value N/E**

1997

18

Bumper Crop, Tender
Touches (set/3)
Handcrafted • SEAL
1495QEO8735 • **Value $27**

	Price Paid	Value
1998 Collection		
1.		
2.		
3.		
4.		
5.		
6.		
7.		
8.		
9.		
10.		
11.		
12.		
13.		
14.		
15.		
16.	5.59	17.00
17.		
1997 Collection		
18.		
Totals		

1

Digging In
Handcrafted • SEAL
795QEO8712 • **Value $16**

2

**Eggs-pert Artist,
CRAYOLA® Crayon**
Handcrafted • TAGU
895QEO8695 • **Value $19**

3

**Garden Bunnies,
Nature's Sketchbook**
Handcrafted • UNRU
1495QEO8702 • **Value $26**

4

Gentle Guardian
Handcrafted • LARS
695QEO8732 • **Value $13**

5

A Purr-fect Princess
Handcrafted • PIKE
795QEO8715 • **Value $16**

6

**Sentimental Valentine™
BARBIE® Doll
(2nd in *Be My Valentine
Collector Series*™)**
Vinyl • N/A
5000QHV8742 • **Value N/E**

7

Swing-Time
Handcrafted • TAGU
795QEO8705 • **Value $16**

8

Victorian Cross
Pewter • N/A
895QEO8725 • **Value $18**

1996

9

**Daffy Duck,
LOONEY TUNES**
Handcrafted • RGRS
895QEO8154 • **Value $17**

10

Easter Morning
Handcrafted • UNRU
795QEO8164 • **Value $16**

11

**Eggstra Special Surprise,
Tender Touches**
Handcrafted • SEAL
895QEO8161 • **Value $19**

12

**Hippity-Hop Delivery,
CRAYOLA® Crayon**
Handcrafted • CROW
795QEO8144 • **Value $18**

13

Look What I Found!
Handcrafted • FRAN
795QEO8181 • **Value $15**

14

Parade Pals, PEANUTS®
Handcrafted • RHOD
795QEO8151 • **Value $18**

15

Pork 'n Beans
Handcrafted • CHAD
795QEO8174 • **Value $14**

16

Strawberry Patch
Handcrafted • SEAL
695QEO8171 • **Value $17**

17

Strike up the Band! (set/3)
Handcrafted • UNRU
1495QEO8141 • **Value $29**

18

**Sweet Valentine™
BARBIE® Doll
(1st in *Be My Valentine
Collector Series*™)**
Vinyl • N/A
4500QHV8131 • **Value N/E**

1997 Collection

	Price Paid	Value
1.		
2.		
3.		
4.		
5.		
6.		
7.		
8.		

1996 Collection

9.		
10.		
11.		
12.		
13.		
14.		
15.		
16.		
17.		
18.		

Totals

1995

1
April Shower
Handcrafted • SIED
695QEO8253 • **Value $15**

2
Baby's First Easter
Handcrafted • PALM
795QEO8237 • **Value $17**

3
Bugs Bunny,
LOONEY TUNES™
Handcrafted • CHAD
895QEO8279 • **Value $19**

4
Daughter
Handcrafted • RGRS
595QEO8239 • **Value $14**

5
Easter Eggspress
Handcrafted • SIED
495QEO8269 • **Value $15**

6
Elegant Lily
Brass • VOTR
695QEO8267 • **Value $14**

7
Flowerpot Friends (set/3)
Handcrafted • ANDR
1495QEO8229 • **Value $26**

8
Ham 'n Eggs
Handcrafted • CHAD
795QEO8277 • **Value $15**

9
High Hopes,
Tender Touches
Handcrafted • SEAL
895QEO8259 • **Value $22**

10
PEANUTS®
Handcrafted • RHOD
795QEO8257 • **Value $26**

11
Picture Perfect,
Crayola® Crayon
Handcrafted • CROW
795QEO8249 • **Value $20**

12
Son
Handcrafted • RGRS
595QEO8247 • **Value $17**

1994

13
Baby's First Easter
Handcrafted • FRAN
675QEO8153 • **Value $21**

14
Colorful Spring
Handcrafted • CROW
775QEO8166 • **Value $32**

15
Daughter
Handcrafted • ANDR
575QEO8156 • **Value $16**

16
Divine Duet
Handcrafted • VOTR
675QEO8183 • **Value $18**

17
Easter Art Show
Handcrafted • VOTR
775QEO8193 • **Value $19**

18
Joyful Lamb
Handcrafted • UNRU
575QEO8206 • **Value $15**

1995 Collection

	Price Paid	Value
1.		
2.		
3.		
4.		
5.		
6.		
7.		
8.		
9.		
10.		
11.		
12.		

1994 Collection

13.		
14.		
15.		
16.		
17.		
18.		

Totals

279

Spring Ornaments

1

PEANUTS®
Handcrafted • UNRU
775QEO8176 • **Value $42**

2

Peeping Out
Handcrafted • UNRU
675QEO8203 • **Value $17**

3

Riding a Breeze
Handcrafted • PALM
575QEO8213 • **Value $18**

4

Son
Handcrafted • ANDR
575QEO8163 • **Value $17**

5

Sunny Bunny Garden (set/3)
Handcrafted • SEAL
1500QEO8146 • **Value $32**

6

Sweet as Sugar
Handcrafted • RGRS
875QEO8086 • **Value $20**

7

Sweet Easter Wishes, Tender Touches
Handcrafted • SEAL
875QEO8196 • **Value $26**

8

Treetop Cottage
Handcrafted • SICK
975QEO8186 • **Value $20**

9

Yummy Recipe
Handcrafted • RGRS
775QEO8143 • **Value $21**

1993

10

Baby's First Easter
Handcrafted • PALM
675QEO8345 • **Value $16**

11

Backyard Bunny
Handcrafted • SICK
675QEO8405 • **Value $17**

12

Barrow of Giggles
Handcrafted • ANDR
875QEO8402 • **Value $21**

13

Beautiful Memories
Handcrafted • UNRU
675QEO8362 • **Value $15**

14

Best-dressed Turtle
Handcrafted • JLEE
575QEO8392 • **Value $16**

15

Chicks-on-a-Twirl
Handcrafted • LYLE
775QEO8375 • **Value $18**

16

Daughter
Handcrafted • ANDR
575QEO8342 • **Value $17**

17

Grandchild
Handcrafted • SIED
675QEO8352 • **Value $19**

18

Li'l Peeper
Handcrafted • JLEE
775QEO8312 • **Value $22**

19

Lop-eared Bunny
Handcrafted • SICK
575QEO8315 • **Value $20**

1994 Collection		
	Price Paid	Value
1.		
2.		
3.		
4.		
5.		
6.		
7.		
8.		
9.		

1993 Collection		
10.		
11.		
12.		
13.		
14.		
15.		
16.		
17.		
18.		
19.		

Totals

1
Lovely Lamb
Porcelain • VOTR
975QEO8372 • **Value $23**

2
Maypole Stroll (set/3)
Handcrafted/Wood
CHAD/FRAN
2800QEO8395 • **Value $50**

3
Nutty Eggs
Handcrafted • JLEE
675QEO8382 • **Value $16**

4
Radiant Window
Handcrafted • UNRU
775QEO8365 • **Value $18**

5
Son
Handcrafted • ANDR
575QEO8335 • **Value $16**

6
Time for Easter
Handcrafted • CHAD
875QEO8385 • **Value $21**

1992

7
Baby's First Easter
Handcrafted • FRAN
675QEO9271 • **Value $22**

8
Belle Bunny
Porcelain • VOTR
975QEO9354 • **Value $20**

9
Bless You
Handcrafted • FRAN
675QEO9291 • **Value $24**

10
Cosmic Rabbit
Handcrafted • SIED
775QEO9364 • **Value $20**

11
CRAYOLA® Bunny
Handcrafted • RGRS
775QEO9304 • **Value $34**

12
Cultivated Gardener
Handcrafted • SIED
575QEO9351 • **Value $16**

13
Daughter
Handcrafted • RGRS
575QEO9284 • **Value $21**

14
Eggspert Painter
Handcrafted • SIED
675QEO9361 • **Value $23**

15
Everything's Ducky
Handcrafted • PIKE
675QEO9331 • **Value $19**

16
Grandchild
Handcrafted • CROW
675QEO9274 • **Value $21**

17
Joy Bearer
Handcrafted • PALM
875QEO9334 • **Value $24**

18
Promise of Easter
Porcelain • LYLE
875QEO9314 • **Value $18**

19
Rocking Bunny
Porcelain/Nickel-Plated • VOTR
975QEO9324 • **Value $23**

1993 Collection

	Price Paid	Value
1.		
2.		
3.		
4.		
5.		
6.		

1992 Collection

7.		
8.		
9.		
10.		
11.		
12.		
13.		
14.		
15.		
16.		
17.		
18.		
19.		

Totals

281

1

Somebunny Loves You
Handcrafted • FRAN
675QEO9294 • **Value $32**

2

Son
Handcrafted • RGRS
575QEO9281 • **Value $19**

3

Springtime Egg
Handcrafted • JLEE
875QEO9321 • **Value $20**

4

Sunny Wisher
Handcrafted • PIKE
575QEO9344 • **Value $18**

5

Warm Memories
Photoholder
Fabric • VOTR
775QEO9311 • **Value $17**

1991

6

Baby's First Easter
Handcrafted • N/A
875QEO5189 • **Value $26**

7

Daughter
Handcrafted • N/A
575QEO5179 • **Value $32**

1992 Collection

	Price Paid	Value
1.		
2.		
3.		
4.		
5.		

1991 Collection

6.		
7.		
8.		
9.		
10.		
11.		
12.		
13.		
14.		
15.		
16.		

8

Easter Memories
Photoholder
Fabric • N/A
775QEO5137 • **Value $17**

9

Full of Love
Handcrafted • N/A
775QEO5149 • **Value $48**

10

Gentle Lamb
Handcrafted • N/A
675QEO5159 • **Value $21**

11

Grandchild
Handcrafted • N/A
675QEO5177 • **Value $20**

12

Li'l Dipper
Handcrafted • N/A
675QEO5147 • **Value $24**

13

Lily Egg
Porcelain • UNRU
975QEO5139 • **Value $23**

14

Son
Handcrafted • N/A
575QEO5187 • **Value $27**

15

Spirit of Easter
Handcrafted • N/A
775QEO5169 • **Value $36**

16

Springtime Stroll
Handcrafted • N/A
675QEO5167 • **Value $23**

Totals

Merry Miniatures

This year there are two new collections in the Merry Miniatures line, featuring a total of 21 new pieces. The Happy Hatters Collection, the first Merry Miniatures annual collection, introduces 12 figurines and a display base. The Madame Alexander® Collection consists of eight pieces based on the famous Madame Alexander® dolls.

2000

1

2000 Happy Hatters Collection Display Base
Handcrafted • N/A
495QMM7003 • **Value $4.95**

2

B.B. Capps (6th)
Handcrafted • N/A
495QMM7008 • **Value $4.95**

3

Bonnie Bonnet (4th)
Handcrafted • N/A
495QMM7006 • **Value $4.95**

4

Booker Beanie (9th)
Handcrafted • TAGU
495QMM7017 • **Value $4.95**

5

Candy Capper (10th)
Handcrafted • N/A
495QMM7022 • **Value $4.95**

6

Cora Copia (11th)
Handcrafted • N/A
495QMM7023 • **Value $4.95**

7

Hattie Boxx (12th & final)
Handcrafted • N/A
495QMM7024 • **Value $4.95**

8

Libby Crown (7th)
Handcrafted • N/A
495QMM7015 • **Value $4.95**

9

Missy Milliner (5th)
Handcrafted • N/A
495QMM7007 • **Value $4.95**

10

Paddy O'Hatty (3rd)
Handcrafted • N/A
495QMM7002 • **Value $4.95**

11

Panama Pete (8th)
Handcrafted • N/A
495QMM7016 • **Value $4.95**

12

Rosie Chapeauzie (2nd)
Handcrafted • N/A
495QMM7001 • **Value $4.95**

13

Tiny Topper (1st)
Handcrafted • N/A
495QMM7000 • **Value $4.95**

14

Fire Fighter Wendy – 1997
Handcrafted • FORS
695QMM7010 • **Value $6.95**

15

Little Red Riding Hood – 1991 (Premiere)
Handcrafted • FRAN
695QFM7062 • **Value $6.95**

16

Mary Had a Little Lamb
Handcrafted • FORS
695QMM7014 • **Value $6.95**

Happy Hatters Annual Collection		
	Price Paid	Value
1.		
2.		
3.		
4.		
5.		
6.		
7.		
8.		
9.		
10.		
11.		
12.		
13.		
Madame Alexander® Collection		
14.		
15.		
16.		
Totals		

1

Mop Top Billy
Handcrafted • FRAN
695QMM7005 • **Value $6.95**

2

Mop Top Wendy
Handcrafted • FRAN
695QMM7004 • **Value $6.95**

3

Mother Goose
Handcrafted • FORS
695QMM7013 • **Value $6.95**

4

Pink Pristine Angel –
1997
Handcrafted • FORS
695QMM7020 • **Value $6.95**

5

Santa's Little
Helper – 1998
Handcrafted • N/A
695QMM7021 • **Value $6.95**

1999

6

Anniversary Edition
(set/2)
Handcrafted • HADD
1295QFM8529 • **Value $19**

7

Bashful Friends Merry
Miniatures® (set/3)
Handcrafted • AUBE
1295QSM8459 • **Value $20**

Madame Alexander®
Collection

	Price Paid	Value
1.		
2.		
3.		
4.		
5.		

1999 Collection

6.		
7.		
8.		
9.		
10.		
11.		
12.		
13.		
14.		

1998 Collection

15.		
16.		
17.		
18.		

Totals

8

Eeyore
Handcrafted • N/A
495QRP8519 • **Value $13**

9

Favorite Friends (set/2)
Handcrafted • KLIN
895QFM8537 • **Value $17**

10

A Kiss For You–
HERSHEY'S™ (set/3, 3rd
& final, HERSHEY'S™)
Handcrafted • BRIC
1295QFM8497 • **Value $21**

11

Park Avenue Wendy
& Alex the Bellhop
Madame Alexander®
(Premiere, set/2)
Handcrafted • FRAN
1295QFM8499 • **Value $20**

12

Piglet on Base
Handcrafted • N/A
495QRP8507 • **Value $13**

13

Tigger
Handcrafted • N/A
495QRP8527 • **Value $13**

14

Winnie the Pooh
Handcrafted • N/A
495QRP8509 • **Value $14**

1998

15

Bride and Groom–1996
Madame Alexander®
(Premiere)
Handcrafted • FRAN
1295QFM8486 • **Value $22**

16

Donald's Passenger Car
Handcrafted • N/A
595QRP8513 • **Value $15**

17

Goofy's Caboose
Handcrafted • N/A
595QRP8516 • **Value $15**

18

HERSHEY'S™
(Premiere, set/2, 2nd,
HERSHEY'S™)
Handcrafted • BRIC
1095QFM8493 • **Value $18**

1

Mickey's Locomotive
Handcrafted • N/A
595QRP8496 • **Value $15**

2

Minnie's Luggage Car
Handcrafted • N/A
595QRP8506 • **Value $15**

3

Pluto's Coal Car
Handcrafted • N/A
595QRP8503 • **Value $15**

4

Rapunzel
(Spring Preview, set/2)
Handcrafted • TAGU
1295QSM8483 • **Value $21**

1997

5

Apple Harvest – Mary's Bears (set/3)
Handcrafted • HAMI
1295QFM8585 • **Value $22**

6

Bashful Visitors (set/3)
Handcrafted • AUBE
1295QFM8582 • **Value $25**

7

Cupid Cameron
Handcrafted • N/A
495QSM8552 • **Value $13**

8

Easter Parade (set/2)
Handcrafted • TAGU
795QSM8562 • **Value $15**

9

Getting Ready for Spring (set/3)
Handcrafted • TAGU
1295QSM8575 • **Value $19**

10

Happy Birthday Clowns
(3rd & final, *Happy Birthday Clowns*)
Handcrafted • N/A
495QSM8565 • **Value $13**

11

HERSHEY'S™
(set/2, 1st, *HERSHEY'S™*)
Handcrafted • BRIC
1295QFM8625 • **Value $22**

12

Holiday Harmony (set/3)
Handcrafted • TAGU
1295QFM8612 • **Value $22**

13

Making a Wish (set/2)
Handcrafted • TAGU
795QFM8592 • **Value $14**

14

The Nativity (set/2)
Handcrafted • N/A
795QFM8615 • **Value $21**

15

Noah's Friends (set/2)
Handcrafted • ESCH
795QSM8572 • **Value $20**

16

Peter Pan (set/5)
Handcrafted • TAGU
1995QSM8605 • **Value $37**

17

Santa Cameron
Handcrafted • N/A
495QFM8622 • **Value $15**

18

Six Dwarfs (set/3)
Handcrafted • ESCH
1295QFM8685 • **Value $24**

19

Snow White and Dancing Dwarf (set/2)
Handcrafted • ESCH
795QFM8535 • **Value $17**

1998 Collection

	Price Paid	Value
1.		
2.		
3.		
4.		

1997 Collection

5.		
6.		
7.		
8.		
9.		
10.		
11.		
12.		
13.		
14.		
15.		
16.		
17.		
18.		
19.		

Totals

1

Snowbear Season (Premiere, set/3)
Handcrafted • ESCH
1295QFM8602 • **Value $21**

2

Sule and Sara – PendaKids™ (set/2)
Handcrafted • JOHN
795QSM8545 • **Value $13**

3

Tea Time – Mary's Bears (set/3)
Handcrafted • HAMI
1295QSM8542 • **Value $22**

4

Three Wee Kings (set/3)
Handcrafted • N/A
1295QFM8692 • **Value $21**

1996

5

Alice in Wonderland (set/5)
Handcrafted • N/A
1995QSM8014 • **Value $33**

6

Bashful Mistletoe (Premiere, set/3)
Handcrafted • N/A
1295QFM8319 • **Value $24**

7

Blue-Ribbon Bunny
Handcrafted • N/A
495QSM8064 • **Value $15**

1997 Collection

	Price Paid	Value
1.		
2.		
3.		
4.		

1996 Collection

5.		
6.		
7.		
8.		
9.		
10.		
11.		
12.		
13.		
14.		
15.		
16.		
17.		
18.		
19.		

8

Busy Bakers (set/2)
Handcrafted • N/A
795QFM8121 • **Value $16**

9

Cowboy Cameron (set/3)
Handcrafted • N/A
1295QFM8041 • **Value $26**

10

Easter Egg Hunt
Handcrafted • N/A
495QSM8024 • **Value $15**

11

Giving Thanks (set/3)
Handcrafted • N/A
1295QFM8134 • **Value $25**

12

Happy Birthday Clowns (set/2, 2nd, *Happy Birthday Clowns*)
Handcrafted • N/A
795QSM8114 • **Value $16**

13

Happy Haunting (set/2)
Handcrafted • N/A
1295QFM8124 • **Value $27**

14

Lucky Cameron (set/2)
Handcrafted • N/A
795QSM8021 • **Value $16**

15

Mr. and Mrs. Claus Bears (set/2)
Handcrafted • N/A
795QFM8044 • **Value $18**

16

Noah and Friends (set/5)
Handcrafted • N/A
1995QSM8111 • **Value $40**

17

PEANUTS® Pumpkin Patch (set/5)
Handcrafted • N/A
1995QFM8131 • **Value $45**

18

Penda Kids (set/2)
Handcrafted • N/A
795QSM8011 • **Value $14**

19

Santa's Helpers (set/3)
Handcrafted • N/A
1295QFM8051 • **Value $24**

Totals

1

The Sewing Club (set/3)
Handcrafted • N/A
1295QFM8061 • **Value $26**

2

Sweetheart Cruise (set/3)
Handcrafted • N/A
1295QSM8004 • **Value $23**

1995

3

Bashful Boy
Handcrafted • N/A
300QSM8107 • **Value $16**

4

Bashful Girl
Handcrafted • N/A
300QSM8109 • **Value $16**

5

Beauregard
Handcrafted • N/A
300QSM8047 • **Value N/E**

6

Birthday Bear (1st,
Happy Birthday Clowns)
Handcrafted • N/A
375QSM8057 • **Value $15**

7

Bride & Groom
Handcrafted • N/A
375QSM8067 • **Value $15**

8

Cameron
Handcrafted • N/A
375QSM8009 • **Value $20**

9

Cameron/Bunny
Handcrafted • N/A
375QSM8029 • **Value $19**

10

**Cameron in Pumpkin
Costume**
Handcrafted • N/A
375QFM8147 • **Value $18**

11

Cameron on Sled
Handcrafted • N/A
375QFM8199 • **Value $15**

12

Cameron Pilgrim
Handcrafted • N/A
375QFM8169 • **Value $16**

13

Cameron w/Camera
Handcrafted • N/A
375QSM8077 • **Value $17**

14

Caroling Bear
Handcrafted • N/A
325QFM8307 • **Value $14**

15

Caroling Bunny
Handcrafted • N/A
325QFM8309 • **Value $14**

16

Caroling Mouse
Handcrafted • N/A
300QFM8317 • **Value $14**

17

Chipmunk with Corn
Handcrafted • N/A
375QFM8179 • **Value $12**

18

Christmas Tree
Handcrafted • N/A
675QFM8197 • **Value $18**

19

Cinderella
Handcrafted • N/A
400QSM8117 • **Value $35**

1996 Collection

	Price Paid	Value
1.		
2.		

1995 Collection

3.		
4.		
5.		
6.		
7.		
8.		
9.		
10.		
11.		
12.		
13.		
14.		
15.		
16.		
17.		
18.		
19.		

Totals

1

Cottage
Handcrafted • N/A
675QSM8027 • **Value $21**

2

Cute Witch
Handcrafted • N/A
300QFM8157 • **Value $13**

3

Fairy Godmother
Handcrafted • N/A
400QSM8089 • **Value $20**

4

Feast Table
Handcrafted • N/A
475QFM8167 • **Value $13**

5

Friendly Monster
Handcrafted • N/A
300QFM8159 • **Value $13**

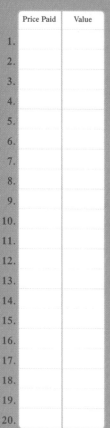

6

Groundhog
Handcrafted • N/A
300QSM8079 • **Value $14**

7

Hamster with Cookies
Handcrafted • N/A
325QFM8319 • **Value $16**

8

Haunted House
Handcrafted • N/A
675QFM8139 • **Value $19**

1995 Collection

	Price Paid	Value
1.		
2.		
3.		
4.		
5.		
6.		
7.		
8.		
9.		
10.		
11.		
12.		
13.		
14.		
15.		
16.		
17.		
18.		
19.		
20.		
Totals		

9

Koala Bear
Handcrafted • N/A
375QSM8019 • **Value $15**

10

Leprechaun
Handcrafted • N/A
350QSM8119 • **Value $15**

11

Lion and Lamb
Handcrafted • N/A
400QFM8287 • **Value $16**

12

Mouse with Cranberries
Handcrafted • N/A
300QFM8189 • **Value $12**

13

Mouse with Pumpkin
Handcrafted • N/A
300QFM8187 • **Value $13**

14

Nutcracker
Handcrafted • N/A
375QFM8297 • **Value $14**

15

Prince Charming
Handcrafted • N/A
400QSM8049 • **Value $33**

16

Pumpkin Coach
Handcrafted • N/A
500QFM8127 • **Value $18**

17

Raccoon and Flower
Handcrafted • N/A
300QSM8087 • **Value $11**

18

Rhino Mummy
Handcrafted • N/A
375QFM8149 • **Value $14**

19

St. Bernard
Handcrafted • N/A
375QSM8017 • **Value $15**

20

Santa
Handcrafted • N/A
375QFM8299 • **Value $14**

1

Selby
Handcrafted • N/A
300QSM8039 • **Value $14**

2

Stepmother
Handcrafted • N/A
400QFM8099 • **Value $16**

3

Stylish Rabbit
Handcrafted • N/A
375QSM8037 • **Value $14**

4

Toymaker Beaver
Handcrafted • N/A
375QFM8289 • **Value $14**

5

Tree
Handcrafted • N/A
675QSM8007 • **Value $20**

6

Turkey
Handcrafted • N/A
375QFM8177 • **Value $14**

1994

7

Basket of Apples
Handcrafted • N/A
275QFM8356 • **Value $12**

8

Bear Letter Carrier
Handcrafted • N/A
375QSM8006 • **Value $13**

9

Bear on Skates
Handcrafted • N/A
375QFM8293 • **Value $15**

10

Bear with Flag
Handcrafted • N/A
375QSM8043 • **Value $24**

11

Beaver
Handcrafted • N/A
375QFM8336 • **Value $13**

12

Beaver
Handcrafted • N/A
375QSM8013 • **Value $12**

13

Birds in Nest
Handcrafted • N/A
375QSM8116 • **Value $13**

14

Black Kitten
Handcrafted • N/A
325QFM8273 • **Value $13**

15

Bunny Alien
Handcrafted • N/A
375QFM8266 • **Value $15**

16

Chick in Wagon
Handcrafted • N/A
375QSM8123 • **Value $16**

17

Chipmunk with Kite
Handcrafted • N/A
300QSM8003 • **Value $15**

18

Corn Stalk
Handcrafted • N/A
675QFM8363 • **Value $18**

19

Dock
Handcrafted • N/A
675QSM8076 • **Value $23**

1995 Collection		
	Price Paid	Value
1.		
2.		
3.		
4.		
5.		
6.		

1994 Collection		
7.		
8.		
9.		
10.		
11.		
12.		
13.		
14.		
15.		
16.		
17.		
18.		
19.		

Totals

1

Document
Handcrafted • N/A
275QSM8053 • **Value $15**

2

Eagle with Hat
Handcrafted • N/A
375QSM8036 • **Value $16**

3

Fence with Lantern
Handcrafted • N/A
675QFM8283 • **Value $18**

4

Flag
Handcrafted • N/A
675QSM8056 • **Value $25**

5

Fox on Skates
Handcrafted • N/A
375QFM8303 • **Value $14**

6

Indian Bunny
Handcrafted • N/A
275QFM8353 • **Value $12**

7

Indian Chickadee
Handcrafted • N/A
325QFM8346 • **Value $15**

8

Lamb
Handcrafted • N/A
325QSM8132 • **Value $12**

9

Mailbox
Handcrafted • N/A
675QSM8023 • **Value $18**

10

Mouse with Flower
Handcrafted • N/A
275QSM8243 • **Value $13**

11

Mrs. Claus
Handcrafted • N/A
375QFM8286 • **Value $16**

12

North Pole Sign
Handcrafted • N/A
675QFM8333 • **Value $21**

13

Owl in Stump
Handcrafted • N/A
275QSM8243 • **Value $13**

14

Pail of Seashells
Handcrafted • N/A
275QSM8052 • **Value $14**

15

Penguin
Handcrafted • N/A
275QFM8313 • **Value $17**

16

Pilgrim Bunny
Handcrafted • N/A
375QFM8343 • **Value $14**

17

Polar Bears
Handcrafted • N/A
325QFM8323 • **Value $16**

18

Pumpkin with Hat
Handcrafted • N/A
275QFM8276 • **Value $13**

19

Rabbit
Handcrafted • N/A
275QSM8066 • **Value $14**

20

Rabbit
Handcrafted • N/A
325QSM8016 • **Value $12**

1

Rabbit with Can
Handcrafted • N/A
325QSM8083 • **Value $13**

2

Rabbit with Croquet
Handcrafted • N/A
375QSM8113 • **Value $11**

3

Raccoon
Handcrafted • N/A
375QSM8063 • **Value $17**

4

Sled Dog
Handcrafted • N/A
325QFM8306 • **Value $16**

5

Snowman
Handcrafted • N/A
275QFM8316 • **Value $12**

6

Squirrel as Clown
Handcrafted • N/A
375QFM8263 • **Value $14**

7

Tree
Handcrafted • N/A
275QFM8326 • **Value $14**

8

Wishing Well
Handcrafted • N/A
675QSM8033 • **Value $22**

1993

9

Animated Cauldron
Handcrafted • N/A
250QFM8425 • **Value $14**

10

Arctic Fox
Handcrafted • N/A
350QFM8242 • **Value $13**

11

Arctic Scene Backdrop
Paper • N/A
175QFM8205 • **Value $7**

12

Baby Walrus
Handcrafted • N/A
300QFM8232 • **Value $11**

13

Baby Whale
Handcrafted • N/A
350QFM8222 • **Value $11**

14

Beach Scene Backdrop
Paper • N/A
175QSM8042 • **Value $7**

15

Bear dressed as Bat
Handcrafted • N/A
300QFM8285 • **Value $12**

16

Bear with Surfboard
Handcrafted • N/A
350QSM8015 • **Value $14**

17

Betsey Ross Lamb
Handcrafted • N/A
350QSM8482 • **Value $16**

18

Bobcat Pilgrim
Handcrafted • N/A
350QFM8172 • **Value $14**

19

Box of Candy
Handcrafted • N/A
250QSM8095 • **Value $17**

	Price Paid	Value
1994 Collection		
1.		
2.		
3.		
4.		
5.		
6.		
7.		
8.		
1993 Collection		
9.		
10.		
11.		
12.		
13.		
14.		
15.		
16.		
17.		
18.		
19.		

Totals

1

Bunny Painting Egg
Handcrafted • N/A
350QSM8115 • **Value $11**

2

Bunny with Basket
Handcrafted • N/A
250QSM8142 • **Value $13**

3

Bunny with Egg
Handcrafted • N/A
300QSM8125 • **Value $12**

4

Bunny with Scarf
Handcrafted • N/A
250QFM8235 • **Value $15**

5

Bunny with Seashell
Handcrafted • N/A
350QSM8005 • **Value $19**

6

**Cat & Mouse (3rd &
final, *Hugs and Kisses*)**
Handcrafted • N/A
350QSM8102 • **Value $15**

7

Chipmunk
Handcrafted • N/A
350QSM8002 • **Value $15**

8

Display Stand
Handcrafted • N/A
675QFM8055 • **Value $9**

1993 Collection

	Price Paid	Value
1.		
2.		
3.		
4.		
5.		
6.		
7.		
8.		
9.		
10.		
11.		
12.		
13.		
14.		
15.		
16.		
17.		
18.		
19.		
20.		

9

Dog with Balloon
Handcrafted • N/A
250QSM8092 • **Value $11**

10

Dragon Dog
Handcrafted • N/A
300QFM8295 • **Value $11**

11

Duck with Egg
Handcrafted • N/A
300QSM8135 • **Value $11**

12

Easter Basket
Handcrafted • N/A
250QSM8145 • **Value $14**

13

Easter Garden Backdrop
Paper • N/A
175QSM8152 • **Value $7**

14

Eskimo Child
Handcrafted • N/A
300QFM8215 • **Value $17**

15

Fox with Heart
Handcrafted • N/A
350QSM8065 • **Value $11**

16

Ghost on Tombstone
Handcrafted • N/A
250QFM8282 • **Value $11**

17

Goat Uncle Sam
Handcrafted • N/A
300QSM8472 • **Value $15**

18

**Haunted Halloween
Backdrop**
Paper • N/A
175QFM8275 • **Value $7**

19

**Heartland Forest
Backdrop**
Paper • N/A
175QSM8082 • **Value $7**

20

Hedgehog
Handcrafted • N/A
300QSM8026 • **Value $12**

Totals

VALUE GUIDE — MERRY MINIATURES

1

Hedgehog Patriot
Handcrafted • N/A
350QSM8492 • **Value $13**

2

Hippo
Handcrafted • N/A
300QSM8032 • **Value $13**

3

Husky Puppy
Handcrafted • N/A
350QFM8245 • **Value $14**

4
Igloo
Handcrafted • N/A
300QFM8252 • **Value $16**

5

Indian Bear
Handcrafted • N/A
350QFM8162 • **Value $13**

6

Indian Squirrel
Handcrafted • N/A
300QFM8182 • **Value $14**

7

Indian Turkey
Handcrafted • N/A
350QFM8165 • **Value $13**

8

Lamb
Handcrafted • N/A
350QSM8112 • **Value $12**

9

Liberty Bell
Handcrafted • N/A
250QSM8465 • **Value $14**

10

Liberty Mouse
Handcrafted • N/A
300QSM8475 • **Value $17**

11

Mouse in Sunglasses
Handcrafted • N/A
250QSM8035 • **Value $14**

12

Mouse Witch
Handcrafted • N/A
300QFM8292 • **Value $14**

13

Owl and Pumpkin
Handcrafted • N/A
300QFM8302 • **Value $15**

14

Panda (3rd & final,
Sweet Valentines)
Handcrafted • N/A
350QSM8105 • **Value $15**

15

Patriotic Backdrop
Paper • N/A
175QSM8495 • **Value $8**

16

Penguin in Hat
Handcrafted • N/A
300QFM8212 • **Value $13**

17

Pig in Blanket
Handcrafted • N/A
300QSM8022 • **Value $17**

18

Pilgrim Chipmunk
Handcrafted • N/A
300QFM8185 • **Value $15**

19

Pilgrim Mouse
Handcrafted • N/A
300QFM8175 • **Value $17**

20

Plymouth Rock
Handcrafted • N/A
250QFM8192 • **Value $17**

1993 Collection

	Price Paid	Value
1.		
2.		
3.		
4.		
5.		
6.		
7.		
8.		
9.		
10.		
11.		
12.		
13.		
14.		
15.		
16.		
17.		
18.		
19.		
20.		
Totals		

VALUE GUIDE — MERRY MINIATURES

1

Polar Bear (3rd & final,
Music Makers)
Handcrafted • N/A
350QFM8265 • **Value $17**

2

Prairie Dog
Handcrafted • N/A
350QSM8012 • **Value $17**

3

Princess Cat
Handcrafted • N/A
350QFM8305 • **Value $17**

4

Raccoon with Heart
Handcrafted • N/A
350QSM8062 • **Value $11**

5

Sandcastle
Handcrafted • N/A
300QSM8045 • **Value $15**

6

Santa Eskimo
Handcrafted • N/A
350QFM8262 • **Value $26**

7

Seal with Earmuffs
Handcrafted • N/A
250QFM8272 • **Value $12**

8

Sherlock Duck
Handcrafted • N/A
300QSM8122 • **Value $13**

9

Skunk with Heart
Handcrafted • N/A
300QSM8072 • **Value $11**

10

Stump & Can
Handcrafted • N/A
300QSM8075 • **Value $12**

11

Super Hero Bunny
Handcrafted • N/A
300QFM8422 • **Value $14**

12

Thanksgiving Feast
Backdrop
Paper • N/A
175QFM8195 • **Value $7**

13

1992

Baby's 1st Easter
Handcrafted • N/A
350QSM9777 • **Value $14**

14

Ballet Pig
Handcrafted • N/A
250QSM9759 • **Value $16**

15

Bear
(2nd, *Sweet Valentines*)
Handcrafted • N/A
350QSM9717 • **Value $22**

16

Bear With Drum
(2nd, *Music Makers*)
Handcrafted • N/A
350QFM9134 • **Value $19**

17

Bunny & Carrot
Handcrafted • N/A
250QSM9799 • **Value $15**

18

Cat in P.J.'s
Handcrafted • N/A
350QFM9084 • **Value $14**

19

Chipmunk
Handcrafted • N/A
250QFM9144 • **Value $11**

1993 Collection

	Price Paid	Value
1.		
2.		
3.		
4.		
5.		
6.		
7.		
8.		
9.		
10.		
11.		
12.		

1992 Collection

13.		
14.		
15.		
16.		
17.		
18.		
19.		

Totals

VALUE GUIDE — MERRY MINIATURES

1

Clown (3rd & final,
Birthday Clowns)
Handcrafted • N/A
350QSM9819 • **Value $17**

2

Clown Mouse
Handcrafted • N/A
250QFM9031 • **Value $14**

3

Cow
Handcrafted • N/A
300QFM9034 • **Value $15**

4

Crab
Handcrafted • N/A
300QFM9174 • **Value $11**

5

Dog
Handcrafted • N/A
300QSM9847 • **Value $17**

6

Dog in P.J.'s
Handcrafted • N/A
350QFM9081 • **Value $14**

7

Ghost with Corn Candy
Handcrafted • N/A
300QFM9014 • **Value $16**

8

Giraffe as Tree
Handcrafted • N/A
300QFM9141 • **Value $14**

9

Goldfish
Handcrafted • N/A
300QFM9181 • **Value $12**

10

Goose in Bonnet
Handcrafted • N/A
300QSM9789 • **Value $15**

11

Grad Dog
Handcrafted • N/A
250QSM9817 • **Value $13**

12

Haunted House
Handcrafted • N/A
350QFM9024 • **Value $14**

13

Hedgehog
Handcrafted • N/A
250QSM9859 • **Value $13**

14

Horse
Handcrafted • N/A
300QFM9051 • **Value $18**

15

Indian Bunnies
Handcrafted • N/A
350QFM9004 • **Value $16**

16

Kitten for Dad
Handcrafted • N/A
350QSM9839 • **Value $15**

17

Kitten for Mom
Handcrafted • N/A
350QSM9837 • **Value $15**

18

Kitten in Bib
Handcrafted • N/A
350QSM9829 • **Value $13**

19

Lamb
Handcrafted • N/A
250QFM9044 • **Value $16**

1992 Collection

	Price Paid	Value
1.		
2.		
3.		
4.		
5.		
6.		
7.		
8.		
9.		
10.		
11.		
12.		
13.		
14.		
15.		
16.		
17.		
18.		
19.		

Totals

VALUE GUIDE — MERRY MINIATURES

1

Lamb
Handcrafted • N/A
350QSM9787 • **Value $15**

2

Lion
Handcrafted • N/A
350QSM9719 • **Value $14**

3

Mouse
Handcrafted • N/A
300QSM9769 • **Value $12**

4

Mouse in Car
Handcrafted • N/A
300QFM9114 • **Value $13**

5

Nina Ship
Handcrafted • N/A
350QFM9154 • **Value $13**

6

Octopus
Handcrafted • N/A
300QFM9171 • **Value $12**

7

Party Dog
Handcrafted • N/A
300QFM9191 • **Value $13**

8

Penguin in Tux
Handcrafted • N/A
300QSM9757 • **Value $16**

1992 Collection

	Price Paid	Value
1.		
2.		
3.		
4.		
5.		
6.		
7.		
8.		
9.		
10.		
11.		
12.		
13.		
14.		
15.		
16.		
17.		
18.		
19.		
20.		

Totals

9
Penguin Skating
Handcrafted • N/A
350QFM9091 • **Value $15**

10

Pig
Handcrafted • N/A
250QFM9041 • **Value $19**

11

Pilgrim Beaver
Handcrafted • N/A
300QFM9011 • **Value $15**

12

Pinta Ship
Handcrafted • N/A
350QFM9161 • **Value $12**

13

Praying Chipmunk
Handcrafted • N/A
300QSM9797 • **Value $14**

14

Pumpkin
Handcrafted • N/A
300QFM9021 • **Value $14**

15

Puppy
Handcrafted • N/A
250QSM9767 • **Value $17**

16

Rabbit & Squirrel
(2nd, *Hugs and Kisses*)
Handcrafted • N/A
350QSM9827 • **Value $19**

17

Rabbit Holding
Heart Carrot
Handcrafted • N/A
350QFM9201 • **Value $14**

18

Rabbit On Sled
Handcrafted • N/A
300QFM9151 • **Value $12**

19

Santa Bee
Handcrafted • N/A
300QFM9061 • **Value $13**

20
Santa Bell (3rd & final,
***Jingle Bell Santa*)**
Handcrafted • N/A
350QFM9131 • **Value $19**

1

Santa Maria Ship
Handcrafted • N/A
350QFM9164 • **Value $13**

2

Seal
Handcrafted • N/A
300QSM9849 • **Value $13**

3

Skunk with Butterfly
Handcrafted • N/A
350QFM9184 • **Value $13**

4

Snow Bunny
Handcrafted • N/A
400QFM9071 • **Value $12**

5

Squirrel Pal (3rd & final, *Gentle Pals*)
Handcrafted • N/A
350QFM9094 • **Value $21**

6

Squirrels in Nutshell
Handcrafted • N/A
350QFM9064 • **Value $14**

7

Sweatshirt Bunny
Handcrafted • N/A
350QSM9779 • **Value $16**

8

Sweet Angel
Handcrafted • N/A
300QFM9124 • **Value $17**

9

Teacher Cat
Handcrafted • N/A
350QFM9074 • **Value $11**

10

Teddy Bear
Handcrafted • N/A
250QFM9194 • **Value $16**

11

Thankful Turkey (3rd & final, *Thankful Turkey*)
Handcrafted • N/A
350QFM9001 • **Value $22**

12

Turtle & Mouse
Handcrafted • N/A
300QSM9857 • **Value $24**

13

Walrus & Bird
Handcrafted • N/A
350QFM9054 • **Value $15**

14

Waving Reindeer
Handcrafted • N/A
300QFM9121 • **Value $15**

1991

15

1st Christmas Together
Handcrafted • N/A
350QFM1799 • **Value $13**

16

Aerobic Bunny
Handcrafted • N/A
250QFM1817 • **Value $18**

17

Artist Mouse
Handcrafted • N/A
250QSM1519 • **Value $16**

18

Baby Bunny
Handcrafted • N/A
350QSM1619 • **Value $13**

19

Baby's 1st Christmas
Handcrafted • N/A
300QFM1797 • **Value $11**

1992 Collection	Price Paid	Value
1.		
2.		
3.		
4.		
5.		
6.		
7.		
8.		
9.		
10.		
11.		
12.		
13.		
14.		
1991 Collection		
15.		
16.		
17.		
18.		
19.		
Totals		

1

Baby's 1st Easter
Handcrafted • N/A
300QSM1557 • **Value $14**

2

Backpack Chipmunk
Handcrafted • N/A
250QFM1809 • **Value $18**

3

Baseball Bear
Handcrafted • N/A
300QFM1827 • **Value $20**

4

Bear
Handcrafted • N/A
250QFM1669 • **Value $23**

5

Bear
(also avail. in Carousel
Set, #2000QSM1667)
Handcrafted • N/A
300QSM1637 • **Value $13**

6

Bear
(1st, *Sweet Valentines*)
Handcrafted • N/A
350QSM1509 • **Value $24**

7

Bears Hugging
(1st, *Hugs and Kisses*)
Handcrafted • N/A
350QSM1609 • **Value $26**

8

Birthday Clown
(2nd, *Birthday Clowns*)
Handcrafted • N/A
350QSM1617 • **Value $20**

1991 Collection

	Price Paid	Value
1.		
2.		
3.		
4.		
5.		
6.		
7.		
8.		
9.		
10.		
11.		
12.		
13.		
14.		
15.		
16.		
17.		
18.		
19.		
20.		

9

Bunny
Handcrafted • N/A
300QFM1719 • **Value $13**

10

Bunny
Handcrafted • N/A
300QSM1537 • **Value $16**

11

Bunny Praying
Handcrafted • N/A
250QSM1597 • **Value $17**

12

Camel
(also avail. in Carousel
Set, #2000QSM1667)
Handcrafted • N/A
300QSM1629 • **Value $13**

13

Carousel Display
(also avail. in Carousel
Set, #2000QSM1667)
Handcrafted • N/A
500QSM1627 • **Value $17**

14

Cat Witch
Handcrafted • N/A
300QFM1677 • **Value $16**

15

Cookie Elf
Handcrafted • N/A
300QFM1769 • **Value $13**

16

Cookie Reindeer
Handcrafted • N/A
300QFM1777 • **Value $13**

17

Cookie Santa
Handcrafted • N/A
300QFM1767 • **Value $13**

18

Daughter Bunny
Handcrafted • N/A
250QSM1587 • **Value $15**

19

Dog in Cap & Gown
Handcrafted • N/A
250QSM1607 • **Value $14**

20

Duck
Handcrafted • N/A
300QSM1549 • **Value $19**

Totals

1

Elephant
(also avail. in Carousel
Set, #2000QSM1667)
Handcrafted • N/A
300QSM1647 • **Value $13**

2

Football Beaver
Handcrafted • N/A
350QFM1829 • **Value $21**

3

Fox
Handcrafted • N/A
350QFM1689 • **Value $13**

4

Frog
Handcrafted • N/A
300QFM1729 • **Value $13**

5

Gentle Pals Kitten
(2nd, *Gentle Pals*)
Handcrafted • N/A
350QFM1709 • **Value $19**

6

Horse
(also avail. in Carousel
Set, #2000QSM1667)
Handcrafted • N/A
300QSM1649 • **Value $23**

7

I Love Dad
Handcrafted • N/A
250QSM1657 • **Value $14**

8

I Love Mom
Handcrafted • N/A
250QSM1659 • **Value $14**

9

Indian Maiden
Handcrafted • N/A
250QFM1687 • **Value $14**

10

Irish Frog
Handcrafted • N/A
350QSM1539 • **Value $15**

11

Jingle Bell Santa
(2nd, *Jingle Bell Santa*)
Handcrafted • N/A
350QFM1717 • **Value $23**

12

Kitten
Handcrafted • N/A
300QFM1737 • **Value $13**

13

Lamb & Duck
Handcrafted • N/A
350QSM1569 • **Value $14**

14

Lion
(also avail. in Carousel
Set, #2000QSM1667)
Handcrafted • N/A
300QSM1639 • **Value $17**

15

Mother Bunny
Handcrafted • N/A
300QSM1577 • **Value $17**

16

Mouse
Handcrafted • N/A
250QFM1789 • **Value $14**

17

Mummy
Handcrafted • N/A
250QFM1679 • **Value $15**

18

Music Makers Bear
(1st, *Music Makers*)
Handcrafted • N/A
300QFM1779 • **Value $23**

19

Pig
Handcrafted • N/A
300QFM1739 • **Value $15**

20

Puppy
Handcrafted • N/A
300QFM1727 • **Value $15**

1991 Collection

	Price Paid	Value
1.		
2.		
3.		
4.		
5.		
6.		
7.		
8.		
9.		
10.		
11.		
12.		
13.		
14.		
15.		
16.		
17.		
18.		
19.		
20.		

Totals

1

Puppy
Handcrafted • N/A
300QFM1787 • **Value $14**

2

Puppy
Handcrafted • N/A
300QSM1529 • **Value $22**

3

Raccoon Thief
Handcrafted • N/A
350QSM1517 • **Value $13**

4

Skating Raccoon
Handcrafted • N/A
350QFM1837 • **Value $20**

5

Snow Bunny
Handcrafted • N/A
250QFM1749 • **Value $13**

6

Snow Lamb
Handcrafted • N/A
250QFM1759 • **Value $13**

7

Snow Mice
Handcrafted • N/A
250QFM1757 • **Value $13**

8

Soccer Skunk
Handcrafted • N/A
300QFM1819 • **Value $20**

1991 Collection

	Price Paid	Value
1.		
2.		
3.		
4.		
5.		
6.		
7.		
8.		
9.		
10.		
11.		

1990 Collection

12.		
13.		
14.		
15.		
16.		
17.		
18.		
19.		

9

Teacher Raccoon
Handcrafted • N/A
350QFM1807 • **Value $11**

10

Turkey
(2nd, *Thankful Turkey*)
Handcrafted • N/A
350QFM1697 • **Value $22**

11

Turtle
Handcrafted • N/A
300QFM1747 • **Value $14**

1990

12

1st Christmas Together
Handcrafted • N/A
350QFM1686 • **Value $12**

13

Alligator
Handcrafted • N/A
300QSM1573 • **Value $11**

14

Artist Raccoon
Handcrafted • N/A
350QSM1543 • **Value $16**

15

Baby's 1st Christmas
Handcrafted • N/A
250QFM1683 • **Value $11**

16

Baby's 1st Easter
Handcrafted • N/A
300QSM1536 • **Value $14**

17

Baseball Bunny
Handcrafted • N/A
250QSM1576 • **Value $11**

18

Bear & Balloon
Handcrafted • N/A
300QFM1716 • **Value $11**

19

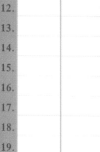

Birthday Clown
(1st, *Birthday Clowns*)
Handcrafted • N/A
350QFM1706 • **Value $20**

Totals

1

Boy Bunny
Handcrafted • N/A
350QSM1682 • **Value $12**

2

Bunny
Handcrafted • N/A
300QSM1593 • **Value $12**

3

Bunny in Tux
Handcrafted • N/A
300QFM1713 • **Value $12**

4

Candy Caboose
Handcrafted • N/A
350QFM1693 • **Value $16**

5

E-Bunny
Handcrafted • N/A
300QSM1726 • **Value $14**

6

Elephant
Handcrafted • N/A
350QSM1566 • **Value $12**

7

Gentle Pal – Lamb
(1st, *Gentle Pals*)
Handcrafted • N/A
350QFM1656 • **Value $21**

8

Get Well Puppy
Handcrafted • N/A
300QFM1703 • **Value $11**

9

Girl Bunny
Handcrafted • N/A
350QSM1675 • **Value $13**

10

Green Monster
Handcrafted • N/A
350QFM1613 • **Value $15**

11

Grey Mouse
Handcrafted • N/A
250QSM1533 • **Value $15**

12

Hippo Cupid
Handcrafted • N/A
350QSM1513 • **Value $20**

13

Indian Chipmunk
Handcrafted • N/A
300QFM1626 • **Value $16**

14

Jingle Bell Santa
(1st, *Jingle Bell Santa*)
Handcrafted • N/A
350QFM1663 • **Value $24**

15

Kangaroo
Handcrafted • N/A
350QFM1653 • **Value $11**

16

Kitten
Handcrafted • N/A
300QSM1516 • **Value $14**

17

Mama Polar Bear
Handcrafted • N/A
300QFM1666 • **Value $14**

18

Mouse
Handcrafted • N/A
250QSM1603 • **Value $14**

19

Mouse & Bunny
Handcrafted • N/A
350QSM1546 • **Value $16**

20

Owl
Handcrafted • N/A
300QSM1563 • **Value $19**

1990 Collection

	Price Paid	Value
1.		
2.		
3.		
4.		
5.		
6.		
7.		
8.		
9.		
10.		
11.		
12.		
13.		
14.		
15.		
16.		
17.		
18.		
19.		
20.		
Totals		

1

Papa Polar Bear & Child
Handcrafted • N/A
350QFM1673 • **Value $14**

2

Pig
Handcrafted • N/A
300QSM1526 • **Value $17**

3

Pilgrim Mouse
Handcrafted • N/A
250QFM1636 • **Value $14**

4

Pilgrim Squirrel
Handcrafted • N/A
300QFM1633 • **Value $15**

5

Puppy
Handcrafted • N/A
250QSM1583 • **Value $13**

6

Raccoon
Handcrafted • N/A
350QSM1586 • **Value $14**

7

Scarecrow
Handcrafted • N/A
350QFM1616 • **Value $15**

8

Snowman
Handcrafted • N/A
250QFM1646 • **Value $14**

9

Squirrel
Handcrafted • N/A
250QSM1553 • **Value $19**

10

Squirrel Caroler
Handcrafted • N/A
300QFM1696 • **Value $18**

11

Squirrel Hobo
Handcrafted • N/A
300QFM1606 • **Value $14**

12

Stitched Teddy
Handcrafted • N/A
350QSM1506 • **Value $28**

13

Teacher Mouse
Handcrafted • N/A
300QFM1676 • **Value $10**

14

Thankful Turkey
(1st, *Thankful Turkey*)
Handcrafted • N/A
350QFM1623 • **Value $24**

15

Walrus
Handcrafted • N/A
250QFM1643 • **Value $14**

1989

16

Baby Boy
Handcrafted • N/A
300QFM1585 • **Value $20**

17

Baby Girl
Handcrafted • N/A
300QFM1592 • **Value $20**

18

Baby's 1st Christmas
Handcrafted • N/A
300QFM1615 • **Value $16**

19

Bear
Handcrafted • N/A
250QSM1525 • **Value $16**

1990 Collection

	Price Paid	Value
1.		
2.		
3.		
4.		
5.		
6.		
7.		
8.		
9.		
10.		
11.		
12.		
13.		
14.		
15.		

1989 Collection

16.		
17.		
18.		
19.		

Totals

1

Bear Baker
Handcrafted • N/A
350QSM1522 • **Value $20**

2

Blue King
(also avail. in Nativity
Set, #3550QFM1685)
Handcrafted • N/A
300QFM1632 • **Value $24**

3

Bunny
Handcrafted • N/A
250QSM1512 • **Value $18**

4

Bunny
Handcrafted • N/A
300QFM1565 • **Value $14**

5

Bunny
Handcrafted • N/A
350QSM1552 • **Value $16**

6

Bunny & Skateboard
Handcrafted • N/A
350EBO3092 • **Value $25**

7

Bunny Caroler
Handcrafted • N/A
300QFM1662 • **Value $20**

8

Dog & Kitten
Handcrafted • N/A
350QSM1515 • **Value $30**

9

Elf
Handcrafted • N/A
300QFM1622 • **Value $16**

10

Grey Mouse
Handcrafted • N/A
250QSM1502 • **Value $22**

11

Joy Elf
Handcrafted • N/A
300QFM1605 • **Value $14**

12

Kitten
Handcrafted • N/A
250QSM1505 • **Value $23**

13

Lamb
Handcrafted • N/A
350QSM1545 • **Value $20**

14

Momma Bear
Handcrafted • N/A
350QFM1582 • **Value $17**

15

Mouse
Handcrafted • N/A
250QFM1572 • **Value $21**

16

Mouse Caroler
Handcrafted • N/A
250QFM1655 • **Value $21**

17

Mr. Claus
Handcrafted • N/A
350QFM1595 • **Value $16**

18

Mrs. Claus
Handcrafted • N/A
350QFM1602 • **Value $16**

19

Owl
Handcrafted • N/A
250QSM1555 • **Value $18**

1989 Collection		
	Price Paid	Value
1.		
2.		
3.		
4.		
5.		
6.		
7.		
8.		
9.		
10.		
11.		
12.		
13.		
14.		
15.		
16.		
17.		
18.		
19.		
Totals		

VALUE GUIDE — MERRY MINIATURES

1

Pink King
(also avail. in Nativity
Set, #3550QFM1685)
Handcrafted • N/A
300QFM1642 • **Value $14**

2

Raccoon
Handcrafted • N/A
350QFM1575 • **Value $14**

3

Raccoon Caroler
Handcrafted • N/A
350QFM1652 • **Value $17**

4

Teacher Elf
Handcrafted • N/A
300QFM1612 • **Value $15**

5

Train Car
Handcrafted • N/A
350QFM1562 • **Value $18**

6

Yellow King
(also avail. in Nativity
Set, #3550QFM1685)
Handcrafted • N/A
300QFM1635 • **Value $14**

1988

7

Dog
Handcrafted • N/A
200GHA3524 • **Value $14**

1989 Collection

	Price Paid	Value
1.		
2.		
3.		
4.		
5.		
6.		

1988 Collection

7.		
8.		
9.		
10.		
11.		
12.		
13.		
14.		
15.		
16.		
17.		
18.		
19.		

8

Donkey
(also avail. in Nativity
Set, #3550QFM1685)
Handcrafted • N/A
225QFM1581 • **Value $11**

9

Indian Bear
Handcrafted • N/A
325QFM1511 • **Value $16**

10

Jesus
(also avail. in Nativity
Set, #3550QFM1685)
Handcrafted • N/A
250QFM1564 • **Value $22**

11

Joseph
(also avail. in Nativity
Set, #3550QFM1685)
Handcrafted • N/A
250QFM1561 • **Value $14**

12

Kitten in Slipper
Handcrafted • N/A
250QFM1544 • **Value $19**

13

Koala & Hearts
Handcrafted • N/A
200VHA3531 • **Value $12**

14

Koala & Lollipop
Handcrafted • N/A
200VHA3651 • **Value $21**

15

Koala & Ruffled Heart
Handcrafted • N/A
200VHA3631 • **Value $62**

16

**Koala with
Bow & Arrow**
Handcrafted • N/A
200VHA3624 • **Value $14**

17

Lamb
(also avail. in Nativity
Set, #3550QFM1685)
Handcrafted • N/A
225QFM1574 • **Value $27**

18

Mary
(also avail. in Nativity
Set, #3550QFM1685)
Handcrafted • N/A
250QFM1554 • **Value $16**

19

Mouse Angel
Handcrafted • N/A
250QFM1551 • **Value $27**

Totals

VALUE GUIDE — MERRY MINIATURES

1

Mouse in Cornucopia
Handcrafted • N/A
225QFM1514 • **Value $16**

2

Mouse/Pumpkin
Handcrafted • N/A
225QFM1501 • **Value $44**

3

Owl
Handcrafted • N/A
225QFM1504 • **Value $18**

4

Penguin
Handcrafted • N/A
375QFM1541 • **Value $23**

5

Santa
Handcrafted • N/A
375QFM1521 • **Value $42**

6

Shepherd
(also avail. in Nativity
Set, #3550QFM1685)
Handcrafted • N/A
250QFM1571 • **Value $14**

7

Snowman
Handcrafted • N/A
350QFM1534 • **Value $18**

8

Stable
(also avail. in Nativity
Set, #3550QFM1685)
Handcrafted • N/A
1400QFM1584 • **Value $17**

9

Tank Car
Handcrafted • N/A
300QFM1591 • **Value $26**

10

Train Engine
Handcrafted • N/A
300QFM1531 • **Value $16**

11

Unicorn
Handcrafted • N/A
350QFM1524 • **Value $34**

1988 Collection

	Price Paid	Value
1.		
2.		
3.		
4.		
5.		
6.		
7.		
8.		
9.		
10.		
11.		

1987

12

Bear
Handcrafted • N/A
450XHA3709 • **Value $26**

13

Boy Lamb
Handcrafted • N/A
295EHA4197 • **Value $20**

14

Bunny
Handcrafted • N/A
200EHA4179 • **Value $140**

15

Bunny
Handcrafted • N/A
250XHA3729 • **Value $20**

16

Bunny Boy
Handcrafted • N/A
250XHA3737 • **Value $21**

1987 Collection

12.		
13.		
14.		
15.		
16.		
17.		
18.		
19.		

17

Bunny Girl
Handcrafted • N/A
250XHA3749 • **Value $21**

18

Chick/Egg
Handcrafted • N/A
350EHA4199 • **Value $15**

19

Clown Teddy
Handcrafted • N/A
200VHA3507 • **Value $18**

Totals

1

Fawn
Handcrafted • N/A
200XHA3757 • **Value $22**

2

Ginger Bear
Handcrafted • N/A
200XHA207 • **Value $25**

3

Giraffe
Handcrafted • N/A
350VHA3519 • **Value $90**

4

Girl Lamb
Handcrafted • N/A
295EHA4187 • **Value $22**

5

Mouse
Handcrafted • N/A
200SHA3467 • **Value $16**

6

Mouse
Handcrafted • N/A
295VHA3527 • **Value $28**

7

Puppy
Handcrafted • N/A
200XHA3769 • **Value $21**

8

Raccoon Witch
Handcrafted • N/A
200HHA3487 • **Value $22**

9

Santa
Handcrafted • N/A
350XHA3717 • **Value $42**

10

Sebastian
Handcrafted • N/A
200EHA4167 • **Value $52**

11

Turkey
Handcrafted • N/A
375THA49 • **Value $19**

1986

12

Boy Bunny
Handcrafted • N/A
295EPF4133 • **Value $20**

13

Bunny
Handcrafted • N/A
350EHA3476 • **Value $21**

14

Bunny Girl
Handcrafted • N/A
295EPF4106 • **Value $20**

15

Cat
Handcrafted • N/A
200HHA3486 • **Value $22**

16

Duck
Handcrafted • N/A
295EHA3463 • **Value $15**

17

Duck Sailor
Handcrafted • N/A
295EPF4113 • **Value $16**

18

Girl Bunny
Handcrafted • N/A
200EHA3503 • **Value $32**

19

Goose
Handcrafted • N/A
200EHA3516 • **Value $16**

Value Guide — Merry Miniatures

1
Katybeth
Handcrafted • N/A
200XHA3666 • **Value $45**

2
Mouse
Handcrafted • N/A
200XHA3533 • **Value $69**

3
Mr. Mouse
Handcrafted • N/A
200XHA3573 • **Value $29**

4
Mr. Squirrel
Handcrafted • N/A
200THA3403 • **Value $21**

5
Mrs. Mouse
Handcrafted • N/A
200XHA3653 • **Value $28**

6
Mrs. Squirrel
Handcrafted • N/A
200THA3416 • **Value $21**

7
Owl
Handcrafted • N/A
200GHA3456 • **Value $16**

8
Pandas
Handcrafted • N/A
350VHA3523 • **Value $22**

9
Penguin
Handcrafted • N/A
295XHA4413 • **Value $24**

10
Rhonda
Handcrafted • N/A
350XHA3553 • **Value $40**

11
Rodney
Handcrafted • N/A
350XHA3546 • **Value $26**

12
Santa
Handcrafted • N/A
350XHA3673 • **Value $40**

13
Sebastian
Handcrafted • N/A
200VHA3516 • **Value $73**

14
Sebastian
Handcrafted • N/A
200XHA3566 • **Value $80**

15
Sheep & Bell
Handcrafted • N/A
295EPF4126 • **Value $15**

16
Unicorn
Handcrafted • N/A
200VHA3503 • **Value $17**

17
Witch
Handcrafted • N/A
300HHS3473 • **Value $95**

1985

18
Basket
Handcrafted • N/A
200EHA3495 • **Value $42**

19
Bears
Handcrafted • N/A
450XHA3392 • **Value $30**

1986 Collection

	Price Paid	Value
1.		
2.		
3.		
4.		
5.		
6.		
7.		
8.		
9.		
10.		
11.		
12.		
13.		
14.		
15.		
16.		
17.		

1985 Collection

18.		
19.		

Totals

1

Bunny
Handcrafted • N/A
200EHA3482 • **Value $35**

2

Cat
Handcrafted • N/A
200XHA3482 • **Value $33**

3

Ceramic Bunny
Handcrafted • N/A
(N/A)EPR3701 • **Value $14**

4

Goose
Handcrafted • N/A
250XHA3522 • **Value $18**

5

Horse
Handcrafted • N/A
350XHA3412 • **Value $11**

6

Kitten
Handcrafted • N/A
200VHA3495 • **Value $30**

7

Lamb
Handcrafted • N/A
350EHA3442 • **Value $20**

8

Mouse
Handcrafted • N/A
350EHA3455 • **Value $24**

9

Mouse
Handcrafted • N/A
350XHA3405 • **Value $25**

10

Mr. Santa
Handcrafted • N/A
200XHA3495 • **Value $22**

11

Mrs. Santa
Handcrafted • N/A
200XHA3502 • **Value $23**

12

Rocking Horse
Handcrafted • N/A
200XHA3515 • **Value $31**

13

Shamrock
Handcrafted • N/A
200SHA3452 • **Value $19**

14

Skunk
Handcrafted • N/A
200VHA3482 • **Value $24**

15

Turkey
Handcrafted • N/A
295THA3395 • **Value $22**

1984

16

Brown Bunny
Handcrafted • N/A
350EHA3401 • **Value $16**

17

Chick
Handcrafted • N/A
200EHA3461 • **Value $30**

18

Dog
Handcrafted • N/A
200VHA3451 • **Value $58**

19

Duck
Handcrafted • N/A
200EHA3474 • **Value $32**

1985 Collection

	Price Paid	Value
1.		
2.		
3.		
4.		
5.		
6.		
7.		
8.		
9.		
10.		
11.		
12.		
13.		
14.		
15.		

1984 Collection

16.		
17.		
18.		
19.		

Totals

1

Duck
Handcrafted • N/A
350EHA3434 • **Value $23**

2

Hedgehog
Handcrafted • N/A
200THA3444 • **Value $20**

3

Jack-O-Lantern
Handcrafted • N/A
200HHA3454 • **Value $26**

4

Kitten
Handcrafted • N/A
200HHA3441 • **Value $24**

5

Koala
Handcrafted • N/A
295XHA3401 • **Value $28**

6

Mouse
Handcrafted • N/A
200THA3451 • **Value $42**

7

Panda
Handcrafted • N/A
200VHA3471 • **Value $26**

8

Penguin
Handcrafted • N/A
200VHA3464 • **Value $32**

9

Puppy
Handcrafted • N/A
200XHA3494 • **Value $53**

10

Redbird
Handcrafted • N/A
200XHA3501 • **Value $46**

11

Rodney
Handcrafted • N/A
295XHA3391 • **Value $40**

12

Soldier
Handcrafted • N/A
200XHA3481 • **Value $35**

1983

13

Angel
Handcrafted • N/A
200XHA3467 • **Value $52**

14

Animals
Handcrafted • N/A
750XHA3487 • **Value $40**

15

Betsey Clark
Handcrafted • N/A
350EHA2429 • **Value $32**

16

Bunny
Handcrafted • N/A
250EHA3457 • **Value $16**

17

Cherub
Handcrafted • N/A
350VHA3497 • **Value $26**

18

Chick
Handcrafted • N/A
250EHA3469 • **Value $195**

1984 Collection		
	Price Paid	Value
1.		
2.		
3.		
4.		
5.		
6.		
7.		
8.		
9.		
10.		
11.		
12.		
1983 Collection		
13.		
14.		
15.		
16.		
17.		
18.		
Totals		

1

Cupid
Handcrafted • N/A
550VHA4099 • **Value $375**

2

Deer
Handcrafted • N/A
350XHA3419 • **Value $52**

3

Duck
Handcrafted • N/A
250EHA3477 • **Value $195**

4

Flocked Bunny
Handcrafted • N/A
350EHA3417 • **Value $16**

5

Kitten
Handcrafted • N/A
200XHA3447 • **Value $43**

6

Kitten
Handcrafted • N/A
350VHA3489 • **Value $110**

7

Mouse
Handcrafted • N/A
200XHA3459 • **Value $45**

8

Mouse
Handcrafted • N/A
350SHA3407 • **Value $21**

9

Penguin
Handcrafted • N/A
295XHA3439 • **Value $70**

10

Polar Bear
Handcrafted • N/A
350XHA3407 • **Value $220**

11

Santa
Handcrafted • N/A
295XHA3427 • **Value $44**

12

Shirt Tales
Handcrafted • N/A
295HHA3437 • **Value $42**

13

Snowman
Handcrafted • N/A
300XHA3479 • **Value $43**

14

Turkey
Handcrafted • N/A
295THA207 • **Value $45**

1982

15

Ceramic Bunny
Handcrafted • N/A
300EPF3702 • **Value $48**

16

Duck
Handcrafted • N/A
300EHA3403 • **Value $32**

17

Kermit
Handcrafted • N/A
395VHA3403 • **Value $33**

18

Kitten
Handcrafted • N/A
395HHA3466 • **Value $57**

19

Miss Piggy
Handcrafted • N/A
395VHA3416 • **Value $35**

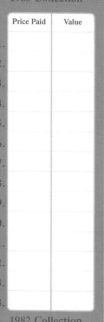

1983 Collection

	Price Paid	Value
1.		
2.		
3.		
4.		
5.		
6.		
7.		
8.		
9.		
10.		
11.		
12.		
13.		
14.		

1982 Collection

15.		
16.		
17.		
18.		
19.		

Totals

1

Mouse
Handcrafted • N/A
450XHA5023 • **Value $66**

2

Pilgrim Mouse
Handcrafted • N/A
295THA3433 • **Value $218**

3

Rocking Horse
Handcrafted • N/A
450XHA5003 • **Value $95**

4

Santa (rigid)
Handcrafted • N/A
450XHA5016 • **Value $185**

5

Tree
Handcrafted • N/A
450XHA5006 • **Value $145**

6

Witch
Handcrafted • N/A
395HHA3456 • **Value $375**

1981

7

Cupid
Handcrafted • N/A
300VPF3465 • **Value $58**

8

Ghost
Handcrafted • N/A
300HHA3402 • **Value $290**

9

Lamb
Handcrafted • N/A
300EPF402 • **Value $32**

10

Leprechaun
Handcrafted • N/A
300SHA3415 • **Value $48**

11

Penguin
Handcrafted • N/A
300XHA3412 • **Value $96**

12

Raccoon Pilgrim
Handcrafted • N/A
300THA3402 • **Value $52**

13

Redbird
Handcrafted • N/A
300XHA3405 • **Value $38**

14

Squirrel Indian
Handcrafted • N/A
300THA3415 • **Value $48**

15

Turkey
Handcrafted • N/A
300THA22 • **Value $50**

1980

16

Angel
Handcrafted • N/A
300XPF3471 • **Value $42**

17

Kitten
Handcrafted • N/A
300XPF3421 • **Value $40**

18

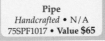

Pipe
Handcrafted • N/A
75SPF1017 • **Value $65**

1982 Collection

	Price Paid	Value
1.		
2.		
3.		
4.		
5.		
6.		

1981 Collection

7.		
8.		
9.		
10.		
11.		
12.		
13.		
14.		
15.		

1980 Collection

16.		
17.		
18.		

Totals

1

Reindeer
Handcrafted • N/A
300XPF3464 • **Value $93**

2

Santa
Handcrafted • N/A
300XPF39 • **Value $35**

3

Sleigh
Handcrafted • N/A
300XPF3451 • **Value $50**

4

Turkey
Handcrafted • N/A
200TPF3441 • **Value $80**

5

Turtle
Handcrafted • N/A
200VPF3451 • **Value $50**

1979

6

Bunny
Handcrafted • N/A
200EPF377 • **Value $90**

7

Duck
Handcrafted • N/A
200EPF397 • **Value $62**

8

Love
Handcrafted • N/A
150VPF1007 • **Value $120**

9

Mouse
Handcrafted • N/A
150XPF1017 • **Value $118**

1978

10

Joy Elf
Handcrafted • N/A
150XPF1003 • **Value $106**

11

Kitten
Handcrafted • N/A
150HPF1013 • **Value $25**

12

Mrs. Snowman
Handcrafted • N/A
150XPF23 • **Value $95**

13

Pilgrim Boy
Handcrafted • N/A
150TPF1003 • **Value $32**

14

Pilgrim Girl
Handcrafted • N/A
150TPF1016 • **Value $32**

15

Turkey
Handcrafted • N/A
150TPF12 • **Value $87**

1977

16

Barnaby
Handcrafted • N/A
125EPF12 • **Value $220**

17

Bernadette
Handcrafted • N/A
125EPF25 • **Value $215**

1980 Collection

	Price Paid	Value
1.		
2.		
3.		
4.		
5.		

1979 Collection

6.		
7.		
8.		
9.		

1978 Collection

10.		
11.		
12.		
13.		
14.		
15.		

1977 Collection

16.		
17.		

Totals

1

Chick
Handcrafted • N/A
125EPF32 • **Value $215**

2

Mouse
Handcrafted • N/A
125XPF122 • **Value $110**

3

Pilgrims
Handcrafted • N/A
150TPF502 • **Value $238**

4

Witch
Handcrafted • N/A
125HPF32 • **Value $185**

1976

5

Betsey Clark
Handcrafted • N/A
125XPF151 • **Value $270**

6

Drummer Boy
Handcrafted • N/A
125XPF144 • **Value $260**

7

Owl
Handcrafted • N/A
100HPF515 • **Value $320**

8

Pilgrims
Handcrafted • N/A
100TPF502 • **Value $220**

9

Pipe
Handcrafted • N/A
89SPF266 • **Value $148**

10

Santa
Handcrafted • N/A
125XPF131 • **Value $90**

11

Scarecrow
Handcrafted • N/A
100HPF522 • **Value $300**

12

Snowman
Handcrafted • N/A
125XPF44 • **Value $65**

13

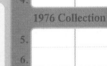

Turkey
Handcrafted • N/A
100TPF512 • **Value $158**

1975

14

Bunny
Handcrafted • N/A
125EPF49 • **Value $675**

15

Devil
Handcrafted • N/A
125HPF29 • **Value $365**

16

Duck
Handcrafted • N/A
125EPF69 • **Value $680**

17

Girl
Handcrafted • N/A
125EPF57 • **Value $560**

18

Indian
Handcrafted • N/A
125TPF29 • **Value $55**

1977 Collection		
	Price Paid	Value
1.		
2.		
3.		
4.		
1976 Collection		
5.		
6.		
7.		
8.		
9.		
10.		
11.		
12.		
13.		
1975 Collection		
14.		
15.		
16.		
17.		
18.		
Totals		

VALUE GUIDE — MERRY MINIATURES

1

Santa
Handcrafted • N/A
125XPF49 • **Value $285**

1974

2

Angel
Handcrafted • N/A
125XPF506 • **Value $425**

3

Bunny
Handcrafted • N/A
59EPF186 • **Value $675**

4

Chick
Handcrafted • N/A
159EPF206 • **Value $665**

5

Child
Handcrafted • N/A
50EPF193 • **Value $665**

6

Jack-O-Lantern
Handcrafted • N/A
75HPF502 • **Value $47**

7

Pilgrims
Handcrafted • N/A
100TPF13 • **Value $300**

8

Raggedy Andy
Handcrafted • N/A
125PF1433 • **Value $110**

9

Raggedy Ann
Handcrafted • N/A
125PF1432 • **Value $110**

10

Reindeer
Handcrafted • N/A
125XPF493 • **Value $475**

11

Santa
Handcrafted • N/A
125XPF486 • **Value $365**

12

Scarecrow
Handcrafted • N/A
100HPF • **Value $425**

13

Snowman
Handcrafted • N/A
125XPF473 • **Value $275**

14

Turkey
Handcrafted • N/A
75TPF13 • **Value $350**

Kiddie Car Classics

More than 130 Kiddie Car Classics have been issued since the line's inception in 1992, including four Artists On Tour pieces. Joining the collection this year are 12 Kiddie Car Classics, five Mini Kiddie Car Classics and six Kiddie Car Corner pieces. Also in 2000, the "Fire Brigade Series" debuts and the "Winner's Circle Collector's Series" comes to a close.

2000

1

1924 Toledo Fire Engine #6 (1st in *Fire Brigade Series*)
Current
6500QHG9053 • **Value $65**

2

1926 Steelcraft Catalog Cover Tin Sign
Current
795QHG5601 • **Value $7.95**

3

1927 Gillham™ "Honeymoon Special"
Don Palmiter Custom Collection
Current
6000QHG7111 • **Value $60**

4

1934 Christmas Classic
Current
5000QHG9061 • **Value $50**

5

1935 American Tandem (LE-24,500)
Current
1QHG9058 • **Value $100**

6

1935 Gillham™ Auburn (3rd in *Vintage Speedster Series*, LE-24,500)
Don Palmiter Custom Collection
Current
9000QHG9059 • **Value $90**

7

1935 Toledo Duesenberg Racer (5th & final in *Winner's Circle Collector's Series*)
Current
5500QHG9057 • **Value $55**

8

1937 Mickey Mouse Streamline Express Coaster Wagon (LE-24,500)
Current
4800QHG6322 • **Value $48**

9

1938 American Graham Roadster (LE-29,500)
Current
7500QHG9060 • **Value $75**

10

1938 Toledo Air King Airplane
Current
5000QHG9052 • **Value $50**

11

1943 Aviator Coloring Book Cover Tin Sign
Current
995QHG5602 • **Value $9.95**

12

1958 Custom Corvette (LE-29,500)
Don Palmiter Custom Collection
Current
6500QHG7112 • **Value $65**

2000 Kiddie Car Classics	
Price Paid	Value
1.	
2.	
3.	
4.	
5.	
6.	
7.	
8.	
9.	
10.	
11.	
12.	
Totals	

1

"Asking for Directions"
Tin Sign
Current
600QHG5603 • **Value** $6

2

Don's Sign
Current
1600QHG3623 • **Value** $16

3

Parking Sign
Current
800QHG3630 • **Value** $8

4

Stop Sign
Current
1000QHG3622 • **Value** $10

5

Street Signs
Current
1000QHG3629 • **Value** $10

6

Streetlamp
Current
1500QHG3624 • **Value** $15

7

1941 Steelcraft Spitfire
Airplane
Current
2500QHG2206 • **Value** $25

8

1950 Murray® Torpedo
Current
2500QHG2209 • **Value** $25

9

1955 Murray® Fire Chief
Current
2500QHG2208 • **Value** $25

10

1956 Garton® Kidillac
Current
2500QHG2210 • **Value** $25

11

1968 Murray® Boat
Jolly Roger
Current
2500QHG2207 • **Value** $25

12

1999

1926 Speedster (2nd in
Vintage Speedster Series,
LE-29,500)
Current
9000QHG9048 • **Value** $90

13

1934 Garton®
Chrysler® Airflow
Current
5000QHG9056 • **Value** $50

14

1937 Steelcraft "Junior"
Streamliner (LE-39,500)
Current
7000QHG9047 • **Value** $70

15

1941 Garton® Field
Ambulance (LE-39,500)
Current
6500QHG9049 • **Value** $65

16

1941 Garton® Roadster
(LE-39,500)
Current
7000QHG9050 • **Value** $70

17

1941 Garton® Speed
Demon
(4th in *Winner's Circle
Collector's Series*)
Current
5500QHG9046 • **Value** $55

18

1949 Gillham™ Special
Don Palmiter Custom Collection
Current
5000QHG7108 • **Value** $50

19

1949 Gillham™ Sport
Don Palmiter Custom Collection
Current
6000QHG7109 • **Value** $60

**2000 Kiddie Car
Corner**

	Price Paid	Value
1.		
2.		
3.		
4.		
5.		
6.		

**2000 Mini Kiddie Car
Collection**

7.		
8.		
9.		
10.		
11.		

**1999 Kiddie Car
Classics**

12.		
13.		
14.		
15.		
16.		
17.		
18.		
19.		

Totals

Kiddie Car Classics

1

1949 Gillham™ Sport
with Golf Bag
(Artists On Tour, yellow)
Current
(N/C) No stock # • **Value N/E**

2

1950 Holiday Murray®
General
Retired 1999
6000QHG9054 • **Value $60**

3

1950 Murray® General
Current
5000QHG9051 • **Value $50**

4

Call Box & Fire Hydrant
(set/2)
Current
2500QHG3618 • **Value $25**

5

"Cinder" & "Ella"
Dalmatians (set/2)
Current
1500QHG3619 • **Value $15**

6

"Cinder Says . . ."
(3rd & final in *Bill's
Boards Series*)
Current
3000QHG3621 • **Value $30**

7

Corner Drive-In
Sidewalk Signs (set/2)
Current
1500QHG3616 • **Value $15**

8

Fire Station #1
(LE-39,500)
Retired 2000
7000QHG3617 • **Value $73**

9

Flagpole
Current
2000QHG3620 • **Value $20**

10

Table & Benches (set/3)
Current
2000QHG3615 • **Value $20**

11

1941 Murray® Pursuit
Airplane
Current
2500QHG2203 • **Value $25**

12

1953 Murray® Dump
Truck
Current
2500QHG2201 • **Value $25**

13

1955 Murray® Champion
Current
2500QHG2202 • **Value $25**

14

1955 Murray® Fire Truck
Current
2500QHG2204 • **Value $25**

15

1955 Murray® Tractor
and Trailer
Current
2500QHG2205 • **Value $25**

16

1951 Hopalong Cassidy™
Velocipede (LE-24,500)
Current
4800QHG6325 • **Value $48**

1999 Kiddie Car Classics

	Price Paid	Value
1.		
2.		
3.		

1999 Kiddie Car Corner

4.		
5.		
6.		
7.		
8.		
9.		
10.		

1999 Mini Kiddie Car Collection

11.		
12.		
13.		
14.		
15.		

1999 Sidewalk Cruisers

16.		

Totals

1998

1

1926 Steelcraft Speedster by Murray® (1st in *Vintage Speedster Series*, LE-29,500)
Retired 1998
9000QHG9045• **Value $130**

2

1929 Steelcraft Roadster by Murray® (LE-39,500)
Retired 1998
7000QHG9040 • **Value $90**

3

1930 Custom Biplane
Don Palmiter Custom Collection
To Be Retired 2000
5500QHG7104 • **Value $80**

4

1930 Spirit of Christmas Custom Biplane
Don Palmiter Custom Collection
Retired 1998
6000QHG7105 • **Value $85**

5

1940 Custom Roadster with Trailer (LE-39,500)
Don Palmiter Custom Collection
To Be Retired 2000
7500QHG7106 • **Value $75**

6

1941 Steelcraft Chrysler by Murray®
Retired 2000
5500QHG9044 • **Value $58**

7

1941 Steelcraft Fire Truck by Murray®
Retired 2000
6000QHG9042 • **Value $63**

8

1941 Steelcraft Fire Truck by Murray® (Convention, silver)
Retired 1998
(N/C) No stock # • **Value N/E**

9

1950s Custom Convertible
Don Palmiter Custom Collection
Retired 1999
6000QHG7101 • **Value $63**

10

1955 Custom Chevy®
Don Palmiter Custom Collection
Retired 2000
5000QHG7103 • **Value $70**

11

1958 Murray® Champion
Retired 2000
5500QHG9041 • **Value $58**

12

1960 Eight Ball Racer (3rd in *Winner's Circle Collector's Series*)
Retired 2000
5500QHG9039 • **Value $58**

13

1998 Nascar® 50th Anniversary Custom Champion
Don Palmiter Custom Collection
To Be Retired 2000
6000QHG7110 • **Value $60**

14

Don's Street Rod
Don Palmiter Custom Collection
Retired 1999
5500QHG7102 • **Value $58**

15

Car Lift and Tool Box (set/2)
Retired 2000
2500QHG3608 • **Value $28**

16

Corner Drive-In (LE-39,500)
Current
7000QHG3610 • **Value $70**

17

Famous Food Sign (2nd in *Bill's Boards Series*)
To Be Retired 2000
3000QHG3614 • **Value $30**

18

KC's Motor Oil
Retired 2000
1500QHG3609 • **Value $18**

19

Menu Station with Food Trays (set/3)
To Be Retired 2000
3000QHG3611 • **Value $30**

1998 Kiddie Car Classics

	Price Paid	Value
1.		
2.		
3.		
4.		
5.		
6.		
7.		
8.		
9.		
10.		
11.		
12.		
13.		
14.		

1998 Kiddie Car Corner

15.		
16.		
17.		
18.		
19.		

Totals

VALUE GUIDE — KIDDIE CAR CLASSICS

1

Newspaper Box &
Trash Can Set (set/2)
To Be Retired 2000
2000QHG3613 • **Value $20**

2

1932 Keystone Coast-to-
Coast Bus (LE-29,500)
Current
4500QHG6320 • **Value $45**

3

1934 Mickey Mouse
Velocipede
Current
4800QHG6316 • **Value $48**

4

1937 De Luxe Velocipede
Current
4500QHG6319 • **Value $50**

5

1960s Sealtest Milk Truck
Current
4000QHG6315 • **Value $40**

1997

6

1937 GARTON® Ford
(LE-24,500)
Retired 1997
6500QHG9035 • **Value $140**

7

1938 GARTON® Lincoln
Zephyr (LE-24,500)
Retired 1997
6500QHG9038 • **Value $140**

8

1939 GARTON® Ford
Station Wagon
Retired 1999
5500QHG9034 • **Value $80**

9

1939 GARTON® Ford
Station Wagon (Artists
On Tour, brown)
Retired 1997
(N/C) No stock # • **Value N/E**

10

1940 Gendron "Red Hot"
Roadster (2nd in *Winner's
Circle Collector's Series*)
Retired 1999
5500QHG9037 • **Value $90**

11

1941 Steelcraft
Oldsmobile by Murray®
Retired 1999
5500QHG9036 • **Value $88**

12

1956 Murray® Golden
Eagle (LE-29,500)
Retired 1997
5000QHG9033 • **Value $95**

13

1941 Murray® Junior
Service Truck
Retired 1999
5500QHG9031 • **Value $88**

14

KC's Garage (LE-29,500)
Retired 1997
7000QHG3601 • **Value $120**

15

Pedal Petroleum
Gas Pump
Retired 1999
2500QHG3602 • **Value $40**

16

Pedal Power Premium
Lighted Gas Pump
Retired 1999
3000QHG3603 • **Value $45**

17

Sidewalk Sales Signs
Retired 1999
1500QHG3605 • **Value $25**

18

Sidewalk Service Signs
Retired 1999
1500QHG3604 • **Value $25**

19

Welcome Sign (1st in
Bill's Boards Series)
Retired 1999
3000QHG3606 • **Value $63**

1998 Kiddie Car Corner		
	Price Paid	Value
1.		
1998 Sidewalk Cruisers		
2.		
3.		
4.		
5.		
1997 Kiddie Car Classics		
6.		
7.		
8.		
9.		
10.		
11.		
12.		
1997 Kiddie Car Corner		
13.		
14.		
15.		
16.		
17.		
18.		
19.		
Totals		

1

1937 Scamp Wagon
(LE-29,500)
To Be Retired 2000
4800QHG6318 • **Value $75**

2

**1939 American
National Pedal Bike**
Retired 2000
3800QHG6314 • **Value $55**

3

**1939 GARTON®
Batwing Scooter**
To Be Retired 2000
3800QHG6317 • **Value $70**

4

**1960 Murray®
Blaz-O-Jet Tricycle**
Retired 2000
4500QHG6313 • **Value $55**

1996

5

**1935 Steelcraft Airplane
by Murray® (LE-29,500)**
Retired 1997
5000QHG9032 • **Value $130**

6

**1935 Steelcraft by
Murray® (LE-24,500)**
Retired 1996
6500QHG9029 • **Value $155**

7

**1937 Steelcraft Airflow
by Murray®
(Artists On Tour, red)**
Retired 1996
(N/C) No stock # • **Value N/E**

8

**1956 GARTON® Hot Rod
Racer (1st in *Winner's
Circle Collector's Series*)**
Retired 1999
5500QHG9028 • **Value $80**

9

**1961 Murray®
Super Deluxe
Tractor with Trailer**
Retired 1998
5500QHG9027 • **Value $100**

10

1964-1/2 Ford Mustang
Retired 1999
5500QHG9030 • **Value $70**

11

**1935 American Airflow
Coaster (LE-29,500)**
Retired 1998
4800QHG6310 • **Value $55**

12

**1935 Sky King
Velocipede**
Retired 1999
4500QHG6311 • **Value $65**

13

**1941 Keystone
Locomotive**
Retired 1998
4500QHG6312 • **Value $60**

14

**1950 GARTON®
Delivery Cycle**
Retired 1999
3800QHG6309 • **Value $55**

15

Late 1940s Mobo Sulky
(LE-29,500)
Retired 1999
4800QHG6308 • **Value $68**

1995

16

**1937 Steelcraft Airflow
by Murray® (LE-24,500)**
Retired 1996
6500QHG9024 • **Value $130**

17

1937 Steelcraft Auburn
(LE-24,500)
Retired 1996
6500QHG9021 • **Value $190**

18

**1937 Steelcraft Auburn
(Artists On Tour,
dark green)**
Retired 1995
(N/C) No stock # • **Value N/E**

1

1948 Murray® Pontiac
Retired 1998
5000QHG9026 • Value **$75**

2

1950 Murray® Torpedo
Retired 1996
5000QHG9020 • Value **$160**

3

1955 Murray® Royal
Deluxe (LE-29,500)
Retired 1999
5500QHG9025 • Value **$78**

4

1959 GARTON®
Deluxe Kidillac
Retired 1996
5500QHG9017 • Value **$115**

5

1961 GARTON® Casey
Jones Locomotive
Retired 1996
5500QHG9019 • Value **$100**

6

1962 Murray® Super
Deluxe Fire Truck
Retired 1997
5500QHG9095 • Value **$85**

7

1964 GARTON®
Tin Lizzie
Retired 1997
5000QHG9023 • Value **$90**

8

1935 Steelcraft
Streamline Velocipede
by Murray®
Retired 1999
4500QHG6306 • Value **$72**

9

1937 Steelcraft
Streamline Scooter
by Murray®
Retired 1997
3500QHG6301 • Value **$60**

10

1939 Mobo Horse
Retired 1998
4500QHG6304 • Value **$77**

11

1940 GARTON® Aero
Flite Wagon (LE-29,500)
Retired 1999
4800QHG6305 • Value **$70**

12

1958 Murray® Police
Cycle (LE-29,500)
Retired 1999
5500QHG6307 • Value **$70**

13
1963 GARTON®
Speedster
Retired 1999
3800QHG6303 • Value **$55**

14

1966 GARTON®
Super-Sonda
Retired 1997
4500QHG6302 • Value **$65**

1994

15
1939 Steelcraft Lincoln
Zephyr by Murray®
(LE-24,500)
Retired 1996
5000QHG9015 • Value **$128**

16
1941 Steelcraft Spitfire
Airplane by Murray®
(LE-19,500)
Retired 1996
5000QHG9009 • Value **$190**

17

1955 Murray® Dump
Truck (LE-19,500)
Retired 1996
4800QHG9011 • Value **$145**

18

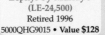
1955 Murray® Fire
Truck (LE-19,500, white)
Retired 1996
5000QHG9010 • Value **$325**

19

1955 Murray® Ranch
Wagon (LE-19,500)
Retired 1996
4800QHG9007 • Value **$135**

1995 Kiddie Car Classics		
	Price Paid	Value
1.		
2.		
3.		
4.		
5.		
6.		
7.		

1995 Sidewalk Cruisers		
8.		
9.		
10.		
11.		
12.		
13.		
14.		

1994 Kiddie Car Classics		
15.		
16.		
17.		
18.		
19.		
Totals		

Kiddie Car Classics *(left margin)*

1

1955 Murray® Red
Champion (LE-19,500)
Retired 1996
4500QHG9002 • **Value $130**

2

1956 GARTON®
Dragnet® Police Car
(LE-24,500)
Retired 1997
5000QHG9016 • **Value $80**

3

1956 GARTON®
Kidillac
Retired 1994
5000QHX9094 • **Value $88**

4

1956 GARTON®
Mark V (LE-24,500)
Retired 1997
4500QHG9022 • **Value $80**

5

1958 Murray® Atomic
Missile (LE-24,500)
Retired 1997
5500QHG9018 • **Value $100**

6

1961 Murray® Circus
Car (LE-24,500)
Retired 1997
4800QHG9014 • **Value $80**

7

1961 Murray® Speedway
Pace Car (LE-24,500)
Retired 1997
4500QHG9013 • **Value $80**

1993

8

1955 Murray®
Fire Chief (LE-19,500)
Retired 1996
4500QHG9006 • **Value $125**

9

1968 Murray® Boat
Jolly Roger (LE-19,500)
Retired 1996
5000QHG9005 • **Value $100**

1992

10

1941 Murray® Airplane
(LE-14,500)
Retired 1993
5000QHG9003 • **Value $440**

11

1953 Murray® Dump
Truck (LE-14,500)
Retired 1993
4800QHG9012 • **Value $300**

12

1955 Murray®
Champion (LE-14,500)
Retired 1993
4500QHG9008 • **Value $360**

13

1955 Murray® Fire
Truck (LE-14,500)
Retired 1993
5000QHG9001 • **Value $420**

14

1955 Murray® Tractor
and Trailer (LE-14,500)
Retired 1993
5500QHG9004 • **Value $385**

1994 Kiddie Car Classics

	Price Paid	Value
1.		
2.		
3.		
4.		
5.		
6.		
7.		

1993 Kiddie Car Classics

8.		
9.		

1992 Kiddie Car Classics

10.		
11.		
12.		
13.		
14.		

Totals

Future Releases

Use this page to record future releases and purchases.

Hallmark Ornaments	Item #	Status	Price Paid	Value

	Price Paid	Value
Page Total:		

Total Value Of My Collection

Record the value of your collection here.

Keepsake Series

Page Number	Price Paid	Value
Page 41		
Page 42		
Page 43		
Page 44		
Page 45		
Page 46		
Page 47		
Page 48		
Page 49		
Page 50		
Page 51		
Page 52		
Page 53		
Page 54		
Page 55		
Page 56		
Page 57		
Page 58		
Page 59		
Page 60		
Page 61		
Page 62		
Page 63		
Page 64		
Page 65		
Page 66		
Page 67		
Page 68		
Page 69		
Subtotal		

Magic Series

Page Number	Price Paid	Value
Page 70		
Page 71		

Miniature Series

Page 72		
Page 73		
Page 74		
Page 75		
Page 76		
Page 77		
Page 78		
Page 79		
Page 80		
Page 81		
Page 82		
Page 83		
Page 84		
Page 85		
Page 86		
Page 87		
Page 88		
Page 89		
Page 90		
Page 91		
Page 92		
Page 93		
Page 94		
Page 95		
Page 96		
Page 97		
Page 98		
Subtotal		

	Price Paid	Value
Page Total:		

Total Value Of My Collection

Record the value of your collection here.

2000-1973 Collections				2000-1973 Collections		
Page Number	Price Paid	Value		Page Number	Price Paid	Value
Page 99				Page 129		
Page 100				Page 130		
Page 101				Page 131		
Page 102				Page 132		
Page 103				Page 133		
Page 104				Page 134		
Page 105				Page 135		
Page 106				Page 136		
Page 107				Page 137		
Page 108				Page 138		
Page 109				Page 139		
Page 110				Page 140		
Page 111				Page 141		
Page 112				Page 142		
Page 113				Page 143		
Page 114				Page 144		
Page 115				Page 145		
Page 116				Page 146		
Page 117				Page 147		
Page 118				Page 148		
Page 119				Page 149		
Page 120				Page 150		
Page 121				Page 151		
Page 122				Page 152		
Page 123				Page 153		
Page 124				Page 154		
Page 125				Page 155		
Page 126				Page 156		
Page 127				Page 157		
Page 128						
Subtotal				Subtotal		

	Price Paid	Value
Page Total:		

Total Value Of My Collection

Record the value of your collection here.

2000-1973 Collections				2000-1973 Collections		
Page Number	Price Paid	Value		Page Number	Price Paid	Value
Page 158				Page 186		
Page 159				Page 187		
Page 159				Page 188		
Page 160				Page 189		
Page 160				Page 190		
Page 161				Page 191		
Page 162				Page 192		
Page 163				Page 193		
Page 164				Page 194		
Page 165				Page 195		
Page 166				Page 196		
Page 167				Page 197		
Page 168				Page 198		
Page 169				Page 199		
Page 170				Page 200		
Page 171				Page 201		
Page 172				Page 202		
Page 173				Page 203		
Page 174				Page 204		
Page 175				Page 205		
Page 176				Page 206		
Page 177				Page 207		
Page 178				Page 208		
Page 179				Page 209		
Page 180				Page 210		
Page 181				Page 211		
Page 182				Page 212		
Page 183				Page 213		
Page 184				Subtotal		
Page 185						
Subtotal						

Page Total:

Price Paid

Value

Total Value Of My Collection

Record the value of your collection here.

2000-1973 Collections			2000-1973 Collections		
Page Number	Price Paid	Value	Page Number	Price Paid	Value
Page 214			Page 243		
Page 215			Page 244		
Page 216			Page 245		
Page 217			Page 246		
Page 218			Page 247		
Page 219			Page 248		
Page 220			Page 249		
Page 221			Page 250		
Page 222			Page 251		
Page 223			Page 252		
Page 224			Page 253		
Page 225			Page 254		
Page 226			Page 255		
Page 227			Page 256		
Page 228			Page 257		
Page 229			Page 258		
Page 230			Page 259		
Page 231			Page 260		
Page 232			Page 261		
Page 233			Page 262		
Page 234			Page 263		
Page 235			Page 264		
Page 236			Page 265		
Page 237			Page 266		
Page 238			Page 267		
Page 239			Page 268		
Page 240			Page 269		
Page 241			Page 270		
Page 242					
Subtotal			Subtotal		

	Price Paid	Value
Page Total:		

Total Value Of My Collection
Record the value of your collection here!

Spring Ornaments

Page Number	Price Paid	Value
Page 271		
Page 272		
Page 273		
Page 273		
Page 274		
Page 274		
Page 275		
Page 276		
Page 277		
Page 278		
Page 279		
Page 280		
Page 281		
Page 282		

Merry Miniatures

Page Number	Price Paid	Value
Page 283		
Page 284		
Page 285		
Page 286		
Page 287		
Page 288		
Page 289		
Page 290		
Page 291		
Page 292		
Page 293		
Page 294		
Page 295		
Page 296		
Subtotal		

Merry Miniatures

Page Number	Price Paid	Value
Page 297		
Page 298		
Page 299		
Page 300		
Page 301		
Page 302		
Page 303		
Page 304		
Page 305		
Page 306		
Page 307		
Page 308		
Page 309		
Page 310		
Page 311		
Page 312		
Page 313		
Page 314		

Kiddie Car Classics

Page 315		
Page 316		
Page 317		
Page 318		
Page 319		
Page 320		
Page 321		
Page 322		

Future Releases

Page 323		
Subtotal		

Page Total:	Price Paid	Value

1999 Year In Review

Each year, certain ornaments stand out from the rest and create a stir among collectors. Here's a look at the pieces that made names for themselves in 1999:

Snowmen were on many collectors' "most wanted" lists for 1999. "The Snowmen of Mitford" was the runaway favorite, while "Millennium Snowman," "Snow Buddies" and "Sew Handy" were not far behind.

As we prepared to enter a new year and a new millennium, anything dated "2000" also leapt off store shelves. In addition to "Millennium Snowman," "Welcome to 2000" and "Father of Time" fall into this category.

Licensed products seemed to be as popular as ever as "Millennium Princess Barbie™," "Pinocchio and Geppetto," "The Cat in the Hat" and The Wizard Of Oz pieces were welcomed into homes across the nation. The miniature ornament "Dorothy's Ruby Slippers" from the *Wonders of Oz* series was especially popular.

The 1999 editions to the *Mischievous Kittens, Fabulous Decade, Colonial Church* and *Harley-Davidson® Motorcycle Milestones* series all did well, while "Best Pals," "Jazzy Jalopy," "Wintertime Treat," "Military on Parade" and the "U.S.S. Enterprise™ NCC-1701 Star Trek™" blown glass were also named as favorites by collectors.

Another hit in 1999 was the availability of pieces in new colors, such as those at the Artists On Tour and Premiere events. "Mischievous Kittens," "Jolly Locomotive" and "A Pony For Christmas" were all re-released in new colors.

Collector's Club News

To date, more than 300,000 collectors have taken advantage of the many benefits that come with joining the Hallmark Keepsake Ornament Collector's Club. Introduced in 1987, the club is not only a great way to meet fellow collectors, but is the key to enjoying exclusive club events and ornaments.

For an annual membership fee of $22.50, collectors who join the club in 2000 will receive the first three ornaments from The Ringing in the Year 2000 Membership Ornaments line, each of which is dated and features a brass bell to help celebrate the new millennium.

"Jingle Bell Kringle," sculpted by Ken Crow, shows Santa Claus leading the parade in true holiday spirit. And what would Santa be without his reindeer? "Ringing Reindeer" can always be found right by his master's side to celebrate the festivities with some music of his own. This adorable ornament was created by Joanne Eschrich.

Not to be left out of the fun, the little mouse in Sue Tague's "A Friend Chimes In" is having a "swinging" good time while playing his part in the musical tribute to Christmas.

Members who join the club for two or three years will receive "Bell-Bearing Elf." This jolly red- and green-clad elf is the perfect complement to your membership set. And since holidays are the time for sharing joy, Hallmark will send "Cool Decade," a color variation of Tammy Haddix's series opener from the general line, to anyone who introduces a friend to the Keepsake Ornament Collector's Club.

Club members who join in 2000 will also have the opportunity to purchase three more exclusive club pieces throughout the year:

"Based on the 1992 Happy Holidays® BARBIE™ Doll," the fifth and final edition in the *Holiday BARBIE™ – Collector's Club* series, looks stunning in her platinum ball gown.

"1938 Garton Lincoln Zephyr" is sure to catch your attention with its fiery red paint and chrome finish. It's a "must" for any classic car lover's tree.

"Angelic Bell," a breathtaking porcelain beauty, depicts an ivory angel accented in gold trim. This delicate bell sculpted by Katrina Bricker reflects the true tradition of the holiday season.

Club members receive other perks of membership, including the "Dream Book" that shows the pieces to be released during the year, and brochures that detail the newest releases in other exciting Hallmark lines. Members also receive an official club membership card and a year's subscription to the "Collector's Courier," the club's quarterly newsletter. And throughout the year, members receive invitations and offers that are only available to club members, including special shows and signings, such as the Artists On Tour events.

To become a member of the club, contact your local retailer or the club at:

Hallmark Keepsake Ornament Collector's Club
P.O. Box 419824
Kansas City, MO 64141-6824
(800) 523-5839
In Canada: (800) 268-3230

A Trip To The
Hallmark Visitor's Center

When Joyce Hall and his growing company moved to Kansas City, Missouri, they were surrounded by vacant parking lots and deserted office buildings. In 1968, the company embarked on an ongoing mission to clean up its surroundings. The result is the Crown Center, an 85-acre complex located on the southern edge of downtown Kansas City.

The Crown Center serves as an entertainment mecca and draws thousands of tourists each year. Not only is it home to Hallmark's world headquarters and the Hallmark Visitor's Center, but it houses local shops and businesses. Two convention hotels, a tri-level shopping plaza, a six-screen movie theater, an ice skating rink, two live theaters and dozens of restaurants all call the Crown Center home.

⁊ The Visitor's Center ✤

There is no admission fee to visit the Hallmark Visitor's Center, which was established for family entertainment. Here you'll learn the incredible success story of greeting card pioneer Joyce Hall and how the company grew from its tiny office in a YMCA to the billion-dollar company it is today. You'll also experience what it's like to be a Hallmark Keepsake Artist through tools that have been enlarged to 15 times their regular size.

You can learn details of the greeting card industry by watching how images are selected and copied onto a card, how engraving and cutting dies are used to shape and design the card and how presses mass produce the items. A museum of how greeting cards have changed over the years is also located in the Visitor's Center, as well as a museum featuring famous artwork, including that of Winston Churchill, Norman Rockwell and Grandma Moses.

Videos, which spotlight past and present Hallmark advertising, line the walls of one room while clips that feature scenes from "Hallmark Hall of Fame" presentations line another. Costumes, props and even the Emmy award won by these productions are on display in the museum. A virtual forest of Christmas trees is also available for your viewing pleasure. Created by Hallmark artists, these decorated trees were all given to Joyce Hall as gifts even before the Keepsake Ornaments Studio was created. A movie about creative workshops finishes out the tour. And don't forget to stop at the Gold Crown store, featuring all kinds of Hallmark products.

🎋 Kaleidoscope 🎋

Next door to the Hallmark Vistor's Center is Kaleidoscope, an entertainment center built just for kids. Here, children ages 5 to 12 can enjoy a one-hour session, creating their own works of art from all kinds of scrap material. Each room in the center features a different theme, from country to outer space, all fashioned to inspire different kinds of creativity from youngsters. Throughout the year, creative workshops are held at Kaleidoscope for a small fee.

Sponsored in part by Crayola®, Kaleidoscope is also free to the public. While reservations are required on weekdays, tickets for Saturday's sessions are distributed in the Crown Center throughout the day until admission for each session reaches full capacity.

Clara Johnson Scroggins Biography

Clara Johnson Scroggins, well known as the country's foremost ornament expert, has been collecting Hallmark Ornaments for nearly 30 years; however, her expertise is not limited to Hallmark. She is knowledgeable about, and collects, all kinds of ornaments. In fact, her passion for the hobby has resulted in a collection of more than 500,000 ornaments to date!

Born and raised in Little Village, Arkansas, Clara was one of nine children in her family. This taught her the importance of family and friends, a value that she still cherishes. She later lived in Illinois, Texas, New York, Connecticut and Washington, D.C. before settling in Tampa, Florida, where she and her husband, Joe Scroggins Jr., reside. Clara has one son, three grandchildren and a great-granddaughter.

"Ornaments are important to help commemorate a passing from the old to the new . . ."

Clara first became interested in ornament collecting in December of 1972, shortly after the death of her first husband. In order to combat a deep depression, she accompanied a friend to a local jewelry store where a Reed and Barton sterling silver cross ornament caught her eye and made her feel closer to her husband and God. After she bought it, she noticed that it was a second edition so she scoured the nation to find the first edition.

Clara has an established tradition of holiday decorating and likes to involve everyone, from family to guests. Each year, she sets up several trees and wreaths that she decorates with themed ornaments. She focuses less on the quantity of ornaments and more on the types of ornaments used in each location. Clara especially enjoys matching ornaments to their surroundings, such as placing dessert-themed ornaments in the kitchen.

In addition to collecting ornaments, Clara has authored seven editions of "Hallmark Keepsake Ornaments: A Collector's Guide" since 1980. She fondly remembers the first time she visited the Keepsake Studio, then called Trim-A-Home, while preparing to write her first book.

Members of the staff were not only surprised that people were beginning to collect their ornaments, but they were amazed at the extent of Clara's knowledge of their product.

Clara travels around the country to share her expertise of Hallmark and ornament collecting at shows and other gatherings, and she has been interviewed by several newspapers and television shows nationwide.

She advises collectors to collect what they love and to remember that ornaments can serve a deeper purpose than just being decorative.

"Ornaments are important to help commemorate a passing from the old to the new," she says, "and will help capture the excitement of this time of change in the year 2000 and beyond."

Clara's Picks

Each year, Hallmark collectors look forward to the release of the "Dream Book" and Clara's predictions of which ornaments will be the favorites in the upcoming year. Here are her picks for the 2000 line:

Collector's Choice
The Good Book

Top Picks
The Great Oz™
The Lone Ranger™
Qui-Gon Jinn™
Kristi Yamaguchi
Joyful Santa
Sleeping Beauty's Maleficent
Together We Serve
Christmas Tree Surprise
Millennium Express
Angel of Promise
Millennium Time Capsule

Secondary Market Overview

Collecting Hallmark ornaments can be quite a challenge. Since general releases can only be purchased for about half a year, usually from July to December, only the most dedicated collectors will be able to buy all of the ornaments they want at retail price. And because most ornaments will never be produced again, with the exception of a few rare pieces scheduled to be re-released, it becomes even harder to complete your collection.

So, how do you find the ornaments that you need after they are no longer on store shelves? Chances are that you will need to turn to the secondary market.

What Is The Secondary Market?

The secondary market is a meeting place where collectors from all over the world can buy, sell and/or swap their ornaments. Once a piece has ceased production and retail stores no longer have it in stock, the secondary market is your best bet for acquiring the coveted piece. However, don't expect to pay retail price for ornaments that are sold on the secondary market, since demand for these pieces is often much greater than the supply. This means prices may rise dramatically if the piece is rare, popular or in demand.

In some cases, Hallmark ornaments can command hundreds of dollars on the secondary market. It may take a while to find a specific ornament, especially if it is a special event piece, limited edition or older item. But even if the piece that you are looking for is not available at your local Hallmark retailer, it's possible that someone out there has the particular piece you want and they may be willing to sell it!

Accessing The Market

The secondary market can seem intimidating at first, and you may wonder where to start your search. Contacting local retailers is a good first step, since they usually keep abreast of information about secondary market events taking place in their areas. Your local retailer may be able to put you in touch with other collectors who know just where to find that elusive ornament.

The Internet has become the most popular, and fastest growing, resource for collectors. To find collectibles sites, search using keywords such as "Hallmark," "secondary market," "ornaments" or "collectibles." Usually the more specific your search terms are, the more likely you are to find pertinent web sites.

A great feature of many Internet sites is the bulletin board. Here you can meet and exchange information with collectors from all over the world, as well as list items that you want to sell or trade. Auction sites are another fast-growing method of finding coveted collectibles.

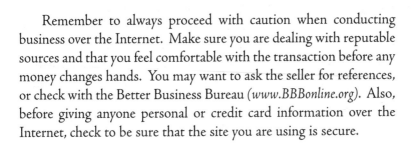

A recent search on one popular auction site resulted in more than 1,500 Hallmark ornaments for sale! Personal web sites, exchanges and on-line secondary market dealers can all be accessed through the Internet. The information on these sites is usually updated quite frequently and reflects the most current market values.

Remember to always proceed with caution when conducting business over the Internet. Make sure you are dealing with reputable sources and that you feel comfortable with the transaction before any money changes hands. You may want to ask the seller for references, or check with the Better Business Bureau (*www.BBBonline.org*). Also, before giving anyone personal or credit card information over the Internet, check to be sure that the site you are using is secure.

Another easy way to search the secondary market is to seek the assistance of a specialist. Secondary market dealers usually focus on one or two types of collectibles and are typically very knowledgeable about those lines. They usually create their own secondary market price listings that they are willing to fax or mail directly to you. Plus, there is the added benefit of being able to communicate directly with them instead of going through a "middle man" or the Internet.

You may also want to consider a secondary market exchange service. These exchanges publish newsletters that are usually available on either a weekly or monthly basis in exchange for a subscription fee. The newsletter provides a listing of items for sale and how much the seller is asking for them. It may also provide space for collectors to post the specific pieces they are looking to buy. However, for the convenience of locating sellers for you, the exchange will most likely charge a fee of between 10 and 20 percent of your purchase price.

Another handy resource, especially if you don't have access to the Internet, is print sources. Taking out an advertisement in the "swap and sell" or classified section of a newspaper or magazine is a sure way to reach a large audience.

☞ What You Should Know ☘

The two most important factors that will affect the value of an ornament are packaging and condition, so keep this in mind when buying or selling on the secondary market. Be sure to keep the original box that came with your ornament. Collectors will pay less for an ornament that doesn't have its original box and packaging. Some even consider the piece to be "incomplete" without these items. The box is also a perfect way to store and protect your ornaments.

It is very important to keep your ornaments in mint condition, especially if you plan to resell them. Store them carefully, preferably in their original packaging, and be sure to avoid exposing them to excessive sunlight, humidity or extreme temperature changes.

Although the monetary value of your collection is an important factor, ornaments are also a sentimental reminder of good times and loved ones. So, remember to enjoy your ornaments, not only at Christmas but all year-round!

Exchanges, Dealers & Newsletters

The Baggage Car
Meredith DeGood
P.O. Box 3735
3100 Justin Drive, Suite B
Des Moines, IA 50322
515-270-9080

Christmas in Vermont
Kathy Parrott
51 Jalbert Road
Barre, VT 05641
802-479-2024
katparrott@aol.com

The Christmas Shop
Shirley Trexler
P.O. Box 5221
Cary, NC 27512
919-469-5264

Collectible Exchange, Inc.
6621 Columbiana Road
New Middletown, OH 44442
800-752-3208
330-542-9646
www.colexch.com

Mary Johnson
P.O. Box 1015
Marion, NC 28752-1015
828-652-2910
maryjorn@wnclink.com

Ron Kesterson
300 Camelot Court
Knoxville, TN 37922
423-675-7511

Morris Antiques
Allen and Pat Morris
2716 Flintlock Drive
Henderson, KY 42420
270-826-8378
prm@dynasty.net

The Ornament Trader Magazine
Judy Patient
P. O. Box 469
Lavonia, GA 30553-0469
800-441-1551
770-650-2726
fax: 770-650-2851
jpat721868@aol.com

Twelve Months of Christmas
Joan Ketterer
P.O. Box 97172
Pittsburgh, PA 15229
412-367-2352

Insuring Your Collection

Now that you've devoted a lot of time, effort and money building up your collection of Keepsake Ornaments, make sure that your collection is covered in the event of theft, flood, fire or other unforeseen circumstances. Insuring your collection is a wise move and it doesn't have to be costly or difficult.

1. Assess the value of your collection. If it is quite extensive, you might want to have it professionally appraised. However, you can determine the current value of your collection yourself by consulting a reputable price guide such as the Collector's Value Guide™.

2. Determine the amount of coverage you need. Collectibles are often covered under a basic homeowner's or renter's policy, but ask your agent if your policy covers fire, theft, flood, hurricanes, earthquakes and damage or breakage from routine handling. Also, find out if your policy covers claims at "current replacement value" – the amount it would cost to replace items if they were damaged, lost or stolen. If the amount of insurance does not cover your collection, you may want to consider adding a Personal Articles Floater or a Fine Arts Floater ("rider") to your policy. Many insurance companies specialize in collectibles insurance and can help you ensure that your collection is adequately covered.

3. Keep up-to-date documentation of your collectible pieces and their values. Save all your receipts and consider photographing each item, taking special care to show color changes, artist signatures and other special features in the photograph. Keep all of your documentation in a safe place, such as a safe deposit box, or make two copies and give one to a friend or relative.

Creating A Keepsake Ornament

The talented artists at the Hallmark Design Studio find inspiration for their ornaments in almost any situation. Whether the inspiration comes from childhood memories or recent travels, each artist can turn an experience into highly detailed and nostalgic ornaments. While each artist has a unique style, the production process is, for the most part, the same.

It all begins at least two years in advance, when all of the Hallmark artists are given the opportunity to submit ideas and drawings for ornaments. Sometimes, the company has its own subject ideas, frequently from movies, television or pop culture. After all of the ideas and drawings have been collected, Hallmark Studio managers and artists review the representations and choose the best one; it is not uncommon to incorporate several drawings into one piece.

The next step is to produce a model, which is photographed. Pictures are given out to the various sculptors so that a minimum of seven duplicate sculptures can be made. Some become the molds for the actual ornament, while others are used to test the different possibilities for color schemes. Once final decisions have been made, the piece is sent to the Hallmark production facility where the ornaments are manufactured.

Thanks to new technology, many new materials have been incorporated into ornaments since the early days of yarn figures and glass balls, including wood, pewter, clay, plastic, porcelain and die-cast metal. In many cases, artists now use a combination of different materials in order to achieve a more realistic representation of their design and to further enhance the unique style of each ornament.

Decorating For Every Season

While Hallmark Keepsake Ornaments have traditionally been linked with Christmas, the variety of pieces within the line provides collectors with the opportunity to assemble creative and original decorations that can be used not only during the holidays, but all year long.

As winter fades and Christmas decorations are put away, why not bring out some festive Spring ornaments to liven up the house and welcome in the warm weather? From Easter bunnies to flower-toting woodland creatures, these Spring and Easter ornaments are sure to scare away the "winter blues" and make the transition between seasons more pleasant.

Decorating can mean anything from setting up an elaborate display of themed pieces on a handmade background to placing a single piece in a strategic location, such as a Kiddie Car Classic in the garage or a "Baby's First Christmas" photoholder near a grouping of family photos or memorabilia of your baby's first milestones.

Here's some other ideas to help you get started:

BARBIE™ Wreath

BARBIE™ fans young and old will love this tribute to the classic American doll – a perfect accent for a child's bedroom or playroom. A styrofoam wreath serves as the backbone for this simple yet beautiful decoration. Wrap the wreath with pink or white ribbon, lace or organza until the styrofoam no longer shows. Next, hang four or five of your favorite BARBIE™ ornaments around the wreath. Finally, decorate the wreath with a few silk flowers or a large floral design at the base.

🍂 Christmas Dinner 🎄

Having guests over for Christmas dinner? Help them get into the holiday spirit with some Hallmark Miniature Ornaments. Attach themed miniature ornaments to wire and tie them onto candlehold-ers or onto napkin holders to display at each guest's place

setting. When doing this, you can use one common theme, such as ornaments in *The Kringles* series, or you can choose ornaments that correspond to each guest's personality or hobbies. For instance, sur-prise a ballerina with a piece from the *Snowflake Ballet* series or honor a seamstress with one of the *Thimble Bells* pieces. Finally, use decora-tive holiday ribbon to attach Miniature Ornaments to the tops of wrapped gifts for an original and eye-catching look.

🍂 Play Ball! 🎄

Here's the perfect idea for the sports fan in the house. Create a tribute to your favorite sports team using some sports-themed Keepsake Ornaments. A corkboard makes the per-fect background for this display, as you can attach

team pennants, ticket stubs from games you've attended and trading cards of your favorite players. This display looks great near a trophy case where you can display game-winning balls, ribbons or trophies. Accent the corkboard with some ornaments related to the particular sport, such as those in the *At The Ballpark* or *Hoop Stars* series.

Boldly Go Where No One Has Gone Before

Find a sizable piece of Bristol board and paint it black. Use white paint to create tiny dots on the board to simulate stars. Paint some thin tree branches white then add white pipe cleaners to simulate alien trees from another planet. Cover a few styrofoam disks with aluminum foil, then attach some colored gems to make it look like a portal. Next, add some planets and stars to the scene by using bent pipe cleaners and styrofoam balls. Finally, add your favorite Star Trek™ and Star Wars™ ornaments for an "outta this world" display!

A Day At The Beach

Keep summer in your house all year long with a beach display! Ornaments in the *Lighthouse Greetings* or *Seaside Scenes* series lend themselves perfectly to this grouping. Cover an oval tray with a thin coating of sand to make the display look authentic. Next, place some seashells directly on the sand or inside a glass jar, then add your summer ornaments. Do not use real water in your beach display as your ornaments may become ruined if they get wet.

When creating displays, have fun and use your imagination. With nearly 5,000 ornaments in the line, the possibilities are endless. And remember – the most important part of creating a new display is not just the end result, but how much fun you have doing it!

Alphabetical Index

All Hallmark Keepsake Ornaments, Spring Ornaments, Merry Miniatures and Kiddie Car Classics are listed below in alphabetical order with the piece's location within the Value Guide section and the box in which it is pictured on that page.

Acknowledgements

CheckerBee Publishing would like to extend a special thanks to Clara Johnson Scroggins, Helen Cherry, Vicki Gilson, Dessie Howard, Mary Johnson, Anne Linville, Kate A. O'Neil, Carol Otto, Judy Patient, Tom Schmidt, Joyce Schroeder, Paula Sheridan, Van Tyner and Diane Zimmer. And many thanks to the great people at Hallmark.